A. S. A. MONOGRAPHS

General Editor: ADRIAN MAYER

12

Urban Ethnicity

URBAN ETHNICITY

Edited by Abner Cohen

TAVISTOCK PUBLICATIONS

London · New York · Sydney · Toronto · Wellington

First published in 1974
by Tavistock Publications Limited
11 New Fetter Lane, London EC4
This book has been set in Modern Series 7
and was printed by Butler & Tanner Limited,
Frome and London

SBN 422 74080 2

This volume derives from material presented at a conference on
'Urban Ethnicity', sponsored by the Association of Social Anthropologists of the Commonwealth, held in London, 31 March to
3 April 1971.

Distributed in the USA by
Harper & Row Publishers, Inc.
Barnes & Noble Import Division

Contents

Contents

Editor's Preface

This volume is a collection of papers presented at the annual conference of the Association of Social Anthropologists of the Commonwealth, which was held in London at Easter 1971, on the theme of 'Urban Ethnicity'. In the planning of the conference it was attempted to have as wide an ethnographic coverage as possible. Dr Charsley's paper is concerned essentially with a rural, not urban setting. But it attempts an analysis of a situation characterized by a great measure of ethnic heterogeneity within a relatively small territory and was thus thought to provide a 'control case' which might throw into relief certain aspects of urban ethnicity. All the papers except one were circulated to the participants in the conference and were later revised in preparation for publication. Professor Bruner's paper was completely changed. Professor Mitchell did not present a written paper at the conference but spoke from notes. He wrote his paper after the conference. My Introduction was read at the opening of the conference but not circulated in its written form.

The gratitude of the participants goes to the many colleagues who helped in organizing the conference. Peter Lloyd, Clyde Mitchell, and David Parkin helped in inviting contributors. A. L. Epstein, Jean La Fontaine, Caroline Ifeka, Paula Brown Glick, Bruce Kapferer, Adam Kuper, and Barbara Ward acted as discussants. John Barnes, Daryll Forde, P. H. Gulliver, Ioan Lewis, Peter Lloyd, and Lucy Mair acted as chairmen for the various sessions. Anthony Forge provided a great deal of help in his capacity as Warden of the Carr Saunders Hall of Residence where the conference was held and accommodated. Miss Helen Hornsey helped me in editing the papers. Miss K. Brown helped greatly in secretarial matters in the organization of the conference.

INTRODUCTION

Abner Cohen

The Lesson of Ethnicity

The papers presented in this volume deal with a number of problems relating to the nature of ethnicity in a variety of situations in different countries. Ethnicity is a ubiquitous phenomenon in both developing and developed countries, past and present. In the Third World the tribes, villages, bands, and isolated communities, which have until recently been our traditional subject-matter, are everywhere today becoming integral parts of new state structures and are thus being transformed into ethnic groupings with varying degrees of cultural distinctiveness. Social anthropologists, whether students of rural or urban areas, are therefore being increasingly forced into dealing with the socio-cultural problems raised by the developing interdependence between these parts and by the processes of socio-cultural change involved in this development. For both heuristic and theoretical consideratons, this interest in the phenomenon of ethnicity is likely to become a major preoccupation in our discipline for many years to come.

Because of its ubiquity, variety of form, scope, and intensity, and of its involvement in psychic, social, and historical variables, ethnicity has been defined in a variety of ways, depending on the discipline, field experience, and interests of the investigators. Many of these definitions are discussed in the papers in this volume. The question is not which definition is the most valid, but which is most helpful in the analysis of certain theoretical problems.

To make a start in this discussion, an ethnic group can be operationally defined as a collectivity of people who (a) share some patterns of normative behaviour and (b) form a part of a larger population, interacting with people from other collectivities within the framework of a social system. The term ethnicity refers to the degree of conformity by members of the collectivity to these shared norms in the course of social interaction. It is obvious that this definition is so wide that it covers collectivities that are not usually described as 'ethnic'. This is a significant point to which I shall return later.

By patterns of normative behaviour I am referring here to the symbolic formations and activities found in such contexts as kinship and marriage, friendship, ritual, and other types of ceremonial. Some anthropologists refer to these patterns as customs or simply as culture. These are not the idiosyncratic habits, hallucinations, or illusions of isolated individuals but largely collective representations, even though they manifest themselves in individual behaviour. They are involved in psychic processes and thus can be subjectively experienced by the actors. They are nevertheless objective in the sense that the symbolic formations representing them, i.e. the stereotypes, mythologies, slogans, 'theories', ideologies, and ceremonials, are socially created and are internalized through continuous socialization. Often it is objective symbolic forms that generate the subjective experience of ethnicity and not the other way round. In terms of observable and verifiable criteria, what matters sociologically is what people actually do, not what they subjectively think or what they think they think. The prophet Muhammad is said to have once remarked that what concerned him was that a good Moslem should go through the act of praying five times a day. As to what went on in the mind of the worshipper, that was between the worshipper and Allah.

Our subjective life is notoriously chaotic, whimsical, vague, shifty, and very largely unconscious. Most people are therefore only too happy to be assisted by 'experts' or 'leaders', parents or teachers, or the culture they inherit, to find definite expressions for their uncertain ideas and feelings. When questioned, though, different men give different reasons for performing certain patterns of behaviour, and the same man may give different reasons for performing the same act at different times.

Symbols are thus essentially objective, not subjective, forms. They may be originally the spontaneous creation of specific individuals going through specific subjective experiences, but they attain an objective existence when they are accepted by others in the course of social interaction within a collectivity. What was originally subjective and individual becomes objective and collective, developing a reality of its own. The symbols become obligatory and thus exercise constraint on the individual. In the field of ethnicity this is manifested, for example, in such a common statement as 'My best personal friends are Jews (or Negroes, Yoruba, Bemba, Catholic) but . . .'. Unlike signs, symbols are not purely cognitive constructs, but are always also emotive and conative. In situations where ethnicity is a relevant issue, labels such as 'Jews', 'Negroes', or 'Catholics' (as the case may be) are not neutral intellectual concepts but symbols that agitate strong feelings and emotions.

The term ethnicity will be of little use if it is extended to denote cultural differences between isolated societies, autonomous regions, or independent stocks of populations such as nations within their own national boundaries. The differences between the Chinese and the Indians, considered within their own respective countries, are national not ethnic differences. But when groups of Chinese and Indian immigrants interact in a foreign land as Chinese and Indians they can then be referred to as ethnic groups. Ethnicity is essentially a form of interaction between culture groups operating within common social contexts.

It is for this reason that the phenomena of ethnicity are so dramatically evident in the cities, in both developing and developed countries. Here the division of labour is usually highly advanced and the struggle for resources, like employment, wages, housing, education, and political following, is intense. But of course ethnicity is not confined to the cities. In both the developed and the developing countries the city is today but a part of the national state. Economically, politically, demographically, and culturally it makes no sociological sense unless we study it within this wider context. Urban anthropology is indeed the anthropology of the complex structure of the new national state.

It is obvious that ethnicity is a complex phenomenon that is involved in psychological, historical, economic, and political factors. A full study of its nature – if this is at all possible – will require giving due weight to these and probably many other factors, and will call for the cooperation of many disciplines. But if we seriously attempt to do this at one and the same time we shall not be able to go far in our analysis. We are therefore forced to concentrate on as few variables as possible at a time, trying to keep the other variables constant in our analysis. This is one of the rudimentary strategies in all research.

ETHNICITY AS A CULTURAL PHENOMENON

Some anthropologists emphasize the cultural nature of ethnicity. One of the earliest and most influential schools of thought in this respect has been that of the former Rhodes Livingstone Institute anthropologists, notably Mitchell (1956), Epstein (1958), and Gluckman (1961), whose views were greatly affected by the special conditions existing in the industrial towns of Northern Rhodesia, now Zambia, during the 1950s. The major social cleavage in those towns ran along racial lines, and the political scene was dominated by a continuous struggle by African workers against White employers. Within the African camp ethnicity, according to this school, was not a live economic or political issue, but essentially an epistemological device developed by the Africans so that they could comprehend, or make sense of, the bewildering complexity and heterogeneity of urban society. They did this by classifying other townsmen in terms of broad tribal categories. In a more recent work, Barth (1969) follows an essentially similar line, seeing ethnic categories as classifying persons in terms of their 'basic most general identity' as determined by their origin and background. Some writers attribute primordiality to this basic identity.

Ethnicity tends to be conceived by this school of thought as an essentially innate predisposition. Barth goes so far as to attribute to it an existence of its own, separate from any social 'content'. He describes ethnic categories as: 'organisational vessels that may be given varying amounts and forms of content in different socio-cultural systems. They may be of great relevance to behaviour, but they need not be; they may provide all social life, or they may be relevant only in limited sectors of activity' (1969: 14).

This approach raises a number of logical, methodological, and sociological difficulties. Its central theme is descriptive and its argument is essentially circular. What it says is that people act as the members of ethnic categories because they identify themselves, and are sometimes also identified by others, with these ethnic categories. How do we know this? The actors say so, or so they act. Such statements and arguments will not become more analytical if we attribute identification and categorization to so-called cognition and begin to construct 'cognitive maps' to 'explain' them. At most, what we are establishing by this procedure is the simple fact that ethnic categories exist. This is of course legitimate if it is taken as the starting-point of an investigation, not as its conclusion. For, by itself it generates no hypotheses and leads to no further analysis. This is why nearly all the anthropologists who approach ethnicity from this angle seek to proceed further beyond this starting-point.

But, as Evans-Pritchard (1951: 19) points out, a continued preoccupation with problems of culture inevitably leads to psychology or history. Some writers thus end up explaining ethnicity in terms of motivation, primordial ideas, or the psychology of identity. Even when no such explanations are explicitly presented there is a tendency to posit ethnicity as a strategy manipulated by *individuals* to advance their personal interests and maximize their power. The difficulty with this kind of explanation is that it is one sided and cannot account for the potency of the normative symbols which the individual manipulates in his struggle for power. An ethnic group is not simply the sum total of its individual members, and its culture is not the sum total of the strategies adopted by independent individuals. Norms, beliefs, and values are effective and have their own constraining power only because they are the collective representations of a group and are backed by the pressure of that group. An individual can manipulate customs if he becomes part of such a group, adopting its current major symbols. He cannot manipulate others without being ready to be manipulated by them. He must pay the price of membership by participating in the group's symbolic activities and by a measure of adherence to the group's aims.

Other writers, on the other hand, end up explaining ethnicity in terms of process in time. Ethnicity here is often associated with migrancy, and is taken to be a stage in the adaptation of the group to its new environment and in the final assimilation of its members within the new society. One of the difficulties with this approach is that it is often not very clear whether one

is concerned with a historical process or a cyclical one. If it is
historical, then the process is unique and our account of it is
descriptive, being a chronological narrative of a migration. If it
is cyclical, then our analysis cannot produce generalizations that
apply to all cases of ethnicity. For, while it is true that many
migrant communities, or ethnic groupings forming a state, go
through a process of mutual adjustment and/or of integration,
and in the process lose their cultural identity, there are many
situations where the reverse can occur. Here a group adjusts to
the new situation by reorganizing its own traditional customs,
or by developing new customs under traditional symbols, using
traditional norms and ideologies to enhance its distinctiveness
within the contemporary situation. As time goes on the group
will become more and more distinct, sometimes even reviving
old customs. This ethnic continuity or revival can be found in
almost all societies, both developed and underdeveloped (Cohen
1969a). In many situations migrancy is not a developmental
phase but a structural status. Among Hausa traders in Yoruba
towns, a Hausa man may operate in the same trading community for many years and yet will remain a 'stranger' performing special roles. On the other hand, a Hausa migrant
who performs the economic roles of a settler will be regarded
as a member of the settled community shortly after joining
it.

ETHNICITY AND POWER RELATIONS

Again, we must remember that ethnicity is a matter of degree.
There is ethnicity and ethnicity. The constraint that custom
exercises on the individual varies from case to case. We may yet
lack the techniques for the exact measurement of the magnitude
of this constraint, but I think that it is common sense that the
ethnicity of a collectivity that manifests itself in the form of an
annual gathering of a few of its numbers to perform a dance or
a ceremonial is different from the ethnicity manifested by, say,
the Catholics in Northern Ireland. In some situations ethnicity
amounts to no more than the exchange of jokes between
different culture groups at the strange and bizarre nature of one
another's customs. In other situations it leads to violence and
bloodshed.

Introduction

The definition of ethnicity as cognition of identity obscures, even nullifies, the conception of differences in degree of ethnicity. Barth's conception of ethnic categories as organizational *vessels* that are fixed, static, always there even when not relevant to behaviour, suffers from the same difficulties. His separation between 'vessel' and 'content' makes it difficult to appreciate the dynamic nature of ethnicity. It also assumes an inflexible structure of the human psyche and implicitly denies that personality is an open system given to modifications through continual socialization under changing socio-cultural conditions. Unless we recognize differences in degree of manifestation we shall fail to make much progress in the analysis of ethnicity. To put it in the idiom of research, ethnicity is a variable.

In any socio-cultural milieu this variable is interdependent with many other variables. But one must tackle one problem at a time, as it is only in this way that the analysis can be developed. For this reason I find the concepts of 'social organization' or 'social structure' difficult to operate with in this kind of analysis because each of them subsumes a large number of variables and is therefore highly ambiguous.

One way to make a start is to analyse ethnicity in terms of interconnections with economic and political relationships, both of which I shall, for brevity, describe as political. One need not be a Marxist in order to recognize the fact that the earning of livelihood, the struggle for a larger share of income from the economic system, including the struggle for housing, for higher education, and for other benefits, and similar issues constitute an important variable significantly related to ethnicity. Admittedly it is not the only relevant variable. What is more, its operation is modified and affected by the processual and psychological factors that I mentioned earlier. But it is a variable that pervades almost the whole universe of social relationships. This holds true of even so-called domestic relationships, which some writers seem to exclude from the realm of politics. Relations like those between father and son or husband and wife have their own aspects of power, and thus form part of the political system in any society. Indeed, in many preindustrial societies the whole political structure is embedded within such 'domestic relationships'. Certainly there are many relationships and activities,

such as friendship or recreation, whose aim is mainly the satis-
faction of personality needs, and which are thus non-political.
But as Marcuse (1964) shows, there is a tendency for the 'big
corporations' to exploit such relations and activities for their
own ends. The non-political becomes thereby politicized. The
youth movements that arose only a few years ago as 'marginal'
enterprises striving for the utopianism of 'non-structure' have
been rapidly drawn into politics (Farren & Barker 1972).
Symbolic activities that are aimed at the solution of such
perennial problems of human existence as those of life and
death, good and evil, fortune and misfortune are exploited in
all societies, whether industrial or preindustrial, by different
political interests, and their dominant symbols are thus loaded
with a multiplicity of political meanings. Indeed I go so far as
to argue that the specialization of social anthropology is this
very political interpretation of what are essentially non-political
formations and activities (Cohen 1969b). The cultures of ethnic
groups are universes of such formally non-political formations
and activities that are politicized in the course of social action.

The relations between ethnicity and politics are discussed, or
touched upon, in some of the papers in this volume, and I myself have done some work on them (Cohen 1965, 1966, 1967,
1968, 1969a, 1971; see also Parkin 1969, and Caplan 1970).
Some writers in this field stress the political factor and even
tend to explain, or rather explain away, the cultural factor as
being of trivial importance. Others put their emphasis on the
cultural side. A few are more concerned with the systematic
interconnections, or dialectical interaction, between the two
variables. What I wish to do here is mention briefly a few
points that are not discussed in the papers presented below, but
which I think bear on our general discussion.

ETHNICITY AND INFORMAL ORGANIZATION

In the course of the organization of economic production,
exchange, and distribution, and more particularly through the
processes of the division of labour and the competition for
greater shares of income between men, a variety of interest
groups emerge, whose members have some interests in common.
To operate successfully an interest group has to develop basic

organizational functions: distinctiveness (some writers call it boundary); communication; authority structure; decision-making procedure; ideology; and socialization. Indeed, organization is *the* group, since we are often dealing here not with a collectivity of total personalities, but with patterns of behaviour developed by a number of people participating with one another in respect of some specific, segmental, roles.

These interest groups can be organized on formal bases. This means that their aims are clearly specified and their organizational functions are rationally planned on bureaucratic lines. As Weber showed, this kind of organization, or association, is the most efficient and effective type of human organization, and in industrial society most groups attempt to make use of it.

But even in the advanced liberal industrial societies there are some structural conditions under which an interest group cannot organize itself on formal lines. Its formal organization may be opposed by the state or by other groups within the state, or may be incompatible with some important principles in the society; or the interests it represents may be newly developed and not yet articulated in terms of a formal organization and accommodated with the formal structure of the society. Under these conditions the group will articulate its organization on informal lines, making use of the kinship, friendship, ritual, ceremonial, and other symbolic activities that are implicit in what is known as style of life.

This strategy of organizing a group on the basis of different types of obligation is likely to be wasteful in time and energy and is not as efficient and effective in achieving the group's end as formal organization. For example, instead of organizing an official meeting for the members of the group to discuss some current problems, the informal group will attend a ceremonial during which these problems are only informally and unsystematically discussed amidst a great deal of what are, for the aims of the group, irrelevant symbolic activities, though these activities may at the same time satisfy some important personality needs.

The use of the term 'informal' to designate group organizations of this type is certainly far from being satisfactory. I have myself been looking for a substitute term for a number of years without much success. The term is highly ambiguous, is negative, and has to be related always to the existence of a formal structure. Some political scientists (see Almond & Powell 1966: 76–7) have used the term 'non-associational' for such interest groups. But it is obvious that this, too, is a negative term and does not seem to solve the terminological problem.

The members of interest groups who cannot organize themselves formally will thus tend to make use, though largely unconsciously, of whatever cultural mechanisms are available in order to articulate the organization of their grouping. And it is here, in such situations, that political ethnicity comes into being. In my view, unless we make this distinction between formal and informal articulation of interest group organization, we shall not be able to understand or to appreciate the nature of ethnicity in either the developed or the underdeveloped countries.

There are, of course, some conceptual problems that will have to be overcome if we want to push our analysis further. The distinction between formal and informal type of grouping is a matter of degree. Some groups are initially formed on formal lines but develop some informal mechanisms of organization later on. Other groups seek from the start to articulate part of their organization on formal lines and part on informal lines. It may be helpful to conceive of the organization of all groups as having two dimensions, the one formal and the other informal; the one governed by contract, the other by moral or ritual obligations or by what we usually call custom. Few groups are wholly formal or wholly informal. Most are in-between on the same continuum.

ETHNICITY IN THE POLITICS OF STRATIFICATION

The literature of social anthropology abounds in cases where we can see the use of ethnicity in articulating the organizational functions of interest groups that for one reason or another cannot organize themselves formally. Examples such as the organization of resistance movements and of trading disporas in underdeveloped countries illustrate the same process.

In order to highlight a few other points in the analysis of this type of organization, I would like to discuss briefly one more situation, this time within the context of such a complex and highly industrialized society as Britain.

I will not choose an apt illustration, such as Protestant and Catholic groupings in Northern Ireland or the formation of ethnic immigrant communities in many parts of the country, but a highly formalized and bureaucratized structure officially governed by purely contractual mechanisms. I am referring here to the now widely known case of the economic elite, or elites, that dominate the City of London, the nerve-centre of the financial system of Britain. No fieldwork by professional anthropologists or sociologists has been carried out in the City, but in recent years, and particularly since the publication of the report of the Bank Rate Tribunal in 1958, some accounts of various features of the organization of business within it have emerged, from a number of publications (see Lupton & Wilson 1959; Ferris 1960; Sampson 1962; Chapman 1968; Parry 1969).

From these it is evident that millions of pounds' worth of business is conducted daily in the City without the use of written documents, arranged mainly verbally, in face-to-face conversations or over the telephone. It is claimed that this is necessary if business is to flow. But as the risks involved are formidable, the business is confined to a limited circle of people who trust one another. Such a high degree of trust can arise only among men who know one another, whose values are similar, who speak the same language in the same accent, respect the same norms, and are involved in a network of primary relationships that are governed by the same values and the same patterns of symbolic behaviour.

For these reasons, City men are recruited from exclusive status groups. They are mostly products of the public-school system. The schools in this system achieve two major tasks: they socialize, or rather train, their pupils in specific patterns of symbolic behaviour, including accent, manner of speech, etiquette, style of joking, play; second, they create a web of enduring friendship and comradeship among the pupils, and these relationships are often continued through periodic old-boy reunions, affiliation with the same clubs, and further interaction in other social situations.

The City is thus said to be a village – barely one square mile in territory – in which everyone of importance knows everyone of importance. *Who* you know is more important than *what* you know. Often, the elite of the City are related to one another not only by a common style of life and by friendship, but also by kinship and affinal relationships. Lupton and Wilson (1959) present a reconstruction of the genealogies of over twenty elite family groupings that are interrelated through marriage and show the connections between top administrative, financial, and industrial 'decision-makers'.

The available reports indicate strongly that the speed and efficiency with which the City conducts its business are made possible mainly by this network of primary, informal, relationships connecting the business elite. This network is governed by archaic norms, values, and codes that are derived from the City's 'tribal past' – as Sampson puts it. It is held together by a complex body of customs that are to an outsider as esoteric and bizarre as those in any foreign culture. Ferris (1960: 58–74) gives a dramatic description of the odd and highly stylized manner in which the stockbrokers – known in the City as the top-hatters because they still wear top hats – make their daily rounds in the City. They queue at a bank sitting on a hard bench, their striped trousers tugged up, exchanging a copy of *The Times* for the *Telegraph*. When they talk to the bank official, they pull up a chair and discuss cricket, television, and politics before mentioning money. This business of 'how-do-you-do', Ferris was told, is to acknowledge: 'we accept the normal rules of society, and we can now start exchanging ideas'. 'If you go to a bank with a top hat they say: "Oh, it's one of the brokers", and you walk right in. If you went in in a homburg there'd be an awful business of "Good gracious me, Mr —, where's your hat this morning?" There'd be a *thing*, which of course you want to avoid at all costs.' For if you behave in an 'abnormal' manner, your bank official will think that there is something 'fishy' about your behaviour, and unless there is an obvious explanation your creditworthiness may suffer – and without unblemished trustworthiness a broker cannot operate.

The Hausa traders in Yoruba towns (Cohen 1969a) conduct their business in much the same way as the City men, though they operate under sifferent structural circumstances and using different symbolic patterns. A Hausa dealer from Northern Nigeria will entrust his goods and money in the South only to a Hausa broker. No matter how long the Hausa broker has been living in the South he will always be anxious to preserve the symbols of his Hausaism, dressing like a Hausa, speaking and behaving like a Hausa. Hausaism is essential for his livelihood. Just as City men in London make use of a series of customs to overcome technical problems of business, so the Hausa use different Hausa customs to create relationships of trust in the trading network. The customs that are implicit in the life-style of the City men are sovereign in their constraining power, as are the customs implicit in Hausa culture.

THE HEURISTIC SIGNIFICANCE OF ETHNICITY

City men constitute an interst group that is part of the system of the division of labour in our society. They use their connections and the symbolism of their life-style to articulate a corporate organization that is partly formal and partly informal, in order to compete within the wider social system for a greater share of the national income. So do the Hausa use their culture to organize and coordinate their effort in order to maintain their share of the profits. In short, City men are socio-culturally as distinct within British society as are the Hausa within Yoruba society. They are indeed as 'ethnic' as any ethnic group can be. But they are not usually described as an ethnic group because the term is principally social and political, not sociological, even though there is massive sociological literature about it, particularly in the USA. To many people, the term ethnicity connotes minority status, lower class, or migrancy. This is why sooner or later we shall have to drop it or to find a more neutral word for it, though I can see that we shall probably have to live with it for quite a while. This is not because it is difficult to find a substitute, but because the term can be of great heuristic significance for the current phase in the development of the anthropology of complex society. The concept of ethnicity throws into relief, or rather dramatizes, the processes by which the symbolic patterns of behaviour implicit in the style of life, or the 'sub-culture', of a group – even of highly individualistic men like members of an elite – develop in order to articulate organizational functions that cannot be formally institutionalized. It is easy to identify an elite when its men are from an ethnically distinct group like the Creoles in Sierra Leone (Cohen 1971), the Americo Liberians in Liberia (Libenow 1969), or the Tutsi in Rwanda (Maquet 1961). But it is difficult to do so with an elite whose cultural distinctiveness within the society is not so visible, and whose members appear to the casual observer to be highly independent individualists.

If in a dynamic contemporary complex society a group of second- or third-generation migrants preserve their distinctiveness and make extensive use of the symbolism of their endoculture, then the likelihood that within the contemporary situation they have become an interest group is very strong. When, in a hypothetical case, two culture groups join together and interact politically and economically, and establish a new political system, they will soon become involved in cleavages on economic and political lines running throughout the extent of the new society. If a new line of cleavage, such as that of social class, then cuts across ethnic lines, ethnic identity and exclusiveness will tend to be inhibited by the emerging countervailing alignments. The poor from the one ethnic group will cooperate with the poor from the other ethnic group against the wealthy from both ethnic groups, who will, on their part, also cooperate in the course of the struggle to maintain their privileges. If the situation develops in this way, tribal differences will weaken and eventually disappear. The people will become detribalized. In time, class division will be so deep that two subcultures, with different styles of life, will develop and we may have a situation similar to that of Victorian Britain, to which Disraeli referred as 'the two nations', meaning the privileged and the underprivileged.

But the situation will be entirely different if the new class cleavage, in our hypothetical example, coincides with tribal affiliations, so that within the new system the privileged will tend to be identified with one tribal group and the underprivileged with the other tribal group. In this situation cultural differences between the two groups will become entrenched, consolidated, and strengthened in order to articulate the struggle between the two social groups across the new class lines. Old customs will tend to persist. But within the newly emerging social system they will assume new values and new social significance.

Introduction

The study of enthnicity will be heuristically important for us also in that it can help us to clarify the nature of socio-cultural change. For it is now clear to us that the formation of an ethnic group in town involves a dynamic rearrangement of relations and of customs, and that it is not the result of cultural conservatism and continuity. The continuity of customs and of some social formations is certainly there, but their functions change dramatically – although to the casual observer it will look as if there is stagnation, conservatism, or a return to the past. This is why a concentration on the study of culture as such will shed little light on the nature of ethnicity.

It is here that the monographs on tribal studies of the 1940s and 1950s can be of immense value. For by the study of the members of those tribes within the context of the developing towns, by either the same or different anthropologists, we shall be able to develop the analysis of the dynamics of cultural and structural changes in response to the complexity of modern society. We shall find out what customs are retained, borrowed, or developed and for what political purposes. More generally we shall be able to develop the dialectical study of socio-cultural interdependence.

Studies of this type will be of immense value in analysis of the more general processes of institutionalization and of symbolization, and will thus provide a unique contribution to social science generally. At the same time they will usher social anthropology into the systematic study of the complexity of contemporary industrial society, without our discipline losing its identity, i.e. without social anthropology becoming sociology, or political science, or history.

REFERENCES

ALMOND, G. A. & POWELL, G. B. 1966. *Comparative Politics*. Boston: Little, Brown.

BARTH, F. 1969. Introduction. In F. Barth (ed.), *Ethnic Groups and Boundaries*, pp. 9–38. London: George Allen & Unwin.

CAPLAN, L. 1970. *Land and Social Change in East Nepal*. Berkeley: University of California Press.

CHAPMAN, R. A. 1968. *Decision-making: A Case Study of the Decision to raise the Bank Rate in September 1957*. London: Routledge & Kegan Paul.

COHEN, A. 1965. The Social Organization of Credit in a West African Cattle Market. *Africa* 35: 8–20.

—— 1966. Politics of the Kola Trade. *Africa* 36: 18–36.

—— 1967. The Hause. In P. C. Lloyd *et al.* (eds), *The City of Ibadan*, 117–27. Cambridge: Cambridge University Press.

—— 1968. The Politics of Mysticism in Some Local Communities in Newly Independent African States. In M. Swartz (ed.), *Local-level Politics*. Chicago: Aldine.

—— 1969a. *Custom and Politics in Urban Africa.* London: Routledge & Kegan Paul; Berkeley: University of California Press.

—— 1969b. Political Anthropology: the Analysis of the Symbolism of Power Relations. *Man* 4: 217–35.

—— 1971. The Politics of Ritual Secrecy. *Man* 6: 427–48.

EPSTEIN, A. L. 1958. *Politics in an Urban African Community.* Manchester: Manchester University Press.

EVANS-PRITCHARD, E. E. 1951. *Social Anthropology.* London: Cohen & West.

FARREN, M. & BARKER, E. 1972. *Watch Out Kids.* Open Gate Books. London: Macmillan.

FERRIS, P. 1960. *The City.* Harmondsworth: Penguin.

GLUCKMAN, M. 1961. Anthropological Problems arising from the African Industrial Revolution. In A. Southal (ed.), *Social Change in Modern Africa.* London: Oxford University Press.

LIEBENOW, J. G. 1969. *Liberia: The Evolution of Privilege.* Ithaca and London: Cornell University Press.

LUPTON, T. & WILSON, S. 1959. Background and Connections of Top Decision-makers. *Manchester University School.*

MAQUET, J. 1961. *The Premise of Inequality in Ruanda.* London: Oxford University Press.

MARCUSE, H. 1964. *One-dimensional Man.* London: Sphere Books.

MITCHELL, J. C. 1956. *The Kalela Dance.* Manchester: Manchester University Press.

PARKIN, D. 1969. *Neighbours and Nationals.* London: Routledge & Kegan Paul.

PARRY, G. 1969. *Political Elites.* London: George Allen & Unwin.

SAMPSON, A. 1962. *Anatomy of Britain.* New York and Evanston: Harper & Row; London: Hodder and Stoughton.

J. C. Mitchell

Perceptions of Ethnicity and Ethnic Behaviour: An Empirical Exploration

Differences, supposed or real, in the customs, beliefs, and practices that are identified as characteristic of particular sets of persons have long been accepted as an almost universal aspect of human behaviour. The awareness of these differences has been referred to as nationalism, as tribalism, and, more generally, as ethnicity. However, these words, when used as anthropological and sociological constructs, have often led to confusion. Much of this confusion, I contend, arises out of the somewhat different epistemological bases of various notions of ethnicity. I wish to distinguish first between 'ethnicity' as a construct of perceptual or cognitive phenomena on the one hand, and the 'ethnic group' as a construct of behavioural phenomena on the other; and, second, between commonsense notions and analytical notions of ethnicity.

There has been a long tradition of anthropology in which cognitive and behavioural phenomena are treated, correctly, as phenomena of different types and therefore not necessarily coincident. Anthropologists steeped in observational fieldwork, for example, frequently point to the contradictions between people's responses to items in race attitude questionnaires and the way in which those people actually behave. The same point has been made by several social psychologists and by none as cogently as by La Piere (1934). He visited a number of hotels and restaurants in America with a Chinese couple and was refused service only once. Subsequently he sent a questionnaire to all the proprietors of these establishments, and found that 93 per cent of the hotels and 92 per cent of the owners said that they would not serve Chinese patrons.

It is too simple, however, to assume that cognitive and behavioural phenomena relating to the same field of activity are either entirely discrepant, or entirely coincident. In the first place the degree of fit should be tested empirically and not

1

J. C. Mitchell

assumed *a priori*. In the second place the discrepancies, where they are manifest, ought ideally to be reconciled by an appropriate theory, either epistemological or substantive.

In general there are not many systematic studies of both cognitive and behavioural data relating to ethnicity. Analysts tend to use ethnicity either as a structural category, that is, as a general principle that illuminates the behaviour of persons in specified social situations or as a cultural phenomenon, that is, as a set of attitudes, beliefs, and stereotypes that people hold about persons identified by some appropriate 'ethnic' label. If the discrepancy between the two is taken to be unproblematic then the logical relationships that may connect them will inevitably remain unexplored. Systematic empirical studies of both cognitive and behavioural data relating to ethnicity, if construed as aspects of the same basic set of phenomena, must of necessity raise questions about the relationships of both types of construct one to the other.

AN EMPIRICAL ANALYSIS OF COGNITIVE AND BEHAVIOURAL ETHNICITY

It is with the intention of attempting an analysis of this sort that I have re-examined some data bearing on ethnicity collected in two very different field situations in Zambia (then Northern Rhodesia) in the 1950s. The first, which I treat as cognitive data, I collected with a formal self-completed questionnaire concerned with the respondent's feeling of social distance from a specified set of ethnic categories. Preliminary analysis of this material has already been published (Longton 1955; Mitchell 1956, 1962). The second set of data is presented here for the first time and concerns the ethnic composition of sets of men living together in 'single-quarter' type of accommodation in the 'line-of-rail' towns of Zambia at about the same time as the social-distance study was conducted. In both sets of data we are concerned basically with 'social distance'. The first (cognitive) set of data refers to the way in which respondents perceived the 'distance' between themselves and a number of designated ethnic categories, and therefore, by implication, the set of 'distances' among the ethnic categories themselves. The second set of data refers to the extent to which 'social distance'

2

is expressed by the degree to which men who have identified themselves in a social survey as belonging to a specified ethnic category are prepared to share residential accommodation with men whom they identify as belonging to other specified ethnic categories.

THE STRUCTURE OF THE COGNITIVE DATA

The recovery of the structure of the perception of ethnic nearnesses and distances has been described more fully elsewhere (Mitchell, forthcoming). Here I merely summarize the procedure so as to make the rest of the analysis intelligible.

In 1954 Miss Janet Longton and I collected data from 329 senior-grade schoolboys on a Bogardus-type 'social distance' questionnaire. The elements in the scale were questions relating to whether the respondent would willingly admit a member from an arbitrarily specified ethnic group into close kinship by marriage, into a village, to the tribal area, work with, share a meal with, or allow as a visitor to his home areas. Twenty ethnic categories were used in the questionnaire.[1] They were selected particularly to include representatives from the major conventional ethnographic clusters and regional areas in Zambia and Malawi. The preliminary results from this inquiry had enabled us to posit a distance-ordering of ethnic categories from the point of view of any particular ethnic group (Mitchell 1956, 1962), which was particularly useful in developing the notion of ethnic categorization that has played such an important part in Epstein's work (1958) and my own.

Access to more advanced analytical procedures subsequently has allowed me to re-analyse the original data in a more refined way.[2] Initially a principal components analysis of the original six social-distance items enabled me to collapse the reactions of each respondent on all of the six in respect of each ethnic category to a single social-distance score. This involved weighting the standardized score of each respondent on each item by a value derived from the principal components analysis, and transforming the score linearly so that a score of zero indicated the greatest possible closeness to the ethnic category involved and a score of 100 the greatest possible distance from that category. This procedure gives greater value to those social-

3

distance items, which correlate highly with the common social-distance dimension underlying all six items, and correspondingly devalues those items that do not correlate very highly with this dimension. Each respondent, then, could be given twenty 'distance' scores, that is, one for each of the ethnic categories involved. These distance scores may be interpreted as reflecting the social distance that each respondent perceived between himself and each of the ethnic categories referred to.

These distances, however, cannot have any objective validity. What we are interested in recovering from the data is whether or not, over all respondents, there are any regularities in the distances perceived among the ethnic categories themselves. To achieve this a set of distances among all twenty ethnic categories was calculated for each respondent. For computational convenience these differences were squared and then summed for all respondents. The appropriate squared differences were then averaged over all 325 respondents.[3] This meant that if, on the average, respondents consistently perceived any specified ethnic category to be close to any other specified ethnic category, however distant they perceived these ethnic categories to be from themselves, then the value of the mean squared differences of distances in the appropriate cell linking these two ethnic groups would be small. Equally if they perceived two ethnic categories to be distant from one another, however distant the respondents perceived these two groups to be from themselves, the value in the appropriate cell would be large. The mean squared differences in distance, therefore, contain within their totality the structure of the perceived distances from one another of all ethnic categories.

Given a matrix of squared distances of this sort there are several procedures available by means of which the implicit structure of the distances among the ethnic groups can be recovered.[4] The method I have chosen here, hierarchical clustering, has several advantages. The most important of these is that the procedures are very simple and are easily understood, the analysis can be presented in simple diagrammatic form, it is non-dimensional, that is, it makes no assumptions about the space in which the elements are contained, and it does not assume interval-type measurements of the relationships among the elements – in fact the procedure I have employed makes use of the ordinal relationships among the ethnic groups only. The procedure is based on that proposed by Johnson (1967), though I have modified it slightly.

Basically, what the procedure does is first of all to find all those pairs of elements – in this case ethnic categories – that are closer to one another than they are to any other element. These are then considered to be linked at the first level of the hierarchy. It then seeks out the elements – or pairs of elements – that are nearest to the pairs linked at the first level, to determine the clusters of elements linked together at the second level. At this stage, and at all subsequent stages, the distance upon which the choice is determined is the median of the distances between the element (or cluster of elements) that is being tested for proximity and the elements that constitute the existing clusters.[5] Clustering in this way continues until finally all the elements are linked together in one hierarchical structure. According to the logic of the procedure the ethnic categories are arranged in clusters in such a way that those that are seen to be socially nearest to one another are linked together successively into sets of clusters which are themselves linked successively according to social distance, one cluster from another. As a whole the diagram prepared by this procedure provides a synoptic representation of the overall way in which the ethnic categories were seen to be related to one another in terms of the social distances (as defined by the original scale) among them. *Figure 1* below sets out a diagram of the hierarchical clustering of the twenty ethnic categories derived from this analysis.

There are four general clusters easily distinguishable at the third level of linkage. First, there is a cluster of people in the extreme western region of Zambia, that is the Chokwe, Luchaze, Lovale, and Western Lunda who are linked together at a median social distance of 20·3 units; second, there is a cluster of Southern Province people, namely the Ila, Tonga, Lenje, and Soli, linked together at a median distance of 18·8 units; third, a cluster of Northern Province peoples, namely the Aushi, Bisa, Bemba, Mambwe, and Nyamwanga, linked together at a median distance of 22·0 units; and, finally, a cluster of Eastern Province and Malawian people, namely the Ngoni, Nsenga, Chewa, and Tumbuka, who are linked together at a median distance of 20·5 units. An interesting point about the perception of ethnic and

5

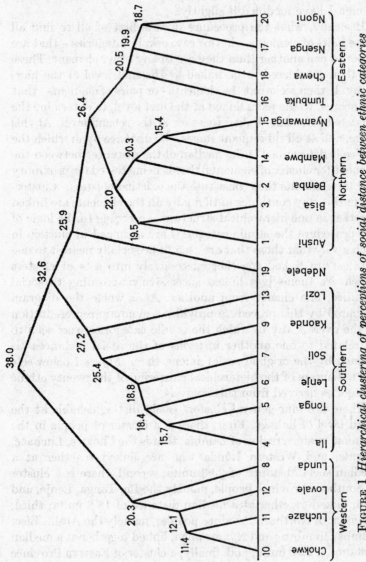

FIGURE 1 Hierarchical clustering of perceptions of social distance between ethnic categories

Source: Mitchell (1972)

social differentiation emerges here. When Miss Longton and I were analysing this material originally we were aware that ethnic and regional identities could hardly be separated, and Miss Longton therefore referred to 'geo-cultural' or 'geo-ethnic' units (Longton 1955) and I to 'two interrelated factors – geographical distance and cultural similarity' (Mitchell 1956: 27). This is presumably the same notion to which Gulliver refers when he writes of 'cultural–regional' distinctions, and about which he says: 'Tribalism in East Africa is more than regionalism: it is regionalism inherently characterized by emphasized cultural distinctions' (1969: 20). The clustering at the third level is almost certainly a demonstration of this point. It is not apparent in the Chokwe/Luchaze/Lovale/Lunda and the Ila/Tonga/Lenje/Soli clusters, for these are both clusters in which the units are culturally similar and which occupy geographically contiguous areas. But the Aushi/Bisa/Bemba/Mambwe/Nyamwanga cluster is a regional cluster in which the Aushi, Bisa, and Bemba on the one hand, share cultural similarities, while the Mambwe and Nyamwanga share them on the other. Within this cluster the Bemba are placed more closely to the Mambwe and Nyamwanga to whom they are closer geographically than to the Aushi and Bisa to whom they are closer culturally. The Ngoni/Nsenga/Chewa/Tumbuka cluster is more varied culturally than the other clusters. The Ngoni and Nsenga, who are linked closest together, in fact speak the same language in the Eastern Province of Zambia. The Chewa and Ngoni speak the same language in Malawi, so that there is some justification for clustering them together. But the inclusion of the Tumbuka in the cluster suggests that the respondents were here working with the notion of 'Nyasa', a regional notion with political significance in which, as has been described several times before (e.g. Mitchell 1956: 30), people associated with Malawi are categorized under a single rubric.

The fact that the respondents' categorization is not simply regional is demonstrated by the placing of the Kaonde. In terms of their general culture these people could be looked upon as interstitial between the Western Lunda (Ndembu) who lie to their west, the Ila who lie to their south, and the Lamba, a Bemba-like people who lie to their east. Their placing, somewhat remotely linked to the Ila/Tonga/Lenje/Soli cluster,

the first opportunity they can to move into rooms where the company is more congenial to them. The administrative officials do not usually raise objections to this procedure since for them it involves merely a transfer within the same type of accommodation. Over time, therefore, the composition of groups of men occupying single quarters reflects to a large extent their choices

TABLE 1 *Distribution of numbers of 'single men' in dwelling units*

Number of persons	Number of units	Per cent*
2	426	48·5
3	234	25·7
4	129	14·3
5	56	6·3
6	23	2·7
7	8	0·9
8	5	0·6
9	2	0·2
10	4	0·5
11	2	0·2
12	1	0·1
13	1	0·1
	891	100·0

Source: Rhodes-Livingstone Institute, Social Survey of Line-of-Rail Towns, 1951–54
* Percentages based on totals raised by reciprocals of sampling fractions

of the companions with whom they prefer to live. The composition of single quarters therefore provides one means of examining whether or not behaviour is influenced by ethnic identity.

There were, of course, many more than the twenty ethnic categories recorded in the survey than were used in the study of the perception of ethnic distance. In fact there were eighty-eight ethnic categories among the men occupying single accommodation, although some of these categories were merely those with slight ethnographic variations from some of the others. All of the twenty ethnic categories used in the study of perception

10

were in fact encountered, although for some of them there were only one or two in the sample. In order to arrive at a measure of social distance based on the ethnic composition of these groups an index of association was calculated for each of the twenty selected ethnic categories in respect of each of the remainder. Because the numbers involved varied, we needed a measure that would vary from say 1·0, when there was as little sharing of accommodation with any specific ethnic category as possible, to say 0·0 when the sharing was exclusively and equally with some specified ethnic category. In order to derive such an index the number of persons from each specified ethnic category in a dwelling unit was squared and the product of all the numbers of persons in different ethnic categories computed. This computation was performed for each unit in the sample, and the squares and cross-products for each dwelling unit summed for all the dwelling units in the sample. It follows that if some ethnic category was never found in a dwelling unit in association with some other category then the value of the aggregated cross-products for these two categories would be zero, but the numbers of these ethnic categories found in association with other ethnic categories would be squared and added together nevertheless. A ratio computed with the sum of cross-products as the numerator in this case must necessarily be zero, so that if the ratio were subtracted from unity the index would itself be unity. This would meet the condition that the index would represent maximum possible distance. Consider now the condition where members of one ethnic category were only found in equal numbers in association with members of some other specified ethnic category, that is, if there are x members of the first ethnic category in the dwelling unit there would be x members of the second ethnic group in the unit. The sum of squares of the number of members of the ethnic groups in the dwelling units would both be $\sum x^2_i$. But the sum of cross-products in the dwelling units would also be $\sum x^2_i$, since there are the same numbers from each ethnic group in each dwelling-house. Hence, if we compute the ratio of the sum of cross-products to the product of the square roots of the two sets of sum of squares, where the numbers from the ethnic groups were entirely equal the ratio would be unity. If this were subtracted from unity then the index would be equal to zero, which is the value that we

11

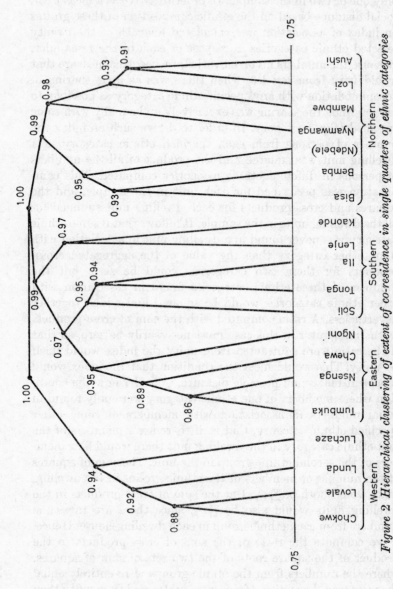

Figure 2 Hierarchical clustering of extent of co-residence in single quarters of ethnic categories. The indices on the figure, however, are shown only to two significant places.

Note: The levels of linkage in the figure were determined from indices to four significant places.

required when the two ethnic groups were always equally associated in dwelling units. The extent to which ethnic categories were proportionately associated in residential units therefore would be reflected by the size of this index, the smaller the index the greater the degree of co-residence.[7]

Given a set of indices of this kind we may now use the same method as was used in the analysis of perceived ethnic distances to recover the structure of co-residence among the men from the twenty ethnic categories. The result of this analysis is set out in *Figure 2*.

Since we are only interested in, and the method of analysis only takes account of, the ordinal relationships among the set of ethnic categories, the actual sizes of the indices do not matter. What is of interest is the patterning of clustering that emerges from the data. The broad similarity with the clustering for the perceptual data is apparent. The same clusters of western peoples and eastern peoples appear. The cluster of southern people is here split into two separate clusters, the Lenje being attached now to the Kaonde in a cluster of their own. The northern cluster also emerges, except that the Ndebele and the Lozi are included in it, whereas in the perceptual data the Ndebele were only very loosely connected to both the northern and eastern peoples and the Lozi were loosely attached to the southern people. As with the perceptual data the western cluster of ethnic categories emerges as being separated from the remainder, who are all linked into a single higher order cluster, before being finally linked to the western cluster at the maximum distance of 1·0. Within the separate clusters there are several disparities with the pattern derived from the perceptual data. Among the western people the Luchaze are less centrally linked to the Tumbuka before they are to the Ngoni; among the northern people the Bemba are linked to the Bisa rather than to the Mambwe and Nyamwanga.

CULTURAL AND STRUCTURAL FRAMEWORKS OF
ETHNICITY

The point at issue in this analysis is the relationship between the way in which people perceive the social alignments and separations among ethnic categories and the way they actually behave towards them, in the restricted sense that we have defined behaviour here. We have pictured the cognitive framework of ethnicity as a set of shared meanings attached to socially identifiable ethnic cues that provide the actors with sets of expectations of behaviour. In so far as association and separation of ethnic categories is concerned the structure of these meanings, which has been presented, represents, as I have pointed out, a generalized or 'average' picture made up of the different perceptions of the component subjects of respondents with different ethnic identities. There are some uncertainties in the structure, as for example the positioning of the Ndebele people about which there was considerable disparity from one ethnic sub-category to another. The clearer the stereotype relating to an ethnic category the more consistent naturally, the overall positioning of that ethnic category was in relation to others. This is no more than saying, in effect, that the set of meanings generally attached to certain ethnic cues is more clear cut when attached to them than to other cues, so that overall there is less ambiguity about the relationship of these ethnic categories to others. In the same way if the number of cases is small the structure of inter-ethnic distances derived from the data on residence may be misleading. If a few persons of a given ethnic identity are distributed in a few dwelling units the method of calculation of the index of association will inflate the value of the index. Consider, for example, the linkage of the Ndebele with the Bemba in *Figure 2*. In fact there were only two dwelling units in the total of 891 in the sample in which Ndebele men were living. In one case the dwelling unit had two men in it – one a Bemba and the other an Ndebele. In the other case there were three men: a Bemba, a Nsenga, and an Ndebele. The fact that both Ndebele men in the sample happened to be living with Bemba men may be socially significant when we consider the large number of possible alternatives open to them. But both of these cases occurred in Livingstone, which is nearer to Southern Rhodesia than any of the other towns and is on the direct railway route from Ndebele homelands around Bulawayo. Although there were very few Ndebele persons as a whole (11 per 10,000 adult males) encountered in the survey most were naturally found in Livingstone (21 per 10,000 adult males). While the Bemba were the largest group (1,238 per

10,000 adult males) they were nevertheless a minority (430 per 10,000 adult males) in Livingstone. The co-residence of Bemba and Ndebele in Livingstone therefore probably arises out of their minority status in that town, and while real in fact represents a contingency that explains to some extent the disparity of behaviour and perception. The data relating to co-residence presented here is combined for all towns from the Copperbelt in the north to Livingstone in the south.

Each town, of course, presents a different demographic ethnic context and the Bemba are a minority in the Lozi-dominated town of Livingstone (1,495 per 10,000 adult males), but the Lozi are a minority on the Copperbelt (103 per 10,000 adult males). Ethnic behaviour is likely to differ in these divergent contexts. A more detailed analysis of ethnic behaviour would need to consider in greater detail the actual ethnic context of each town, but the structure represented in *Figure 2*, like that for the cognitive data, relates to general ethnic behaviour.

CONSTRUCTIONS OF ETHNICITY

The problem now presents itself: what is the analytical relationship between the patterns of cognitive and behavioural ethnicity? A suitable departure-point for the exploration of this problem is the distinction between ethnicity as a structural concept and ethnicity as a cultural concept.

Earlier I made the distinction between ethnicity as a structural as compared to a cultural phenomenon. As a structural concept ethnicity has been taken to be an abstract attribute of actors by means of which an analyst is able to provide some general understanding or explanation of the conduct of these actors. If an analyst was able to label any actor as being a member of some designated 'ethnic group' therefore, taking into account the situation in which the actor was placed, this predicated a more or less determinate set of actions. For a man to be identified as a member of a certain 'ethnic group', for example, justified the expectations of those interested in political behaviour that he would support, and vote for, some political party with which that 'ethnic group' was connected.

Not unnaturally, those concerned with wider order social relationships, political scientists for instance, are likely to use

15

ethnicity in this structural sense. Anthropologists, such as Cohen & Middleton (1970), concerned with behaviour of the same order appear to view ethnicity in the same light. Here they are concerned with 'incorporation' by which they mean the processes by which groups merge, amalgamate, and develop into new collectivities with new and/or emergent identities (Cohen/ Middleton 1970: 10). Cohen and Middleton clearly recognize the structural basis of ethnicity in this context for they point out that 'anthropologists have always been aware that their methodological isolation of the tribal or ethnic group is in large degrees an abstraction, useful for both the gathering of field data and the comparative analysis of ethnographic material' (Cohen/ Middleton 1970: 5). Abstract concepts of this kind are, of course, primarily analytical devices and as such are structural in the sense that I am using that word here.

On the other hand, ethnicity may be conceived of as a cognitive or cultural phenomenon in terms of which actors themselves may structure their experiences. This approach, which has a respectable place in anthropological thinking,[8] instructed my own studies of ethnicity in industrial towns (Mitchell 1956) but several other writers have also adopted it. Mercier, for example, warns against 'any schematic and rigid definition of the ethnic groups' and emphasizes that it is necessary to 'stress how its present manifestations are far from having always the same significance'. Instead he writes of ethnicity as 'a kind of "particularism" which is a *form* of expression common to oppositions which can in fact be quite different in nature'. The study of ethnicity he concludes 'must be to a large degree at the level of *symbols* and *justifications*' (original italics) (Mercier 1965: 485). Wallerstein argues on much the same lines. He states for example that 'membership in an ethnic group is a matter of social definition, an interplay of the self-definition of members and the definition of other groups' (Wallerstein 1965: 474). Cohen has made the same point in connection with his notion of retribalization, which he describes as:

'a process by which a group from one ethnic category, whose members are involved in a struggle for power and privileges with the members of a group from another ethnic category,

16

within the framework of a *formal* political system, manipulate some customs, values, myths, symbols and ceremonials from their cultural tradition in order to articulate an *informal* political organization which is used as a weapon in that struggle' (original italics) (Cohen 1969: 2).[9]

I take this to imply that whatever the oppositions and divergence of interests of individuals, they may mobilize their perceptions and understandings of ethnic diacritica in order to express those oppositions and divergences. Gulliver is much clearer on the distinction. In discussing 'tribalism' as a factor in the problems of unity and identity in East Africa, for example, he writes that 'to some extent ['tribe'] represents real divisions of people on the ground: to some extent it is a mental concept, strongly coloured by emotion, made use of to "explain" or to justify divisions which have their sources elsewhere' (Gulliver 1969: 2). The 'real divisions of people on the ground' would here relate, I presume, to what I have referred to as ethnicity as a structural concept. The 'mental concept of "tribe" ' would refer to the cognitive or perceptual concept of ethnicity. The necessary relationships between these two somewhat different aspects of the notion of ethnicity remain for Gulliver, however, problematical, and he likens the controversy between those who use ethnicity as a structural and those who use it as a cognitive category to the age-old 'nature–nurture' debate. He rejects any necessary 'either-or' dichotomy and points out that 'both concrete interests and cultural forms and symbols are inherent in tribal differentiation' (Gulliver 1969: 34). He then goes on to quote La Fontaine to emphasize the point made earlier that people may use language and culture to signify their opposition to others from whom they are divided on other grounds.

The most sophisticated treatment of ethnicity as a cognitive category thus far has been that of Barth and his colleagues (1969). Barth argues that by concentrating on 'what is *socially effective*' ethnicity becomes a principle of social organization (original italics) (1969: 13). But the 'socially effective' turns on a self-ascribed and other-ascribed membership to an ethnic category which 'classifies a person in terms of his basic most general identity, presumptively determined by his origin and

17

background' (1969: 13). Ethnic groups, therefore, appear because people utilize these ascriptive identities in their relationship with others. Barth goes to some trouble to separate these cognitive identities from the 'objective' categories that the ethnographer may establish on the basis of his analyses of the cultural characteristics exhibited by people whom he considers to be members of some designated ethnic group. The assumed identity is based upon certain diacritica which the actors are able to recognize and they imply some evaluation of the behaviour of the persons so categorized in terms of what people expect of them by reason of the label they have attached to them. Barth points out that: 'Neither of these kinds of cultural "contents" follows from a descriptive list of cultural features or cultural differences: one cannot predict from first principles which features will be emphasized and made organizationally relevant by the actors'. 'In other words', he goes on, 'ethnic categories provide an organizational vessel that may be given varying amounts and forms of content in different sociocultural systems. They may be of great relevance to behaviour, but they need not be; they may provide all social life, or they may be relevant only in limited sectors of activity' (1969: 14). This emphasis on ascription then shifts the attention of Barth and his colleagues from ethnicity as a structural characteristic to the definition and maintenance of the ethnic boundaries. The individual contributors to the book then devote their attention to aspects of this problem.

The position I have taken on ethnicity utilizes both the cognitive and the structural approaches. The real problems of analysis lie, however, in the combination of the two types of approach rather than inside either. This devolves from the approach I had taken in the early 1950s concerning the nature of what I then called 'tribalism' in towns in Central Africa (Mitchell 1956) and which I developed more explicitly in a subsequent paper (Mitchell 1970). At that time it was still common for urban administrators and for some anthropologists to conceptualize the behaviour of migrants in towns in terms of 'detribalization' by which they meant the falling into desuetude of customs, beliefs and practices to which the migrant had firmly adhered before he had come to town. There were several objections both in relation to facts and in relation to analytical rigour to this sort of approach. While it was patently and some-what trivially true that migrants from rural areas could not follow some of the practices of their erstwhile homes in towns, at the same time they were able to continue others, such as for example, those related to domestic life, without too much difficulty. This led me to suggest, following Gluckman's lead (1940) that the practices which migrants followed could be understood by relating them to the social situation in which they appeared. This approach had the advantage of treating the behaviour of persons who were following what might be con-strued as 'tribal' modes of behaviour in one social situation, within the same framework of analysis that could be applied to these people in the situations in which they were acting as town-dwellers. The norms, beliefs and customs in terms of which the behaviour might be construed may have differed widely as a migrant moved from situation to situation but regularities in similarly defined situations allowed some system-atic analysis of behaviour. This was developed particularly in Epstein's work on the growth of trade unions and political organizations on the Copperbelt (1958).

At the same time a manifestation of ethnic behaviour of a different kind was apparent in everyday behaviour in Central African towns. This was the way in which ethnic identities provided the basis for certain types of public behaviour. The fact that these identities were often in terms of the rural or 'tribal' origins, led easily to the assumption that the identities, irrespective of the public situation in which they were involved implied practices, beliefs and customs associated with the rural origin to which the identity referred. In fact, however, it was not difficult to show that these identities were categorical and were in fact a labelling process which related primarily to expectations of behaviour in that public place rather than to basic customs, beliefs and practices. A detailed knowledge of the actual origin of participants involved in categorical ethnic behaviour in typical urban situations, soon showed that people from quite dissimilar ethnic groups were being labelled in terms of some wider more inclusive category and behaviour was appropriately adjusted to this label. Thus, in one instance a Chewa person was identified with the ethnographically dis-similar, but geographically close, Ngoni by a Lungu person who, in turn, was identified by the Chewa person as the ethnographically similar but nevertheless distinct Bemba who also like the Lungu, live in the Northern Province of Zambia (Mitchell 1956: 39). This behaviour could only be understood, first, in terms of the expectancies of behaviour rooted in the urban institution of ethnic joking relationships in which the Ngoni and Bemba are expected to express their hostilities in ribaldry, and, second, in terms of the process of categorical

FIGURE 3 *Different levels of analytical and commonsense abstractions of ethnic phenomena*

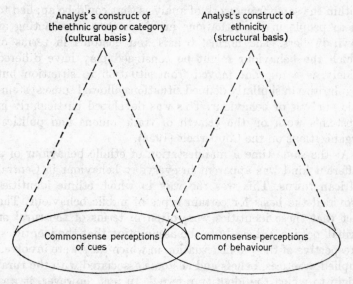

labelling in which the Chewa were identified with the Ngoni and the Lungu with the Bemba.

The common origin of people in towns and the extent to which because of their common origin they share norms, beliefs and customs, particularly language, provides them with a set of understandings in terms of which they are able to interact in the towns. This means that in personal, as against public, behaviour the ethnic origin of a person in town is likely to have a distinct significance. It now becomes the basis upon which he is able to share experiences with someone else if they have the same origin, or to become absorbed as one facet of a multiplex

relationship with the other.[10] In either case the perception of
ethnic identity becomes an understanding which has meaning
for the social action of the people concerned, but this meaning
clearly is contained in the social situation in which the interaction is taking place.

Situational ethnicity has been noted in several other field
studies particularly in towns. Paden, for example, referring to
Kano, speaks of an ethnic regrouping in the city based on urban
categories of migrant ethnic units (1970: 245).[11] But when
phenomena which derive from ethnicity are used in analytical
writings their origin in the perceptions and actions of people involved in different social situations, may in fact have quite varied
epistemological statuses. This arises because social phenomena
may be subsumed into analytical categories often at differing
levels of analysis or based upon abstractions from different
aspects of the phenomenon in question. Failure to recognize
these differences in levels or types of abstraction lead at least
to misunderstandings, or at worst to analytical confusions.

I find it useful to distinguish four different types and levels
of abstraction relating to ethnic phenomena which may be
diagrammatically represented as in *Figure 3*.

Initially there are the actors' perceptions of differing customs,
practices, costumes, beliefs, and other cultural phenomena
which become the basis of their appreciation of 'ethnicity' as an
everyday phenomenon. There is also a set of folk interpretations
of behaviour in terms of perceived or assumed ethnicity, such
as, for example, assumed 'tribal' voting in political elections.
The 'commonsense' understandings of ethnicity are represented
in *Figure 3* by overlapping ellipses because from the actors'
point of view some aspects of behaviour and of culture are in-
separable. The members of an ethnic category who are performing a folk-dance in a multi-ethnic situation, for example, both
exhibit their ethnic identity in the dance that they perform and
the dance is explained by their ethnic identity. Ethnic characteristics, however, need not necessarily imply expectations of
'ethnic' behaviour as for example when a folk-dance is performed as part of normal recreation in an ethnic region where
the dance is taken to be part of everyday activity and has no
additional meaning to its performers or its spectators. Equally
ethnic explanations of behaviour need not in the first instance

necessarily involve conscious perception of ethnic criteria. Attendance at particular dance clubs, for example, might possibly coincide with ethnic identities but the attendance may have arisen from the tight-knit sets of personal relationships among members of ethnic groups. Later the dance clubs may become identified with particular ethnic groups and so become part of the conscious perception of the actors but until this happens the ethnic identity of the attenders may well serve as a preliminary explanation to the analyst without its necessarily being a commonsense ethnic phenomenon. Out of the two overlapping sets of folk perception the analyst may abstract two rather different analytical constructs. From the *ethnic* categorization he may abstract an *ethnographic* categorization which has relevance for the sort of analytical operations he wishes to perform with it. The ethnographer's construct of a culturally homogeneous 'people' is such an abstraction. Equally he may arrive at an abstract interpretation of ethnic behaviour by a detailed analysis of the actions of people in which ethnicity is only one component and of which, in fact, the people themselves may not be fully aware. Patterns of inter-ethnic marriage may be such a construct where, among many marriages an ethnic bias in the choice of spouses may be apparent while to the individuals concerned ethnicity may not appear to be involved at all.

The characteristics of these four types of ethnicity in more detail are as follows:

(a) *Commonsense Constructs*

In the first instance ethnicity may be construed as the set of meanings which actors attribute to certain symbols, signs or cues by means of which they are able to identify other persons as members of 'cultural' sets or categories. This is similar to the notion of the 'native model' (Ward 1965, quoted by Barth 1969: 120). At this phenomenological level the ethnic category exists as part of the framework of social perceptions of the actors. The symbols, signs and cues may be costume, hairstyle, language, facial scarifications, diet, or any combination of similar diacritica by means of which the actor is able to 'label' or categorize the person who presents these cues. Once the cues have been recognized and interpreted and the ethnic identity thereby established then the actor has available to him a set of expectations of the person's behaviour towards him. Note that the perception of the ethnic category, although fundamentally a psychological process, from the point of view of social analysis is significant for its *consequences* for behaviour and how people construe that behaviour. The actual process of perception might properly be studied by a social psychologist. Our interest is mainly in the fact that perception has a social referent. The 'ethnic category' therefore has significance in that it exists as a 'collective representation' which is not only common among a designated set of people but is also shared by them so that the shared perceptions can become the basis of an understanding between them in their social relationships.

The ethnic meaning which may be accorded to some set of signs, symbols and cues is not necessarily attached rigidly to those diacritica throughout all social situations in which they may be present. Meanings exist as cognitive *referents* which actors are able to mobilize in different ways and in different social situations to validate their behaviour. A person identified as Catholic 'Irish' in Boston, for example, is expected to behave in a particular way in the context of United States society and in Boston society in particular. The same person identified in the same way in Belfast in 1970 would be subject to a somewhat different set of expectations. The social meanings of ethnicity, therefore depend directly on the wider social context of which it is only a part, since the meanings have social significance in that they enable behaviour to be predicted. This view of ethnicity as a set of situationally determined meanings leaves open, of course, the possibility that there could be several contradictory definitions of ethnicity possible for a set of actors in a social situation so that the meaning which comes to prevail will need to be negotiated by the actors. This happens sometimes in relation to ethnic joking behaviour on the Copperbelt where one party may address his behaviour towards another in terms of his perception of the joking relationship. When this happens in public life the somewhat unexpected and aggressive behaviour so presented may surprise the other until he

23

accepts the definition of the joking situation. Sometimes he refuses to accept the proffered definition in which case the hostility is not dissipated by the joking and a tense encounter ensues. The joking relationship must therefore be negotiated by the actors before they can accept it as a frame of public interaction.[12]

(b) *The Ethnographer's Construct: the Ethnic Group*

These folk-perceptions of ethnic diacritica constitute part of the raw material from which the analyst is able to construct his abstract model of the 'ethnic group'. The ethnographer systematically records the ethnic meanings that people attribute to specified sets of diacritica whether they exhibit these themselves or they are the attributes of people ascribed to some other ethnic category. To the extent to which these meanings are shared by the actors and are not simply idiosyncrasies of a limited number of people the ethnographer may run across, they may be treated as part of the culture of the people concerned. The 'shared meanings' of ethnic diacritica then become a first order abstraction which the ethnographer makes from his field notes in order to record one aspect of the 'culture' of the people he is describing. Usually, however, he takes the process of abstraction several steps further. He is able not only to identify the socially perceived diacritica but to check and reinforce these by observations he is able to make directly of the customs, practices, and values of the various peoples concerned. From his observations he may be able to isolate particular combinations of these identifiable features which he may then use to classify peoples as a whole into ethnographic types. These theoretical ethnographic categories, as distinct from the ethnic categories at the common-sense level, are then second order abstractions which the ethnographer may use to state propositions, for example, about the distribution of peoples in some region of the world or to set some people he is describing in a framework of comparison with other peoples. This seems essentially to be the procedure that Naroll (1964) is describing for Ethnic Unit Classification.

The processes by which ethnographic categories are arrived

at are sometimes a little obscure. Sometimes formal procedures of analysis or ethnographic traits may be used as for example by Driver & Schuessler (1957) who used factor analysis to separate peoples into ethnographic categories by the extent to which a specified set of practices and customs had or had not been reported for them. I am not here concerned with the validity of formal procedures of this kind: my purpose is merely to suggest that the category that an ethnographer may eventually establish for his analytical purposes must be a different order of abstraction from the ethnic categories of the people themselves and, of course, it will be put to a completely different use. It is possible, therefore, that the ethnographer's classification may be quite unrecognizable to the people themselves. He is likely to come up with a set of diacritica of an ethnographic category which is meaningless to the people concerned for their own perceptions arise out of a different process of abstraction in a different context and are directed towards a different end. Yet it is necessary to make this elementary point since the danger that the unwary may slip from the analytical level of ethnographic categorization to that of commonsense ethnic categorization is very real. If they should do this and try to use the latter analytically when only the former is appropriate for this purpose, then confusion is sure to ensue. This is what I fear has happened when Moerman criticized the procedure advocated by Naroll and several others who recommend similar procedures. He writes of these procedures: 'none of them helps me to discover who the Lue are; none "tends towards a sharper crystallization" in situations of continuous variation; none relates as directly to social and cultural patterns as they exist in the minds of culture bearers, and none are as easy to discover as is ethnic identification expressed by the existence of an ethnic label used as a means of describable procedures for applying that label and its contrast labels' (1965: 1221). But Moerman is talking about ethnicity as it exists, in his words, 'in the minds of the culture bearers', whereas Naroll and those who are concerned with similar problems is concerned with valid conceptualization of ethnicity as an analytical construct, which is a construct of an entirely different epistemological status.

(c) *Ethnicity as a Commonsense Interpretation of Behaviour*

Thus far I have been concerned with the meanings that actors and analysts separately give to their perception of phenomena which are primordially defined as ethnic.[13] These meanings as collective representations in turn, however, may become commonsense interpretations for the actions of people, for which the analyst may have different interpretations. I am referring here to the process whereby an ethnic categorization becomes a dominant element in public perception and so comes to be taken as an adequate explanation for the behaviour of the people so defined. This is what Parkin describes as 'a blame-pinning' device (Parkin 1969: 274). The tribal identity of an actor in these circumstances overrides all others and becomes sufficient explanation for his behaviour to the others involved. As Epstein and I described, the struggle for power within the African Mineworkers Union in Zambia (then Northern Rhodesia) in the 1950s was interpreted by many participants and observers at the time, as due to the ethnic oppositions of the actors concerned (see Epstein 1958, and Mitchell 1956). Here ethnicity is a commonsense construct which makes people's actions intelligible to observers. In the sense that all perceptions and understandings are real to those who have them, then this folk-concept of ethnicity is a valid explanation of behaviour at a certain level of analysis. But for the analyst's purpose it must be treated not as an explanation in these terms but merely as a datum from which he can begin to develop explanatory propositions of a somewhat different order of abstraction. Ethnic explanation then at the commonsense level is a cognitive phenomenon of the same order as the perception of ethnic diacritica and amenable to use by the analyst in a similar way.

(d) *Analytical Ethnic Explanation*

The analyst, however, when seeking an explanation of behaviour in terms of general principles must necessarily separate commonsense explanations from those which have validity at the level of interpretation at which he is operating. There are likely to be several identifiable strands in any social

action, any of which the analyst may consider has explanatory significance in terms of his set of theoretical postulates.
For he may choose to see the struggle for power within the
trade union in terms of the positions of antagonists in the
trade union structure as a whole in which ethnic identities
become for each merely one way in which to mobilize support.
The real roots of the struggle lie not in ethnicity as such but
in oppositions which arise in all associations in which office
is accorded by elective procedures.

Nevertheless the analyst may find that irrespective of the
interpretation that the actors put on actions, certain patterns
of behaviour emerge which he might find convenient to
express in capsule form as ethnicity. These patterns may in
fact arise out of the behaviour of the actors in terms of their
appreciation of ethnic diacritica, or they may arise when the
actors themselves are not conscious of the presence of 'ethnic'
elements in the actions involved. The essential point is that
just as there is no necessary connection between ethnic and
ethnographic categorization so there may be none between
ethnicity as a folk category and ethnicity as an analytical
category.

The abstract analytical constructs are in fact properties
which are emergent from the perceptions and actions of the
people involved and have the same abstract qualities of
all emergent properties described by Blau as 'relationships
between elements in a structure which are not manifest in the
elements themselves'. A triangle, for example, is a property
which emerges from the lines joining three points which are
not in a straight line. But the property of triangular shape is
not contained in any of these lines considered independently
of the other two lines (1964: 3). The abstract constructs of
ethnicity and ethnographic classification thus are relational
properties of the perceptions and actions of actors which the
analyst finds convenient to use as a general explanation for
a specified class of phenomenon. He concludes, for example,
to revert to the earlier example, that irrespective of the
perceptions and understandings of the people involved and
taking into account other factors at the same level of abstraction, people consistently choose their spouses from people whom
they identify ethnically with themselves, or at least from

ethnic categories that are 'socially' close to them. Or in terms of the sort of phenomenon used in this analysis that, irrespective of other factors operating in the situation, men who have no wives with them in the town choose to live with people from ethnic categories similar to their own although to do so may not appear problematic to them. Ethnicity here is a general abstract property of empirically observed relationships which is amenable to observations only to those who are prepared systematically to conduct the basic theoretic analysis of the phenomenon to reveal that property.

Equally the ethnographer may arrive at an ethnographic map of a region through a detailed and systematic analysis of the cultural traits of the peoples in the area. The inhabitants of the region are unlikely to have the detailed information at their command to make a similar analysis and in any case unless they were interested in problems of ethnographic taxonomy would be likely to see little point in the exercise. The 'ethnic group' here is essentially a property of the concatenation of cultural traits and as such it is a useful tool for the ethnographer's purposes. But it should not be confused with the people's own perception of ethnic identities from which it could differ quite radically.

SITUATIONS, MEANINGS, AND ACTIONS

The purpose in separating these different orders of ethnic phenomena and abstract constructions of ethnicity is primarily to clarify the analytical problems involved in appreciating the significance of ethnicity in everyday social actions. The empirical data have shown that the regularities in the over-all 'distance' relationships among ethnic categories recovered from cognitive material coincide substantially with those recovered from observations of the behaviour even though the sets of respondents were very different in composition. An examination of the discrepancies between the cognitive and behavioural structures of ethnic distance in *Figures 1* and *2* suggests that some of them, furthermore, may be explained by special circumstances such as the small number of representatives of some of the ethnic categories involved or the relative numerical minority of members of some ethnic categories in particular towns. This suggests that both abstractions have arisen from a common

28

ethnic component of social life which was a reality in the daily lives of the people of Zambia at the time of the study.

The reality, however, manifests itself in the sequences of social situations through which individuals pass in the course of day-to-day urban existence. The fusing of structural and cultural constructions of ethnic behaviour, therefore, must occur in the interpretations of sequences of actions of people involved in social situations. At this level, however, the distinction between action and social perception is a convenience of which the analyst may avail himself in order to achieve a particular type of theoretical understanding of the situation. For the people themselves there will probably be no point in distinguishing them.

The instrumental character of analytical commonsense abstractions is brought out by a more detailed examination of some of the data used earlier. When we consider the set of circumstances which lead to a number of unattached men sharing accommodation together we become aware of the complexity of factors influencing their choices. There are, however, difficulties in separating out the independent effect of ethnicity from these factors. For one thing because of the housing policy at the time when the survey was conducted, employers provided the accommodation for the workers even in local authority housing (that is, by paying the rent for the dwelling which houses their workers) so that one condition of accommodation together was that the men should work together. The analysis of the co-residence data was made within such a framework so that most of the men were co-workers almost by definition. Similar restrictions apply to other factors. Because of the way in which Christian missionary activities were conducted in Central Africa in the past there is a close correlation of religious affiliation and area of origin and hence ethnic identity. The vast majority of the men in the sample were unskilled workers with little education so that differentiation of residence in terms of these factors is also likely to be difficult. Similarly there was a strong tendency for young men to be single. All in all there is likely to be a concatenation of social characteristics distinguishing one set of co-residents of single quarters from another. I happen to have chosen, because of its relevance to the topic of discussion, to examine the way in which the pattern of

29

co-residence coincides with certain perceptions of the social distance among ethnic categories. It is possible, however, that substantially the same composition of single quarter residential units would be explained by age, occupational, educational or religious affiliations.[14] Whether the actors themselves would identify age, occupation, education and religious beliefs as the basis upon which they choose to share accommodation I cannot say. Certainly I can confirm that sometimes when men were found sharing accommodation with others whose ethnic category in terms of the cognitive paradigm represented in *Figure 1*, would be considered to be distant from their own category, they seemed conscious of it and said that they were merely waiting for the opportunity to move to a household of ethnically more congenial fellows. But the essential point is that this represents their own 'construction of reality' in terms of which they thought the general public would likely find their desire to move perfectly reasonable. In this instance ethnicity had been selected from a variety of other possible constructions to justify a particular intended action. But the contrary process is also possible. In a previous paper I argued that it was not that ethnic differences led to political divisions but rather that political oppositions are phrased in ethnic terms and in so doing provide the sentiments in terms of which social actions may be justified. A challenger, for example, can accuse his opponent of favouring people of his own 'tribe' and by so doing mobilize support from those who come from different 'tribes'. The meaning given to the notion of 'tribe' here is that it provides the sentiment in terms of which personal services may be claimed and acceded to. In time the association of the tribe of a leader with the organization he leads may become so strong that the contradictions between the belief and reality tend to become ignored or explained away. This point was neatly demonstrated in an incident from Kapferer's fieldwork when a respected political leader was being discussed. Although a staunch supporter of independence and an influential member of the governing party he came nevertheless from a tribal group which was opposed to the government and hence to the tribal group commonly associated with the government. Those discussing the leader, all of them from the tribe with which the ruling party was associated, however, excused the leader saying that all his behaviour demonstrated that in fact he was not really a person from his own tribe but was in fact operationally defined as a member of the tribe associated with the party in power (Mitchell 1970 : 98). Here the actors selected the political identity in contradistinction to ethnic identity to relate themselves to the leader in question. The inconsistency between ethnic group and party was thus resolved by expanding the meaning they gave to ethnicity to make party membership coterminous with it.

The selection of ethnic identity as a means of organizing the meaning of social action, therefore, depends heavily upon the context in which the social action takes place. As yet the particular processes through which an acceptable definition of a social situation is negotiated by the actors involved are poorly understood. The analyst, however, should be able to approach this theoretically because he is able to appreciate the instrumental advantage to the actors of alternative justifications of action and he is able to explain logically why the actors chose one frame rather than another in terms of which to construe their social actions.

From this point of view 'ethnicity' at the commonsense level is simply the significance that is attributed to perceptible cultural distinctions in so far as public action is concerned. As such it is beyond further analysis and must remain a primordial basis of definition in the same way that sex or occupation is: it cannot be reduced to more elemental form. There is no point from a sociological point of view to enquiries as to why a particular ethnic group has certain characteristics attributed to it. In so far as social action is concerned the analysis must start rather from the fact of these attributes and proceed to show how they are used or ignored by actors in different situations. Neglect of the primordial character of ethnicity in this sense has led to much fruitless and unilluminating debate over what is meant by ethnicity. What is meant by ethnicity is what it implies for the behaviour of the actors concerned.

When ethnicity is treated as an emergent property, however, its epistemological status is different from that of ethnicity at a commonsense level of analysis and the basis of its logical coherence is also different. The analyst's construct of ethnicity, as a property which is emergent from everyday perceptions and actions, as Cohen and Middleton imply (1970 : 5) is logical

31

because he makes it so by the way he arrives at it. The utility of an analytical tool of this kind depends upon the extent to which other scholars are able to take it up and to arrive at its implications for their material by the ordinary rules of logic. The actor's construct is consistent through his selection of appropriate referents from a set of beliefs and values – often inconsistent among themselves – through which he is able to order his appreciation of the outside world. The actor's interpretation of another's behaviour in terms of ethnic stereotypes can be taken to be a manifestation of the process whereby he orders the reality of the outside world in a meaningful way by choosing the appropriate 'meanings' whereas the regularities that the analyst perceives linking his abstract ethnic categories with the social behaviour he observes is a demonstration rather of the plausibility of his sociological analysis.

ACKNOWLEDGEMENTS

I am grateful to Drs G. Kingsley Garbett and Bruce Kapferer and to Hilary Mitchell for constructive comments on an earlier draft of this paper.

NOTES

[1] The groups used are as set out in *Figure 1*.

[2] Details are set out in Mitchell (forthcoming).

[3] Thus, the entries in the $n(n-1)/2$ cells were

$$\frac{\sum_{i,j=1}^{20}(S_i - S_j)^2}{325} \quad i \neq j$$

where the subscripts i and j refer to the ethnic categories used in the analysis. The diagonal cells by definition, of course, would be zero. Four respondents of the original 329 were lost in the transcription from the original data to the computer record.

[4] For example, if we are prepared to assume that the scores on our scale are true interval measures we could transform the interpoint distances to distances from the centroid and use any appropriate procedure for determining the axes of the multi-dimensional space which could contain those points. If we are prepared to accept only the ordinal relations among the ethnic groups we could use the Lingoes-Guttman smallest space procedures. I have successfully used this latter procedure in Mitchell (forthcoming) but I have not used it here because the data relating to the behavioural aspect of ethnic distance led only to a degenerate solution since there were too many tied distances at the extreme distance of 'no shared accommodation'.

[5] It is here that the procedure which I have used differs from that suggested by Johnson (1967). He suggested either the distance to the nearest element, or alternatively the distance to the most distant element.

[6] They are taken up in Mitchell (forthcoming).

[7] Symbolically the value of the index of association is

$$I = 1 - \frac{\Sigma x_i x_j}{\sqrt{\Sigma x_i^2 x_j^2}}$$

where x_i is the number of members of the first ethnic group in the dwelling unit and x_j the numbers of the second ethnic group in the dwelling. I am grateful to Dr David Peizer of the Center for Advanced Study in the Behavioral Sciences, Palo Alto, who suggested this measure to me.

[8] It underlies Nadel's (1942, 1949) analysis of the social structure of Nupe and Nuba, for example, and Fortes's (1945) of the Tallensi.

[9] We may well cavil that Cohen understands ethnicity too narrowly in terms of political relationships, but that is not the point at issue.

[10] I have discussed the role of 'meanings' in personal relationships more fully in connection with the nature of social networks, see Mitchell (1969).

[11] Paden quotes as his authority Anderson, von der Mehden, and Young (1967), but their reference appears to be indirectly to my own work, so that the confirmation is less direct than may appear at first sight.

[12] I have been stimulated here by a paper by D. Handelman and B. Kapferer (1972) on joking frames.

[13] I explain what I mean by primordial definitions below, on page 31.

[14] Of course, this may to some extent be tested empirically but I have not yet had an opportunity of trying to do so.

REFERENCES

ANDERSON, C. W., VON DER MEHDEN, F. R., YOUNG, C. (eds). 1967. *Issues of Political Development*. Englewood Cliffs, NJ: Prentice-Hall.

BARTH, FREDERICK (ed.). 1969. *Ethnic Groups and Boundaries: The Social Organization of Culture Differences*. London: George Allen & Unwin.

BLAU, PETER M. 1964. *Exchange and Power in Social Life*. New York: John Wiley.

COHEN, ABNER. 1969. *Custom and Politics in Urban Africa: A Study of Hausa Migrants in Yoruba Towns*. London: Routledge & Kegan Paul.

COHEN, RONALD, & MIDDLETON, JOHN. 1970. Introduction. In R. Cohen and J. Middleton (eds), *From Tribe to Nation in Africa: Studies in Incorporation Processes*: 1–34. Scranton, Penn.: Chandler Publishing.

DRIVER, H. E., & SCHUESSLER, K. F. 1957. Factor Analysis of Ethnographic Data. *American Anthropologist* 59: 655–63.

EPSTEIN, A. L. 1958. *Politics in an Urban African Community*. Manchester: Manchester University Press for Rhodes-Livingstone Institute.

FORTES, M. 1945. *The Dynamics of Clanship among the Tallensi*. London. Oxford University Press.

J. C. Mitchell

GLUCKMAN, M. 1940. The Analysis of a Social Situation in Modern
Zululand. *African Studies* **14**: 1–30; 147–74. Reprinted (1958) as
Rhodes-Livingstone Paper No. 28. Manchester: Manchester
University Press.

GULLIVER, P. H. 1969. Introduction. P. H. Gulliver (ed.), *Tradition
and Transition in East Africa: Studies in the Tribal Element in
the Modern Era:* 5–40. London: Routledge & Kegan Paul.

HANDELMAN, DON, and KAPFERER, BRUCE. 1972. Forms of
Joking Activity: A Comparative Approach. *American Anthropologist* **74**: 484–517.

JOHNSON, S. C. 1967. Hierarchical Clustering Schemes. *Psychometrika* **32**: 241–54.

LA PIERE, R. T. 1934. Attitudes *v.* Actions. *Social Forces* **12**: 230–7.

LONGTON, JANET. 1955. A Study of Social Distance in a Secondary
School. Paper given to the Ninth Conference of Research
Officers, 22 March 1955. Rhodes-Livingstone Institute. Lusaka.

MERCIER, PAUL. 1965. On the Meaning of 'Tribalism' in Black
Africa. In Pierre Van den Berghe (ed.), *Africa: Social Problems
of Change and Conflict:* 483–501. San Francisco: Chandler
Publishing.

MITCHELL, J. C. 1956. *The Kalela Dance. Aspects of Social Relationships among Urban Africans in Northern Rhodesia.* Rhodes-Livingstone Paper No. 27. Manchester: Manchester University
Press.

—— 1962. Some Aspects of Tribal Social Distance. In A. Dubb, ed.,
The Multi-tribal Society, 38. Proceedings of the Sixteenth Conference of the Rhodes-Livingstone Institute. Lusaka: Rhodes-Livingstone Institute.

—— 1969. The Concept and Use of Social Networks. In J. C. Mitchell
(ed.), *Social Networks in Urban Situations*, 1–50. Manchester:
Manchester University Press for Institute of Social Research,
Zambia.

—— 1970. Tribe and Social Change in South Central Africa: A
Situational Approach. *Journal of Asian and African Studies* **5**:
83–101.

—— Forthcoming. *Cities, Society, and Social Perception.* London:
Longmans.

MOERMAN, M. 1965. Ethnic Identification in a Complex Civilisation: Who are the Lue? *American Anthropologist* **67**: 1215–1230.

NADEL, S. F. 1942. *A Black Byzantium.* London: Oxford University
Press.

—— 1949. *The Nuba.* London: Oxford University Press.

NAROLL, R. 1964. On Ethnic Unit Classification. *Current Anthropology* **5**: 283–91, 306–12.

PADEN, JOHN N. 1970. Urban Pluralism, Integration and Adaptation of Communal Identity in Kano, Nigeria. In R. Cohen and J. Middleton (eds.), *From Tribe to Nation in Africa: Studies in Incorporation Processes*, 242–70. Scranton, Penn.: Chandler Publishing.

PARKIN, DAVID J. 1969. Tribe as Fact and Fiction in an East African City. In P. H. Gulliver (ed.), *Tradition and Transition in East Africa: Studies in the Tribal Element in the Modern Era*, 273–96. London: Routledge & Kegan Paul.

SOUTHALL, A. W. (ed.) 1961. *Social Change in Modern Africa*. London: Oxford University Press for International African Institute.

WALLERSTEIN, IMMANUEL. 1965. Ethnicity and National Integration in West Africa. In Paul Van dan Berghe (ed.), *Africa: Social Problems of Change and Conflict*, 478–82. San Francisco: Chandler Publishing.

WARD, B. 1965. Varieties of the Conscious Model: The Fishermen of South China. In Michael Banton (ed.), *The Relevance of Models for Social Anthropology*. ASA Monographs 1. London: Tavistock Publications; New York: Barnes & Noble.

Ulf Hannerz

Ethnicity and Opportunity in Urban America

The study of ethnicity in urban communities has as its focus
the strains and the congruences between two principles of
organization. On the one hand there are the cultural, historical,
and geographical groupings of people who have come to regard
themselves or to be regarded by others as being of the same
kind, irrespective of the roles they play in the urban social
system. On the other hand there is the functional differentiation
of that system itself, with its distribution of tasks and resources,
with slots to which personnel must be recruited in one way or
other, which will determine the interests of that personnel to a
considerable extent. It is true that we have been told often
enough that some ethnic groups in African cities are not as
traditional as we might have thought but have in fact emerged
as urban phenomena because the consciousness of kind has been
aroused by the encounter with people of a variety of backgrounds. Even so, however, the distinction remains. We realize
that a Yoruba is a Yoruba regardless of whether he is a politician
or a streetsweeper, at the same time as we have come to accept
that urbanism itself may have an impact which outweighs that
of such extra-urban or quasi-urban factors – that is, 'an African
townsman is a townsman, an African miner is a miner' (Gluckman 1961: 69). As students of urban ethnicity, then, we aim at
throwing light on the variety of social arrangements in which
ethnicity and urban functional differentiation co-exist, with or
without difficulty, temporarily or in a more stabilized fashion.
Here I will attempt to show how different contexts of urban
opportunity structures in the United States have influenced
expressions of ethnic identity and social relationships within
ethnic groups. It is an exercise in which I will try to embellish
my argument with a minimum of ethnographic detail. If on the
other hand I seem to stray repeatedly to consider the work of
Africanists, it is not only to show proper respect for their
dominance in the study of urban ethnicity but also because

37

experience in one area may give insight into the other. As Banton (1965: 131) and others have noted, African and American cities have something in common in that they tend to constitute recently established and at least for some time rapidly expanding social systems which have recruited their personnel from a variety of ethnic groups. Beyond this similarity there are certainly also some important divergences which I am afraid have not always received the recognition due to them as scholars with an African base have occasionally raided American cities for comparative materials. But I would hope that by drawing attention to similarity as well as variation, these notes could be a step toward more systematic considerations which could advance our understanding of urban ethnicity.

INTEREST AND ETHNICITY

For some theoretical preliminaries before turning to American materials, I would like to use as a point of departure Cohen's (1969) study of the Hausa community of Ibadan which, besides being lucid and enjoyable ethnography, suggests a comparative framework for the study of ethnic organization in cities. The inhabitants of this community form a political and religious unit as subjects of the Hausa chief and (generally) members of the Tijaniyya order, while the greater number of them are also participants, in one way or other, in the long-distance cattle and kola trades. With the members of the community thus integrated around and dependent upon a common enterprise, which they dominate, it is certainly in their interest to ward off threatening incursions into that sphere of livelihood by outsiders. They do so by maintaining a high degree of ethnic solidarity; while relationships within the community are multiplex, based on ties of religion, politics, residence and other factors, providing a diffuse sense of identification, its members engage in few relationships with outsiders in which strong bonds of solidarity are likely to arise.

From an analysis along such lines, to the precision of which this summary regrettably cannot do justice, Cohen derives two main theoretical points:

(1) Urban ethnic groups are interest groups engaged in struggle with other groups for resources in the public arena;

38

(2) The peculiar contribution of ethnicity to this struggle is to provide an idiom which promotes solidarity as a moral duty – the specific common interests for which the battle is waged are embedded in a much wider, more complete unity.

Cohen even takes this argument so far as to define ethnicity as the strife between ethnic groups, in the course of which their members emphasize their identity and exclusiveness (1969: 4). While preferring a wider definition of ethnicity as the phenomenon whereby people are categorized in terms of those most general group identities presumptively revealed in behaviour and background (cf. Barth 1969: 13) regardless whether the situation is one of conflict, I share his concern with the uses of ethnicity in the advancement of interests, and it is on these I will continue to dwell. To begin with, I want to elaborate on the two points above.

When Cohen describes the Ibadan Hausa as an interest group there is a quite obvious basis for this characterization. Since the Hausa have concentrated in one socio-economic niche, there is a high degree of overlap between the Hausa ethnic group and the cattle and kola trading group. The sharing of interests arises from a situation in which ethnicity is at the basis of extensive role summation, so that economic, political, and religious alignments overlap with it. This is also what Glazer and Moynihan note as they make the point that ethnic groups in New York may be seen as interest groups:

> 'This is perhaps the single most important fact about ethnic groups in New York City. When one speaks of the Negroes and Puerto Ricans, one also means unorganized and unskilled workers, who hold poorly paying jobs in the laundries, hotels, restaurants, small factories or who are on relief. When one says Jews, one also means small shopkeepers, professionals, better-paid skilled workers in the garment industries. When one says Italians, one also means homeowners in Staten Island, the North Bronx, Brooklyn, and Queens.' (Glazer & Moynihan 1963: 17).

There is, however, one sense in which the point that urban ethnic groups are interest groups is somewhat ambiguous. This may become most apparent if we return to the two principles

39

of organization originally outlined. On the basis of them we can arrive at a distinction between two kinds of groups which may be involved in the struggle for resources in the urban social system. One, exemplified here by the ethnic group, is not intrinsically defined by a position somewhere in the urban opportunity structure but may attempt to gain access to or secure control over attractive niches in it. In this case the allocation of resources among these niches need not be at issue. The other kind of group may be seen as consisting of the people in a given niche, who are concerned with the definition of niche boundaries and who want to ensure that the greatest possible amount of resources is to be found within them. The members of this group may engage in disputes with the occupants of other niches in the advancement of this kind of interest; in such instances internal differences of one kind or other are seen as irrelevant. The typical example of this kind of interest group is the trade union, concerned with the allocation of resources between its members and the employers.

Now obviously an ethnic group which is an interest group in the first sense need not be an interest group in the second sense; whether it is or not depends on the positions of its members in the opportunity structure.[1] In the case of the Hausa community of Ibadan, Cohen has no difficulty because although there is some differentiation and competition within the group, there is little or no reason for interest groups of the second kind to form across its boundaries. But in his brief general discussion of the interrelations between ethnicity and social stratification the problem emerges more clearly; if we view the strata as superniches in the opportunity structure, so that a class struggle may be regarded as the conflict between interest groups over the allocation of resources among the niches, we may tie this discussion to the argument above. Cohen makes the distinction between situations in which ethnic boundaries coincide with those of social strata and situations in which ethnic groups are parallel units extending vertically across a pattern of hierarchical differentiation (Cohen 1969: 193–4). In the former case, the ethnic group obviously becomes an interest group much of the same kind as the Ibadan Hausa, in that it is located in a common niche; in so far as solidarity within the group is helpful in the conflict with other groups, idioms of ethnicity can be used

40

as expressions of the conflict between privileged and under-privileged. In the case of ethnic groups cross-cutting social strata, however, Cohen notes that

'manifestations of ethnic identity and exclusiveness will tend to be inhibited by the emerging countervailing alignments of power. The less privileged from one ethnic group will co-operate with the less privileged from other ethnic groups against the privileged from the same ethnic groups.' (Cohen 1969: 193.)

This may be a point which needs some further discussion. In this case it would seem that the ethnic group is not an interest group in the sense that the Ibadan Hausa constitute such a group. On the other hand it is questionable whether ethnicity may not still play a part in the promotion of the interests of ethnic group members, in line with the delineation above of the first kind of interest group. The rise of class struggle and the simultaneous decline of ethnic struggle may not follow quite so automatically from the growth of inequality within ethnic groups. In other African contexts we have seen how relationships between the elites and the masses within ethnic groups have often taken precedence to class alignments in politics, leading many observers (e.g. Sklar 1967: 6; Lloyd 1968: 302; Gulliver 1969: 32–3) to suggest, in stronger or more restrained terms, that the 'new men of power' in Africa support ethnic divisiveness to prevent the emergence of class struggle. If this leads us to a rather one-sided picture of the exploitation of ethnic solidarity for sectional interests, it may be noted on the other hand that the ethnic power elite may be able to distribute jobs and other resources from the public arena as patronage to ensure the continuity of the support of its followers. There is thus an alternative mode of interest group organization in a situation characterized by inequality; there is competition over resources *within* the niches of the opportunity structure, and in these struggles the com-petitors are aided by alliances with people in other niches who have complementary interests. Scarcity of resources combined with ethnic consciousness may lead to continuous ethnic rivalry and the vertical integration of ethnic groups on some form of exchange basis.[2] Of course, we may prefer to restrict the use of the term 'interest group' to groups with a common interest focus in a single niche or an interrelated set of niches, such as the Ibadan Hausa. In that case, we may perhaps describe the ethnic group scattered over the opportunity structure but still co-operating in certain situations as a coalition of interests where members can use to some extent the diverse resources controlled by their partners in the advancement of their personal interests. Shared ethnicity is counted as credit toward access to these resources, although it may have to be complemented in some instances by additional reciprocity.

The consequence of this argument is the recognition that ethnicity may be employed strategically by members of groups distributed in a variety of ways over the urban opportunity structure, although the ethnic group can probably function most unambiguously as an interest group when its members share a niche in that structure and have no real or potential cross-cutting allegiances. Ethnic solidarity as a generalized moral obligation provides a particular form for relationships between group members: it ascribes them regardless of situation to a relationship of incorporation, in which gains are sought for the sum of partners, at the possible expense of outsiders (cf. Barth 1966: 4). This form, however, can be used for many purposes. It can be used to strengthen the unity of persons with shared interests; it can be used to favour certain persons over others in recruitment to relationships of complementarity; and, since the relationship is not systematically governed by recipro-city, it can be used as a gloss to cover a more or less exploitative relationship, where one party makes real gains in exchange for the other party's sense of conducting himself in line with a moral duty. In the latter case, ethnicity is used strategically by the person making claims on the solidarity of the other; but from the point of view of the latter, ethnicity need not be particularly advantageous in this situation. It is this latter fact which makes ethnicity a power on its own, at least partially beyond the principle of situational selection. Interests served by ethnic solidarity may thus be those of all involved group members, in which case outsiders may be the losing parties, or those of certain individual members making their gains at the expense of other members within the limits of the moral duty. In short, ethnic strategies come in many shapes.

ETHNICITY IN THE UNITED STATES: SOME
GENERAL CHARACTERISTICS

Having sketched my theoretical concerns, I can now turn to
discussing them more specifically in the urban American context. Since the varieties of ethnic strategies have been indicated
to relate to different structural matrices, however, I will begin
by pointing to some characteristics of American ethnicity of a
more general kind, which can both show a few of the similarities
and variations between Africa and the United States and provide a basis for the understanding of the management of ethnicity in strategic action.

There are indeed some notable parallels between developments in the two continents; on the American side they seem
particularly to involve those ethnic groups whose members
arrived in the greatest numbers from Southern and Eastern
Europe in the decades between 1880 and 1920. Like in Africa,
some of their concepts of ethnic identity only emerged in the
new urban environment, as the immigrants were not used to
identifying themselves in terms of nationalities of origin which
were in some cases recently established and rather artificial.
As many of the immigrants came from relatively isolated rural
areas, they were more apt to identify themselves as the people
of certain villages, towns, or provinces, and this was evident
quite frequently in the early stages of ethnic organization. Perhaps the Italians, coming from a young nation, were the group
where such local allegiances were and have remained the
strongest. The concept *paesani*, countrymen, was mostly used
to refer to people of the same region. In New York the Italians
clustered regionally in their neighbourhoods; there was a pre-
dominance of Calabrians and Neapolitans for some time in the
Mulberry Bend area, while there were Genoese on Baxter Street
and Sicilians on Elizabeth Street. North Italians were in the
Eighth and Fifteenth wards west of Broadway, while those of
Austria and the Tyrol congregated on Sixty-ninth Street (Jones
1960: 224). Zorbaugh (1929: 224) describes a similar situation
in Chicago in the 1920s, and according to Whyte, whose study
Street Corner Society depicts an Italian neighbourhood in Boston
in the late 1930s, there were also concentrations of people from
the same area in that city, although they tended to weaken in

43

later generations (Whyte 1943: xvii). Voluntary associations were also first of all based on village and provincial ties. In 1910, according to Ware (1965: 155), 50 per cent of the men in the Italian quarter of New York's Greenwich Village were estimated to have held membership in town or provincial associations. Such smaller associations of *paesani* still existed, holding picnics in the summer and dances in the winter, when Suttles (1968: 105–106) did his study in an ethnically mixed working-class and lower-class area of Chicago in the early 1960s, although they had then joined in a common summer festival. Earlier, as Whyte (1943: xvii) also notes, each group of *paesani* had its own *Festa* for the patron saint of its home area.

There was from the beginning a somewhat similar division among the East European Jews, who began to arrive in the United States in large numbers during the last decades of the nineteenth century as conditions worsened for their people in Eastern Europe. There they had identified themselves by town or region or by dialect, and they formed their *lantsmanshaftn* on this basis; however, having been an identifiable ethnic group in frequent contact with non-members already in these areas of origin, they were also more conscious of the Jewish identity overarching these lesser groups even from the beginning of their life in the United States (cf. Herberg 1955: 37; Wirth 1956: 222–4). But again, as we shall see, this wider ethnic identity was not unproblematic.

The voluntary associations based on such common ties of origin have also resembled those formed in African cities, serving purposes of sociability and welfare. Smaller groups have provided good company and mutual aid in rather informal ways; larger-scale organizations, often with a federal structure, have had more ambitious projects. Glazer and Moynihan have summarized the developments in New York:

'American social services grew up in large part to aid incoming immigrant groups. Many of these were limited to a single religious or ethnic group. Ethnic groups set up hospitals, old people's homes, loan funds, charitable organizations, as well as churches and cultural organizations. The initial need for a separate set of welfare and health institutions became weaker as the group became more prosperous and as the government took over these functions, but the organizations nevertheless continued. New York organizational life today is in large measure lived within ethnic bounds. These organizations generally have religious names, for it is more acceptable that welfare and health institutions should cater to religious than to ethnic communities. But of course religious institutions are generally closely linked to a distinct ethnic group' (Glazer & Moynihan 1963: 18–19).

We must keep in mind, however, that these voluntary associations are designed to make optimal use of resources which are already under the control of group members, in meeting their acute needs. This may entail some redistribution on the basis of ethnic solidarity, which may either take the form of more or less balanced reciprocity or of a flow in which some members make a net gain and others a net loss. But in these cases, where the similarities between African and American urban ethnicity may seem striking, ethnic organization does not primarily involve resources which would otherwise be available in the public arena and thus also to members of other groups. It is only when ethnicity is used in attempts to secure control over resources of the latter kind that an expansive ethnic strategy is pursued, and an ethnic struggle for power may take place. In this situation insights into the uses and non-uses of ethnic strategies must be built on some understanding of the distribution of ethnic groups over the opportunity structure, as it is necessary to consider whether the group is in such a position as to make ethnic strategies feasible. Here the American situation seems much less similar to the African situation as the latter is commonly delineated in urban anthropological studies. While African urbanism is to a great extent a colonial phenomenon, shaped and for a long period controlled by expatriates, studies of ethnicity in African cities have mostly been concerned with indigenous ethnic groups and their competition either in spheres of activity in colonial society which have not been fully controlled by expatriates, or in postcolonial society where expatriate influence is receding. In these cases, the African ethnic groups have commonly been in relatively equal positions with regard to access to resources, most of them being spread over many niches and social strata.[3] In the United States, on the other hand, the study of ethnicity is most often taken to involve the relationship between one socially and culturally dominant group and other less privileged groups. The Anglo-Saxons have been the host group to other immigrants from the beginning of colonization; other groups from Northwestern Europe have merged with it to form a wider white Protestant bloc which continues to dominate the society in such a way that the members of all other ethnic groups are considerably more constrained by its influence than by that of any other group. It is important to note here that even in a case such as present-day New York, where white Protestants form a numerical minority and are because of this in some ways on a more equal footing with others, they may still have an unproportionately great influence through their control of the 'strategic heights' of the economy and the centres of power on the national level. Their special status is also indicated by the fact that they usually seem not to be considered an ethnic group at all; they are non-ethnic 'real Americans', while those usually thought of as 'ethnic' are the later immigrants – those from Ireland, from Eastern and Southern Europe, from Puerto Rico and from Mexico – and their descendants, as well as the blacks and the Indians. For the sake of convenience I will largely follow this established usage here, tainted though it is with white Protestant ethnocentrism, and the groups with whose more or less recent past in urban American life I will be more particularly concerned are the Italians, the Jews, and the blacks. But as the dominant external relationships of these groups are with the white Protestant group, and since many of their internal relationships are also influenced by these contacts, one can hardly avoid giving that group a prominent place in any interpretation of American ethnicity.

The groups which entered urban America from the latter part of the nineteenth century and onwards were generally ushered into parts in the expansion of American industry and commerce as members of an unskilled lower-class work force; Berger notes that

'we have no clear images of *American* 'working-class style' precisely because the lowest positions on our socioeconomic ladder were traditionally occupied by the most recent groups of European immigrants, each of which, as they arrived, pushed earlier groups of immigrants up. Our images of working-class life, consequently, are dominated by ethnic motifs.' (Berger 1960: 95).

Class and ethnicity have thus both coloured the relationships of members of immigrant ethnic groups to other Americans. During the period of large-scale immigration in the latter part of the nineteenth and the first decades of this century, labourers of more settled groups were suspicious of the newcomers as their entry into the labour market kept wages down and as they could be used as strike breakers. Ethnic cleavages were thus at the basis of conflict within the class to which most immigrants belonged.[4] At the same time, members of the upper strata saw the division between themselves and the more recently arrived groups as simultaneously one of class and one of ethnicity. While some of the immigrants had indeed proven easier to deal with than labourers of older American stock, there was constant worry, with some basis in reality, that others among them might introduce into American society the more radical conceptions of class struggle which were appearing in Europe. A series of events was rightly or wrongly taken to demonstrate the subversive inclinations of radicals of foreign birth or descent, including the Haymarket Affair of Chicago in 1886, when a bomb exploded as the police were closing in on a meeting called by anarchists, as well as the trial of Sacco and Vanzetti which, extending through most of the 1920s, marked the end of the large-scale influx of Europeans. If these conflicts tended to be understood in class terms, however, there was also the area of discord where ethnicity itself was seen as the issue. During the same period of immigration, many Americans of more well-established descent in the country, as well as of higher class, doubted that the Southern and Eastern Europeans then arriving in large numbers could be assimilated, because of their physical and cultural characteristics. This kind of nativism was propagated intensively for example by the Immigration Restriction League founded in 1894 by upper-class Bostonians, and it was supported by such works of popular science as Madison Grant's *The Passing of the Great Race* (1916). Some of its basis was to be found in the unfavourable stereotyping of character traits of immigrant

47

ethnic groups, and there was also the occasional suspicion of disloyalty in favour of some foreign supra-national power – the Papacy in the case of the Catholic groups, some such conspiracy as the Elders of Zion in the case of the Jews (cf. Higham 1955; Solomon 1956).

Finding themselves in the lower strata of the urban social system, then, and also finding the members of the dominant group for various reasons reluctant to disregard ethnic boundaries, the members of American ethnic minorities have obviously had to take their ethnicity into consideration when they have attempted to advance their interests in society. This has not meant, however, that their strategies have always involved ethnicity in a similar fashion. In the following I will attempt to relate the handling of ethnicity to some of the varieties of constraints and opportunities which have existed in urban America.

ETHNIC HEGEMONIES

The first kind of opportunity situation of which I want to take note here is one toward which we can make a nod of recognition, as it has already been discussed in the case of the Ibadan Hausa – it is the situation in which one ethnic group dominates a niche and finds it attractive enough to wish to maintain control over it. In the early stages of their lives in the United States, of course, most ethnic groups cannot be said to have been in such a position except perhaps in a quite limited sense. Although some groups dominated numerically in particular occupations – the lake seamen of Chicago, for example, were Scandinavians in the late nineteenth century, the apartment janitors were Flemish, and the labourers in the garment industry were Eastern European Jewish (Pelling 1960: 87–8) – they may have valued them largely because these jobs were better than nothing, and they were in them because they were excluded from more advantageous positions. To the extent that there was competition for jobs among immigrants, of course, groups might use such means as they had at their disposal to exclude non-members from these occupations. Frequently, however, these means were also limited as access to the jobs was controlled by businessmen and officials of older American groups, so that recruitment along ethnic lines could occur largely at their discretion. Furthermore, group members with greater ambitions could hardly realize them in these positions, so that some degree of ethnic control over relatively low-ranking occupations could only provide some temporary security, while access to more satisfactory resources could only be gained by moving beyond the early niches of immigrant groups. The problem here, naturally, was that these more attractive niches which had already been developed in the urban opportunity structure were usually controlled by white Protestants.

One avenue of advancement in this situation was to develop new niches from which one could get access to resources in the public arena by providing new goods and services to those members of the society at large who wanted them. It is generally acknowledged that Jewish enterprise has had a large share in the development of the American garment and movie industries; in New York, the Italians are said to dominate the trucking business (Glazer & Moynihan 1963: 206). It is difficult to determine, however, what role ethnic solidarity as such has played in these developments.

But there is another field which has traditionally been left open to members of ethnic minorities, to the extent that it has indeed been open at all: the field of organized crime. Here I want to point out some facts concerning the alliance nowadays known as the Cosa Nostra which are perhaps particularly relevant to the study of ethnicity in society-wide enterprise.

Bell (1961: 127–50), in a well-known essay on crime as an American way of life, has discussed the prominence of Italian-Americans in organized crime as a consequence of their late arrival and original position in the American opportunity structure. Immigrating in large numbers later than most European groups and having no particular sponsors among those who had preceded them there, they had to start from the bottom of the socio-economic system like many others before them, but they found their progress even more completely blocked in most areas by these other groups. Even in crime they had been preceded by the Irish and the Jews who had for some time been in similar disadvantaged positions, but for various reasons these groups had later been able to advance themselves more legitimately. Thus those Italians who entered the sphere of illicit activities were relatively soon able to establish themselves there, co-existing, uneasily or in symbiosis, with a few remaining large-scale criminal entrepreneurs of other ancestry but carefully excluding members of later arriving groups from any foothold in the niche (cf. Cressey 1969: 51 ff., 195 ff.). The majority of their compatriots, I need hardly point out, have continued to struggle in legitimate fields; the character of the Italian community as such is thus only secondarily at issue here. The fact that it formed close-knit, encapsulated neighbourhoods, however, may have had some effect on the growth and persistence of organized crime. The inhabitants, mostly Sicilians and Southern Italians, had few contacts with the representatives of the wider society and were not very knowledgeable about it. This may have made them vulnerable to the extortionists within their community who may have been inspired by the *mafia* of their homeland and who were known in the United States as the Black Hand. The beginning of organized crime in the community was thus turned inward, but soon enough it also operated in the wider society, engaging for example in gambling, prostitution, and labour racketeering. The breakthrough by which Italian-Americans established their dominance in organized crime came with the prohibition years, in the 1920s. Cressey, whose study *Theft of the Nation* provides some noteworthy information on activities and organization in more recent years, concludes that their organizations now control most of the illegal gambling in the country and that they are the major loan sharks and providers of narcotics. They have also infiltrated many labour unions, extorting money from the employers while at the same time cheating the union members. Besides, they are involved in many legitimate enterprises financed originally by illegal activities (Cressey 1969: xi).[5]

What we are interested in here, however, is of course the role of ethnicity in the organization of this business empire. An inevitable question, to begin with, is its relationship to the mother country. Although such a relationship exists, just as it does in the case of the Ibadan Hausa trading with Northern Nigeria, Cressey (1969: 35) is just as emphatic as Cohen (1969: 48–9) in pointing out that the organization is autonomous and adapted to the local opportunity structure rather than a mere extension of homeland culture; that is, it is not a part of the *mafia*. The

Cosa Nostra, then, must be understood in its American context. Perhaps we may organize our understanding of its use of Italian ethnicity under four major headings.

1. *Ethnicity has provided extraterritorial resources.* The Italian-American criminal entrepreneurs have had some considerable advantages from a continuous contact with their country of origin. The traffic in narcotics has benefited greatly from the existence of a stable and trustworthy network of contacts who have been able to provide a steady supply, and links of ethnicity and even kinship have certainly been useful in the construction and maintenance of this network. Furthermore, it has been possible to go back to the country of origin occasionally to get out of the public view, and organized crime in the United States has also occasionally drawn on the personnel resources of the Sicilian *mafia*.

2. *Ethnicity has provided a basis for cohesion.* Not only is there the general sense of fellow ethnics having a common background and shared values, thus basically 'playing the same game' (cf. Barth 1969: 15); there are also shared cultural idioms such as that of extending fictive kinship to cement close working relationships with non-kin. Cressey (1969: 151 ff.) notes that the hierarchical units of which the Cosa Nostra is an alliance are described as 'families', drawing on this idiom to maintain cohesion and exclusiveness. There are also frequent marriage alliances within the organization, both within 'families' and between them, and these are said to play a great part in recruitment to top offices. If marriages are not within the organization, there is a strong tendency at least to marry inside the Italian-American community, so that the organization maintains the ethnic boundaries more generally.

3. *Ethnicity has provided a basis for recruitment.* The traditional means of recruitment to criminal organizations in the Italian-American community has had a great deal to do with its localized, inward-turning character. In a working-class neighbourhood, the people who are recognizably best off are often those engaged in criminal activities, and thus they come to stand as models for one kind of personal advancement. The members of criminal organizations have lived in close

51

face-to-face relationships with their neighbours, they may have had some patronage to dispense such as paying boys for minor errands, and to keep their organization intact they may have been looking out for young men around them who have seemed to display the right character for a job (Whyte 1943: 140 ff.; Cressey 1969: 238 ff.).

4. *Ethnicity has provided protection.* While on the one hand Italian-Americans tend to be singled out for suspicion of criminal involvements by other Americans, the professional criminals in the group are in some ways able, on the other hand, to use their ethnic membership as a cloak. The code of honour and trustworthiness of the Cosa Nostra has roots in the culture of small-scale Mediterranean village society, which to some extent also colours life in Italian-American urban enclaves, and in the eyes of community members it makes organization members appear morally superior to many of their enemies in the wider society (Cressey 1969: 171). This code, the relative success of organization members, and their ability both to provide certain benefits and to enforce sanctions against those within the community who act contrary to the will of the organization, seem together to have given the Cosa Nostra a relatively safe harbour in the Italian-American communities, the members of which may in any case have been somewhat reluctant to cooperate with outsiders against their own countrymen. The other members of the ethnic group have also protested against intimations of a connection between their group and organized crime, seeing it as an injury to their reputation, and an organization like Americans of Italian descent, formed to protect the group from such attacks, has thus to some extent seemed to hold a protective umbrella over the criminal entrepreneurs as well (Cressey 1969: 10–11). Other ethnic organizations, outwardly supposed to have quite different functions, have occasionally also been captured and made to provide an acceptable front for illicit business. During the prohibition years, the Italo-American Union in Chicago, ostensibly a welfare association, was used to control the sugar supply to the secret distilleries in and around the city (cf. Allsop 1961: 266; Nelli 1970: 220).

* * * *

The Italian-American criminal organization thus seems to have been able to use ethnicity to ensure solidarity, to organize recruitment, to win the assistance of a wider group in warding off attacks and maintaining a non-criminal front, and to build up a system for the supply of resources. In such ways, it seems to be the most extreme case of an entrepreneurial interest group operating on an ethnic basis in the United States. It is possible, however, that its traditional form, outlined here in a kind of 'ethnographic present', has become the victim of its own success, and new tendencies appear as the organization enters another phase. One of them has to do with its internal structure; whether legitimate or illegitimate, a large-scale business easily takes on a more bureaucratic form and requires a great deal of specialized expertise not easily found in the Italian-American community as traditionally constituted. The Cosa Nostra has thus had to recruit some outsiders to fill responsible positions, and when the positions are given to Italian-Americans the latter are often persons who have qualified by entering the wider society to acquire the necessary education rather than people who have worked their way up through the organization. Ethnic solidarity may thus become less important and organized crime is no longer the opening for personal advancement it once was (Anderson 1965; Cressey 1969: 242 ff.). The other side of the matter is one of external image. Because criminal enterprise is now best protected by being as inconspicuous as possible, the leaders of the organization attempt as much as they can to appear as average respectable American businessmen, and this may require a de-emphasis on the kind of impression management which has earlier attracted favourable attention in the Italian-American community and enhanced ethnic solidarity there. Possibly, then, strategies of ethnicity are becoming less important in organized crime.

Another factor with some significance of its own is the branching out into legitimate business by the members of the organization (cf. Lopreato 1970: 131 ff.). This, of course, is also a development favouring respectability and more normal business procedures. But furthermore, it shows that while dominance of the niche of organized crime may be seen as an adaptation which has now achieved a measure of stability, it has also been a phase in the advancement and diversification of the ethnic group into other niches more favourable than that originally assigned to Italian-Americans. As Whyte (1943: 145) has pointed out in *Street Corner Society*, the resources amassed through organized crime have provided both the participants themselves and other persons whom they have chosen to sponsor with chances of upward mobility in the opportunity structure which have otherwise been available only on a limited scale. A strategy involving a first stage of ethnic mobilization of strength in a niche where competition is limited has thus served as an alternative to direct unsponsored advancement on an individual basis in which case ethnicity, as we shall see later, has more often been a handicap.

ENTREPRENEURSHIP WITHIN ETHNIC BOUNDARIES

The second variety of ethnic strategy occurring in urban America which I want to point out is one which we may deal with more briefly. In this case the relationship between ethnic group members is not of such a clearly corporate character as in the case of the Italian-Americans in organized crime, not being oriented toward dealings with the outside world. Instead the relationship is basically transactional, and the element of shared ethnicity is important principally in the recruitment of the parties to the relationship. As far as access to resources is concerned, ethnicity has here served to provide protected niches for entrepreneurs within the ethnic groups, in that non-members have been more or less disadvantaged in competing for the same customers. Thus, even when most of the members of the group have been restricted to the positions in the lower strata originally assigned to them by the dominant group in the society, some members have been able to advance themselves through enterprises of this kind without becoming heavily dependent on the patronage of outsiders. Again we may find examples in the Italian immigrant community; Ware (1965: 155) mentions an Italian-American physician who in 1930 was the 'lodge doctor' of twenty-five provincially or locally based Southern Italian voluntary associations in New York, and she notes that even as this kind of arrangement became more difficult to maintain when ethnic neighbourhoods dissolved,

'some few of the old professional men managed to retain a

practice after their clientele had moved away by exploiting
their common ethnic origin and keeping their people as nearly
as possible in the old traditional mould.' (Ware 1965: 165.)

Similarly, Whyte (1943: 201) notes that in the Italian-
American community in Boston there has generally been one
undertaker for each Italian region from which many immigrants
have come, and this undertaker maintains his position by taking
an active part in social relationships within his group of *paesani*.
The same pattern occurs in other ethnic groups as well. It is
generally acknowledged, for example, that fragile as black-
owned business is in American cities, its basis has largely been
within the black community. There are some banks and insurance companies, but most of the businesses are smaller: real
estate agencies, funeral homes, beauty parlours, etc. In some of
these instances, there is really no competition with outsiders
whatsoever. But when such competition has existed, there have
been conscious attempts to take advantage of such ethnic
solidarity as may be aroused. Drake and Cayton, in their classic
study of the black community in Chicago first published in
1945, describe the doctrine of the 'Double-Duty Dollar', according to which members of the community should use their money
not only to purchase whatever they themselves desired but also
to 'advance the race' by making their purchases in black-owned
businesses. This doctrine was supported from the pulpits of
many black churches as well as by other community organizations, and Drake and Cayton conclude:

'This endorsement of business by the church simply dramatizes, and brings the force of sacred sanctions to bear upon,
slogans that the press, the civic organizations, and even the
social clubs repeat incessantly, emphasizing the duty of
Negroes to trade with Negroes and promising ultimate racial
"salvation" if they will support racial business enterprises.'
(Drake & Cayton 1962: 431).

It may be hard to find a more clearcut example of the use of
ethnic solidarity in the advancement of individual entrepreneurial interests. Yet black business even in the ethnic community is generally recognized as rather weak. Among the
explanations set forth to account for this fact I will mention

only one (suggested e.g. by Glazer & Moynihan 1963: 33), for the sake of its wider implications in the study of ethnic entrepreneurship: the culture of black Americans entails few specializations on which business may be based, and in which outsiders would be handicapped by a lack of know-how. Italian and Jewish food habits, for example, could become the basis of small enterprises in which cultural expertise is at least as important as ethnic solidarity, but there are hardly any counterparts to such possibilities in the black community. What this should lead us to recognize is that entrepreneurship directed toward the entrepreneur's own ethnic group need not be wholly based on the moral imperative of solidarity but may also be based on ethnic technical competence.

One more point may be added to this discussion of ethnic entrepreneurship. What leads the entrepreneur and the customers within his ethnic group to one another need not be the positive sense of ethnic solidarity as much as their exclusion from relationships with other partners. Because white people tend not to go to black doctors, the latter must seek black patients; because black people are not or do not feel very welcome in the offices of white physicians, they may have to seek out the black doctors. In these cases, then, the niche for ethnic enterprise is created neither by solidarity within the group nor by special cultural skills but by considerations of ethnicity on the part of outsiders, perhaps most likely to become relevant in enterprises involving personal services.

ETHNIC BROKERS

From the type of entrepreneurs who promote their individual interests largely in relationships within the ethnic group through the exploitation of solidarity, it is only a rather short step to the third kind of ethnic strategy I want to outline. This is what we may term ethnic brokerage, where the ethnic relationship of incorporation enters as an element in tying members of a group as clients to a person or an organization using this clientele as a resource in relationships to outsiders. It may be exemplified by the *padroni* of the Italian-American communities at the height of the immigration period; these men were above all labour bosses who used their ties of origin in an Italian town or province to form work squads among their compatriots for American employers with whom they had profitable contracts. They also served as mediators in a variety of other ways, but the profits they derived from the dependence of their country-men on them were such that their brokerage role could not last as the Italian-Americans began to become more assimilated into American society (cf. Jones 1960: 191–2; Glazer & Moyni-han 1963: 190–1; Lopreato 1970: 93–8; Nelli 1970: 56 ff.).

The most prominent form of ethnic brokerage in urban America, however, which I want to discuss at somewhat greater length, has certainly been 'machine' politics. In its traditional form as a stabilized order of exchange of votes, jobs, contracts, and economic support, the machine was by no means founded only on the basis of immigrant ethnic blocs, as for example the muckraker-journalist Lincoln Steffens pointed out in his famous report, *The Shame of the Cities* (1904). It can hardly be denied, however, that the conditions of the ethnic groups which were later to arrive in the great American cities were particularly conducive to machine organization. On the one hand, politics was one area in which the growing number of their members could relatively easily be converted into strength, while com-merce and industry continued to be dominated by white Protestants; on the other hand, the immigrants could use the aid of a strong organization in their adaptation to an otherwise frequently hostile environment. While public assistance and the means of voluntary associations were often insufficient, the machine to which the immigrants gave their votes could offer some assistance such as food, fuel, and clothing to those whose needs were most acute. The men in power in City Hall could also find jobs in local government operations for some of their supporters, and if many of these jobs may have been in un-qualified manual labour, the structures of local government and political machine also offered some opportunities for social mobility.

In these ways, the relationship between machine bosses and ethnic voters has obviously involved reciprocity in terms of some quite specific interests. These, however, have been com-plemented by considerations of ethnicity as the machines have employed ethnic solidarity and ethnic institutions to make themselves integral parts of the organization of ethnic groups.

As Ware (1965: 161) and Whyte (1943) both show, the Italian
voluntary associations which were originally of a non-political
nature were used by politicians to secure the support of their
members, and Handlin, the leading American historian of
immigration, takes care to point out that the multiplex grass-
roots ties of the machine representative played an important
role even if his position as an employment broker was perhaps
his major source of strength:

'The job was at the center of the boss's attractiveness. But
he was also able to call forth a more general sense of attachment. Often the feelings of group loyalty focused upon him.
He was a member of many associations, made friends on every
block. In the columns of their own newspapers his name
appeared frequently. His achievements cast their reflected
glory on the whole community and he in turn shared its sense
of solidarity. In that respect he stood at an advantage over
every competitor for the immigrants' leadership. He had
sprung from among them and substantially remained one
with them.' (Handlin 1952: 210–11.)

From what has been said so far, there might seem to be little
difference between the American political machine and an
ethnic organization in which solidarity serves to unite the group
in the pursuit of common interests. It does not seem wise, however, to regard them as similar in a stricter sense. First of all,
it seems not usually to be possible for a machine to base its
strength on one ethnic group alone; more often it must build a
coalition of ethnic groups. Because the Irish were the first of the
ethnic minorities to arrive and to reach a significant number of
voters, they were quite frequently able to put the machines
together and to maintain control over them for decades to come.
Whyte's *Street Corner Society* (1943) shows the difficulties encountered by Italian politicians in Boston as they attempted to
wrest control over their own neighbourhoods from Irish incum-
bents, only to run into other Irishmen at higher levels of the
machine when they were successful. In their turn the Italians
may be equally concerned with retaining control over the whole
or a part of a machine in which other groups also have an interest, as is evident in Suttles' (1968: 119–20) study of a multi-

ethnic area of Chicago. The result of such problems of coalition
is often that the ethnic broker may use his multiplex ties within
the group to retain his hold on it but presents its claims within
the machine with a soft voice to decrease risks of conflict and
competition. The late Congressman William L. Dawson, for
example, head of the Negro segment of the Democratic party
machine in Chicago, could use both ethnicity and patronage to
stay in control in his group, but he frequently opposed black
interests when this was in line with the stand of the machine as
a whole (cf. Wilson 1960). In such cases, the ethnic broker is less
the leader of his people than the agent of the machine, managing
its interests among a particular target group.

Furthermore, the objectives of machine bosses may not even
be the results of bargaining between the interests of stronger
and weaker groups as such. Alternatively or in a complementary
fashion, the machine may promote individual or sectional
interests with which the bosses are aligned. The connection with
the world of business is most important here. While the machine
needs financial support to keep its operations going, businesses
may need local government contracts or at least the goodwill of
City Hall, and there has thus been a basis for a reciprocal
relationship between the two in which the ability to organize
voters and keep control over public business has given the
machine its strength. At times this relationship has had an
ethnic strand, as politicians and businessmen of the same group
have been able to work together or as the machine has been
more or less controlled by ethnic business interests. Bell (1961),
in the essay cited above, notes the simultaneous rise in business
and in politics of Irishmen and Italians as an example of ethnic
preferential treatment. Frequently, however, the businessmen
who have influenced the ethnic bosses of the machines most
strongly have been white Protestants who have thereby indirectly maintained some of the control over politics which they
have lost in elections. Glazer and Moynihan describe the relationship between the early Irish bosses and white Protestant
business as a symbiotic one. The businessmen profited and the
machine profited, but the bosses

'never thought of politics as an instrument of social change –
their kind of politics involved the processes of a society that

was not changing.' (Glazer & Moynihan 1963: 229; cf. Baltzell 1964: 21).

In such a case it seems reasonable not to view the machine as the political expression of a united underprivileged interest group but rather as a broker between that group as a whole and other interests, within it or outside it.

THE BURDEN OF ETHNICITY

The three types of spheres of operation in which we have just found that members of American minorities have at one time or other been able to put ethnic strategies to successful use, on individual or group basis, show in which areas white Protestant dominance can be modified or avoided. One may find an unoccupied niche in the general division of labour and resources, one may raise the barriers around one's own group and make it a special niche for some of its members, or one may use whatever strength it has in particular areas, such as in the labour market or in the competition for votes. There is no way of escaping the fact, however, that ethnic minority status is frequently a handicap as minority members attempt to gain access to the more attractive niches controlled by white Protestants. The best strategy in such situations is most likely to try not to involve ethnicity at all in the advancement of individual interests, and this is indeed the line of action frequently chosen.[6] But the decision to define ethnicity as irrelevant cannot always be made unilaterally; one still has to take into account white Protestant conceptions of ethnicity, which seem to be characterized by considerable ambivalence. On the one hand there can be little doubt that the dominant group regards its own culture as the national culture of the United States. On the other hand there is doubt whether the achievement of mainstream cultural competence is sufficient to eradicate the stigma of ethnicity. In an analysis of recruitment to the American elite, Baltzell (1964) has described this ambivalence as a wavering between principles of aristocracy and caste. The former emphasizes achievement according to standards which can in some ways be regarded as universalistic, whereby it would be possible for members of any group in society to accumulate credits toward elite membership, while the latter would allow recruitment only on the basis of ascribed identity, of which ethnic identity is a major part. This ambivalence is a recurrent phenomenon in the white Protestant view of ethnicity on other levels of society as well. The combined effect has been to make the advent of other ethnic groups into spheres of activity dominated by white Protestants an uncertain trickle of individuals who have largely been culturally assimilated but who have continued to find their ethnic identity an unpredictable influence on their lives. As Gordon has put it,

'What at a distance seemed to be a quasi-public edifice flying only the all-inclusive flag of American nationality turned out, on closer inspection, to be the clubhouse of a particular ethnic group – the white Anglo-Saxon Protestants, its operation shot through with the premises and expectations of its parental ethnicity.' (Gordon 1964: 113).

While we cannot go into detail in considering the burden of ethnicity of American minority groups here, I would like to raise one point involving the relationship between ethnicity and social stratification. We have already quoted Berger to the effect that American images of working-class life have been dominated by ethnic motifs; for our purposes, I want to suggest, it is equally important to understand that the images which the members of the dominant group have of ethnic minorities have been strongly influenced by their experiencing ethnics as inhabitants of the lower strata of society. Some of the dislike and distrust may well result from the modes of behaviour derived from a foreign culture, but it is highly probable that the general conditions of life in the lower strata have also been regarded as disreputable. Ethnic minority newcomers to the American city, from the late nineteenth century until today, have had their lives shaped to a significant extent by poverty and bad living conditions in overpopulated slums, and they seem often to have reacted or adapted to these circumstances in quite similar ways. For that reason they have also been stereotyped in much the same fashion by the inhabitants of higher strata. It has been frequently noted in recent years that the terms now used to characterize lower-class blacks bear a strong resemblance to those used to describe the Irish when they constituted the major

61

lower-class immigrant group. Here, of course, I am paraphrasing an argument from the American 'culture of poverty' debate of recent years; the behaviour of lower-class people which is often taken to express values deviating from those of mainstream society should not be taken to signify such values but merely constitutes a realistic adaptation to the particular constraints on life in the most unfavourably placed sectors of the urban opportunity structure (cf. Valentine 1968). But the problem is that people customarily attribute values to others on the basis of overt behaviour, and if these latter people have little opportunity to dispute effectively the truth of these attributions, these understandings of values and value differences may be used to complement other markers of ethnic dichotomization (cf. Barth 1969: 14–15). Furthermore, precisely because these adaptations to the urban opportunity structure are made by groups which are also identifiable on the basis of other criteria as ethnically distinct, they tend to be defined, by non-members at least, as parts of an indivisible ethnic character. Or to put it another way, because class and ethnicity have so often coincided in American society, the pivotal ethnic identity attribute of descent, as signalled by a surname and possibly by other overt characteristics, is held to have entailing attributes which are actually those of class (cf. Nadel 1957: 32 ff.). This, in turn, has obvious implications as the members of the ethnic group are considered as candidates for access to more advantageous positions. In social mobility which is not complicated by ethnic factors a person may leave the life style of his former social class and need not worry more than intermittently about its continued impact on his public identity. When an undesirable lower-class way of life becomes identified in the public mind with an ethnic group, on the other hand, the ascriptive nature of ethnic identity may force a member of the group to carry with his identity baggage the ineradicable stigma of this life style in which he no longer has a part.

SOLIDARITY AND STRATIFICATION

Although social mobility in urban America has tended to be based on the acceptance of mainstream middle-class culture and on the understatement of ethnicity, it is clear that this has not involved complete de-ethnicization. To some greater or lesser extent, the member of an ethnic minority continues to be identified with his group, and this has inevitably meant identifications across the boundaries of social strata, as most groups have at least passed through long periods of time when the greater part of the membership has remained in the lower strata while another number has achieved middle-class status or even better. This pattern of distribution of ethnic groups has not been entirely unproblematic, and as studies of the relevance of ethnicity to urban social organization have tended to emphasize the uses of ethnic solidarity, I want to devote the final part of this discussion of varieties of American urban ethnicity to situations which have arisen as such solidarity has become more tenuous.

When members of ethnic minorities have depended for greater opportunities on the acceptance of the dominant group, they have found it desirable to decrease the impact of the ethnic stigma. They may be acutely concerned with denying parochial ethnic allegiances; they may also involve themselves in efforts which would make their ascribed ethnic identity less burdensome by improving the image of the group. If they are to vote for a political candidate of their own ethnic group, it had better be one who does not seem to cater too exclusively to members in the lower strata and who does not seem to conform to the ethnic stereotype held by the dominant group but who can give desirable 'recognition' to the group in the wider society (cf. Dahl 1961: 35–6; Banfield and Wilson 1963: 43). They may also participate in 'uplift' institutions and organizations for those lower-class members who seem to contribute to the stigmatization of the entire group. But this may still appear to be rather a residual kind of ethnic solidarity, and the majority of the group remaining at the lower levels of society have frequently viewed the life style and the relationships of members in more advantageous, non-ethnic niches of the opportunity structure as expressions of disloyalty. As Spiro has concluded in a review of studies of the acculturation of American ethnic groups, 'intraethnic conflict, as well as ethnic acculturation, is associated with social mobility' (Spiro 1955: 1243), and this conflict has often been stated in very clear terms by the ethnics themselves. Warner and Srole, discussing ethnicity in a volume of the

63

Yankee City series, note the vocabulary of stratification among the Irish:

> 'The growing identification with class level and the usual manifestations of extreme class distance have served to break up the Irish group's inner cohesion. The result is seen in the sharp antagonisms which exist between the Irish of the two lowest classes (lower-lower and upper-lower) and of the two higher classes (upper-middle and lower-upper). The former refer to the latter as "lace-curtain Irish", a term with reproachful connotations . . . The higher-class Irish, when aroused, will apply to the Irish of the lower classes the familiar epithet, "shanty Irish".' (Warner & Srole 1945: 93).

This discord, however, does not always involve only social mobility and social stratification as such. In some groups it is intimately connected with differences of regional background within the ethnic group and with the length of urban American residence of its various segments. Some capsule descriptions of cleavages within the Jewish, Italian, and black groups may give some insights into the particular influence of such factors on relationships in some ethnic minorities.

1. *The Jews.* The period of greatest interest as far as conflict within the American Jewish group is concerned is that between the late nineteenth century and the 1930s. In 1880 there were about one quarter of a million Jews in the United States; by 1900 another half million Jews had arrived from Eastern Europe, and another one and a quarter million followed before World War I (Glazer 1957: 60). Due to an unprecedented rate of social mobility between generations, the Jews were already to a considerable extent a middle-class group by the time of World War II. But in the preceding years, when the effect of the massive influx of new group members into the lowest strata of society was strongest, the Jewish group was characterized by the considerable difference between two segments.

While the first and originally most prestigious Jewish settlers had been Spanish and Portuguese Sephardim, the early and middle decades of the nineteenth century brought a considerable number of German Jews to the United States. Because of their cultural background and a still rather open opportunity structure, the members of these groups were relatively soon able to establish themselves in quite favourable situations, often in the fields of commerce and finance, and they did not encounter very significant discrimination from the majority group. By the beginning of the great urban immigration period toward the end of the nineteenth century, the American Jews were thus largely of German origin and in rather comfortable circumstances. From then on, however, the Jewish immigrants were overwhelmingly Eastern European, and these soon outnumbered the German Jews. They were of a very different cultural background, much more concerned with their ethnic identity as they came from areas where there was little assimilation and where they had been subjected to persecution, and among them were represented forms of Orthodoxy, Zionism and political radicalism which were foreign to the German Jews. To this, then, was added lower-class status.

In this situation there was a strong negative element in the reaction of the German Jews to the newcomers. As other Americans worried about the immigrants changing the character of American society, the established Jewish community, with equally limited sympathy for the ways of life of the Eastern Europeans, feared that the latter might arouse anti-Semitism. In the 1880s some Jewish organizations urged a halt to the immigration from Eastern Europe, occasionally in terms reminiscent of Gentile stereotypes of Jews. The derogatory term, *kike*, is said to have been invented in the United States by German Jews aiming it at Eastern European Jews, many of whom had names ending with -*ki*. On the other hand, the new immigrants often expressed hostility toward German Jews because of their status and way of life. Reform Judaism was regarded as one example of the disloyalty of the Germans toward their Jewish heritage, and particularly the more radical Eastern Europeans saw the German Jews as members of an exploiting class (cf. Glazer 1957: 66 ff.; Weinryb 1958: 16 ff.; Baltzell 1958: 282–3).

As social mobility began within the Eastern European group, similar expressions protesting apparent betrayal of ethnicity appeared aimed at those who were leaving the ghetto, figuratively speaking or in a literal sense. Wirth (1956: 191) notes that

the Eastern Europeans derisively gave the name *Deutshland* to
the area inhabited by the prosperous German Jews, and the
name *Deitchuks* to the Eastern Europeans who later joined
them there, deserting old customs to emulate *'goyische* ways'.
Just as cutting is the Yiddish epithet *allrightnick* for the man
who 'in his opportunism has thrown overboard most of the
cultural baggage of the group' (Wirth 1964: 101). Perhaps the
development of such concepts may show some of the concern
with which the Jews of the lower classes viewed the relative
de-ethnicization (in terms of cultural markers) that went with
social mobility.

However, before long, a great many of the Eastern European
Jews had been able to climb to higher social strata. It has been
argued that their ethnic culture provided an unusually good
basis for such mobility; some part in the process was certainly
also played by the German Jews who had soon begun to provide
opportunities for advancement as well as a variety of other
forms of assistance. Glazer (1957: 88) notes that many well-to-
do Jews spent much of their lives administering and raising
money for philanthropic organizations catering largely to the
newcomers. Thus the split between those who had appeared
disreputable and those who had appeared disloyal was gradually
healed, and the distinction between Germans and Eastern
Europeans decreased in importance.

One question readily arises out of these facts. Why did the
Eastern European and the German Jews come to form a single
group in the United States at all? Most new ethnic groups which
emerge in urban communities seem to have a wider base of
cultural similarity than that shared by these two groups,
coming from different countries, entering the United States at
different times, and occupying, originally, quite different niches
in the opportunity structure. Perhaps one part of the answer
involves the peculiar power of the dominant group in the United
States to decide what people should share, willingly or unwillingly, one ethnic label. The German Jewish group, which
could conceivably have desired not to become identified with
the later arrivals, was not free to define its ethnic boundaries.
As Glazer and Moynihan note,

'two wills make a group – the self-will that creates unity, and
66

the will of others that imposes a unity where hardly any is felt.' (Glazer & Moynihan 1963: 139).

2. *The Italians.* Similar circumstances provided for division and unity in the Italian group. The Northern Italians had come first, in relatively small numbers. They came from the more developed part of the mother country, they were frequently more skilled occupationally when they arrived in the United States, and they often brought considerably greater funds with which to establish themselves in the new habitat (cf. Glazer & Moynihan 1963: 184). Thus they had often already adapted themselves rather successfully as the greater number of Southern Italians and Sicilians began to arrive around 1900, unskilled farm labourers among whom illiteracy was common. While as we have already noted, the strong local ties and the distrust of all who were not *paesani* in the most narrow sense limited cohesion on a national basis within the Italian community, the deepest split was between Northerners and Southerners. It was a distinction recognized to begin with in immigration statistics, by the social services, and even by American nativists (cf. Solomon 1956: 163 ff.; Glazer & Moynihan 1963: 183–4). And the Northern Italians did what they could to maintain it. As Ware notes, writing of Greenwich Village Italians in the 1920s:

'Whenever a North Italian thought that a question implied criticism of something which was not American, he took pains, often gratuitously, to insist that the particular thing was done by the South Italians and to turn the question into a criticism of the latter.' (Ware 1965: 160).

When Whyte (1943: xvii–xviii) studied an Italian neighbourhood in Boston in the late 1930s, the difference between Southerners and Northerners still existed, but it was beginning to become less obvious. The Northern Italians were not able to define themselves as a separate group in the eyes of the wider society, and as the Southern group improved its situation and became more internally differentiated a common ethnic identity may have become less objectionable. On the other hand, however, the relationship between Italianism and Americanism has continued to be problematic in the organization of the group as

67

a whole. The American-born members of the group have contemptuously referred to the less acculturated Italian-born as 'greasers', and generational conflict, in this as in many other immigrant groups, has revolved around the greater acceptance of American ways of life and rejection of the life style of the newcomers by the younger members. But this is a matter of degree and context. To adapt to the new circumstances in ways by which one leaves the Italian community and becomes an assimilated part of the wider society is not a manner of advancement which is widely accepted. Whyte points out that

'to get ahead, the Cornerville man must move either in the world of business and Republican politics or in the world of Democratic politics and the rackets. He cannot move in both worlds at once; they are so far apart that there is hardly any connection between them. If he advances in the first world, he is recognized by society at large as a successful man, but he is recognized in Cornerville only as an alien to the District. If he advances in the second world, he achieves recognition in Cornerville but becomes a social outcast to respectable people elsewhere.' (Whyte 1943: 273).

And Suttles, whose study of ethnic minorities in Chicago is about twenty-five years younger, shows that while assimilation has proceeded, considerations of ethnic loyalty still have an impact on behaviour within the community:

'Actually, many of the Italians are quite "americanized". Frequently, however, these people lead something of a double life. During the daytime they leave the neighborhood and do their work without much thought of their ethnicity. When they come home in the evening, however, they are obliged to reassume their old world identity . . . there are still many "old-timers" in the neighborhood, and it would be very ill-mannered to parade one's americanism before them. Thus, within the bounds of the local neighborhood, an Italian who "plays" at being an American runs the risk of being taken as a snob, phony, opportunist, coward, or fink.' (Suttles 1968: 105).

3. *The blacks.* Frazier (1962: 8) begins a later edition of his well-known *Black Bourgeoisie* with a new preface discussing the

original reception of the book, in which he notes how working-class blacks, under the impression that the book was an attack on upper-class, light-skinned members of their group, stopped him on the street to shake his hand for performing this long overdue service. This incident reveals much about the lasting tensions between social strata in the black community. Once more the strain arises partially because one segment of the group may have established itself reasonably successfully as a great number of new members arrive in the cities to threaten its positions and its respectability. Green, writing the history of the black community in Washington, D.C., mentions how in the 1860s the older inhabitants, often of partially white ancestry, freed from slavery somewhat earlier, and even during slavery often in the more favoured position of house slaves, worried over the fact that

'alien blacks seemed about to engulf them all, as whites appeared increasingly prone to make no distinction between educated, responsible colored people and the mass of ignorant, often shiftless freedmen flooding in from the South.' (Green 1967: 65).

The chasm between the lighter-skinned upper strata of the group and the lower-class newcomers has been the most widely-known expression of the problem of ethnic solidarity in the black community as the stream of migrants has continued to flow, with greater or lesser force, since Emancipation (cf. Frazier 1966: 295 ff.). The former have reacted, as have the more advantaged in other groups, by trying to maintain the social distance as well as by extending some assistance to the less fortunate through philanthropic and 'uplift' organizations. But discord seems to have been strong during most periods, and since such a great proportion of the black group is even now in the very lowest stratum of the society it is noticeable between segments which are not far apart in socio-economic terms. Members of the lower middle class and the stable working class, forced because of ghettoization to live as neighbours of the lumpenproletariat, show dislike for the behaviour of the latter and try to shield themselves from its influences. But in the eyes of those whose way of life seems disreputable, their neighbours, trying to live in line with mainstream American notions of respectability, are disloyal to the poorer blacks, and the common epithets of 'Uncle Tom', 'handkerchief head', or 'house nigger' are aimed at them (cf. Hannerz 1969: 34–6). While countervailing tendencies of solidarity appear at times and have been strong in recent years, the black community is thus another one where the behaviour associated with social mobility has been seen as an expression of alienation from the ethnic group.

In all these cases, then, crises in intra-ethnic relationships, of greater or lesser magnitude, have arisen on the basis of the distribution of group members over the opportunity structure. Obviously ethnicity has not been untouched by the fact that some group members have been in positions where ethnic solidarity has been largely irrelevant to or even inimical with their interests. While these members have tried to avoid the effects of ethnic stigma, the many members of the group in the lower strata have regretted the lack of ethnic cohesion and interpreted strategies of non-ethnicity as strategies of anti-ethnicity. As an afterthought, I want to note the possibility of looking at this resentment of non-ethnic avenues of advancement as an expression of a lower-class ideology of solidarity as outlined by Jayawardena (1968). Members of groups of low status in the wider social system, Jayawardena suggests, while irreconciled with their position and antagonistic to the dominant strata, attach high value to an egalitarian ideology based on the relative absence of status differences within the group. This ideology emphasizes inalienable human worth rather than social, economic or political criteria of evaluation.[7] As an organizing principle for relationships within the group, it provides for a loosely structured solidarity which may prove highly efficient as the group engages for example in spontaneous collective protests against the dominant forces of the wider society. While satisfying to the sense of worth and recognition, however, the ideology is vulnerable to the intrusion of status definitions from the outside. As long as membership categories are distinct and expressions of status differences emanate only from non-members, it is to some extent possible to discount them, or at least to compensate for them with the egalitarianism within the group. But as people to whom is ascribed the identity of group members bring the definitions of the outside world into relationships within the group, the ideology of egalitarianism arouses outrage at those who have betrayed the group by questioning its moral universe from within. If this analysis is accepted, it is not surprising if the predominantly lower-class members of American urban ethnic groups have at times been resentful of compatriots seemingly acting as agents of the dominant group in denying them, if only by implication, their worth.

AMERICAN URBANISM AND THE ANALYSIS OF ETHNICITY

It is obviously not possible in an essay like this to do justice to the complexity of American urban ethnicity or to the richness of the scholarship concerned with it. Even the few facets which have been discussed here have certainly been given a most parsimonious treatment. But then my aim has not been to give a complete account of the topic, or to provide original ethnography, but rather to indicate some areas over which at least Americanists and Africanists with an interest in urban ethnicity might be able to conduct a fruitful dialogue. Obviously there is no lack of work on the subject in the United States; but it may be unfortunate that while so much research on urban ethnicity has been carried out there, under that or any other name, so little cross-fertilization has occurred between it and the body of theory and knowledge built up by Africanists. Clearly there have been separate research traditions at work, most of the studies of ethnicity in Africa having been conducted in the tradition of British social anthropology while the work in America has mostly been in the hands of historians, sociologists, and political scientists, with anthropologists playing only a limited and generally rather recent part. If the concern with the understanding of contemporary ethnicity which has developed so encouragingly in social anthropology in recent years is to lead toward a general analytical framework, however, we ought to make a genuine attempt to look at all the materials available from the same point of view, using their variety to make our framework both more detailed and more flexible.

Here I have tried to sketch some general types of strategies of ethnic solidarity on the basis of American urban opportunity structures, occasionally indicating or implying limited African parallels. I have also wanted to draw attention to the constraints on the use of ethnic strategies by minorities in a situation where one group is clearly dominant, at the same time as I have noted that the problem of ethnic solidarity does not become unimportant simply because the members who are most successful in advancing their interests may not use it. We have also touched on the problem of the definition of ethnic boundaries as understood by members of the community: when there is a dominant group, does its definitions take precedence over those of others, leaving minorities little freedom to make their own distinctions? Finally, we have seen that the different segments of an ethnic group may have varying conceptions of their ethnicity and its relevance for social organization depending on the length of their stay in the city and on their relationship to the urban opportunity structure. This shows that we may sometimes be wise to view urban ethnicity in a diachronic perspective, and that we should be aware of the possibility of similar developments in cities which are yet younger and less permanently settled than those of the United States.

Perhaps these considerations point to some of the things we should take into account as we try to make the study of urban ethnicity one of careful comparison and disciplined generalization; and while they can undoubtedly be elaborated in more intensive ethnography, it may be useful at this stage of the growth of urban anthropology to begin by charting only the general features of a cityscape in which we are to continue work.

NOTES

[1] Even if it is not, of course, it could be striving to become an interest group of the second kind, but this is not necessarily the objective, as a satisfactory spread over many attractive niches could also be a desirable goal.

[2] Ethnicity thus appears to provide examples of the kind of vertically integrated units in hierarchical social systems which Wertheim (1968, 1969) views as an alternative to class conflict.

[3] It would seem, however, that the Creoles of Freetown and the Americo-Liberians of Monrovia have played a role somewhat similar to that of American white Protestants as standard setters of civilization, hesitatingly offering some opportunity for assimilation (cf. Porter 1963; Fraenkel 1964: 224; Banton 1965: 137).

[4] While American social scientists frequently attribute the relative absence of class consciousness among American workers to opportunities for social mobility, it thus appears that ethnic cleavages should also be mentioned as a contributing factor. Even a recent observer like Leggett (1968), sharply critical of tendencies to underestimate American working-class consciousness,

finds it most strongly expressed when embedded in the ethnic consciousness of a group relatively restricted to one class level.

[5] A partially autobiographic account of life in the Cosa Nostra can be found in the celebrated *Valachi Papers* (Maas 1970).

[6] According to Cohen (1969: 201–2), 'a privileged status group will try to prevent men, from underprivileged status groups, from infiltrating into its ranks. An underprivileged status group, on the other hand, will have to define its membership because it is only by organizing itself tightly that it can struggle effectively with the other status groups'. The privileged status group, however, will not inevitably close its boundaries to prevent infiltration; and the underprivileged group may have better chances for advancement by infiltration than by conquest.

[7] It is interesting to note that the kind of ideology outlined by Jayawardena bears considerable resemblance to the conception of 'soul' of recent years in the black ghetto (cf. Hannerz 1968; 1969: 156 ff.).

REFERENCES

ALLSOP, KENNETH. 1961. *The Bootleggers*. London: Hutchinson.

ANDERSON, ROBERT T. 1965. From Mafia to Cosa Nostra. *American Journal of Sociology*, **71**: 302–10.

BALTZELL, E. DIGBY. 1958. The Development of a Jewish Upper Class in Philadelphia: 1782–1940. In Marshall Sklare (ed.), *The Jews: Social Patterns of an American Group*. Glencoe, Ill.: Free Press.

—— 1964. *The Protestant Establishment: Aristocracy & Caste in America*. New York: Random House.

BANFIELD, EDWARD C., & WILSON, JAMES Q. 1963. *City Politics*. Cambridge, Mass.: Harvard University Press and MIT Press.

BANTON, MICHAEL. 1965. Social Alignment and Identity in a West African City. In Hilda Kuper (ed.), *Urbanization and Migration in West Africa*. Berkeley and Los Angeles: University of California Press.

BARTH, FREDRIK. 1966. *Models of Social Organization*. (Occasional Papers no. 23) London: Royal Anthropological Institute of Great Britain and Ireland.

—— 1969. Introduction. In Fredrik Barth (ed.), *Ethnic Groups and Boundaries: The Social Organization of Culture Difference*. Bergen and Oslo: Universitetsforlaget; London; George Allen & Unwin.

BELL, DANIEL. 1961. *The End of Ideology: On the Exhaustion of Political Ideas in the Fifties*. New York: Collier Books.

BERGER, BENNETT M. 1960. *Working-Class Suburb*. Berkeley and Los Angeles: University of California Press.

COHEN, ABNER. 1969. *Custom and Politics in Urban Africa*. London: Routledge & Kegan Paul.

CRESSEY, DONALD R. 1969. *Theft of the Nation: The Structure and Operations of Organized Crime in America*. New York: Harper & Row.

DAHL, ROBERT A. 1961. *Who Governs? Democracy and Power in an American City*. New Haven, Conn.: Yale University Press.

DRAKE, ST CLAIR, & CAYTON, HORACE R. 1962. *Black Metropolis: A Study of Negro Life in a Northern City*. New York: Harper & Row. (First edition 1945.)

FRAENKEL, MERRAN. 1964. *Tribe and Class in Monrovia*. London: Oxford University Press.

FRAZIER, E. FRANKLIN. 1962. *Black Bourgeoisie: The Rise of a New Middle Class in the United States*. New York: Collier Books. (First edition 1957.)

—— 1966. *The Negro Family in the United States*. Chicago: University of Chicago Press. (First edition 1939.)

GLAZER, NATHAN. 1957. *American Judaism*. Chicago: University of Chicago Press.

—— & MOYNIHAN, DANIEL PATRICK. 1963. *Beyond the Melting Pot*. Cambridge, Mass.: MIT Press.

GLUCKMAN, MAX. 1961. Anthropological Problems Arising from the African Industrial Revolution. In Aidan Southall (ed.), *Social Change in Modern Africa*. London: Oxford University Press.

GORDON, MILTON M. 1964. *Assimilation in American Life*. New York: Oxford University Press.

GREEN, CONSTANCE MCLAUGHLIN. 1967. *The Secret City: A History of Race Relations in the Nation's Capital*. Princeton, NJ: Princeton University Press.

GULLIVER, P. H. 1969. Introduction. In P. H. Gulliver (ed.), *Tradition and Transition in East Africa*. London: Routledge & Kegan Paul.

HANDLIN, OSCAR. 1952. *The Uprooted: The Epic Story of the Great Migrations that Made the American People*. Boston: Little, Brown.

HANNERZ, ULF. 1968. The Rhetoric of Soul: Identification in Negro Society. *Race*, **9**: 453–65.

—— 1969. *Soulside: Inquiries into Ghetto Culture and Community*. New York: Columbia University Press.

HERBERG, WILL. 1955. *Protestant – Catholic – Jew: An Essay in American Religious Sociology*. Garden City, NY: Doubleday.

HIGHAM, JOHN. 1955. *Strangers in the Land: Patterns of American Nativism 1860–1925*. New Brunswick, NJ: Rutgers University Press.

JAYAWARDENA, CHANDRA. 1968. Ideology and Conflict in Lower Class Communities. *Comparative Studies in Society and History,* **10**: 413–46.

JONES, MALDWYN ALLEN. 1960. *American Immigration.* Chicago: University of Chicago Press.

LEGGETT, JOHN C. 1968. *Class, Race, and Labor: Working-Class Consciousness in Detroit.* New York: Oxford University Press.

LLOYD, P. C. 1968. *Africa in Social Change.* New York: Praeger.

LOPREATO, JOSEPH. 1970. *Italian Americans.* New York: Random House.

MAAS, PETER. 1970. *The Valachi Papers.* London: Panther Books. (First edition 1968.)

NADEL, S. F. 1957. *The Theory of Social Structure.* Glencoe, Ill.: Free Press.

NELLI, HUMBERT S. 1970. *Italians in Chicago, 1880–1930: A Study in Ethnic Mobility.* New York: Oxford University Press.

PELLING, HENRY. 1960. *American Labor.* Chicago: University of Chicago Press.

PORTER, ARTHUR T. 1963. *Creoledom: A Study of the Development of Freetown Society.* London: Oxford University Press.

SKLAR, RICHARD L. 1967. Political Science and National Integration – A Radical Approach. *Journal of Modern African Studies,* **5**: 1–11.

SOLOMON, BARBARA MILLER. 1956. *Ancestors and Immigrants: A Changing New England Tradition.* Cambridge, Mass.: MIT Press.

SPIRO, MELFORD E. 1955. The Acculturation of American Ethnic Groups. *American Anthropologist,* **57**: 1240–52.

SUTTLES, GERALD D. 1968. *The Social Order of the Slum: Ethnicity and Territory in the Inner City.* Chicago: University of Chicago Press.

VALENTINE, CHARLES A. 1968. *Culture and Poverty: Critique and Counter-Proposals.* Chicago: University of Chicago Press.

WARE, CAROLINE F. 1965. *Greenwich Village 1920–1930: A Comment on American Civilization in the Post-War Years.* New York: Harper & Row. (First edition 1935.)

WARNER, W. LLOYD, & SROLE, LEO. 1945. *The Social Systems of American Ethnic Groups.* New Haven, Conn.: Yale University Press.

WEINRYB, BERNARD D. 1958. Jewish Immigration and Accommodation to America. In Marshall Sklare (ed.), *The Jews: Social Patterns of an American Group.* Glencoe, Ill.: Free Press.

WERTHEIM, W. F. 1968. Patronage, Vertical Organization, and

Populism. *Proceedings of the VIIIth Congress of Anthropological and Ethnological Sciences*, II: 16–18. Tokyo: Science Council of Japan.

—— 1969. From Aliran Towards Class Struggle in the Countryside of Java. *Pacific Viewpoint*, 10 (2): 1–17.

WHYTE, WILLIAM FOOTE. 1943. *Street Corner Society: The Social Structure of an Italian Slum*. Chicago: University of Chicago Press.

WILSON, JAMES Q. 1960. *Negro Politics: The Search for Leadership*. Glencoe, Ill.: Free Press.

WIRTH, LOUIS. 1956. *The Ghetto*. Chicago: University of Chicago Press. (First edition 1928.)

—— 1964. *Louis Wirth on Cities and Social Life*. Edited by Albert J. Reiss, Jr. Chicago: University of Chicago Press.

ZORBAUGH, HARVEY. 1939. *The Gold Coast and the Slum*. Chicago: University of Chicago Press.

Badr Dahya

The Nature of Pakistani Ethnicity in Industrial Cities in Britain

I INTRODUCTION

Studies conducted during the past two decades show that immigrants from Commonwealth countries tend to settle in the slums of the inner wards of our industrial cities (Glass 1960, Desai 1963, Rex & Moore 1967, Aurora 1967, Thompson 1970). Some writers (e.g., Rex & Moore) explain this pattern of settlement in terms of racial discrimination. They argue that discrimination in the private sector of the housing market (e.g., lack of credit facilities) forces coloured immigrants to live in 'twilight zones'; and discrimination practised by local authorities (e.g., the differential system of allocation of council housing) prevents them as newcomers from access to housing in the public sector. That is, the immigrants' concentration in the inner wards of towns and cities is said to be an outcome of various structural constraints exercised by the host society.

I wish to examine this hypothesis and to discuss how and why the process of settlement developed in the form now familiar to us. I look at the patterns of Pakistani immigrants' settlement in Bradford and Birmingham, and provide relevant data from a selected number of the immigrants' villages of origin. My acquaintance with Pakistani immigrants in the Midlands dates from the summer of 1956, I was therefore able to establish close relationships with them in the Balsall Heath, Moseley and Sparkbrook areas of Birmingham during 1959–61 (when I made a study of Arab immigrants in those areas),[1] and to observe the growth of the immigrant community there. During 1964, when an opportunity arose for a study of Pakistanis in Britain, I found myself a base in the community in Sparkbrook and carried out fieldwork among Pakistanis in Bradford, Birmingham and in other selected areas of Britain. I should like to mention that my fieldwork in Sparkbrook

77

(1964–67) overlapped with the survey carried out in that area by Rex and Moore (op. cit.). Although I focus primarily on the situation in Bradford, the material has a bearing on the immigrant settlements elsewhere.

In analysing the material I have found it necessary to look at the situation from 'the actor's frame of reference',[2] for it is my belief that the immigrants' perception of the situation in the context of their socio-economic background, their motives for migration and their ideology or myth of return are essential for a meaningful understanding of their behaviour. To say this is not necessarily to deny the existence of external constraints – such as racial discrimination practised by the various socio-economic and political institutions of the dominant society (PEP 1967, Burney 1967, Abbot 1971) – which impinge upon the immigrants. As I show at a later stage, an observer's interpretation of the situation, in the light of his own perspectives can give us a distorted picture regarding the settlement of Pakistani immigrants (Rex & Moore, op. cit.; Butterworth 1967; Krausz 1971) and does not really help us to disentangle the various forces which have brought about the concentration of immigrants in certain areas of our industrial cities and towns.

I begin with a description of the settlement patterns in Bradford in terms of various ethnic groups and their distribution within the city, and trace the historical growth of the patterns and changes over a period of time. I then relate the material to the immigrants' perception of the situation and discuss the inadequacies of the thesis put forward by Rex and Moore (op. cit.).

II BRADFORD

The city of Bradford (see *Map 1*) is widely known as the centre of the wool textiles industry. In addition, it has a number of expanding ancillary industries, notably light and heavy engineering, building and electrical engineering, and other allied industries, all of which are[3] in strong competition for labour. This is probably why the figures for unemployment in Bradford since the Second World War have been below the national average.

According to the 1961 Census, Bradford had a population

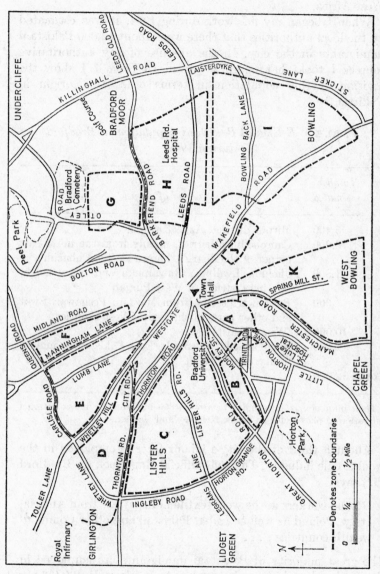

Map 1 Map of Bradford showing the areas of immigrant settlement divided into various zones (see text)

of 295,768 which included: 3,457 Pakistanis, 1,512 Indians, 984 West Indians and a small number of Africans, mainly from West Africa.

When I began my fieldwork during 1964, it was estimated by the local authorities that there were about 12,000 Pakistani immigrants in the city. In the absence of any authoritative sources I took that figure as given. In *Table 1* I show the division of this population in terms of area of origin in Pakistan.[4]

TABLE 1 *Estimated Pakistani population in Bradford during 1964*

Number estimated	*Area of origin*
5,400	Mirpur district, Azad Kashmir
3,000	Campbellpur district, mainly from the north-east corner of the district, known as 'the Chhachh'
1,800	Jhelum, Lyallpur, Rawalpindi and other neighbouring districts of West Punjab
300	Pathan tribesmen from Mardan, Peshawar, Swat and other parts of the North-West Frontier
10,000	(West) Pakistanis
1,500	Bangladeshis* (formerly East Pakistanis), mainly from Sylhet district
Total: 12,000	

* Their number has since fallen to around 850–900, mainly due to internal migration to places such as Leeds, Keighley and Halifax.

About a third of the city's labour force is employed in the wool textile industry. The 1964 Official Handbook for Bradford (62) says:

'15,465 workers in the wool textile industry are from Austria, Italy, Poland as well as India, Pakistan and other Commonwealth countries . . .'.

The great majority of Pakistani immigrants are employed in the wool and engineering industries. Approximately 400 (33 per cent) of the platform staff in the city's Transport Department are Commonwealth immigrants, mainly of Indo-Pakistan origin.

III IMMIGRANTS' BACKGROUND

In terms of socio-economic background, the majority of the immigrants from the Chhachh, the Punjab and Mirpur are small landholders. The size of landholdings for most of those in the Chhachh and the Punjab is between 10 and 12 *kanāls* (8 *kanāls* = 1 acre), and around 5 to 6 *bighās* (4 *bighās* = 1 acre) for those in Mirpur district. I also came across four immigrants from Lyallput, Jhelum and Sahiwal (formerly Montgomery) districts whose landholdings were between 30 and 40 acres; but these were exceptional cases.[5] While the landholdings of a majority of the immigrants may appear to be meagre, the immigrants cannot be identified with the industrial proletariat in this country or with the landless category in their society of origin. One has only to witness the plight and the depressed status of the landless category in Pakistan (and, indeed, in the subcontinent as a whole) in order to appreciate the socio-economic significance of ownership of even small landholdings such as the immigrants and their families possess. Generally speaking, small landholders in the immigrants' villages tend to eat what they obtain by means of sharecropping, and occasionally barter some of the produce for other goods. But it is difficult even for a moderate farmer to lay aside cash for acquiring consumer goods such as clothes, shoes and kerosene, or for meeting emergencies such as illness or family disasters. The landholder in Pakistan is most reluctant to part with his land, although in money terms it may be worth between £4,000–£6,000, the price one would pay for 1 acre of agricultural land in the Chhachh and Lyallpur. A similar attitude is known to prevail among pastoral people who rarely and unwillingly kill or sell their cattle or other livestock, since they represent to the owner a far more real expression of wealth than cash in hand or in the bank. The immigrants' and their families' attachment to land and their interest in increasing the size of their landholdings is a characteristic they share with peasants generally. Such attachment is not a matter of sentiment, as Redfield (1956: 19 and Chap. IV) holds. Nor is it so much a matter of the

81

mystical attributes associated with land. But it is a common concern for social standing within one's village community which is based on land ownership. One's landholding, no matter how small its size, is a scarce economic resource. Ancestral land, which is more highly esteemed than newly-acquired land, is often spoken of in mystical terms as a sacred heritage, but any land is better than none. Completely to abandon one's attachment to the village of origin and to one's landholding means giving up one's claims to membership of one's village-and-kin network. Their attachment to their landholdings, then, gives the immigrants a firm root in their village-kin groups both in Pakistan and in Britain. Further, their traditional bias for land ownership is the basis of their predilection for real estate in Britain.[6]

IV THE MOTIVE FOR MIGRATION

Like Indians (A. C. Mayer 1971, Thompson, op. cit., 80; Evans 1971), Pakistanis emigrate not in order to earn a livelihood but to supplement the economic resources of their families of origin, so that their landholdings may remain intact and their remittances may be invested, as indeed they are, to improve their existing landholdings and/or to extend them, to improve their family homestead by building a *pakkā* (lit. solid) house, and so on. In short, from the immigrant's and his family's point of view, migration is an economic investment. For example, in the mid-1950s, travel agents in Pakistan used to charge between £250 and £300 for a passport and fares to Britain, and during 1960–65 these charges went up to as much as £800. In a country like Pakistan, where *per capita* income is £30 p.a., the money which the immigrant's family spent in financing his migration represents a substantial amount and is an indication of the family's expectations in the form of remittances. That is, migration is undertaken for raising the immigrant's family's socio-economic status back home, and not for the immigrant's immediate gratification in the receiving country. It is important to bear this fact in mind, for the immigrant's behaviour patterns in Britain, especially with regard to living conditions, consumption, etc., are influenced by this motive for migration. To that extent, the motive provides the immigrant with a scale of values and preferences which differ from those of other coloured immigrants and from those of the host society in general. These values and preferences markedly differ from those of the native proletariat, with whom the immigrants are mistakenly identified. For example, according to Krausz (op. cit., 121), Rex holds that the coloured proletariat together with other underprivileged groups, such as the newer Irish immigrants and poorer sections of the indigenous population, comprise a distinct housing class. The fact that the politically dominant group of the host society judges the immigrants as belonging at the bottom of the class structure in Britain is not a valid reason for a sociologist to assume that the immigrants and the native proletariat share a single scale of values and preferences.

Closely related to the motive for migration is the myth or ideology of return. The immigrants come with the firm intention of returning home where they hope to enjoy the fruits of their labour in retirement. That is, the immigrants consider themselves to be transients and not settlers. However, this is not to imply that the immigrants, or any significant number of them, will in fact return home. None the less, this myth or ideology of return is an important factor that has consequences with regard to the immigrant community's social organization, the immigrants' willingness to endure hardship in work and living conditions, and their emphasis on savings which are remitted to their families in Pakistan.

There is no primogeniture in Pakistan and every generation sees increasing fragmentation of land and the division of other forms of property. While actual division of the property as such need not take place, the allocation of shares among the heirs is effected immediately. Because of this fragmentation of property, every man regards it as his duty to work hard to build up his landholding and other forms of property during his working life to pass on to his children after his death. Therefore the motivation for a man and his sons to build up their economic resources is very strong, for the more there is of land and other forms of property at the time of the man's death, the more there will be to share out among his heirs. This is a very strong motive that drives a man to great endeavour to accumulate resources.

Badr Dahya

The first Indo-Pakistanis to settle in Bradford were former seamen who, during 1941, were directed from seaports such as Liverpool, Middlesbrough and Hull to munition factories and essential wartime industries in the Bradford and Leeds areas. These were the pioneers whose arrival in the city and whose economic success there led to the subsequent emergence and development of the immigrant communities.

Around 1944–45, there were some thirty-odd Indo-Pakistanis, all of whom were former seamen, who lived as lodgers in houses owned by Poles in Howard Street, which is in zone 'A' (see *Map 1*). During 1964, there were about half a dozen Polish houses in the zone and there are found in the zone today a Polish social club, the Polish Roman Catholic Church and an East European delicatessen. The presence of these institutions in the zone suggests that the zone was at some time in the past inhabited by Poles and other East Europeans, that it was an area of transition and marginal to the local people.

According to the pioneer immigrants, the first Pakistani-owned houses were in William Street which was sandwiched between rows of warehouses at the corner of Manchester Road and Little Horton Lane (zone A), about a couple of minutes' walk from the Town Hall. (This street was demolished around 1963–64 and replaced by a modern block with a pub, a few shops and an ice rink.) During 1949–50, some Pakistanis bought two houses in Howard Street. At that time houses in Howard Street used to cost about £250 and those in William Street, being smaller and older, cost less than £150. As the pioneers gradually settled down and began to buy houses, their economic success attracted deserting seamen and other Pakistanis who had hitherto stayed in places such as Nottingham, Newcastle upon Tyne, Sheffield, Birmingham, Leeds and Manchester. It is said that during the war Indo-Pakistanis at Leeds outnumbered those at Bradford, and it was largely due to the success of the early settlers in Bradford that former seamen from other cities and seaports moved to Bradford.

The pioneer settlers were not immigrants but former seamen who had found themselves stranded during the Second World War. Over the next few years they were joined by a flow of their fellow countrymen who were not immigrants but seamen who had jumped ship on arrival and duly moved to Bradford, either directly or via their intermediate contacts in other cities. On arrival in Bradford, they would go to Howard Street where they were sure to find lodgings and help through their country-men. A retired police officer told me that in those days if you happened to come across an Indo-Pakistani looking for help you could not do better than show him to Howard Street.

VI SELECTIVE MIGRATION AND SPONSORSHIP

Up to about 1950 the new arrivals were mostly deserters from the merchant navy or former seamen who had previously settled elsewhere. But soon the settlers in the city began to sponsor their kinsmen, though a substantial proportion of the new arrivals continued to be seamen.

In terms of area of origin, Pakistanis among the pioneers were from the Chhachh area in a sub-district of Campbellpur, and from Mirpur district, Azad ('Free') Kashmir (which, for all practical purposes, is a part of Pakistan). In the Chhachh area there has been a well-established tradition for males to emigrate abroad for a few years and eventually to retire in their villages. According to the Punjab District Gazetteer, 1907 (51):

> 'From the northeast corner of the Chhachh very large num-bers of men go out as stokers on the P. & O. and British India boats and come back shattered in health, but full of money'.

The Gazetteers for Jammu and Kashmir (of which, until 1947, Mirpur was a part) do not give information about emigration from Mirpur district. However, during fieldwork both in Britain and in Pakistan I came across descendants of former seamen from whose accounts it appears that men in that dis-trict, like those in the Chhachh, used to go abroad and serve in the merchant navy.

The pioneer settlers in Bradford sponsored their kinsmen by arranging for their recruitment as seamen in the hope that eventually the sponsored kinsmen would find their way to this country. Most of them indeed did so after a year or two of service at sea. The pioneers had settled in Bradford with the intention of working for a few years to accumulate savings and eventually retire in their natal villages. This kind of settler tended to return home, but made arrangements for a kinsman (usually a younger brother or a son) to replace him. Thus, from the early days of settlement, the migration of Pakistanis has been selective in terms of specific areas and specific families of origin. This selectivity was not affected by the Commonwealth Immigrants Act, 1962. In fact, the terms of the Act reinforced selectivity because the immigrants in Britain were favourably placed to sponsor their kinsmen and fellow-villagers by obtaining vouchers for them, by raising cash for their passports and air fares, and in the last resort by helping them with loans and guarantees for the travel agents in Pakistan. This selectivity in migration has affected the growth of the community in Britain generally and enabled the immigrants to create small-scale units based on village-kin ties.

VII ETHNIC GROUPS AND THEIR DISTRIBUTION[7]

At the end of 1964 there were 1,265 houses owned and occupied by Asian immigrants in the city.[8] After classifying the various ethnic groups in Bradford, I divided the areas of immigrant settlement into various zones as shown on *Map 1*. My analysis of the housing records shows that there were 983 Pakistani (including Bangladeshi) houses, sub-divided in approximate numbers along ethnic lines as in *Table 2*.

On the basis of case histories of Pakistanis in Bradford, Birmingham, and elsewhere, it is possible to formulate a developmental cycle (Goody 1958) with regard to changes in the character of the immigrant house as an institution. During the early stages of their settlement in Bradford, Indo-Pakistanis (that is, Hindu, Muslim and Sikh immigrants) from undivided India used to stay together. With the division of the sub-continent into two national entities in 1947, and with the arrival of fresh immigrants, older settlers began to differentiate themselves on the basis of national/ethnic origins. Later on, as a result of sponsorship the number of immigrants increased and new forms of sub-groups based, at first, on regional identity and, later, on the basis of village-kin group, emerged. Since 1960, with the arrival of wives and children, the village-kin group as a residential unit has very gradually begun to ramify into nuclear households. Broadly speaking, the process of growth and subsequent development of the immigrant community is one of fusion of immigrants from different areas leading to a fission and segmentation on the basis of village-kin ties. That is, the process begins with the fusion of members of various ethnic/sectarian/national groups during which stage traditional attitudes of inter-ethnic/sectarian hostility are tem-

TABLE 2 *Pakistani houses in Bradford, December 1964*

489	Mirpuri houses
190	Chhachhi houses
135	Punjabi houses
24	Pathan houses
3	Gujarati Muslim houses
841	
142	Bangladeshi houses
Total: 983	

The division of Pakistani houses along ethnic lines is based on the following facts:
1. Bangladeshis live exclusively apart from Pakistanis, and similarly Pathan tribesmen maintain their exclusiveness.
2. Chhachhis and Mirpuris avoid one another and from 1964 onwards I did not come across a single instance of Mirpuris and Chhachhis living together either in Bradford or Birmingham.
3. A great majority of Punjabis likewise exclude themselves from non-Punjabis and there were only a few isolated cases of Punjabis from Jhelum district who lived either in Mirpuri or Chhachhi houses.

porarily shelved. During 1964–66 it was possible to observe this process in places such as Bedford, Luton, Watford and Crawley. It was not unusual to find Mirpuris, Chhachhis, Pathans and Punjabis, and, in some cases Sikh immigrants also, living together in these towns. In the GLC area, because of housing shortage and the capital expenditure involved in buying a house, a similar situation obtains. But in all cases, Pakistanis tend to stay apart from Bangladeshis. Fission and segmentation of the immigrant community from fortuitous sub-groups into sub-groups of choice is a form of developmental cycle where the immigrants exclude themselves from those outside their village-kin groups and express their preference for living with those of their own kind. Where immigrants have set up family households, they move away from areas where all-male dormitories predominate and take up residence in areas (or streets) where there are other immigrant family households. If the present trends continue, a situation might arise where the all-male dormitory as an institution might become marginal to the immigrant community.[9]

VIII ETHNIC PREFERENCE

The pattern of immigrant settlements over the city and also on streets within the zones reflects the immigrants' preferences along ethnic lines. For example, the Gujarati immigrants are concentrated in A, B, and C zones; their shops and cultural institutions (e.g., the *Bhāratiya Mandala*) are located there. The Sikhs are concentrated in zones G and H and their economic, social and cultural institutions, e.g., the *Gurdwāra* (temple), are likewise found in those zones. Among the Pakistanis, the Pathan houses are located on some three streets in zone G. The Chhachhis are found, in the main, in zones A, B, C, E, and K; the Punjabis are concentrated mainly in A, B, C, D, and E zones. The Mirpuris are, on the other hand, fairly widespread except that only a few of them live in zones G, H, and K. The Bangladeshi houses are confined to certain streets in zones A, B, C, E, F, and I, where they form more or less closely clustered settlements.

A further preference with regard to settlements occurs along sectarian lines. For example, in a private square off Lumb Lane (zone E), there are four *Shī'a*[10] dormitories (with the *Shī'a* mosque in a house nearby). Another four *Shī'a* houses are in a street opposite the square. Also, in zone A, there are four *Shī'a* dormitories in a row on one street, and in zone G there are three *Shī'a* dormitories located on one street.

There are several reasons why the immigrants chose to settle in the zones they did. The area within the inner ring of the city is characterized by back-to-back artisan cottages, old terrace houses and large late Victorian and Edwardian houses, mills, warehouses, factories, workshops, stores, shops, and schools, public houses, and places of worship. The area is close to the central business and commercial districts in the city. The zones are thus centrally situated with easy access to the city centre and to the main arterial routes of public transport. Buses linking the city to other towns in the woollen textile belt run along the roads which radiate from the city centre. Further, the area had previously served as an area of transition for East and Central European immigrants who, in successive waves, had made good and moved away. Similarly the more mobile elements among the working classes who lived in the back-to-back cottages, like most of the middle-class occupants of the large Victorian and Edwardian houses (e.g., in Ashgrove, zone B; Southfield and Hanover Squares, zone E) had moved out to the suburbs or left the city altogether.[11]

When the pioneer immigrants arrived on the scene, they readily found accommodation in houses owned by their predecessors, namely, the Poles and Ukrainians. Case histories of the pioneers show that they were able to obtain relatively cheap lodgings in the Howard Street area in zone A, and it was in the same street that they established the first mosque in the city. Once the pioneers had settled in zone A, they attracted other immigrants to the adjoining streets and gradually the boundaries of the immigrant settlement began to stretch. Over the last few years, changes in the social structure and in the demographic features of the immigrant community have gradually pushed the 'frontier' outwards. In brief, there were a number of factors such as environment, cheap housing, and easy access to transport and communications, which, taken in conjunction with the economic circumstances and motives of the immigrant population, made for their settlement in the inner ring. Further, there was no competition for the houses there, where no one, other than the immigrants, wanted to live. It must be mentioned that the immigrants had arrived during the period of full employment. Also, the majority of new arrivals were for the first time in their lives earning wages and handling cash. Their living and eating requirements were broadly the same as before migration, and consequently greater was the margin of their savings.

The immigrants did not find it necessary to obtain loans from building societies or other agencies for the purchase of old back-to-back cottages and old terrace houses in the zones because the houses were 'cheap'. In any case, building societies in Bradford, as elsewhere, are reluctant to give loans for old houses which, in this case, were built between 1880 and the First World War, and some of the back-to-back cottages date back to the middle of last century. Also, some building societies are known to draw the line at houses built before the Second World War and, as a rule, they do not give loans for houses under £2,000. During the early 1960s it was possible to buy back-to-back cottages for £80 or so without a loan. (Indeed, during 1964–66, there were many cottages selling for £45 to £60.) The most that is required of the purchaser is a deposit of £10–£12 and a weekly instalment of 15s. (75p) to £1 to be paid to the vendor or his solicitor. More or less similar terms were available for purchasing old terrace houses. This form of purchase is fairly widespread in the North and is known as 'rental purchase'. In the circumstances in which the immigrants found themselves on their arrival, they could not have been expected to buy modern houses in the suburbs and, therefore, their settlement in the zones of transition was a form of adaptation to the problems they faced.

IX ECONOMIC ENTERPRISE AND ETHNICITY

Over the last decade, the immigrant community has grown from a few thousand to approximately 21,000 (1970 estimate), including children born in this country. This growth has been accompanied by a parallel growth of ethnic socio-economic institutions. In 1959, the only Pakistani-owned economic concerns were 2 grocery/butchery businesses and 3 cafés. By 1966, the number of Pakistani concerns had grown to 133, which included 51 grocers/butchers and 16 cafés. In 1970, there were over 260 immigrant-owned and -operated businesses, all of which were located in the areas of immigrant settlement. The number of food businesses has risen to over 180, which includes 11 wholesale premises, 1 canning factory, 112 grocery and butchery businesses, 25 cafés, 15 private clubs, and 2 confectioners and bakers.

The ethnic establishments which serve the needs of the immigrant community comprise grocers and butchers, cafés and clubs, restaurants and cinemas, places of worship and a public house, travel agencies, laundry and drycleaning businesses, income tax consultants, information and advisory bureaux, herbalists and astrologers, booksellers, photographic dealers, car and van hire firms, driving schools, secondhand furniture dealers, importers and exporters, drapers and tailors, barbers, jewellers, Pakistan-based banks and insurance companies, plumbers, estate agents, bakers and confectioners, coal merchants, and electrical goods and gramophone records dealers. The presence and proliferation of such a vast range of ethnic concerns in the zones has an important bearing on the nature of Pakistani ethnicity and on the quality of interpersonal relations among the immigrants. It helps, *inter alia*, to keep the immigrant community a relatively closed one as the immigrants do not have to cross the ethnic boundaries to satisfy most of their everyday needs.

Pakistani shops and cafés are distinguished from their native counterparts by means of Urdu signs and notices on the fascias and shop-windows. Also, as a rule, posters bearing pictures of famous Muslim shrines, such as those at Mecca and Medina, wreathed and ornamented with verses from the Qur'an, pictures of Pakistani national heroes such as Iqbal and Jinnah, and the Muslim calendar are displayed inside the shops and cafés. Consequently, some of the streets in the areas of settlement tend to acquire a peculiar character and remind the immigrants of their ethnicity, and at the same time they make the natives aware of the immigrants' separate identity. Further, apart from selling goods and services, Pakistani shops and cafés disseminate information about the various Muslim feasts and about the beginning and the end of the Ramadan fast, sell Pakistani newspapers and magazines, distribute handbills regarding Pakistani social and cultural activities, and circulate literature regarding Indo-Pakistani film shows. Thus, every time an immigrant visits a Pakistani shop or café, he is exposed to various influences emanating from such an environment which remind him of his distinct identity.

Ethnic entrepreneurs need an ethnic clientele and, therefore, it is in their interest that during periods of economic recession the immigrants should not remain unemployed for long and that the number of unemployed immigrants at any given time should be as low as possible. To that end, ethnic entrepreneurs act as 'clearing houses' for information regarding opportunities for employment within the city and in other towns. They have village-kin links both within and beyond the city, and among items of news and gossip they exchange with their fellows information relating to employment. Also, Pakistani wholesalers and travelling salesmen carry messages to their clients, such as grocers and drapers, from one town to another. Further, weekend and holiday visiting among kinsmen and fellow-villagers, often taking a group of kinsmen to another town, provides an opportunity for carrying messages, especially information regarding employment, to and fro. During such visits, after the normal greetings and formalities have been exchanged, the very first topic discussed relates to wages and overtime, and the local situation regarding employment. Thus, the immigrant is indirectly linked by the ethnic entrepreneurs to his fellows all over the country and given access to information relevant to his interests. He utilizes these links when he or any of his fellows become unemployed. During the period of his unemployment, the immigrant does not wander randomly in search of a job; rather, he relies on the various sources of information which are at his disposal. He sifts such intelligence as comes his way, and deliberates with his fellows at home whether to move to another town, or to stay put in the hope that the employment situation in his locality may take a turn for the better. Since the motive for migration is economic, and since the immigrant regards his stay in Britain as temporary, he is keen to deploy his time to his best advantage. Accordingly, he remains mobile and does not hesitate to move to another town in search of a job. During such moves he stays with fellows who are known to him either through his village-kin network or through an intermediary, such as the ethnic entrepreneur. Thus, village-kin and ethnic ties are potentialities for social participation and mutual aid. These potentialities are activated, *inter alia*, during economic recession and are among the factors that help to keep the number of unemployed immigrants down to a low level. Thus, village-kin ties and ethnicity help to bridge physical distance between members of the immigrant community who may be scattered all over the country, and in spite of its numerical size and geographical distribution, the immigrant population turns out to compose a small-scale society.

That is, it consists of small interlocking and interdependent groups whose members are bound to one another by virtue of their shared past, their experiences and interests in Britain and their orientation to the country of origin.

Ethnic institutions emerge to provide the immigrants with a wide range of goods and services and thereby part of the resources earned by the immigrants in the host society's economic organization are channelled into the hands of the ethnic entrepreneurs and kept within the bounds of the ethnic group. However, since the ethnic institutions depend on ethnic patronage, they acquire a vested interest in the immigrants as their clientele. That is, the ethnic entrepreneur's interest lies in ensuring that the immigrants continue to remain Pakistanis, or that they do not give up their Pakistanihood, for only then can the entrepreneur be secure in the knowledge that the immigrants will continue to patronize his business. Accordingly, one role of the entrepreneur in the immigrant community is to remind immigrants of their traditional culture and values, that is, to perpetuate and defend their ethnicity. Some of the entrepreneurs (e.g., travel agents, bank officials, insurance agents, grocers, and butchers) and religious functionaries, such as the Imams of the local mosques, sit on the local Mosque Committee. In their capacity as members of the Committee, they act as a pressure group, for example, on the local education authority and emphasize their religious and cultural traditions in order to seek concessions with regard to female dress and the content of education, especially physical education. Thus, ethnic entrepreneurs take steps to ensure that some aspects of their community's traditional forms of family organization and values may be transmitted to the second generation. Also, the fact that the immigrant settlements are concentrated in certain areas means that the entrepreneurs as 'leaders' are often able to mobilize public opinion in the immigrant community and influence its political behaviour. During the 1971 local elections, the Mosque Committee was one of two immigrant organizations which exhorted the immigrants to vote against a Bangladeshi who contested Manningham Ward, which includes one of the main areas of immigrant settlement, on a Labour Party ticket (*The Times*, 11.5.71: 2). The effectiveness with which the immigrant organizations were able to mobilize the immigrant vote

(3,000 voters, mainly Pakistanis, out of 12,600) can be seen
from the fact that the Manningham Ward returned the Conservative candidate when there was an anti-Conservative swing
all over the country. Further, in view of their vested interest in
the immigrant community, it is not surprising that Pakistani
'leaders', including entrepreneurs, who appeared as spokesmen
for the community to give evidence before the Select Committee
on Race Relations and Immigration during March 1971, came
out against a policy for dispersal.

The immigrants' participation in their own socio-cultural
activities and their patronage of ethnic institutions reduces their
chances of meeting non-immigrants. By taking hold of the
immigrants' allegiance, the ethnic institutions bring about their
relative encapsulation and reduce the potentialities for interpersonal relations across the ethnic boundaries. The immigrants'
support for ethnic and their avoidance of native institutions is
not simply a matter of voluntary decision on their part; rather,
it is an obligation ('If we do not patronize our own people, who
else will?'). Indeed, it is an expression of one's loyalty to the
homeland. The fact that all transactions over the counter are
carried on in one's own language and dialect, and that one
meets one's fellow countrymen there with whom one exchanges
news about matters of common interest in an environment
peculiar to Pakistani shops, are among the factors that remind
the immigrants of their shared past, their cultural characteristics, their motives for migration, their low social status in the
wider host society and their separate identity. In brief, participation in ethnic institutions increases their pride in their
traditional culture and nationality and is an expression of their
ethnicity. Unlike its native – British – counterpart, the Pakistani shop fulfils extra-economic functions which could not be
fulfilled by the former. The specific role played by ethnic
entrepreneurs in the immigrant community make the ethnic
shop and the entrepreneur unique institutions in the context of
Pakistani ethnicity.

Also, the range and variety of ethnic institutions are an index
of the 'institutional completeness' (Breton 1964) of the immigrant community; the whole complex of ethnic institutions
manifests the community's wish not merely to express but also
to defend and perpetuate their traditional social forms, values,

beliefs and ethnic identity. To put it negatively, the ethnic institutions are a means of making explicit to outsiders the immigrant community's refusal to adopt local norms or to surrender its ethnic identity. Ethnic institutions in the areas of settlement serve as an anchorage for the immigrant community, and as a brake on whatever tendencies there may be on the part of individual immigrants towards geographical dispersal.

To sum up the material to this stage, the immigrant community's ecological base serves several important functions which are related to the community's need to create, manifest and defend its ethnic identity. During the early stages of the community's settlement, the ecological base is closely interwoven with the immigrants' participation in ethnic socioeconomic institutions and mutual aid, and with the community's need to define its identity, both for its members and outsiders. Reinforced by endogamy, the ecological base with its concomitant institutions serves as an instrument for the transmission of the community's culture, values and identity to the second generation, and for maintaining ethnic boundaries and for avoiding (or minimizing) ambiguities with regard to ethnic identity. Further, during local elections, the ecological base is transformed into the community's political base, and generally it enables the community to act as a pressure group on local, as well as national, civic, and political institutions. That is, the various dimensions of ethnicity which the immigrant community defines, expresses and defends in a number of different contexts make it one among several interest groups in British society. Several recent studies (e.g., Morris 1968, Cohen 1969, Glazer & Moynihan 1970) show ethnic groups to fulfil more or less similar functions in the wider societies of which they form a part.

X SETTLEMENT IN BIRMINGHAM

The settlement of Pakistanis and other Asian immigrants in the city of Birmingham began during January/February 1940, with the arrival from Cardiff[12] of some thirty-odd Asian merchant seamen (among whom were Sikhs and Muslims from undivided India, and Yemenis). They were directed to Birmingham by the Ministry of Labour to work on essential wartime production in local factories. Initially they were housed in a government hostel, but within two to three months of their arrival, most of them had left the hostel to live in private lodgings in the Balsall Heath area; some of them lived in East European houses and others in houses owned by Turkish Cypriots. By June 1940, two of the Muslims (Yemenis) managed to buy an artisan cottage towards the Balsall Heath Road end of Mary Street and there established the first mosque in the city. Thus, Balsall Heath as the primary area of settlement with the mosque as its base began to attract Muslim merchant seamen – as did the Howard Street area in Bradford – and their numbers increased during the post-war period when deserting seamen made for Balsall Heath to join their fellows. From then onwards, the pattern of growth and settlement is broadly similar to that described for Bradford. The settlement began to extend outwards from the primary area to places which afforded the immigrants easy access to their place of employment. On a spatial distribution based upon access to work place was superimposed a concentration into ethnic neighbourhoods caused by sponsorship of kinsmen and fellow-villagers; both these phenomena were parallel developments during the second stage.

By 1956, when I happened to visit Birmingham, the immigrants had already 'sorted' themselves out on the basis of national origins and ethnicity (that is, on factors such as language/dialect, religion/sect, and area of origin). Pakistanis had moved across to Moseley/Sparkbrook, and to Small Heath and Aston; most of the Jat Sikhs (landowning castes by origin) had moved to places such as Smethwick and Wolverhampton and a few had gone to Sparkbrook, whereas Ramgarhia Sikhs (artisan castes by origin) had settled a little to the south of the primary area and established themselves in two or three streets off Edward Road where they are found to this day with their *Gurdwāra* on the corner of Mary and Hallam Streets (their previous *Guardwāra* having been on Cannon Hill Road). Similarly, most of the Yemenis moved to the area south of Edward Road and to parts of Moseley (e.g., to some of the streets east of Moseley Road). Immigrants from Sylhet district (formerly East Pakistanis) were the only ones who for the next few years decided to stay put in the primary area which as far as residence is concerned became marginal to Pakistanis, Sikhs, and Yemenis.

XI ATTITUDE TO REAL ESTATE

There is no housing shortage in Bradford and the local authority does not discriminate against immigrants in the allocation of houses and flats. The qualifying period for joining the waiting list for council houses is six months' residence in the city. Burney (op. cit., p. 35) tells us that council houses in Bradford 'are going begging'. Asian immigrants generally, and Pakistanis in particular, are not interested in renting flats and houses. Their attitude in this respect was expressed by one informant who remarked:

'Why pay rent for property which can never be yours? Better to save money and buy a house, so that you can live in it and also make more money.'

Another informant, this time from Sparkbrook, observed:

'What is the status of a fifteen-shilling tenant?[13] Does anyone respect him? He is always at the mercy of the landlord and his 'party' [faction] and dare not express himself openly lest he offend them . . . and he can be kicked out at a week's notice.'

The immigrants are thus guided by their traditional criteria of status, namely, that as a tenant the immigrant has a subordinate status *vis-à-vis* the landlord and his kinsmen. In other words, the position of the tenant in Britain is broadly similar to that of a client in their traditional patron-client relationships back home. As a tenant, the immigrant is subject to the landlord's influence and is indebted to him and his kinsmen and fellow-villagers by virtue of the fact that he stays with them at the landlord's pleasure. Further, the landlord has the power to give or withhold accommodation and to control his tenant's credit (i.e. mutual aid) relationships, for the immigrant's credibility in the immigrant community depends, among other things, on his status (i.e., whether he is a tenant or a landlord), and, most important, on the quality of his relationship with the landlord, and by implication with the latter's kinsmen and fellow-villagers. In brief, the immigrant's status as a tenant is a negation of the traditional values associated with the status of a 'free' person. However, for a couple of years after his arrival, the immigrant compromises over his status because he needs his fellows' help which eventually enables him to become an entrepreneur in Britain and/or in Pakistan.

During 1965–67 I registered an informant's name as a prospective buyer with three estate agents in Bradford, giving details about his employment, length of stay in the country, earnings, nationality, etc., and had his application lined up with a building society. On two occasions he was offered semi-detached houses in the suburbs of Bradford at prices ranging between £3,250 and £4,000. But neither he nor any of the numerous prospective buyers from among my informants were interested in buying houses in the suburbs at those prices. They refused these offers on the ground that immigrant-tenants could not be expected to pay more than 75p per week in rent; that there would be the problem of getting transport to work and of visiting their fellows in the city; and that the houses in question were a long distance away from the immigrant areas and, therefore, getting provisions from Pakistani grocers and butchers would be a further problem. Also, from time to time I used to obtain lists of houses for sale from various estate agents and carry these around for the benefit of my informants, many of whom had asked me to be on the look-out for a 'decent' house. However, their notion of a 'decent' house meant a dwelling that was easily accessible by bus, within easy reach of the immigrant shops and, most importantly, within the price range of £175 to £550. Further, on several occasions I tried to test the immigrants' reaction by advising them to buy modern houses. Their reactions, which were more or less similar, are illuminating:

'What is the use of spending so much money on a house in this country? We are not going to live here for ever.'
'Will the English people think better of me if I buy a modern house? Better to build a *pakkā* house in the village where there are people who know you and respect you. They are the people who matter.'

Thus, from the immigrant's point of view, the 'significant others' are his kinsmen and fellow-villagers back home who will recognize his achieved status and he accordingly seeks their esteem and approbation.

On numerous occasions when I tried to dissuade my informants in Birmingham and Bradford from buying cheap property with short leases, usually thirty to thirty-five years, and in a few cases twelve years and less, they invoked their myth of return:

'We shall have gone by the time the lease expires.'
'I shall get more than the price of the house in rent over the next six years as well as free accommodation for all of us, and I shall still make a profit if I decide to sell it then.'
'God knows what will happen in nine or ten years' time.'

That is, the immigrants consider that cheap houses with short leases would suit their short-term interests and at the same time earn them extra money with which they intend to return home. In other words, the immigrants' preference for a particular type of housing is a form of response to their immediate needs and interests, and an expression of their non-committal to Britain. In keeping with their myth of return, the immigrants do not regard the house in Britain as a 'home' but as a short-term expediency related to a particular goal or goals. It cannot be overemphasized that the immigrants came to Britain with the firm intention of earning and saving money and eventually returning to their homeland. They did not come in order to enjoy a comfortable life here. Thompson (op. cit., 112) provides similar evidence with regard to the settlement of Sikh immigrants in Coventry.

XII LANDLORDS AS ENTREPRENEURS

One more reason why the immigrants are favourably disposed towards cheap housing is that as a form of investment they require a relatively small outlay and are an easy source of extra income derived from lettings. An immigrant labourer who owns a house is at the same time an entrepreneur, investing in primary relationships in anticipation of future rewards. As a landlord he provides cheap lodgings to his kinsmen and fellow-villagers. He gives free hospitality to the latter's kinsmen and friends during weekends and holidays and, further, he charges no rent when a fellow-tenant becomes sick or unemployed. Similarly, a newly-arrived immigrant, or one who moves from another town seeking work as is the practice among the immigrants during economic recession, is not charged any rent at all until such time as he lands himself with a job. The landlord sees his tenants and their friends in the form of investment and is able to reap benefits when they give him interest-free loans for generating capital with which to undertake some form of economic enterprise in this country or in Pakistan.

Mutual aid is an important aspect of interpersonal relationships among the immigrants. Every immigrant is both a borrower and a lender to a number of his fellow-immigrants within his network which is 'bounded' (A. C. Mayer 1966: 101) in terms of village-kin ties. Loans given as mutual aid are an informal arrangement and *always* free of interest. No documents are signed, nor are there any witnesses. Further, there is no stipulation about the date by which such loans have to be repaid. A lender makes no specific demand on the borrower for the repayment of the loan. However, it is expected that the borrower repays it within six months to a year, depending on the amount involved. There are several instances where loans have been paid three, and sometimes four, years after they had been contracted. Where an immigrant happens to have borrowed a fairly large sum, say, £1,000, the usual practice among the immigrants is for him to subsequently borrow varying sums from different people within his network in order to repay the loan in question. This form of mutual aid is broadly similar to rotating credit associations which have been reported from a wide range of societies in Africa, South-East Asia and the Caribbean (Ardener 1964; Jain 1970: 160–74, and *passim*; Katzin 1959). But unlike the rotating credit associations, the immigrants' network as a mutual aid group is not formally organized into a group with rules and regulations, office-bearers and so on. Further, mutual aid is not referred to as a loan or a debt (*qarzā*), nor as help (*imdād*). Mutual aid is spoken of as *lévā-dévī*, or *léndén* (lit. 'give-and-take', reciprocity) and is regarded as a social obligation (*farz*) between kinsmen and friends. That is, mutual aid comprises economic transactions or what are in effect reciprocal obligations which have repercussions in social and economic spheres.[14]

Mutual aid is given, for example, for purchasing a house and/or for getting it repaired, for sending remittances to Pakistan, for air fares for an immigrant when he wants to return to Britain after visiting his family, and so on. It is not, however, given for the acquisition of luxury goods, such as a motor car or a camera. I came across numerous instances where immigrants who wanted to buy a house were able to raise sums of over £2,000 among their kinsmen and friends within two to three weeks. Sometimes loans are raised along similar lines for opening a business in this country and for shipping a truck, for example, to Pakistan or for investment there. When one of the tenants wishes to purchase a house, he meets with his landlord, fellow-tenants and their friends to put out 'feelers' and he gets a ready response in the form of interest-free loans which enable him to become a landlord. Not only does he receive financial help to launch him in a business enterprise, but also help to provide him with a small nucleus of tenants who will go to live with him, and with whose help he will recruit other tenants. In places such as Birmingham and the GLC area, the immigrant-landlord lets only a part of the house to his fellows whom he charges a nominal rent, and lets the rest of the house, usually converted into furnished rooms and flats, to non-Pakistanis, mainly West Indian and Scottish/Irish immigrants, at high rents. In Bradford and the rest of West Yorkshire, the situation is different and only a few immigrant landlords take non-Pakistanis as tenants. The prospective landlord receives help from his fellows because loans are reciprocated and he benefits from the help he has given them in the past. Those who come to his help now wish to become landlords and/or businessmen themselves at a future date. In other words, the immigrants are following the classical path to entrepreneurship, which Schumpeter (1934: 101–2) expressed in these terms:

> 'The entrepreneurial function is not, in principle, connected with the possession of wealth, as analysis and experience equally teach, even though the accidental fact of wealth constitutes a practical advantage. . . . [An individual] can only become an entrepreneur by previously becoming a debtor.'

We see from the foregoing discussion that the immigrant house as an institution is a means of mobilizing socio-economic resources within the immigrant community and as such it is of considerable significance for an understanding of immigrant settlements. It was mainly for this reason that the Bradford hostel plan for single immigrants failed to evoke any response on the part of Pakistanis (the *Guardian*, 9.2.65; *Daily Telegraph*, 8.7.65).

XIII THE SPARKBROOK STUDY

In their study of Sparkbrook, Rex and Moore (op. cit.) make a number of propositions which are not the outcome of their study at all but are none the less presented as 'findings'. I mention the following propositions for their relevance for this paper:

1. The immigrants fail to obtain mortgages and are thus prevented from becoming owner-occupiers (37).
2. The immigrants are an underprivileged group who seldom qualify for council houses. And when they sometimes do, they are offered 'patched' rather than council-built houses (26-7, 37).
3. Since the immigrants find it difficult to obtain accommodation, they have two choices, namely, either to be lodging-house landlords or lodging-house tenants (30-1, 38, 133-4).

While I do not hold any brief for the Birmingham Corporation, and have no desire to whitewash its discriminatory policy regarding the allocation of council houses to coloured immigrants, I feel it must be pointed out that as early as 1959-61, I came across a number of Pakistani and Adenese immigrants in Balsall Heath, Moseley, and Sparkbrook who had been successful in getting mortgages from the local council (see Birmingham Corporation, 1969). During those years and from 1964 onwards, I was often asked by my informants from among these two communities to act as intermediary in which capacity I accompanied them to various estate agents, solicitors, building societies, and the local council offices. An overwhelming majority of the immigrants I accompanied showed no interest in any other form of dwelling other than large Victorian and Edwardian houses. Further, I know at least seven immigrants who, for various reasons, chose to buy post-1945 houses and were granted mortgages by some of the nationally well-known building societies during 1960-61. However, in each case the immigrant-landlord set up a lodging-house although the local council and the building societies concerned were told on the application form that the immigrant-borrower was expecting his wife and children to join him in this country. That is, the immigrant-landlord's main interest in buying a house was to run a lodging-house. The questionnaire for the Sparkbrook study contained no fewer than a hundred questions and, in their study, the authors provide us with sixty-one tables and an appendix on sampling methods adopted by them. But they fail to give us any data which prompted them to make the above assertions. For example, one would like to know what percentage of their Pakistani sample did in fact apply for a mortgage in order to buy, say, a modern semi-detached house but had been turned down.

I have already dealt with the Pakistani immigrants' attitude to rented property in general and so do not feel there is any need for me to discuss the authors' second assertion regarding council houses. According to Plant (1971: 325), to date no Asian immigrant in Birmingham has put his name down for a local council house whereas some West Indian immigrants have done so. In this respect, it ought to be mentioned that in other parts of the country where some of the Pakistanis affected by slum clearance have been allocated council houses, they have turned these into lodging-houses by taking kinsmen and friends as lodgers. Further, when an immigrant buys a house, he does not think of a house that is going to be a 'comfortable home' where he may hope to spend his days in retirement. Among his main interests in buying a house are:

1. To save the amount which he would have to pay in rent as a lodger;
2. To obtain a steady source of income from rents by taking lodgers; in this way he is able to supplement his income and eventually when he decides to sell, he makes a further profit as a result of rising prices;
3. To recruit supporters from among his kinsmen and fellow-villagers by giving them cheap lodgings and securing well-paid (that is, with plenty of overtime) jobs for them; and
4. To express his achieved status as an immigrant who has made good.

The immigrants buy cheap housing because the returns through rents are a fruitful investment. They do not buy houses in order to enjoy personal freedom or privacy; rather, as house-owners they have their eyes on the number of *lājers* (lodgers) they can accommodate.

Rex and Moore (op. cit., 30) assert that because the immigrant has to pay out a large sum of money borrowed from friends, he has to fill the house with tenants in order to discharge his debts as quickly as possible. Again, the authors do not provide any data to support their assertion. In a previous section I discussed the role of mutual aid as an institution among the immigrants and mentioned the fact that no immigrant pays interest on loans received from kinsmen and fellow-villagers, and that there is no stipulation with regard to the payment of such loans. In this respect, the authors' assertion about 'heavy charges' and quick repayments are not based on internal evidence. According to my information relating to the immigrants in Birmingham, Bradford, and elsewhere, the immigrant-landlord uses the house as a source of extra income. In fact, this is one of the main reasons why he buys a house in the first place. For example, several big Pakistani landlords, who are well known among the immigrants in Sparkbrook, are known to have lived there since the early 1960s. Although they live in some of the streets to the east of Stratford Road, that is, in the area studied by the authors, they do not appear among Rex and Moore's sample of thirty-nine male Pakistanis, nor is there any information relating to their economic activities as *rentiers*. At the time of the authors' study, there were among the big landlords: two immigrants who are joint owners of some eighteen houses, a further two owning eight houses each, one owning eleven houses and another six, some eleven immigrants owning three houses each and several others who own two houses each. The houses owned by these big landlords are located in Sparkbrook, Moseley, Small Heath, Aston, Edgbaston, Balsall Heath and King's Heath. That is, they are absentee landlords who did not buy houses in order to house themselves, as Rex and Moore assert (30, 133–4), but purely to earn extra income.

Rex and Moore write as if they were surprised to see the immigrants in Sparkbrook, for they tell us:

'What we did observe was a process of discriminative and *de facto* segregation which compelled coloured people to live in certain typical conditions. . . .' (20).

'Virtually the only houses these immigrants could buy were the late Victorian and Edwardian terrace houses. . . .' (30).

Again, no empirical evidence is provided to support these statements. In fact, in this respect, it ought to be mentioned that since the mid-1950s, about a dozen Indo-Pakistani professionals are known to have lived in the 'green belt' of Birmingham, in places such as Solihull (where two-car families are said to be a norm) and Sutton Coldfield. Similarly, at least four Indo-Pakistani professionals are known to have lived in places such as Allerton and Shipton which are within Bradford's 'green belt' and where, during 1964–66, a modern house cost between £4,500 and £6,000. Indo-Pakistani professionals, however, differ from the immigrant labourers with regard to their socio-economic background, motives for migration, style of life, aspirations and so on, and therefore their differential patterns of settlement need not surprise us. As I mentioned earlier on, the latter immigrants were not interested in buying modern semi-detached houses and their preference for cheap housing is related to their impermanent intentions, and to their desire to save as much money as they can within as short a time as possible before retiring.

According to Rex and Moore (30, 134), overcrowding in the immigrant houses is a consequence of the high rate of interest which the immigrant landlord has to pay on loans obtained and the 'many debts' incurred in purchasing the house. The landlord buys a house in order to find a shelter for himself and then overcrowds it in order to meet 'the [heavy] weekly charges' (30) and repay the loan as quickly as possible. Since there is a housing shortage in Birmingham, the immigrant landlords 'as a pariah group' (40) fulfil a need by providing accommodation for newcomers, that is, for both white and coloured immigrants, who are discriminated against with regard to the allocation of the local council houses. In other words, overcrowding is a local factor and is an outcome of conflict of interests between the politically and economically dominant group (the white natives) and the newcomers (white and coloured immigrants). However, a logical inference of such an assertion by Rex and Moore is that places like Bradford, which have plenty of old housing stock and where there is little demand for council houses, should not have any overcrowding in the immigrant houses. Yet the immigrant houses in Bradford are overcrowded. During the period 1957–63, over 1,000 immigrant houses were found overcrowded and were served with notices for the abatement of overcrowding. At the end of 1970, several immigrant houses are known to have been overcrowded (Select Committee on Race Relations and Immigration, 1971, Vol. I, Report, para. 158; Minutes of Evidence, para. 1645) and, during my visit there in 1971, the position was found to remain more or less unaltered.

The authors of the Sparkbrook study make no secret of the fact that they were deeply involved in local political issues and, in my view, they have imposed their own political perspectives on the immigrants' housing situation in Sparkbrook without providing any significant data to support some of their various statements. Accordingly, the assertions which they make are not 'findings' but statements which need to be tested and verified. Evidence from studies of Asian immigrants (e.g., Davies and Taylor 1970) shows that the Rex and Moore thesis has little, if any, bearing on the housing conditions of Asian immigrants. Thus, it is necessary to distinguish the housing needs of West Indian immigrants from those of Asian immigrants. The two cannot be subsumed under the blanket category of 'coloured immigrants'.

Like Rex and Moore, both Butterworth (op. cit.) and Krausz (op. cit.) are among those who have imposed their perspectives on the immigrants' housing situation. With regard to the housing situation in West Yorkshire, Butterworth writes:

'. . . much housing is available if [the migrant] is prepared to accept a low standard of amenity' (7–10).

Here, we see that there is an assumption on the part of Butterworth that the immigrants are used to a high standard of amenities in their villages of origin, and there is also the implication that their settlement in back-to-back artisan cottages and Victorian and Edwardian terrace houses represents a fall in the immigrants' standards. A reference has already been made to the incidence of overcrowding in the immigrant houses in Bradford. Butterworth explains it thus:

'[Migrants] are often in areas where there is much overcrowding, but it should be remembered that this existed before. The wards which were the most overcrowded in 1961 had been . . . the most overcrowded in 1951 – before migrants had come to the country in any numbers' (10).
'There is often a conflict between the demands of hospitality which requires that a person from the same area should be given a bed, and the local standards of overcrowding' (33).

According to this form of reasoning, overcrowding in Bradford (and West Yorkshire) occurs not through lack of cheap housing, but is a local characteristic found among the natives and immigrants alike, and is also a result of the cultural patterns among the immigrants. Thus, instead of providing a sociological explanation for the incidence of overcrowding, Butterworth has merely explained it away. The reasons advanced by him show a lack of knowledge about living conditions in the immigrants' villages of origin, and an assumption on his part that the immigrants are used to low-density housing. Similarly, one could go on multiplying with quotations from various people (e.g., Goodall) who have contributed to Butterworth's study of West Yorkshire.

In his recent study of ethnic minorities in Britain, Krausz's (op. cit.) value assumptions become apparent at several places, of which I take a selection to illustrate my point. With regard to the housing conditions of the Poles in London, he tells us:

'. . . the Poles first settled in poorer districts like Paddington and Lambeth, where they could get accommodation cheaply' (39).

and, later on, cites Sheila Patterson (1968: 28) to the effect that the Poles'

'. . . poorer housing in Brixton, Peckham and Battersea . . . was all [that] the majority had been able to afford in the first years of settlement' (114).

However, the author's perspective takes on a different turn

when he discusses the housing situation of coloured immigrants. For example:

'. . . [coloured] immigrants are as a rule given opportunities . . . for housing in the decaying areas in the older parts nearer the centre of cities' (43).
'As a rule new [i.e., coloured] immigrants have to put up with housing both qualitatively and quantitatively inferior' (88).

The contrast between Krausz's differential perspective with regard to the Poles and the coloured immigrants is obvious. However, he does not tell us why if it was right for the Poles to exercise their choice and live in poorer housing, 'which was all the majority had been able to afford in the first years of [their] settlement', why the coloured immigrants could not exercise their choice similarly and live in poorer housing to suit their economic circumstances. One wonders if Krausz imagines that the coloured immigrants came to Britain with a hoard of money and wanted to live in modern semi-detached housing but because of racial discrimination were forced to live 'in the decaying areas in the older parts nearer the centre of cities'.

It is clear from the above examples that the authors in question have interpreted the immigrants' housing situation in the light of their own (that is, the authors') perspectives. They have assumed that the immigrants and the authors share a single frame of reference, a similar perspective; so that what appears to the observer to be poorer housing with low amenities and overcrowding is similarly viewed by the immigrants. But the situation as seen from the inside, that is, by the immigrants, and contrasted with living conditions in the immigrants' villages of origin presents a different picture, as I show below.

XIV CONDITIONS IN PAKISTAN

In the rural areas of Pakistan the villagers are used to high-density conditions. Privacy is alien to the villagers' way of thinking and what we would call overcrowding is a permanent phenomenon and forms part of the villagers' experience. Gregariousness in everyday life is valued because, among other things, it helps to keep a check on a person's movements and is a means of social control.

Families live in *kachchā* houses (lit. crude, made of mud bricks) which have two rooms, an enclosed courtyard and a flat roof. During the hot season (from April to mid-September), female members of the household sleep in the open in the courtyard, while men and boys carry their *chārpoys* (string cots) to the flat roofs to sleep there. During the monsoon and winter months, when the night temperature in the immigrants' villages (especially in Mirpur, the Chhachh and the North-West Frontier Province) often drops to below freezing point, the two rooms are turned into bedrooms where male members sleep separately from the females. Further, during the winter months there is no heating in the bedrooms, and villagers keep warm by keeping all doors and windows shut, and by curling up under a *razā'ī* (a heavy quilt, a bedroll). The *pakkā* houses built with remittances from immigrants in Britain tend to be large with one to three storeys, yet only the two ground-floor rooms are used, and the rest of the house is kept locked. As before, during the hot season, women sleep in the open in the courtyard, while men and boys sleep on the open verandah or balcony. During the monsoon and winter months, they retreat to the two rooms on the ground floor and men sleep apart from women.

Houses lack sanitation and there is no piped water. It is one of the tasks of women and girls to draw water from the wells, village ponds, lakes, or streams, and there is no short cut to obtaining water supplies. Fuel for cooking purposes comprises firewood, which has to be collected and chopped by women and boys, stubble from wheat, maize and other crops, and cowdung. The latter is collected by women who flatten it into round cakes which they plaster on walls and roofs to dry in the sun.

Until recently, there was no electric supply in the villages. It has, however, reached a few villages in the Punjab and the Chhachh, but none in Mirpur, during the last few years. Nevertheless, it remains beyond the means of a vast majority of the rural population to have electricity installed. The hurricane lamp (*lāl-tin*, probably derived from lantern) is used universally.

The houses in the villages lack lavatories and bathrooms. Villagers resort to the fields to defecate early in the morning; and usually the bathroom consists of a roofless cubicle in the courtyard or one of the ground-floor rooms. Cold water is used for bathing and washing. For villagers, these experiences are part of everyday life, and are taken as a matter of course.

XV   FROM *KACHCHĀ* TO *PAKKĀ* HOUSES

The immigrants do not think of the localities in which they live as decaying areas or slums. The back-to-back cottages and old Victorian and Edwardian houses which they occupy are, from their point of view, *pakkā* structures with modern plumbing, electricity, sanitation, gas supply, lavatory and so on. That is, the contrast between their *kachchā* houses and those in the zones of transition cannot be overemphasized. In other words, their translation from *kachchā* houses to places such as Spark-brook, Birmingham, and Lumb Lane, Bradford, does not represent a fall in their standards of living, nor is there a sense of deprivation in terms of amenities. The immigrants do not look for modern semi-detached houses, with a garden, garage and other amenities such as inside lavatories, central heating and so on because, as the immigrants repeatedly emphasize, their motive for migration is to save money and not to live in comfort. No matter how old and dilapidated the immigrant houses in Britain may be, they are regarded as infinitely superior to those left behind in the villages. Further, the ownership of such a house immediately raises the immigrant-landlord's status both here and in the village of origin. It is a sign of that economic achievement which is the main motive for migration. To an outsider, an artisan cottage with an outside lavatory or a terrace house in an industrial town may not appear to be a desirable residence in a well-appointed situation. However, the immigrants' evaluation of the areas of their settlement rests on different perspectives. The immigrants' perspectives in this respect are similar to those reported by Philip Mayer with regard to Red (rural-oriented) Xhosa migrants in the shanty town of East London:

'However horrible the shack, its ownership immediately puts a Red man a cut above his fellows. Even in the country it is admired as a sign of thrift and economic success' (1963: 147).

On the basis of these observations it is not surprising that the immigrants in Birmingham and Bradford have no desire to disperse and are content with their existing patterns of settlement (Select Committee on Race Relations and Immigration, op. cit. Vol. I, Report, para. 80; Minutes of Evidence, Birmingham and Bradford; paras. 613, 656, 762, 1845, and 1861).

The immigrants' attitudes towards physical environment, overcrowding and sharing rooms differ from those of the local people. Since the immigrants live in more or less similar circumstances, and since from their perspective settlement in the inner wards of industrial cities and towns is a tremendous improvement over what they have been accustomed to in their villages back home, the immigrants do not thereby feel deprived nor do they experience 'status dislocation' (cf. Richmond 1967). Further, they do not attempt to create good impressions on their fellows, say, by weeding the front gardens or the backyard, drawing the curtains, cleaning the windows and so on. Like the natives, the immigrants also have symbols for expressing their status and for creating impressions on others, but the people they wish to impress, that is, their fellow-immigrants, and the way in which they do so, differ. An immigrant-visitor evaluates his host not on the basis of the type of his house and its layout, the kind of furnishings and amenities provided in it, and the social reputation of the area in which it is located, but on the basis of his hospitality, his friendliness and his qualities as a fellow-immigrant.

Views about the areas inhabited by the immigrants depend on a person's emotional involvement and experience in the locality. Outsiders tend to regard the areas as 'twilight zones'; but to the immigrants it is not a 'problem' area but a home from home. The immigrants regard their way of life in the areas of their settlement as 'different' from but certainly not 'inferior' to the natives'. As an immigrant observed:

'What is wrong with the place [i.e., Bradford's Lumb Lane]? The English used to live here before we came, so what makes it 'low' now? It is just that we live differently. That is all.'

XVI   CONCLUSION

I have tried to show in this paper that the patterns of Pakistan immigrant settlement in the zones of transition in English industrial towns and cities cannot be explained adequately in terms of racial discrimination. The immigrants' choice of poorer housing in the inner wards of industrial cities and their preference for living there is related to their motives and orientations and is not an outcome of racial discrimination, as writers like Rex and Moore, and Krausz have asserted. This is not to deny that there is racial discrimination against Pakistani immigrants but to point out that during the early stages of their settlement, the immigrants voluntarily segregated themselves because they realized that their economic goals were more likely to be achieved through conformity to group norms, by means of mutual aid and under austere living conditions than through dispersal into the wider society. In other words, during the early stages of their settlement, the immigrants needed an ecological base for achieving their goals. Here, we have to note the factor of sponsorship which through selective migration has brought about the emergence of sub-groups based on village-kin ties, and the binding character of obligations between kinsmen and friends which in turn make for the immigrants' preference for living with kinsmen and fellow-villagers.

The kind of housing towards which the immigrants are attracted provides them with an ecological niche which they are exploiting to their economic advantage by becoming landlords and, in some cases, *rentiers*. In this respect, given their economic circumstances, their motive for migration and their predilection for living in their own houses rather than in rented accommodation, their choice is voluntary and rational, and irrespective of whether racial discrimination occurs or not. In their study of Asian immigrants in Rye Hill, a twilight area of Newcastle upon Tyne, Davies and Taylor (op. cit.) found that Asian immigrants there bought houses in order to save money and to earn extra income and, further, declined to move into council houses.

I mentioned earlier the immigrants' emphasis on savings and austere living conditions. The evidence collected by the Select Committee on Race Relations and Immigration in Pakistan in 1970 shows that the immigrants are known to remit £60m sterling every year. 'For these reasons,' the Select Committee's Report on Housing (op. cit., para. 80) adds, 'it would be natural for immigrants, many of whom are in lower paid, unskilled employment, to seek the cheapest housing available. The cheapest housing available will tend to be the poorer housing in the centres of towns and cities. Many immigrants will therefore buy or rent old, decaying houses and live in them in over-crowded conditions.' In this respect it seems worth noting that during January 1972, that is, the first full month since East Pakistan became the new nation state of Bangladesh, an estimated population of 110,000 Pakistani immigrants (excluding some 100,000 women and children) remitted £5m sterling to Pakistan through official channels (*Akhbār-é-Watan*, 23.2.72; 1). The significance of this sum should be seen in the context of the fact that the remittances in question came hard on the heels of the immigrants' contributions to the Pakistan Defence Fund during the Indo-Pakistan war in December 1971. It is probable that there may be as many as 7,500 immigrants unemployed at present but their unemployed status as such may be ignored for the purposes of remittances. For, while technically they may not be in receipt of regular earnings, they are none the less able to save as much as half of their social security benefits, as I found during my fieldwork. During the period of his unemployment (and sickness), the immigrant-tenant is charged no rent by the immigrant-landlord and may be asked to contribute only a token sum, if at all, towards his weekly grocery bill, and mutual aid within the immigrant house sees to his other needs. Further, where an unemployed immigrant happens to have his wife and children with him in this country, he does not, like his native counterpart, have 'council house' rents to pay nor, like him, does he have to meet weekly instalments for, say, dining-room or bedroom suites, vacuum cleaner, and so on. The immigrants' remittances to Pakistan clearly indicate:

1. the extent to which the immigrants are prepared to make sacrifices and endure hardship in order to save money for fulfilling goals back home;
2. the immigrants' scale of preferences which differ in a significant manner from that of the native proletariat with regard to consumption patterns, aspirations, prestige symbols, etc.; and
3. that for the present the immigrants' priorities are geared to raising their status, and that of their families, in the society of origin.

Further, the evidence collected by the Select Committee shows that the immigrants' concentration in central areas of towns and cities in cheap housing and overcrowded conditions is a pattern that was adopted, among other ethnic groups, by Italians in Bedford. During the first stage of their settlement in Bedford, the Italians, like the Pakistani immigrants, chose to live in cheap houses in overcrowded conditions, because 'they could not afford more than that' (para. 939). Thus, the immigrants' settlement in poorer housing is a form of adaptation – a response, one might say – on their part to the situation which they face on their arrival here. Crucial to their response in this respect are their motives for migration, the ethnic preference, the nature of sponsorship and the immigrants' perception of the situation.

The analysis offered above relates to the early stages of Pakistani immigrants' settlement in England. It is not intended to forecast that the immigrants will continue to see their present housing conditions as an improvement over those in their villages in Pakistan. Nor do I wish to suggest that the emphasis which the immigrants place on hard work, austere living, savings and remittances to Pakistan will persist over time, or that the immigrants will continue to live in the areas which they now inhabit. It is likely that at a later stage, the immigrants may begin to re-evaluate their position *vis-à-vis* Britain/ Pakistan and, accordingly, adopt new values and aspirations and seek recognition in British society or, alternatively, modify their present perspectives and yet, given external constraints as suggested by Rex and Moore (op. cit.), may find their residential mobility blocked; that is, their settlement could be in more or less the same or similar areas (but see Collison 1967, Deakin & Cohen 1970).

ACKNOWLEDGEMENTS

An earlier version of this paper was presented to the ASA Conference. Fieldwork in Britain (1964–67) was carried out under the auspices of the Survey of Race Relations in Britain; that in Pakistan (1968–69) was part of the Social Science Research Council Project HR 331/1. I am grateful to these two bodies for their generous grants. I wish to thank Professors M. Banton, Abner Cohen, and Adrian Mayer, and Mr Simon Abbott who read an earlier draft of this paper and made valuable comments.

NOTES

[1] See my *Religion and Society amongst Arabs in Britain* (forthcoming).

[2] Cf. Thomas's 'the definition of the situation' (1923; 41–4), and Schutz, 1967.

[3] The present tense refers to the situation that obtained during 1965–66.

[4] The estimates are based on: (a) internal inquiries made by me during the course of fieldwork; (b) observations and attendances at annual religious festivals, such as the *'Id* festival; and (c) on estimates by local Pakistani entrepreneurs (grocers, butchers, bank officials, and travel agents).

[5] See Thompson (op. cit., 115) for data relating to size of landholdings among Sikh immigrants in Coventry.

[6] According to Adrian Mayer (1959; 25), Sikh immigrants in Vancouver, who are predominantly of landowning castes by origin, exhibit a similar bias for real estate and 'seem far more eager to buy property than other Canadians'.

[7] I should like to express my gratitude to Dr John Douglas, OBE, formerly Medical Officer of Health, Bradford, for giving me access to records in his department, and to various members of his staff for their kind cooperation. The classification of various ethnic groups in this section was verified with the help of Mr Manzoor Ahmed, formerly liaison officer and health visitor (1963–67) in the local health department.

[8] By April 1965 the number of Asian immigrant houses in the city had risen to 1,398 and a year thence the figure was 1,565. According to the local health department, there were about 4,250 houses owned and occupied by Asian immigrants at the end of 1970.

[9] One of the marked features of the Pakistani immigrant population in Bradford, and in Britain as a whole, is its high sex ratio. It has been estimated that over 60 per cent of adult male immigrants in Bradford are either unmarried or without their wives and live in all-male dormitories. That is, the family household is at present marginal to the immigrant community. According to a recent editorial in *Akhbār-ė-Watan* (26.4.72; 3), 60 per cent of Pakistani immigrants in Britain are estimated to be single men.

[10] *Shī'a* is a heterodox sect in Islam. See Hollister 1953.

[11] Since 1951 the population of Bradford has remained stable around the 290,000 mark. The fact that the growth of the immigrant population (estimated to be around 30,000 in 1971) over the two decades since then has not led to an increase in the size of the local population suggests that the immigrant population is displacing the indigenous population and that the exodus of the latter is more or less matched by the growth of the immigrant population.

[12] See Little (1948) on pre-war Colonial seamen in Cardiff.

[13] The immigrants in Birmingham pay a weekly rent of 15s. (75p) for bed in a room shared between two or more fellows; in Bradford, the rent varies between 50p and 60p a week.

[14] A discussion of social control aspects of this form of mutual aid remains beyond the scope of this paper.

REFERENCES

ABBOTT, S. (ed.). 1971. *The Prevention of Racial Discrimination in Britain*. London: Oxford University Press for UNITAR/IRR.

Akhbār-ė-Watan. (Urdu.) 23.2.72; 26.4.72. London.

ARDENER, S. 1964. The Comparative Study of Rotating Credit Associations. *J. R. anthrop. Inst.* **94**, 2, 201–29.

AURORA, G. S. 1967. *The New Frontiersmen*. Bombay: Popular Prakashan.

BIRMINGHAM CORPORATION. *Immigration*. 14.5.68.

Bradford Official Handbook. 1964. The Corporation of the City of Bradford (ed. J. Burrow).

BRETON, R. 1964. Institutional Completeness of Ethnic Communities and the Personal Relations of Immigrants. *Amer. Jnl. Sociol.* **70**, 2, 193–205.

BURNEY, E. 1967. *Housing on Trial*. London: Oxford University Press for IRR.

BUTTERWORTH, E. (ed.). 1967. *Immigrants in West Yorkshire*. London: Institute of Race Relations, Special Series.

BUTTERWORTH, E. (ed.). 1967. *Immigrants in West Yorkshire*. London: Institute of Race Relations, Special Series.

COHEN, A. 1969. *Custom and Politics in Urban Africa*. London: Routledge & Kegan Paul.

COLLISON, P. 1967. Immigrants and Residence. *Sociology*. **1**, 3, 277–92.

Daily Telegraph, London. 8.7.65.

DAVIES, J. G. & TAYLOR, J. 1970. Race, Community and No Conflict. *New Society*. 9.7.70, 67–9.

DEAKIN, N. & COHEN, B. G. 1970. Dispersal and Choice: towards a strategy for ethnic minorities in Britain. *Environment and Planning*. **2**, 193–201.

DESAI, R. 1963. *Indian Immigrants in Britain*. London: Oxford University Press for IRR.

EVANS, P. 1971. For an Indian there is nothing like having a son in Britain. *The Times*, 12.11.71, 6.

GLASS, R. 1960. *Newcomers*. London: Allen & Unwin for Centre for Urban Studies.

GLAZER, N. & MOYNIHAN, P. 1970. *Beyond the Melting Pot*. Cambridge, Mass.: The MIT Press. 2nd edition.

GOODY, J. (ed.). 1958. *The Developmental Cycle in Domestic Groups*. Cambridge Papers in Social Anthropology, No. 1. Cambridge: The University Press.

Guardian, the. 9.2.65.

HOLLISTER, J. H. 1953. *The Shi'a of India*. London: Luzac.

JAIN, R. K. 1970. *South Indians on the Plantation Frontier in Malaya*. New Haven and London: Yale University Press.

KATZIN, M. F. 1959. 'Partners': An informal savings institution in Jamaica. *Soc. and Econ. Stud*. 436–40.

KRAUSZ, E. 1971. *Ethnic Minorities in Britain.* London: Mac-Gibbon & Kee.

LITTLE, K. 1948. *Negroes in Britain.* London: Routledge & Kegan Paul. Revised ed. 1972.

MAYER, A. C. 1959. *A Report on the East Indian Community in Vancouver.* (Mimeo.) Vancouver: University of British Columbia.

—— 1966. The Significance of Quasi-Groups in the Study of Complex Societies. In M. Banton (ed.), *The Social Anthropology of Complex Societies.* ASA Monographs, 4. London: Tavistock Publications, 97–122.

—— 1971. *A Study of Selected Indian and Pakistani Communities in Britain.* Final Report on SSRC Project HR 331/1. Available at the National Library, London.

MAYER, P. 1963. *Townsmen or Tribesmen.* Cape Town: Oxford University Press.

MORRIS, H. S. 1968. *The Indians in Uganda.* London: Weidenfeld & Nicolson.

PATTERSON, S. 1968. *Immigrants in Industry.* London: Oxford University Press for IRR.

PEP (Political and Economic Planning Research Services Ltd) 1967. *Racial Discrimination.* London: PEP.

PLANT, M. A. 1971. The Attitudes of Coloured Immigrants in two Areas of Britain to the Concept of Dispersal. *Race.* **12**, 3, 323–328.

PUNJAB DISTRICT GAZETTEERS, 1907. *Attock District.* Part A. Vol. XXIX. With Maps. Lahore: The Civil and Military Gazette Press, 1909.

REDFIELD, R. 1956. *Peasant Society and Culture.* Chicago: University of Chicago Press.

REX, J. & MOORE, R. 1967. *Race, Community and Conflict: A study of Sparkbrook.* London: Oxford University Press for IRR.

RICHMOND, A. H. 1967. *Post-War Immigrants in Canada.* Toronto: University of Toronto Press.

SCHUMPETER, J. A. 1934. *The Theory of Economic Development.* New York: Oxford University Press.

SCHUTZ, A. 1967. *The Phenomenology of the Social World.* Trans. by George Walsh and Frederick Lehnert. Evanston: Northwestern University Press.

SELECT COMMITTEE ON RACE RELATIONS AND IMMIGRATION. 1971. *Housing.* Minutes of Evidence. Bedford, Birmingham, Bradford. Session 1970–71. *Report.* Vol. I. Session 1970–71. London: HMSO.

THOMAS, W. I. 1923. *The Unadjusted Girl: With Cases and Standpoint for Behavior Analysis.* Boston: Little, Brown.

THOMPSON, M. A. 1970. *A Study of Generation Differences in Immigrant Groups with Particular Reference to Sikhs.* Unpublished M.Phil. Thesis, University of London.

Times, The. Bradford's Pakistani heads plump for Conservatives. 11.5.71; 2.

David Parkin

Congregational and Interpersonal Ideologies in Political Ethnicity

We can grapple with a number of definitions of ethnicity. I will
make my standpoint clear. Following Abner Cohen (1969a), I
would put my view in the form of a simple equation: ethnicity = a) the articulation of cultural distinctiveness in b) situations of political conflict or competition. I can anticipate some
objection to this inclusion of politics. A first counter-view may
be that ethnic differences can distinguish groups or categories
who are not necessarily in either competition or conflict and may
actually cooperate. We all accept that one is a corollary of the
other and so it is really a question of which we most focus on.
I take the anthropologically conventional view that if we study
self-perpetuating groups or categories over time interacting
with each other, we are bound to observe that their most critical
organizational problems arise from conflicts over rules of procedure and from competition for human and material resources.
A second counter-view may be that we can profitably study
ethnicity as a folk-system based on an ordered set of cultural
themes: we compare the thematic sets of different societies in an
ultimate search for a fundamental and universal code. Ethnicity
to structuralists and cognitive anthropologists will in this case
invite the study of the different cultural statements which
peoples use to define themselves, and their opposition to,
alliance with, or social distance from each other. These may well
be 'manifestations' of something more fundamental, but for my
present purposes their usefulness is that they can be shown to
vary as a result of political change. In short, I want here to
discuss some of the different cultural themes or idioms most
useful to competing ethnic groups under a number of different
structural conditions. I conclude by suggesting that a simple
distinction between two types of ideology, congregational and
interpersonal, has relevance beyond this particular study of
ethnicity.

David Parkin

My focus is on the use of kinship and descent. I suggest that kinship, seen as a network or reticulum (to use Kapferer's term, 1969) of interpersonal relations radiating from an individual, is an excellent medium for communicating political messages between members of an ethnic group in a way that insulates the messages from observation or comprehension by other ethnic groups. This 'private' message-carrying quality of kinship contrasts with that of descent, which as I hope to show lends itself to more 'public' and therefore less-insulable proclamations of group identity and political aims.

PRIVATE AND PUBLIC DOMAINS

It is now some years since the theme of urban studies in the Zambian Copperbelt was so well summarized by P. Mayer (1961) in the phrase 'Trade unions transcend tribes'. Epstein (1958) was the classic example. Mayer also reminded us that there was sometimes an explicit and always an implicit distinction in the work of the Manchester/Rhodes-Livingstone 'school' between (a) urban politico-economic organization and (b) urban domestic life. In the former 'tribe' was not a dominant principle of organization (trade union members closed ranks to confront the common enemy) and was not to be taken as a starting-point for analysis; while in urban domestic life certain customary procedures, which might vary according to ethnic group, were adhered to – i.e. marriage was primarily intra-tribal, and domestic disputes, even at the urban local court level, were settled by reference to customary expectations where possible.

Independence has brought an alteration of power relations in these and other African nations. There is now no longer any need to close ranks against the common enemy, or at least no visibly apparent need. Ethnic cleavages and competition, which were previously held in abeyance and never fully expressed, are now focal points of political conflict in many important African towns. Now, more than before independence, perhaps, urban struggles for power reflect the politics of the nation. Epstein appears to have recognized the potentiality of ethnic cleavage in describing the way in which, *within* the unions, offices were fought for along the lines of 'tribe'. Cohen (1969a) has pointed to this as an example of how, even when united on the wider issues of higher wages and labour conditions, trade union and political leaders will look to their own ethnic group for much of the support on which their positions depend. Probably the most efficient method of recruiting and maintaining ethnic support is by emphasizing community of custom (Cohen 1969a and b, and Parkin 1969). Both these studies, and those by Banton (1965) and Grillo (1969a and b), are concerned with the problem of urban ethnicity in post-independent African nations.

If there is now a genuine problem of ethnicity in African towns and nations, no one is claiming that Africa, or the Third World generally, is alone in this. In more industrialized nations, minority groups are using their cultural distinctiveness to express political consciousness. I would argue that much, though not all, of Africa is distinguished by a more marked discontinuity of social system between town and country: the urban and rural systems generate their own forms, yet are inextricably interrelated. In Kampala, Uganda, to take an example, the rural lineage-based social structure of the Kenya Luo was associated with a distinct form of urban domestic life (Parkin 1969). A strong ideology of kinship operated in Kampala at the level of informal personal networks while one of patrilineal descent operated at the level of a hierarchy of ethnic associations and association branches. These institutions enabled the Luo to foster and retain political consciousness, which was most obviously expressed at the time of Uganda's independence (1962). In short, the study suggests that the urban domestic life of an ethnic group with a deep and extensive lineage organization may provide a framework of relationships which are politically useful.

Later in the paper I continue to apply this approach to material collected in 1968–69 in Nairobi, Kenya. As in Kampala I focus on Luo and on their most distinctive urban cultural features: (a) their urban domestic and kinship organization, characterized by strong control over women and ethnic endogamy, and another factor, not previously discussed, a high polygamy rate; and (b) a remarkable pyramidal system of ethnic, 'sub-tribal', and clan and lineage associations, which are faction-ridden and run by constantly changing sets of leaders, yet constitute a stable structure and include many people in their activities. As in Kampala also, Luo in Nairobi claim that they have been under political pressure. Indeed, on the surface the situation of Luo in Nairobi in 1968–69 is very similar to the situation of Luo in Kampala in 1962–64. Why then should I concern myself with basically similar situations? In justification I echo the exhortation made by Southall (1965) that we study 'differences arising from similarities', i.e. that by analysing variants of a basic system we are able to isolate the range of forms which the interaction of the same key variables may produce. The alternative is a useful, easier but perhaps endless classification of types of urban ethnic response, whose dissimilarities are given undue attention.

The distinction between urban politico-economic organization and urban domestic life describes *manifest* organizational differences. It leaves open the question of how much *latent* politico-economic significance urban domestic life may have. A similar analytical distinction is the classical one by Fortes (1959) between politico-jural and kinship domains and by Smith (1969: 38–9) between the public and private domains.

These also describe manifest role differences and, as such, are important for their heuristic value. For example, one of the problems confronting many ethnic groups is how to promote or defend its interests in a manner which is discrete and hidden, so to speak, from wider disapproving authorities. A people's interests can be advanced through seemingly 'harmless' kinship relations. They are less likely to be marked out as an obtrusive entrepreneurial or exploitative group than if they rely solely upon formal organizations to deal with their economic and political specializations. In most cases of ethnic economic differentiation the network of kinship relations supplements the formal organizations by allowing decisions to be made in a private domain when they cannot for reasons of expediency be taken publicly. Where members of an ethnic group do not significantly monopolize an economic sphere but compete with members of other ethnic groups for the same limited number of economic opportunities, then the network of kinship relations would seem to be of crucial importance. One important sociological task is to identify the particular properties of kinship which make or do not make it a suitable ideology for informal political organization.

I should point out here my awareness of the now familiar

anthropological argument that kinship relations are relations which may be talked about in other ways, such as locality, neighbourhood, friendship, and religion. We can argue, also, that these are all possible idiomatic aspects of any one relationship: monks verbally express their ritual ties as 'brotherhood', a woman may be 'Auntie' to her unrelated neighbour's child, a biological kinship tie may be temporarily denied and referred to as one of neighbourhood or friendship, Quakers call themselves Friends, and so on. But, controlling, if we can, for cross-cultural semantic variations we can discern certain sets of ties which are *consistently* expressed as being mainly one or other of these and which may provide the relational context for a specific sphere of activities. Thus a business run by alleged friends tells us something different about the notion of obligations underlying its organization than one run by say, alleged relatives, co-worshippers, or neighbours.

KINSHIP AND DESCENT

In his seminal study (1969a) Cohen distinguishes kinship and religion as alternative modes of informal political organization. He argues that kinship is likely to become less practicable as a principle of informal political organization as members of an ethnic group settle and reproduce themselves in towns and lessen the extensiveness of their original rural ties (209). Religion is then likely to produce a more viable and practicable principle.

Cohen suggests that where the transition from kinship to religion does occur, it is 'because as a result of migration even those migrants who come from tribal societies which have traditions of extensive kinship organization tend to become bilateral as they settle in town' (209). This immediately suggests that a 'bilateral' kinship system is a less effective piece of cultural equipment than religion for informal political organization in town. But it also suggests another issue. When Cohen here talks of 'extensive kinship organization' he refers to the fictional use of *unilineal descent* by Luo in Kampala. His argument would be that as Luo settle in Kampala they will make increasingly less use of unilineal descent. They are then left with (a) 'bilateral' kinship and (b) the possibility of articulating a religious ideology for political purposes.

I think that if we talk loosely of 'extensive' kinship organization instead of unilineal descent and bracket it together with
'bilateral' kinship as a phenomenon of the same order differing
only in degree, we may miss an important criterion of our
delineation of informal political ideologies. I would regard a
religious and a unilineal descent ideology as having more in
common than have unilineal descent and bilateral kinship. As
a general statement we can say that religions emphasize unambiguous membership of 'congregations'. Similarly, unilineal
descent rests on an ideal rule of unambiguous descent group
membership, sometimes even expressed in 'congregational'
contexts such as ancestor worship. By contrast, even where
corporate kindreds arise, systems of 'bilateral' kinship tend to
emphasize the egocentric, optative element of membership:
ambiguity of membership enables the system to work, and
membership itself is often expressed as a network of interpersonal kin ties. Ties of friendship (see La Fontaine 1970:
172, on Leopoldville), god-parenthood (e.g. *compadrazgo*), and
patron-clientage are other possible examples of basically non-
congregational, interpersonal ideologies. By contrast, again,
locality and neighbourhood ties have a specifically territorial
referent and, if ever they acquire informal political significance,
tend to involve congregations (e.g. tenants' and ratepayers'
associations as in Frankenburg 1966 and Parkin 1969).

Ideologies of this kind are rarely, if ever, mutually exclusive
and it depends very much on a society's particular cultural
prescriptions as to which is emphasized for specific activities.
Much more could be written on this[1] but for the purpose of the
present discussion I suggest the simple division between (a)
congregational and (b) non-congregational or, hereafter, interpersonal (or perhaps reticular) ideologies. The 'world' religions
and unilineal descent are congregational. Bilateral kinship is
interpersonal.

Returning to the Luo in Kampala, Cohen was quite correct if
he was suggesting that any simple transplantation of the
principle of unilineal descent from the rural area to the town
was impracticable. That is to say, we would not expect Luo in
town to organize themselves for residential and subsistence
purposes through the idiom of unilineal descent as is partly the
case in rural areas where even nowadays lineages are frequently

localized and may comprise corporate, property-owning descent groups. But it is clear that the somewhat remarkable system of Luo urban ethnic associations *does* make use of a generalized principle of unilineal descent. The qualification is that unilineal descent *alone* is unlikely to be a widely effective principle by which people organize themselves in town. This is different from saying, as Cohen does, that the principle is unsuited to urban settlement by an ethnic group. If unilineal descent cannot operate alone, then what is likely to supplement it? Religious, friendship, and other ties undoubtedly *do* supplement descent ties among Luo in town. But Luo religious sectarian activities involve few Luo while their concept of friendship lacks distinctiveness by soon becoming merged with 'brotherhood'.

As has been long demonstrated in anthropology a deep and widely ramifying unilineal descent system, such as typifies a segmentary lineage system, generates a correspondingly extensive web of kinship and affinity. And it is an ideology of kinship (including affinity) which undoubtedly informs Luo interpersonal relations to an extent which quantitatively and in qualitative 'usefulness' exceeds that of other ethnic groups living and working with them in town, as I shall show. Putting it simply we can say that what religion does for the Hausa of Ibadan (Cohen 1969a), unilineal descent plus kinship do for Luo in Kampala and Nairobi.

If we look at the situation of the Hausa in Ibadan, we can see how Cohen felt able to place so much importance on the use of religion for political purposes. The marked Hausa corporateness owed much more to religious than kinship and descent principles of organization. Their concentration into one local area corresponded with a strong congregational ideology. The Luo in Kampala were perhaps no more than quasi-corporate, being endogamous, recognizing common spokesmen and consciously sharing a single culture and political identity, but nevertheless differentiated occupationally and residentially. Their occupational, socio-economic, and residential dispersion in Kampala corresponded with an equally dispersed web of kinship and affinity. Through a multiplicity of individual kinship and affinal ties, which could be regarded as communicating a common language of custom, Luo were linked to each other in recognition both of their political exposure and, through their spokesmen, of the means to cope with the problem. Kinship was here a non-congregational ideology. It supplemented their congregational structure of voluntary associations which were organized on a modified but recognizable principle of unilineal descent.

Let me list the differences between the situations of the Hausa in Ibadan and the Luo in Kampala in order to pick out the distinctive features which make kinship and descent useful to Luo. I then move on to look closely at Luo in Nairobi.

DIFFERENCES BETWEEN HAUSA IN IBADAN AND LUO IN KAMPALA

(a) The Kampala Luo depend on the public and private sectors of employment. They are *not* a self-sufficient urban economic community. The Hausa *are* economically self-sufficient.

(b) The Luo have to live in ethnically mixed housing areas. They are not an exclusive local grouping, though their public activities (e.g. association meetings) are held in areas in which they predominate. The Hausa *are* a local grouping, deriving from a 'colonial' policy of residential segregation.

(c) There is considerable occupational, educational, and income *heterogeneity* among Luo, but they come together on public occasions through their associations and are inter-linked by recurring informal networks of kin.

The Hausa are more *homogeneous* with regard to these attributes and show more interchangeability of roles. The key ritual roles in the Islamic Tijanniya congregation are seen to correspond with the key political and economic ones.

(d) Luo are *involved* in what one might call the conventional urban prestige and status system, whose symbols of conspicuous consumption ('modern luxuries', etc.) are important at the individual level.

Hausa are *insulated* from such 'Western' status aspirations.

(e) Luo are simultaneously involved in *both* a rural and an urban economic system: they run farms through wives and relatives and also have urban wage employment.

Most Hausa have their economic relations centrally located in Ibadan and have a higher proportion actually born in the city.

(f) The Luo emphasized the *already useful* rural-based ideologies of kinship and descent, in order to deal with changing
political conditions. The Hausa *switched* to an Islamic Order
which suited their need to remain corporate better than their
previous Islamic ritual beliefs and practices.

Summarizing the first three differences, we can confirm that
Hausa are a highly corporate grouping (or, in Cohen's terms, an
informal political interest group), while the Luo fall further
along the continuum and are no more than quasi-corporate
(Parkin, 195) or, in Cohen's terms, a pressure group rather than
a solid political block.

Another way of expressing this contrast is to view Hausa in
Ibadan in the context of a back-to-back or even caste-like
relationship with Yoruba, i.e. the 'strata' coincide with ethnic
divisions, and to view Luo as at a kind of cross-road: on the one
hand, public crises draw Luo together; on the other hand, socio-
economic status and life-style groups cut across ethnic ties
(differences (c) and (d)). Which way will Luo go? Will they
become formed into classes which eventually cut across ethnic
affiliations, or will they eventually become economically and
politically differentiated from other ethnic groups in a back-to-
back manner, so showing structural affinities with the Hausa of
Ibadan (Cohen 1969a: 193 f.)? In the case of Kampala, this
question will never be answered, because, as illustrated in the
study, Luo had to turn their attentions to their home nation,
as must all expatriates (Parkin, 11). Latest figures in 1969
showed a marked drop in the proportion of Luo in the area
originally studied in Kampala. To follow up this question for
a possible answer, we must focus on Luo in Nairobi, the capital
of their nation.

This is where difference (e) comes in. In spite of land registration and enclosure schemes in Luoland, the 'traditional' descent
group and clan system is remaining intact and is perhaps
strengthened in its new functions (Sytek 1965). I have figures
which do *not* suggest a significant decrease in the high polygyny
rate among most young Nairobi Luo compared with their
fathers. Polygyny is a core feature of the extended family or
local descent group of Luo (see Southall 1952): it helps Luo in
town maintain an economic foothold on the farm as well.

It is only a small Luo elite of high education and income who appear to be decidedly monogamous. Though they cannot therefore utilize the informal relations radiating from a polygynous union to protect rural investments in land and business, they draw more randomly from home local ties and use these instead. Since Luo lineages and clans are frequently highly localized, with specific local areas designated by an individual into those in which he may or may not marry, it is almost inevitable that many, though not all, such ties are also expressed as being those of kinship and affinity.

As a result of these factors there is a highly maintained system of rural-urban ties among Nairobi Luo. Occupational mobility does not necessarily weaken kin ties. Indeed, Ross (1968) suggests that the higher his socio-economic status, the more substantial a townsman's rural links may be: he may invest in a larger and better equipped farm or in a business. Luo seem to be the most likely among Nairobi's four main ethnic groups to use 'relatives' to protect these rural investments. Under these conditions we can expect Luo in Nairobi to continue for a long time to use the ideologies of kinship and descent as principles of organization (difference (f)).

My task now, then, is to present a brief case study of a section of Luo in Nairobi based on recent fieldwork (1968–69). First, I describe the housing estate accommodating the Luo who were studied. Second, I discuss the 'meaning' of kinship for these urban Luo. Third, I show how a kinship ideology was indeed a crucially important component in their political organization.

A LUO HOUSING ESTATE

Nairobi is East Africa's largest town, with a population at the 1969 Census of 509,286. Africans are some 82 per cent of this population, Asians nearly 14 per cent, and Europeans nearly 4 per cent. The four main ethnic groups of this African population are Luo (nearly 15 per cent), Luhya (just over 15 per cent), Kamba (just over 14 per cent), and Kikuyu (over 45 per cent), with thirty-odd other ethnic groups making up the rest. We see, therefore, that Kikuyu are much more heavily represented in Nairobi than the other three groups. But in Kaloleni, which has a population of nearly 5,000 and is one of about a dozen city council housing areas accommodating between a quarter and a third of the Nairobi African population, it is Luo who are over-represented. Proportions for Kaloleni are Luo 39 per cent, Luhya 26 per cent, Kamba nearly 16 per cent, Kikuyu 14 per cent, and 'others' 5 per cent. This is the only city council housing estate in which such a large Luo proportion is found. Indeed, Nairobi people frequently refer to it as a 'Luo' area.

How has this situation come about and what is its present significance? During the Kenya Emergency of 1952–59 the British detained, restricted, and imprisoned many Kikuyu on the grounds that the Mau Mau nationalist movement was led by them. In Operation Anvil of 1952–53 Kikuyu in Nairobi were removed from ethnically mixed housing estates and concentrated in guarded areas on their own. After the removal of Kikuyu, Kaloleni estate became predominantly Luo. It had previously been an important area for Luo welfare and soccer associations and activities. After Operation Anvil it became even more of a 'headquarters' for Luo activities. Since the ending of the Emergency in 1959 the proportion of Kikuyu residents in Kaloleni has gradually increased while that of Luo has declined, but, as shown, Luo are still by far the most numerous.

The two resources which are so critically scarce that they constitute spoils of competition between individuals and groups in Nairobi are jobs and housing. Most jobs are in the private and public sectors of employment but a substantial proportion are of a self-employed nature. Housing has always been scarce in Nairobi as in most towns of relatively recent British 'colonial' creation. Scarce housing limits a man's opportunities for having his wife and family live with him in Nairobi.

Within an ethnic group those men who have the luck or persistence to acquire (rented) housing are key figures. Through their own and their wives' relatives they are stable contact points for men and women who move to Nairobi from a home area or another town and for those who, lacking accommodation, circulate within the city from one temporary lodging to another. A man (rarely a woman) who is the acknowledged head of an urban household is thus thereby marked out as likely to be in secure employment. The constant stream of lodgers who call upon his hospitality do constitute a drain on his resources but, in certain circumstances, they can constitute useful contacts or 'message-carriers' within the city, between town and country, and between towns. Together with wives and children, these lodgers can be deployed strategically to protect the household head's rural and other 'investments'. When these lodgers are almost invariably of his own ethnic group, the overall consequence is an institutional mechanism which, together with a very low outmarriage rate, defines the group's membership boundaries and also sustains the mutual usefulness of its members.

Under what conditions can this institutional mechanism emerge and in what ways is it conveniently expressed in the idioms of descent, kinship, and affinity? When we look at a 100 per cent numerical profile of Kaloleni's household heads (see *Table 1* in Appendix), we see that Luo more than hold their own in any ranking of the four ethnic groups by the usual socio-economic criteria of education, occupation, and income. Though the Luo median income is slightly less than that of the Kikuyu, they have far fewer household heads in unskilled employment. They easily out-rank the Kikuyu in white and blue collar occupations and almost equal them in the proportion of self-employed, which is a category otherwise dominated by Kikuyu in Nairobi. Their higher median length of residence in Nairobi suggests further that we are dealing here with a category of Luo who have developed a strong economic commitment to Nairobi.

Moreover, their high median length of residence in Kaloleni estate itself is in striking contrast to the very much lower one for Kikuyu, giving empirical support to the popular Luo complaint that Kaloleni has been 'losing' its Luo population since independence, while Kikuyu have been moving in. This kind of complaint is also made with reference to wage- and self-employment in Nairobi generally. The proportion of Luo to Kikuyu in the rapidly increasing Nairobi population, even allowing for boundary extensions, has indeed changed drastically in favour of Kikuyu since the ending of the Emergency. Figures on the ethnic distribution of the labour force in Nairobi are unavailable but the changed population proportions probably mean than an improportionately large number of *newly* created jobs in the expanding labour force have gone to Kikuyu. An independent 100 per cent survey of four important city council markets certainly suggests this.

Similarly, with regard to housing there are specific examples of this post-independence (or more properly, post-Emergency) 'dominance' by Kikuyu. The case of Kaloleni has been given. The new and important Uhuru housing estate, still being constructed, is already 99 per cent Kikuyu. Other examples can be given.

It can justifiably be argued that these increasing proportions of Kikuyu in housing and employment merely represent a return to the situation in Nairobi as it was before the declaration of the Emergency and of Operation Anvil in 1952. This may well be so. But, from the viewpoint of ordinary Luo, it is hardly surprising that the current situation is seen as a threat. In sociological analysis we *are* to a large extent dealing with the situation as people themselves perceive it and their conscious and unconscious responses to it. Fed by rumour and gossip as well as accurate report, people consistently refer to the situation in different conversations. It is part of the Nairobi dweller's 'world-view', the explanatory and evaluative aspects of which are critically shaped by his membership of a specific ethnic group. Certain political developments, which I later describe, substantiate this ethnic slant to popular modes of explaining and evaluating the problem of job- and house-finding.

It is not possible to show statistically how 'typical' or 'untypical' Kaloleni householders are of their respective ethnic groups in Nairobi. All one can say is that the Luo in Kaloleni are settled townsmen in relatively secure jobs and with above average incomes and that many are long-term residents in an area which has for a long time been regarded by all groups as a kind of Luo 'headquarters'.

By focusing on activities in which these particular Luo engage it seems legitimate to assume that I can analyse core features of Luo ethnic response to supposed Kikuyu domination. To repeat, the two most important modes of response are first, the interpersonal ideology of kinship and second, the congregational one of unilineal descent. I want to show, first, how the interpersonal ideology of kinship was an important instrument in this response and so I now turn to describe the distinctiveness of this important piece of Luo cultural equipment.

FORMAL PROPERTIES OF URBAN KINSHIP
AMONG LUO

Some key properties of kinship among urban Luo derive from (1) the low divorce and separation rate; (2) the low rate of marriage by both males and females into other ethnic groups (i.e. the high rate of ethnic endogamy); (3) the wide range of informal but effective sanctions exerted on women's status before and after marriage and (4) the high polygyny rate. In Kampala the two 'rival' groups, the Ganda and Luo, contrast strikingly in all four respects. But in Nairobi it is only with regard to the fourth property, the high polygyny rate, that the Luo stand in marked and isolated contrast (see *Table 2* in Appendix). It is on the consequences of this formal difference that I focus here.

A third of all married Luo household heads have more than one wife and their total 'pool' of wives is considerable. In both respects they greatly exceed other ethnic groups and particularly the Kikuyu, who have virtually abandoned polygyny. This marked difference cannot be explained by a significant discrepancy in median age between the four groups (see *Table 1* in Appendix). Nor, from other surveys, does a difference of this order seem 'untypical'. It is true that the older a Luo is, the more likely he is to be polygynous, but the apparent Luo propensity for polygyny cannot be explained away as a custom only followed these days by older men and spurned by younger. Over a third of the polygynous are under forty (most of these in their thirties but some in their twenties), and nearly half of them are still only in their forties (see *Table 3*).

Polygynists tend to be a little less educated than monogamists but this, too, is a function of their age. Among younger educated men, education *per se* is not a significant factor of difference. There is only a slight tendency for polygynists to be less well represented in clerical and skilled occupations, and this, too, seems to correspond with their age and lesser education and training. There is, however, a definite tendency for polygynists to be self-employed; Luo wives are important sources of labour in private enterprise such as market stalls, shops, etc. Another significant difference is of income. Polygynists earn on average about Shs. 100s. more than monogamists (see *Tables 4* and *6*).

To some extent this difference can be explained by the fact that, though less educated and skilled, many older men came to Nairobi in the years when jobs were more plentiful and their now limited paper qualifications no handicap. Some have worked their way up the ladder by acquiring on-the-job experience and command handsome incomes as relatively skilled men and even as clerks. *Within* the separate age categories, however, polygyny *is* associated with a higher than average income. In summary, then, we can make three observations about the propensity for polygyny among Luo in Kaloleni.

First, as a 'customary' pattern it is followed by all age and socio-economic categories and there is no evidence of it being discarded as a result of long urban residence. This fact invites us to ask whether this persisting customary form has altered its functions in urban and rural relations among Luo over the last half-generation or so. Second, polygynists tend to be over-represented in self-employment. Relevant to this also is the fact not yet mentioned, that some men in wage employment also run 'businesses' as a side-line, using a wife or wives to run it on their behalf while they themselves work in a factory or office. Third, and more generally, polygynists tend to have higher incomes than monogamists.

Clearly, the institution of Luo polygyny is not atrophying under contemporary conditions. Are we to call it an investment sphere which enables men to retain an economic stake both in town and at home? Or is it as likely to be a kind of consumption sphere, which drains a man's resources by first requiring him to provide the considerable cash bridewealth for an extra wife and then to provide for her and her offspring, and then, almost inevitably, certain of her own kin? If we look at individual polygynists at any one time, we can indeed divide such men up into those for whom many wives have strained their resources and those for whom definite economic benefits appear to have accrued. But if we look back over their life histories, we find the same men oscillating through alternate periods of success and failure, not always determined by life cycle factors. There is thus no simple equation of polygyny with either success or failure.

We can, however, look at the overall consequences of this strongly persisting institution as it has constantly readjusted

133

to changing conditions. In doing this we are in a position to analyse what part it has played in maintaining Luo ethnic distinctiveness.

It would perhaps be tedious to produce many more figures. Some general points can be made. There is evidence from observation and discussion that polygynists 'deploy' wives between town and country, and even between different towns. More Luo have a wife in both Nairobi and their rural home than any other ethnic group. Skilful deployment means that a Luo polygynist is rarely without a wife in Nairobi, where she can help him run a business or provide hospitality for a succession of visitors and lodgers. Luo households abound with lodgers and are larger than those of other ethnic groups. They include proportionally far more 'relatives' than others. These Luo 'relatives' include a proportionally larger number of (a) women, both married and unmarried, and (b) affines.

These women lodgers fall into a number of categories and fulfil a variety of functions. An important one centres on marriage arrangements. All married Luo males in Kaloleni have provided or are in the process of transacting valuable cash bridewealth for their wives. They will almost certainly have undergone a rural ceremony with a wife 'chosen' from an approval rural area. But urban contacts are important in these rural 'choices'. Men in Nairobi establish friendships and suggest sisters and daughters as possible wives. A main stated criterion for selecting a possible husband for a sister or daughter is the ability of the man to 'provide' for the girl. From observation of individual cases, it would seem that the prime expectation is that the groom be in a financial position to meet the valuable bridewealth which is given in return for rights over all children born to the wife. Full brothers cooperate in arranging marriages. They also constantly warn each other of the alleged possibilities of being cuckolded or being deserted by a wife in Nairobi. In fact the divorce and separation rates are both very low. But this does not seem to minimize Luo concern at the possibility of marital breakdown in Nairobi. Like obsessional witchcraft beliefs, an exaggerated or unfounded concern about conjugal instability symbolizes a key relationship for the maintenance of group boundaries.

It follows that domestic quarrels between husband and wife

134

frequently become family affairs, with kin, mostly agnates but also matrilaterals, from both sides brought in to mediate. Even where these notions of conjugal responsibility exist in the other ethnic groups, as among the Luhya for instance, the sheer fact of a higher polygyny rate among Luo ensures that marriage and kinship rules are talked about more frequently among Luo. For the same reason, they involve partially recurring and partially overlapping networks of kin and affines.

There are many other ways in which it can be shown both quantitatively and through case studies that Luo have more 'dense', 'reachable' and 'multiplex' ego-centred networks of kin and affines (see Mitchell 1969) than other ethnic groups. Lack of space prevents me from discussing these. But, by focusing on some of the consequences of the high Luo polygyny rate, I have illustrated something of this Luo distinctiveness. The most apt way of summarizing this distinctiveness is, to repeat my earlier phrase, to say that Luo rules of kinship and marriage are always being talked about or, more properly, being thrashed out in argument. Like ritual among Kachin, kinship is indeed a language of argument (Leach 1954: 278). But as a language of argument among an extensive spread of overlapping and interlinked networks, it has the overall consequence if not of promoting Luo harmony, then at least of marking off their cultural and thereby ethnic distinctiveness in Nairobi. Much the same can be said with regard to the use of descent by Luo in establishing urban associations. But before turning to this use of descent, I have to answer the obvious question: in what way is a markedly distinct Luo ideology of kinship politically useful to . them?

The most obvious answer is that, simply by stressing Luo ethnic distinctiveness in the important domestic domain, Luo group boundaries are drawn, the badges of membership are assigned, and communication between revolving sets of individual Luo is assured. As Cohen has shown, to solve or partially solve such problems as distinctiveness, discipline, and communication is to win half the battle to become an informally organized ethnic polity. We can see how the other half is won if we look at the way these interpersonal networks function alongside the pyramidal structure of Luo associations. I first describe this structure and then discuss how the informal networks and the formal associations operate together in the wider political context.

As in Kampala there is in Nairobi a three-tiered structure of associations. At the top is the widest level Luo Union. Second are the so-called location associations, which are based on home administrative 'locations' but which invariably have their own myths of origin and ancestry, and third are the 'clan' (*sic*) and lineage associations which frequently are based on actual exo- gamous clans but which may also rest on clan sections and even smaller lineages. As in Kampala also, location associations have over the years segmented to form lower order clan associations as more Luo have settled in Nairobi.

At the time of fieldwork this segmentation was continuing. In a few cases even relatively small lineage associations were segmenting. The process is segmentation rather than fission because the location associations continue to function and the overall 'authority' of the Luo Union as the seat of administra- tion is rarely questioned. It is the Luo Union which organizes recreational (soccer) and welfare activities. These are extremely popular and bring together large numbers of Luo as organizers, players, and spectators. Luo Union officials and notables usually have top clerical and professional jobs and rub shoulders with senior Luo politicians.

These senior politicians, including in the past the former Vice-President of Kenya, Odinga, the late Tom Mboya, and now others, often speak at public events organized by the Union. Since the Luo vernacular is almost invariably the language of discussion at these public meetings and also at the smaller association meetings, matters affecting the Luo community in Nairobi can be discussed freely, and Luo politicians, whose positions may rest firmly on the support of people of their home areas, are able to gauge opinions and act as representatives.

None of this is to say that there are no Luo rival factions and that all Luo are conscious of these overall expressions of ethnic distinctiveness. Indeed, both in the interpersonal kin networks mobilized to deal with disputes over rights in women and in the disputation and rivalry characterizing segmenting associations and competing soccer teams, Luo themselves will point to examples of Luo divisiveness: it is always the other party which is breaking the ideal rules of Luo behaviour. But, as anthropo-

logists have laboured to demonstrate, provided the legitimacy
of the ideal rules is accepted by all, then this kind of internal
disputation among sections of a community can actually under-
line the broad customary forms of behaviour which distinguish
that community from others. As an example of this, men may
segment from a location association to establish their own clan
association, but they may still remain members of the former,
as well as of the wider Luo Union. A few figures can be used to
demonstrate this multiple association membership as well as
the extensiveness of membership generally. (*Table 7* in the
Appendix).

Of the 333 Luo household heads in Kaloleni, only 133 or 40
per cent are not at present members of any of the three kinds
of association: Union, location, and clan. But a number of these
have at some time in the past been members and/or, on the
evidence of their own and other life histories, are likely to be so
again. There is, in other words, a fairly rapid turnover of
individual members of associations as a direct result of disputation. But the turnover of personnel does not, of course, reduce
the actual number of associations at any one time, so that the
overall structure may be said to persist. By membership I mean
here regular participation in the running of these associations,
which meet once a month or more in the hall or one of the rooms
in the Kaloleni community centre.

If we look at the distribution of associations of which these
200 Luo at Kaloleni are members, we see some interesting facts
(see *Table 7* in the Appendix).

We find that 33·5 per cent are members of more than one of
the three types of association (columns 4–7 in *Table 7*). These 67
men hold between them 148 membership positions, more than
two for each man. Multiple membership of this kind is a common method by which individuals manipulate ethnic support
from a number of different quarters. There are at least two
evident benefits. First, this support can be used by the entre-
preneurially gifted to find better jobs or employment for
their own relatives, or to provide their small businesses with
customers. Second, it can also be used to climb the ladder of
leadership *within* the Luo community: a number of Luo have
climbed from clan, to location, and finally to Union leadership.
It can be argued, though perhaps teleologically, that this

internal struggle for economic and minor political status and the
inevitable intra-ethnic patron-clientage that goes with it, de-
flects Luo away from similar involvement with other groups.
It is extremely rare, almost unheard of, for economic partner-
ships or patron-client relations in Nairobi at the present time
to occur between Luo and Kikuyu or Kamba. Even where they
occur with Luhya, Luo are almost invariably the senior party.
As with marriage, the idiom of fraternity and descent, sanctioned by continuing rural economic and social interests, is an
obviously powerful 'moral' weapon with which to dissuade a
man from lasting involvement of this kind with people of other
ethnic groups (see case on p. 133 of Parkin 1969).

It is significant therefore that it is the smaller associations
based on home local divisions of clan and location which are by
far the most popular (see *Table 8*). The Luo Union by contrast
involves the regular active participation of only a minority of
Luo, though many more Luo attend the recreational and welfare
meetings which it sponsors. The clan associations are explicitly
based on localized home descent units, while the location
associations in town make use of the same sentiments of common local and ancestral origins. Mythical ancestors are sometimes revived or 'discovered'. Indeed, even at the higher level
the recent switch in name from the Luo Union football team to
that of Gor Mahia made use of a venerated Luo war hero.

I have briefly described the structure of Luo associations in
Nairobi. Let me now show how informal kin networks, already
described, supplement these formal associations to raise Luo
cultural distinctiveness to a level of political significance. This
is best done by letting some illustrative material speak for itself,
in the form of an extended case.

LUO UNDER POLITICAL PRESSURE

At least four developments provide the basis of the belief held
by Luo in Nairobi that since Kenya's independence the Kikuyu
are acquiring political power, in the nation as well as the city,
at their expense. But let me first give the pre-independence
situation.

The Kenya Emergency of 1952–59 resulted in the imprisonment, detention, and restriction of Kikuyu. In Nairobi they

were removed from ethnically mixed housing estates, which are by far the most typical places of residence available. One such estate is Kaloleni. After the removal of Kikuyu it became a predominantly Luo estate and is still popularly referred to as such. It was and still is the scene of many Luo political meetings and activities. A second consequence of restrictions on Kikuyu was that Luo increased their hold on small business enterprises, especially market stalls, of which there are many in Nairobi. A third consequence was that the proportion of Luo in Nairobi, and in the labour force, increased markedly. But Luo and Kikuyu could not be said at that time to have been in direct competition, because they formed a strong alliance in the political party which came to power at Kenya's independence after defeating a rival party largely made up of ethnic groups other than Kikuyu and Luo.

In the recent post-independence years, these four developments have been completely reversed. Kaloleni has seen a steady increase in the proportion of Kikuyu and a decrease in Luo. This reflects the situation in other housing areas and in Nairobi as a whole, and also in the labour force. It probably also reflects the situation in the structure of trade union leadership, though, not surprisingly, details here are lacking. Luo are losing their hold on market stall enterprises, while Kikuyu are increasing theirs, and, even more recently, it is mainly Kikuyu, apparently, who are buying up the more lucrative larger businesses vacated by non-Kenyan Asians who leave Kenya. Finally, the alliance of Kikuyu and Luo in KANU (the Kenya African National Union) gave way to an at first superficially ethnic division between two parties: KANU and KPU (the Kenya People's Union). Recent events show how this superficial ethnic division has hardened into something much more fundamental.

And this is the point at which I can describe the process of informal political organization among Nairobi Luo as a variation of the process documented for Kampala.

In Kampala I showed how (a) the pyramidal structure of Luo associations based on unilineal descent and (b) frequent and overlapping kin networks enabled Luo to retain political consciousness *before* independence in competition with Ganda, and *after* independence in competition with representatives of the Uganda nation.

139

In Nairobi, *before* independence, the Luo/Kikuyu alliance of the political party KANU was reflected beforehand in other more inter-personal alliance relationships. I give two examples of this. When Kikuyu were rounded up during Operation Anvil early in the Emergency in 1952–53, many had to cede their small businesses, including market stalls. I have case histories and a few non-random figures which demonstrate that many Kikuyu allowed Luo 'friends' ('Are we not allies in the common struggle?') to run the businesses for them, though the licences continued to be in the name of the original Kikuyu.

Similarly, at the time of Operation Anvil, Kikuyu would retain tenancy rights in the housing estates (remember housing is, and always has been, in chronically short supply) in the following way: sisters would be 'allowed' to set up home in a common menage with Luo 'temporary husbands'. This pattern is said to have been pronounced in Kaloleni. The house would have been registered originally in the name of a Kikuyu brother or father, but the occupants would now be a Luo male household head and his 'wife', a Kikuyu. A few of these mixed marriages have survived to the present time, but most broke up with the ending of the Emergency and with the approach of independence. With the ending of the temporary 'marriage', Kikuyu families were able to reclaim tenancy rights, just as many Kikuyu were able to reclaim rights to run the market stalls and other small businesses which had been temporarily ceded to Luo. There are various methods by which these rights were effectively reclaimed, but I shall not discuss them in this short case-study.

At the time when these rights were being reclaimed, which was also the time when, more generally, the proportion of Kikuyu in Nairobi and in the labour force increased considerably (or, more accurately, swung back to pre-Emergency levels), the Luo Union and its branch associations became much more active. On the surface these associations are non-political. They are concerned with welfare, home-improvement, and recreational activities and schemes. But, as explained, they constitute an informal arena for leadership and a political platform.

In the early days of the Kikuyu/Luo alliance (as expressed particularly in the formation of KANU), the Luo Union and its chain of subordinate associations constituted an occasional but very useful means by which, on the one hand, the ordinary man in the street could be informed of the progress of negotiations with the British for independence and, on the other hand, senior Luo could make representations to the colonial authorities on behalf of both Luo and Kikuyu. On the basis of joint interests, some senior Luo became incorporated in the KANU and therefore government 'establishment'. It became inevitable that when the period of Kikuyu reclamation of rights began, Luo should be divided, or appear to be divided, on the future of their role as allies in KANU. In 1966, Odinga vacated the nation's vice-presidency and left KANU to form an opposition party, KPU, while the late Tom Mboya remained in KANU. The Luo Union became a public forum for debate and discussion among Luo, between those who claimed to side with each of these two leaders. As the proportions of Kikuyu in Nairobi, the labour force, housing estates, and small businesses, reverted swiftly to pre-Emergency levels, the KPU factions within the Luo Union became more popular, seeming to signify and confirm the common-sense observation that KPU had increased significantly the size of its Luo membership. This trend continued, with subordinate association branches playing a greater part in this process, as evidenced in a famous by-election campaign in 1969 in which the KPU candidate vanquished the KANU one (see Okumu 1969). I shall not concern myself with even more recent developments, except to say that I believe that they demonstrate a logical continuation of the process I am describing.

In short, we can discern two eras and three stages of Luo political process. In the pre-independence era, Luo and Kikuyu were allied and the activities and informal means of representation of the Luo Union and its subordinate branches reflected this alliance. This is stage one. Stage two is marked by a return by Kikuyu to their pre-Emergency numerical, commercial, and residential dominance in the Nairobi African population. This marked the ending of the 'formal' alliance and gave rise to a transitory period during which Luo leaders took stock of their place in the alliance. The Luo Union provided the forum in which this stock-taking took place and became communicated to ordinary Luo, both in Nairobi and elsewhere, through the subordinate associations. This was a time for 'internal' Luo political debate. Stage three is wholly a product of the post-independence era, when Kikuyu 'dominance' is seen by Luo to have reached inordinate proportions. KPU was formed and, increasingly, the Luo Union and branches became media by which the party's political 'messages' were communicated.

At the level of urban domestic life, there has been an almost total halt to Luo-Kikuyu 'marriage' or cohabitation. During the period of the alliance, this had been rising, apparently causing outside observers to see this as an interesting example of 'inter-tribal' harmony. These mixed unions had almost always involved Luo men and Kikuyu women and rarely the other way round, possibly because Kikuyu women, unlike their menfolk, were much less restricted during the Emergency. By stage three, representatives of each ethnic group now used the exhortations of 'custom' to bring moral sanctions to bear, respectively, on Kikuyu women and Luo men in a successful attempt to discourage mixed conjugal unions. Thus, at the personal, egocentric level as well as at the level of formal associations and political parties, people were constantly reminded of their 'moral' obligations to their own ethnic group and of the political significance of these obligations.

The crucial difference in the essentially similar political process in the Kampala and Nairobi situations is as follows: in Kampala the Luo structure of associations and their kin network and emphasis on ethnic endogamy enabled them, at the time of Uganda's independence, to acknowledge publicly their expatriate status and their withdrawal from Uganda politics. This was an example of political acquiescence as an expedient measure; in Nairobi these same urban cultural institutions had been used *not* to express political withdrawal but the opposite, the formation of an opposition party. (The recent banning of this opposition party need not alter the trend towards further ethnic polarization. But it is a matter of intelligent speculation as to what may happen.) In Kampala, Luo expatriates had the alternative of reclaiming rights to jobs in their country of Kenya, which was not yet independent but seemed to Luo to offer greater opportunities in alliance with the Kikuyu. Their political withdrawal from Uganda was not only expedient but seemed, to Luo leaders at least, a better alternative. In Nairobi, no such alternative was available. Few Luo ever seriously contemplated a Biafra-type secession. Opposition was inevitable.

It is perhaps clear from this comparative analysis of Luo in Kampala and Nairobi that (a) informal interpersonal kin networks and (b) formal associations established on the basis of descent, together provided Luo with their most immediately useful cultural resource with which to meet political changes. They used the same dominant cultural apparatus to formulate contrasting political responses, one of withdrawal and the other of confrontation.

To return to some comparative material, I now look at a few other ethnic groups in African towns which appear to show similarities with Luo in (a) lacking the degree of economic self-sufficiency and residential exclusiveness of the Hausa of Ibadan, and (b) utilizing what appear on the surface to be 'traditional' idioms of social organization in the formation of urban ethnic associations. The purpose of this exercise will be to assess further the range and viability of non-religious ethnic institutions in the promotion or defence of common urban interests.

ETHNIC ASSOCIATIONS IN AFRICAN TOWNS

The widespread occurrence of ethnic associations in African towns has attracted the attention of many writers. Cohen points out that the significance of such associations has been greatly exaggerated by some scholars (1969a: 195). He cites their sometimes low membership and attendance figures and implies that this illustrates their peripheral relevance for central political and economic activities. There are many examples to support this view, but it is perhaps better to regard the politico-economic significance of ethnic associations as highly variable.

The Luo Union of East Africa (together with its branch and subordinate associations), the sometime Ibo Union of Nigeria, the Kru Corporation of Monrovia, and possibly the Kru 'Committee' of Freetown, do seem to provide central or at least significant support for the group's political and economic interests. Moreover, none of those are 'new' urban migrant groupings. The Luo were among the first to supply labour to urban centres in East Africa at the turn of the century. There have been numerous religious sectarian movements among them and neighbouring peoples. But none of these movements has provided a unitary structure linking virtually all Luo in

143

all main East African towns, as has the Luo Union and its branches.

The Kru, similarly, traded from the Liberian coast with passing European vessels more than a century before the Americo-Liberians arrived. Liebenow (1969:33) calls theirs an ambivalent case, in that they managed to resist Americo-Liberian control until the 1930s yet were more involved in the cash economy than any of the other so-called 'tribal' peoples. In particular, the Kru successfully controlled the stevedoring profession along long stretches of the West African coast, both within and beyond Liberia. From Fraenkel's account (1964) of Monrovia, in contemporary times they have done this largely through their Kru Corporation and its branches in a manner I shall shortly describe. The Ibo Union would also appear to have had considerable significance of this kind.

We must, then, distinguish ethnic urban-based associations as to their politico-economic significance. Epstein (1967) has made a useful fourfold distinction both of ethnic and non-ethnic voluntary associations according to their manifest stated functions. But, to emphasize a point made earlier in the paper, it seems to me that if our task is to be problem-focused, i.e. if we are to dwell on ethnicity as a sociological problem, then we should consider both their latent and manifest functions. That is to say, we need to understand the extent and nature of political and economic functions performed by ethnic associations, whether or not they are so labelled, which use a variety of ostensibly 'indigenous' cultural traditions, symbols and units of recruitment and organization. At the risk of making what is perhaps now an obvious point, it should be emphasized that I am here not dealing with a simple transplantation of traditional rural phenomena to urban conditions, but with persisting cultural *forms* taking on new meanings and functions in constantly changing conditions (see Cohen 1969b).

Let me now construct a simple hierarchy of ethnic associations according to their politico-economic significance. At the bottom we have in Freetown the young men's 'companies' of such ethnic groups as the Temne and Mandinka. These 'companies' have had limited political and economic significance. Throughout his description of them Banton (1957, 1965) refers to their function of 're-socializing' individual migrants to urban life. Mention is made of the way post-independence political leaders in Sierra Leone appeal to 'tribal loyalties' to amass followings, but no mention is made of any part played by the 'companies' in this process. Urban ethnic associations of apparently negligible political and economic significance are also described by Little (1965).

I do not wish simply to let the matter of these weakly developed, and probably nowadays atrophied, associations rest here. It is clear that the 'companies' did not become any more than a minor component, if that, in the formation of an ethnic political interest group. During the 1930s when they were probably at their most viable, there was simply no apparent need for Temne or Mandinka to organize themselves for economic and political purposes. The significance of the 'companies' is not so much in what they did or did not become, but more in what they might have become. Under different structural conditions in the early days of, say Temne migration to Freetown and incorporation in wage employment, the use of both 'traditional' and 'modern' cultural features in these societies might have constituted the corner-stone of a more economically and politically significant association. The Temne did not, it seems, exploit an economic 'niche', to use Barth's metaphor (1963), at a time when their otherwise socially useful 'companies' developed.

The Kru, however, were already well placed to exploit new economic opportunities along parts of the West African coast. Their Kru Corporation established, expanded and defended their hold on an occupational monopoly. Unlike among most of the West African urban ethnic groups, the Kru Corporation has been very much more than merely a component in the organization of Kru corporate interests. The Kru Corporation has more politico-economic significance than even the Luo Union and, probably, the Ibo Union. This is my interpretation of Fraenkel's descriptive material on Kru in Monrovia.

Thus, the Kru dominate the stevedore profession. They provide the dock-workers and many dock hands along the coast of West Africa. They are recruited into jobs through their sub-tribal and other local associations in Monrovia. Kru are kept in contact with each other under the organizational umbrella of the Kru Corporation and branch associations. They pay dues at the end of each sea trip; they establish ties through soccer competitions; their urban tribal head, called the Kru Governor, and their urban tribal court are recognized by the Monrovia municipal authorities. The Kru Corporation also distributes 'tickets' for work on the ships, and has some of the functions of a trade union in so far as it may offer protection to its members against employers. Indeed, it did so in the 1930s during the depression when it introduced the 'ticket' system, and again in 1958 when it hired a lawyer, himself a Kru, to negotiate with the shipping companies over wages and conditions. Similar functions are ascribed by Banton to the Kru 'Committee' in Freetown.

The bricks of this administrative system among a huge and widely dispersed ethnic group are the *dako* or localized home sub-tribes. Fraenkel notes with interest that the *dako* were traditionally autonomous and did not cooperate, were even bitter rivals and might war with each other. This is a long time ago. What is remarkable is that the same could be said for the Luo of East Africa in towns like Kampala, Nairobi and Mombasa, and, possibly, the Ibo of Nigeria. The Luo are not associated predominately with a single occupation, though they are well represented in docks and railways and do preserve quasi-corporate interests in town. Yet they too have local groups at home which were previously autonomous and which warred with each other. The data are slender but do seem to suggest that these uncentralized structures first allow migration to operate through the fiercely autonomous local groups, be they sub-tribes, clans or lineages, and then, due to external pressure or competition, bring about a loose confederacy of these groups in town, so that the ethnic hierarchical structure of Kru, Luo and others comes into being.

This is of course historical speculation. But it is quite feasible to suggest that these units, whether they are believed by the people to be based on descent or on common locality or both, provide convenient units in the urban situation for mobilizing people and organizing them for economic and administrative purposes as among Kru, or for informal political purposes, as among the Luo of Kampala and Nairobi. Just as the Tijanniya Order fitted well the need of the Ibadan Hausa to retain their corporate structure, so the hierarchy of traditional units among

Luo and Kru in towns was the most convenient way of establishing common interests and, in the case of Kru in particular, of defending them.

It will be remembered that I first used the continuum of situations of political ethnicity proposed by Cohen. At one end of the continuum we have highly corporate political groups such as the Hausa of Ibadan, whose considerable political autonomy is accompanied by a trading monopoly, preferred residential segregation, and religious and cultural exclusiveness. At the other end are ethnic groups, or rather categories, whose members recognize and interact among themselves by references to their cultural affinity but who do not otherwise hold significant corporate interests in common. The Temne of Freetown is one such category discussed here. As Cohen says (1969a: 196), most situations lie between these two extremes. The Luo in Kampala and Nairobi and the Kru in Monrovia and elsewhere would certainly fall in the middle area of the continuum. Indeed, the evidence suggests that the Kru, in so far as they have marked residential and occupational exclusiveness and independent or 'privileged' forms of political representation, may even move some way towards the Hausa end of the continuum. Both Kru and Luo have made constant use of their ethnic associations for political purposes.

The Hausa, Kru, and Luo all encourage and practise a high rate of ethnic endogamy: out-marrying by females in particular is discouraged. By contrast, Temne have a high outmarriage rate for their women (Banton 1965: 138).

Though there is not the same amount of evidence available, the Kru in Monrovia compare in some respects with Luo in kinship relations as well as in type of ethnic association structure. Thus, we learn from Fraenkel that among Kru in Monrovia 'close ties of kinship' bind households to each other in different and sometimes ethnically mixed areas of Monrovia (76). Separate residences for wives in polygamous unions is one way in which dispersed households are linked to each other. Unlike other ethnic groups in Monrovia, Kru never followed the custom of sending their children to live as wards in the homes of the politically dominant Creoles. As explained, Luo too see control over children, as well as over women, as an instrument of corporate identity and independence. Additionally, there is a slight tendency for Kru residential enclaves and communities in Monrovia to accommodate members of specific sub-tribes.

Neither Kru nor Luo can be regarded as newcomers to urban conditions. An interesting feature does apply to them both, however, and not to the Ibadan Hausa. This is that, though a high proportion of Kru and Luo are in any conventional sense 'townsmen', they have until the present time shown a propensity for migration, not simply back and forwards between rural area and town in the cyclical manner analysed by Mitchell (1959),[2] but between towns over wide areas. Fraenkel explains that some new Kru arrivals to Monrovia within the last ten years have lived previously in other West African ports, especially Accra and Freetown (74). Luo, similarly, are, or until very recently were, found in large numbers in all major towns in Kenya, Uganda, and Tanzania, and have shown the same tendency to inter-city migration, especially but not solely as railway employees (see Grillo 1969b).

Luo and Kru have thus established themselves as corporate or quasi-corporate sections of urban populations, yet have shown some internal turnover. Somewhat paradoxically, they are 'settled' urban communities yet have been internally fairly mobile. It seems to me that an intensified, congregational religious organization of the Tijanniya type does indeed fit well the needs of a small ethnic group who are both occupationally and also residentially exclusive. By contrast, the kinship links which I have described for Luo and Kru are clearly non-congregational. They are activated for minor domestic matters in recurrent and overlapping networks of 'kin'. Taken diachronically, they thus splay out in different directions but yet are controlled and regularized by a kinship ideology which, in the case of the Luo at least, exercises its discipline ultimately through the dogma of rural-based descent. This controlled splaying out of kinship links seems to suit admirably the needs of a larger yet clearly politically conscious ethnic group like the Luo, by linking its residentially and occupationally heterogeneous population within and between towns. It probably does the job better than an exclusively congregational ideology requiring a fixed and settled locus for the activities it mandates. Nevertheless, the Luo and Kru associations provide a *supplementary* though not predominant congregational ideology. They constitute a regularly recurring structure enabling people to come together and arrive at decisions, and to communicate information about political developments. By observing and participating in association activities, ordinary Luo could tell who were Luo 'leaders' and could judge for themselves the issues between KPU and KANU.

While interpersonal networks communicate information by way of 'private' gossip and rumour, the persisting and coherent structure of associations communicate information by publicly displaying leadership rivalries and factions within the Luo community. This combination of formal associations and culturally valued interpersonal kin networks, which is a balance between congregational and non-congregational ideologies, is possibly more typical of ethnic groups in plural urban situations than we have realized. Hindu urban and rural caste associations, which are a response to contemporary circumstances and by no means a mere persistence of rural *jati* castes (Bailey 1963: 121–3), also frequently operate in conjunction with economically important joint family structures with correspondingly extensive kin networks (see Srinivas and Singer in Singer & Cohn (eds) 1968; Gould 1963; Rudolf, L. & S. 1960, 1965).

Let me attempt the following hypothesis. Where an urban ethnic group attempts to create its autonomy but has its members residentially and occupationally dispersed, then it will tend to overcome the problem of dispersal by making extreme, even 'exaggerated' use of interpersonal kin networks for the solution of a range of domestic problems. The notion of kinship is likely to be phrased also in terms of friendship or neighbourhood, etc., according to the group's cultural repertoire of important relationships and idioms. This use of network has two functions. One of constantly 'reminding' people of their common language of custom. Another of communicating information about matters of common ethnic interest, thus keeping people alert to the possibility of more mobilized, collective action. Here, some kind of formal association structure would seem to be a necessary condition of actual mobilization.

We know, for instance, from various parts of the world that bilateral kinship networks can persist as important mechanisms by which people, sometimes of specific ethnic and cultural categories, can find jobs, housing, and political privilege (Leeds 1964 for Brazil, Whitten 1969 for Ecuador and Colombia, Boissevain 1966 for Sicily, *et. al.*). But such networks do not by themselves seem to provide a sufficient ideology for the political organization of categories and their transformation into interest or pressure groups. The congregational associations which provide this necessary supplementary role may be articulated through a wide variety of cultural idioms and activities such as religion, unilineal descent, welfare, recreation and others.

By contrast, Van Velsen (1964: 313) was able to report for rural Tonga that 'Overall social and political cohesion' was achieved through interpersonal kin networks alone, unaided by any 'structural ranking and coordination of clearly defined and permanent local or kinship groups'. Situations of stark ethnic confrontation seem to require more than this sole use of an interpersonal ideology.

In many parts of the third world regional differences of income and political opportunity frequently correspond with acknowledged ethnic differences. In many parts, also, as in much of Africa, rural and urban economic and political interests complement each other and really constitute a single sphere rather than dual ones. In such situations of continuing interdependence of rural and urban interests, we may expect the rural areas positively to charge, so to speak, urban organizational ideologies, and also for the latter to feed back into the ethnically distinctive rural areas. In situations of ethnicity (not just urban) and other situations of cultural resistance or assimilation we should aim to look for possible examples of different interdependencies of *both* congregational and interpersonal organizational ideologies.

Let me conclude by suggesting some theoretical implications of this analysis. Empirically, congregational and interpersonal ideologies have each to be seen as extremes of a continuum. Conceptually, the distinction has some theoretical significance. Anthropologists have for a long time had difficulty in classifying different types of social relations: when is a kinship relationship

150

also one of friendship, neighbourhood, patronage and so on; is there a special 'meaning' to, or content of, kinship which is distinctive of other kinds of relationship (see especially the lively exchange between Beattie and Schneider 1964 and 1965)?

This concern will re-emerge and is far from dead. We shall continue to distinguish relations in this conventional way for purposes of straightforward communication if little else. But it is worth pausing to consider whether we should not temporarily dismantle this conceptual apparatus for certain types of holistic study. We can look instead at how group or collective interests are articulated through variously emphasized congregational and interpersonal ideologies: some cultures emphasize the legitimacy, acceptability, or sanctity of 'private' dyadic face-to-face transactions for certain key activities and deprecate 'public' congregational or associational transactions in these same contexts. Other cultures reverse this order of preference. A variety of such cultural combinations of preferences may operate in different societies under different conditions of political confrontation, exposure, or self-advancement. Within a single society it may be possible to observe a change from emphasis of one type of ideology to the other or to a different combination in response to such changing conditions.

This approach is part of the search for a fuller understanding of the *communicative* aspects of cultural systems which, in the end, make up the common thread binding all branches of anthropology. Its distinctive feature is that it assumes that ultimate reference must be made to the crucial significance of groups, collectivities, or status categories as interest-bearing units. The problems of self-perpetuation confronting these units and their largely unconscious solutions to these problems through adjustment are of central concern.

APPENDIX

TABLE 1 *Numerical Profile of the Household Heads of Kaloleni estate*

	Luo (333)	Luhya (222)	Kikuyu (122)	Kamba (133)	Others (42)
% of household head population	39·0	26·0	14·3	15·6	4·9
Median age	37.3	36·4	37·1	37·0	38·7
Median education (in yrs)	8·2	6·6	7·1	6·2	6·0
Median formal instruction in Swahili (yrs)	1·4	1·1	1·3	1·2	—
Median Income (Shs.)	539/–	75/–	549/–	450/–	542/–
Median length of residence in Nbi (yrs)	17·6	15·2	16·7	14·2	16·9
Median length of residence in Kaloleni	11·3	9·1	6·7	8·3	7·6
% proportions in:					
(a) white collar employment	36·3	30·2	39·3	27·1	30·9
(b) blue collar/manual	38·1	39·2	23·8	43·6	40·5
(c) unskilled employment	10·2	24·3	21·3	23·3	19·0
(d) self-employed	13·2	4·5	15·6	5·3	4·8
(e) unemployed	2·1	1·8	—	0·7	4·8

TABLE 2 *Polygyny rate by ethnic group of married men*

	Total No. of Household heads	No. married	Proportion with two or more wives	Total No. of wives	Ratio of wives to married heads
LUO	333	309	33·3 (103)	435	148%
LUHYA	222	210	17·1 (36)	249	118%
KAMBA	133	123	16·3 (20)	144	117%
KIKUYU	122	102	6·9 (7)	109	107%

TABLE 3 *Polygynists and Monogamists by Age*

Age	Categories	20–29	30–39	40–49	50–59	60+		(Total Number)
LUO	Polygynists	8	25	46	18	3	100%	(103)
	Monogamists	20	45	26	7	2	100%	(204) (2 n.a.)
LUHYA	Polygynists	17	22	47	14	—	100%	(36)
	Monogamists	20	43	28	7	2	100%	(174) (1 n.a.)
KIKUYU	Polygynists	—	42	29	29	—	100%	(7)
	Monogamists	24	30	40	6	—	100%	(94) (1 n.a.)
KAMBA	Polygynists	—	20	75	—	5	100%	(20)
	Monogamists	16	49	29	6	—	100%	(101) (2 n.a.)

This *Table 3* compares polygynists and monogamists by age *within* ethnic groups. *Tables 4–8* following focus on Luo alone.

TABLE 4 Luo Polygynists and Monogamists by Income

	Shs 100+	200+	300+	400+	500+	600+	700+	800+	900+	1000+		(Total No.)
Polygynists	2	6	8	24	9	16	10	6	3	16	100%	(102)
Monogamists	3	7	17	22	11	10	7	6	5	12	100%	(204)

TABLE 5 Luo Polygynists and Monogamists by Education

No. of years education	None	Up to 3 yrs	4-7 yrs	8 yrs	9	10	11	12	13	14+		(Total No.)
Polygynists	21	9	28	19	5	7	6	2	—	3	100%	(102) (1 n.a.)
Monogamists	9	10	23	27	6	7	8	6	1	3	100%	(204) (2 n.a.)

TABLE 6 Luo Polygynists and Monogamists by Occupation

	Professional Technical & Supervisory	White Collar	Blue Collar Skilled	Semi-Skilled	Unskilled	Self-Employed	None		(Total No.)
Polygynists	10	20	14	23	11	19	3	100%	(102)
Monogamists	12	27	19	21	9	10	2	100%	(204)

153

TABLE 7 Range and Types of Membership of Luo Ethnic Associations

Association Type	1 Clan/ lineage only	2 Location only	3 Union only	4 Clan & Location	5 Clan & Union	6 Location & Union	7 Clan, Location & Union	(Total)
Proportion of Members	30·5	29	7	23·5	1	2	7	100% (200)

TABLE 8 Proportionate Membership of the three Luo Association Types

Association Type	Clan/Lineage	Location	Union	(Total)
No. of Members	124	123	34	(281—i.e. includes 81 cases of multiple membership)
As a proportion of all 200 members	62·0	61·5	17·0	

154

NOTES

[1] Certain analytical concepts correspond with this heuristic distinction. For example the by now familiar identification of ego-centred network rather than group and, more recently, the contrast of 'grid' and 'group' elegantly presented in Douglas 1970. These concepts are not identical, however, and while 'group' but not 'grid' is a boundary-maintaining mechanism, I am interested in the extent to which *both* congregational and interpersonal ideologies set up and maintain ethnic and other socio-cultural boundaries.

[2] Compare here Weisner's findings in Nairobi on a section of Kisa Luhya who continue to operate this kind of migration cycle (1969).

REFERENCES

BAILEY, F. G. 1963. Closed Social Stratification in India. *European Journal of Sociology* 4, 107–24.

BANTON, M. P. 1957. *West African City*. London: Oxford University Press.

—— 1965. Social Alignment and Identity in a West African City in Kuper, H. (ed.). *Urbanization and Migration in West Africa*. California University Press.

BARTH, F. (ed.). 1963. *The Social Role of the Entrepreneur in Social Change in Northern Norway*. Bergen: Norwegian University Press.

BEATTIE, J. 1964. Kinship and social anthropology. *Man* 64, 130: 101–3.

—— 1965. The content of kinship. *Man* 65, 38: 51–2; 109: 123.

BOISSEVAIN, J. 1966. Patronage in Sicily. *Man* (NS) 1, 1.

COHEN, A. 1969a. *Custom and Politics in Urban Africa*. London: Routledge & Kegan Paul.

—— 1969b. Political Anthropology. *Man* (NS) 4, 2.

DOUGLAS, M. 1970. *Natural Symbols*. London: Barrie & Rockcliff.

EPSTEIN, A. L. 1958. *Politics in an Urban African Community*. Manchester UP.

—— 1967. Urbanization and Social Change. *Current Anthropology* 8, 4.

FORTES, M. Descent, Filiation and Affinity: a rejoinder to Dr Leach. *Man* 59 (Nov. 1959) 193–7; (Dec. 1959) 206–12.

FRAENKEL, M. 1964. *Tribe and Class in Monrovia*. London: Oxford UP.

FRANKENBERG, R. 1966. *Communities in Britain*. Harmondsworth: Penguin.

GOULD, H. A. 1963. The Adaptive Function of Caste in Contemporary Indian Society. *Asian Survey*.

GRILLO, R. D. 1969a. The Tribal Factor in an East African Trade Union, in P. H. Gulliver (ed.) *Tradition and Transition in East Africa*. London: Routledge & Kegan Paul.

—— 1969b. Anthropology, Industrial Development and Labor Migration in Uganda, in D. Brokensha and M. Pearsall (eds). *The Anthropology of Development in Sub-Saharan Africa*. Kentucky UP.

KAPFERER, B. 1969. Norms and the Manipulation of Relationships in a Work Context, in Mitchell, J. C. (ed.), *Social networks and urban situations*. Manchester University Press.

KUPER, LEO, & SMITH, M. G. (eds). 1969. *Pluralism in Africa*. Berkeley: California UP.

LA FONTAINE, J. S. 1970. *City Politics: a Study of Leopoldville 1962–1963*. Cambridge University Press.

LEACH, E. R. 1954. *Political Systems of Highland Burma*. London: Bell.

LEEDS, A. 1964. Brazilian Careers and Social Structure in a case history and model. *American Anthropologist* 66.

LIEBENOW, J. G. 1969. *Liberia: The Evolution of Privilege*. Ithaca: Cornell UP.

LITTLE, K. 1965. *West African Urbanization*. Cambridge University Press.

MAYER, P. 1961. *Townsmen or Tribesmen*. Cape Town: Oxford University Press.

MITCHELL, J. C. 1959. The Causes of Labour Migration, in *Migrant Labour in Africa South of the Sahara*. CCTA 6th International Labour Conference. Abidjan. Reprinted in Middleton, J. (ed.) *Black Africa*. Toronto: Macmillan.

OKUMU, J. J. 1969 (June). The By-election in Gem: An Assessment. *East African Journal*. Nairobi.

PARKIN, D. J. 1969. *Neighbours and Nationals in an African City Ward*. London: Routledge and Kegan Paul, and California UP.

ROSS, M. 1968. *Politics and Urbanization: Two Communities in Nairobi*. PhD Dissertation for Northwestern University.

RUDOLF, L. and S. 1960. The Political Role of India's Caste Associations. *Pacific Affairs*, 33.

—— 1965. The Modernity of Tradition: the Democratic Incarnation of Caste in India, *American Political Science Review*.

SCHNEIDER, D. M. 1964. The nature of kinship, *Man* 64, 217: 180–1.

—— 1965. The content of kinship, *Man* 65, 108: 122–3.

SINGER, M. 1968. The Indian Joint Family in Modern Industry, in Singer & Cohn (eds).

SINGER, M. & COHN, B. (eds). 1968. *Structure and Change in Indian Society*. Chicago: Aldine Publishing Company.

SMITH, M. G. 1969. Institutional and Political Conditions, in Kuper & Smith (eds).

SOUTHALL, A. W. 1952. Lineage Formation among the Luo. IAI *Memorandum* No. 26. Oxford.

—— 1965. A Critique of the Typology of States and Political Systems, in M. Banton (ed.), *Political Systems and the Distribution of Power*. ASA Monograph No 2. London: Tavistock Publications.

SRINIVAS, M. N. 1968. Mobility in the Caste System, in Singer & Cohn (eds).

SYTEK, W. 1965. Luo Land Consolidation Schemes. Paper for the Makerere Institute of Social Research, Kampala.

VAN VELSEN, J. 1964. *The Politics of Kinship*. Manchester University Press.

WEISNER, T. S. 1969. One Family, Two Households: A Rural-Urban Network Model of Urbanism. Unpublished Paper.

WHITTEN, N. E. 1969. Strategies of Adaptive Mobility in the Colombian-Ecuadorian Littoral. *American Anthropologist* **71**, 228–42.

R. D. Grillo

Ethnic Identity and Social Stratification on a Kampala Housing Estate

It is necessary to begin with terminology, definition, and orientation. For although one prominent writer has asserted that 'Few scholars have tried to define the ethnic group' (Mercier 1965: 487) anyone familiar with this field will realize that most of those who venture into it offer their own definitions which usually entail, explicitly or implicitly, whole theories of ethnic relations.[1] In a paper such as this it is possible only to state one's preferences with little discussion of divergences from and similarities to those of others. So here, for example, the word 'ethnicity' is used to refer to all matters pertaining to relations between those with the same or different ethnic identities living in a poly-ethnic system. This usage differs from that suggested by Cohen who defines ethnicity as 'strife . . . between ethnic groups' (Cohen 1969a: 4) but is closer to that preferred by others (Gans 1962: 32; Greenberg 1965: 57; Wallerstein 1965: 477). This, however, leaves the real problem untouched, for what is meant by 'ethnic'? This concept would seem to imply, in the first place, a classification or ordering of the human world into a comprehensive set of categories defined by reference to an idea of common origin, ancestry, and cultural heritage. Underpinning this classification is usually an ideology that specifies the relationship between those with the same or different identities. Such ethnic ideologies often, perhaps always, enjoin an idea of solidarity, even equality, among those who share an identity, and opposition, even superiority, towards those whose identities differ. These ideologies may be considered not so much as prescribing solidarity as providing a set of ideas and symbols by reference to which a claim to solidarity (or opposition) may be made in inter-group and interpersonal relations. A major problem of ethnic studies is to understand how and when such claims come to be made and accepted or rejected. This is one of the themes explored in this paper.

159

A second terminological issue relates to the distinction between an ethnic group and an ethnic category. In anthropology the word category has two meanings. It may refer to an item in a classificatory system, but it may also refer to a pragmatically defined set of people who, to follow Cohen, fall short of forming a 'corporate political group' (Cohen 1969a: 4). Similarly, Williams distinguishes between aggregates, categories, collectivities, groups, and societies and raises the question 'how do aggregates become collectivities?' (Williams 1964: 18). Most anthropologists use the word group to refer to all these phenomena, and since I wish to retain the word category in the first sense noted above, the usual anthropological convention will be followed here. This is not to imply that the distinction raised by Cohen and Williams is insignificant. On the contrary the issue – the extent to which those who share an ethnic identity form a corporate group – is of paramount importance for many ethnic studies. This relates to a third point.

A concept which has gained currency in recent work on ethnicity is that of the 'boundary' (Barth 1969: 15; Cohen & Middleton 1970: 15). This refers generally to the extent to which relations between those with different ethnic identities are restricted and formalized, and interaction is confined within the bounds of the ethnic group. In certain respects the discussion of boundaries and the discussion of the formation of corporate groups referred to above run parallel, each generating important questions and propositions. The boundary analogy, however, has a number of advantages. First, it provides a convenient framework through which one may analyse the emergent properties of informal interaction. Second, it enables us to talk about the strong and weak points on the boundary between groups. Numerous studies have already demonstrated the importance of such variations in definition – which may be temporal, systematic or situational – and this is another theme examined in this paper (cf. Cohen 1969a; Epstein 1958; Williams 1964). Third, through the concept of the boundary our attention is focused not only on the formation and properties of aggregate social entities, but also on the behaviour of individual actors. The significance of this for the present paper lies in the following. Among the people with whom this study is concerned ethnic identity cannot or should not be considered

separate from another set of identities that derive from other
sources, mainly from principles of ranking or stratification that
operate in their community. These principles provide an alternative set of claims to solidarity and opposition, an alternative
series of points along which boundaries may emerge. There are
thus two systems, ethnicity and socio-economic status, by
reference to which relationships may be ordered. We are forced,
therefore, to recognize that any actor has some degree of choice
as to which system he will employ in any particular relationship.
The form of social aggregates both affects and is affected by the
outcome of these choices.

It will be realized that the last point touches on a general
theoretical problem the discussion of which is beyond the scope
of this paper. I refer to the debate between two approaches
which have been termed 'methodological holism' and 'methodological individualism' (cf. Blau 1964; Lukes 1968; Ryan 1970:
chap. 8). For some, these methodologies are seen as incompatible, theoretically and even morally. In fact, total adherence
to one approach or the other poses the problem that both have
their limitations and advantages. So that while the orientation
adopted in this paper derives mainly from what Cohen (1969b:
223) calls the 'action theory' school of British anthropology it
is recognized that we must also be concerned with the properties
of the general context within which action takes place and with
the general structure that emerges from our analysis of individual action. To the extent that this paper is thus theoretically eclectic it follows in the time-honoured tradition of British
social anthropology.

ETHNICITY AND STRATIFICATION: SOME
COMPARATIVE MODELS

This paper, then, is concerned with the interplay of two principles of organization and systems of identity: ethnicity and
stratification. The ethnographic material to be considered
derives from fieldwork undertaken in 1964–65 among African
employees of the East African Railways and Harbours (the
'Railways') stationed in Kampala, Uganda, and resident on the
railway-owned housing estate at Nsambya, on the southern edge
of the City. In the literature on urban Africa both ethnicity

('tribalism') and systems of socio-economic status taken separately are well documented. There is less evidence as to what kind of structure emerges when we consider both variables simultaneously. *Tribe and class in Monrovia* (Fraenkel 1964) does not live up to its promising title from this point of view. If one examines the possible combinations of the two principles of organization with a holistic approach in mind, at least two ideal type systems may be distinguished. In one, ethnic and stratum boundaries coincide, i.e. ethnic groups are themselves stratified; in the other, ethnic groups are internally stratified on principles of ranking common to all the groups in the system. Both types may occur simultaneously as the obvious examples of South Africa or Ulster show. The first type of system is frequently associated with imperial conquest, though it may also be the result of migration. It is well known that in the USA wave after wave of migrants have moved into the lowest level of American urban society, each wave replacing its predecessor, often in employment, frequently in place of residence (see Warner & Srole 1945: chap. 3, and many other studies). A recent account of the English town of Bedford (Brown 1970) revealed the same pattern. The possibility that in urban Africa something similar may have occurred is often overlooked, though Banton notes explicitly that in Freetown, Sierra Leone, in contrast with the cities of northeastern America, the migratory process was such that 'ethnic differences did not get built into the economic structure' (Banton 1965: 139). Nevertheless, with regard to the African populations of the major East African cities, there are good reasons for believing that the early involvement of Ganda, Luo, Luhya, and Kikuyu in migration and the cash economy and thence in the educational system was responsible for their relative success in benefiting from the process of Africanization that occurred in the 1960s. Bearing this in mind the attempt by one sociologist to convey a general picture of the structure of contemporary American society, especially in the cities, may have some value as a model of the emerging situation in some African towns. 'Each ethnic group may be thought of as being divided into subgroups on the basis of social class, and . . . theoretically each ethnic group might conceivably have the whole spectrum of classes within it, although in practice some ethnic groups will be found to contain only a partial distribution of social class subgroups' (Gordon 1964: 48).

The fact that there may be a relatively unequal distribution of socio-economic statuses – wealth, prestige, power – between ethnic groups may obviously be significant for the understanding of ethnic conflict. It is clearly a point about which the members of an ethnic collectivity may rally and form an interest group. Equally it is a ready-made theme available for those aspiring to leadership. This aspect is not, however, the concern of this paper. For the moment the issue is the structural significance of the existence of ranking systems that operate both within and between ethnic groups. The American literature again suggests some points of comparison and some hypotheses. Gordon, for example, has proposed that the intersection of class and ethnic boundaries has produced what he terms 'ethclasses' in which are located the individual's primary relationships. These ethclasses are not localized communities, their representatives are to be found, in varying degrees, across the United States, and there is an important principle of transferability involved; this he defines as: 'The ability of each person in a given ethclass to move to another community and take his place within the same segment of the population marked off by ethnic group and social group' (Gordon 1964: 162).

This model conflicts with an older view of American society in which it was thought that class and ethnic identities and values were incompatible, and that the internal differentiation of ethnic groups on class lines would undermine ethnicity. The following may be taken as representative of that viewpoint: 'Our class system functions for a large proportion of ethnics to destroy the ethnic sub-system and to increase assimilation. The mobile ethnic is much more likely to be assimilated than the non-mobile one' (Warner & Srole 1945: 284).

It is not the purpose here to discuss the relative merits of these models of the American social system (all else considered a survey of the literature would raise more questions than the available evidence can apparently answer), but simply to suggest some lines which might guide the analysis of data from another area. Thus, in Kampala does the existence of principles of stratification that cut across ethnic groups result in the breakdown of ethnic boundaries, and if so in what way and why? Or do we find the emergence of ethclasses of the kind suggested by Gordon? Or does something entirely different occur?

SOCIAL STRATA, ETHNIC GROUPS, AND BOUNDARIES AT NSAMBYA

In two previous publications (Grillo 1969a and 1969b) I showed that African employees of the railways are relatively 'committed' to an urban and industrial way of life. For example, the average length of service in the industry is about thirteen years and most married men keep their wives and children with them in the town for much of the year. At the same time significant links are retained with the rural area of origin where most workers claim they will retire when their working days are over. In Kampala itself railwaymen form a relatively closed community with life centring largely around the workplace and the housing estate, though most individuals have at least some ties which link them with residents of other parts of the city. Railwaymen at Kampala form part of a wider 'railway community' representatives of which are to be found throughout East Africa, wherever the railways operate. This community is bound together by the formal and informal ties that arise from the work process, the system of inter-depot transfers, and from the fact that all railwaymen share a common sub-culture derived from the structure of the industry. This manifests itself in a number of ways, but the most significant for present purposes is the idiom through which differences of status are articulated.

Within the community, as perhaps throughout urban Africa, there is an intense interest in relative status. An individual's rank is largely determined by reference to the following variables: occupation, income, education, and 'grade'. Occupation generally involves four categories, unskilled, skilled, clerical, and 'officer', and is a measure of status shared with other Kampala residents, as is education and income. The fourth variable is peculiar to the railways which operate a complex grading system. This consists of four 'groups' – Superscale, Group A, Group B, and Group C – each with its own internal divisions. Thus Group B includes an executive division and eleven grades, eleven up to one (at least at the time of the study). All railway

164

posts from a porter to the general manager are graded, the grade determining basic salary and rights to a number of perquisites. Of these the most important is the 'class' of free housing to which the worker is entitled. There are seven 'classes' ranging from single room 'landies' to the most lavish colonial-style bungalows. The houses in each class are located in different parts of the estate. Each of the four status variables are partially independent – a man could have high educational qualifications, but a low grade, or a low grade but a high income derived from non-railway sources – but there is in fact considerable covariation. Where discrepancies occur they tend to become points of conflict. Taken as a whole the status variables indicate what kind of work a man does and with whom, his position in the industrial hierarchy in relation to others, where he lives on the estate and who his neighbours are, what his spending power is, and what he can consume in a community setting much store by conspicuous consumption. There are also expectations about the behaviour appropriate in relationships between those at the same or different levels and a series of stereotypes which are thought to indicate the personalities of those in different statuses.

The detailed documentation of these status differences will not be undertaken here, though some evidence on their significance in interaction may be found in the case studies considered later. Briefly it may be stated that in the first instance the community can be thought of as divided into strata between which there are differences of culture and increasingly of interest – those Africans at or above a certain level in Group B are seen to be, and often see themselves as, on the management side of industry, Bwana Railway. From the actors' viewpoint the status variables provide a kind of grid or map by reference to which any railwayman can locate the position of any other and thus determine what form their relationship should take. This, however, is not the only map available. Each individual has an identity or set of identities deriving from his supposed ethnic origin or ancestry. I include here not only 'tribe', but also sub-divisions of tribes, groupings of tribes and nations. Thus, as a Luo a man comes from a particular location that will be in either Central or South Nyanza. He is also, as a Luo, a Nilotic and thus linked to Acholi, Alur, and others. He is also a Kenyan and thus shares a common identity with a Luhya who is a Bantu and so on. These identities imply or may be used to imply common heritage, culture, and interest. They may also be seen, by the people themselves, as entailing common values and a common type of personality. Kenyans, for example, often see themselves as industrious, go-ahead people determined to succeed, whilst Ugandans are out to enjoy themselves and abjure hard work. I reiterate that these are perceived differences. These identities also imply relative degrees of solidarity and opposition to those with other identities. Thus ethnic identity, like grade or education, may be used to locate an appropriate mode of behaviour for two people to employ in a relationship. Ethnic identity therefore entails a set of statuses and a set of roles with which the individual operates in the related spheres of inter- and intra-ethnic relations.

It has been stated that the assertion of common ethnic identity will be understood to imply a claim to solidarity and equality. Epstein, writing of the Copperbelt, makes a similar point when he notes that: 'Membership of a tribe . . . imposes an obligation, vaguely defined though it may be, to give mutual aid and support' (Epstein 1961: 51). This formulation is too imprecise. What form do these obligations take, how are they fulfilled, and what are the consequences for the emergent structure? In order to narrow the focus of this study we will concentrate attention on the tribal ethnic group, leaving aside other levels of ethnic identity. Analytically it is very difficult to separate general obligations to fellow ethnics from the more specific obligations derived from kinship, friendship, and neighbourhood back home, i.e. the rural areas from which individuals come. Their significance for inter and intra-ethnic relations derives from the way in which the exercise of the obligations is interpreted and the extent to which, as a result, ethnic boundaries are created or maintained in the urban areas. In a previous publication I showed that the members of different ethnic groups are not randomly distributed through the departments and sections of railway organization (Grillo 1969a: 302–3). There are in fact throughout the industry ethnic enclaves that persist through time and apparently arise through a process similar to that which has been described as 'chain-migration' (MacDonald 1964: 90; Price 1969: 210), that is by recruitment through networks of kinsmen and friends from back home. Other unpublished data indicate that the process appears to be widespread in other industries in Kampala. In the publication cited I argued that these ethnic enclaves are not the result of ethnicity but of 'kinship'. This was naïve, since the process and the result are interpreted by others – by members of other ethnic groups, and by the European management – in undeniably ethnic terms, as when the high incidence of Ankole in jobs involving sweeping and cleaning is explained by reference to the value system of that particular ethnic group. While those who benefit from this system may often deny its implication of 'tribalism' they will in certain circumstances interpret the situation as a manifestation of ethnic solidarity or interest or even personality, as when it is argued that Ganda are too 'soft' to undertake work in the locomotive shed and that it has to be done by Luo and Luhya.

A similar point may be made with respect to housing. Many people use ethnic ties to establish their first foothold in the urban area. In a 10 per cent sample of household heads conducted at Nsambya in April 1965 it was found that 15·4 per cent of the estate population consisted of relatives and friends of working railwaymen. This section of the community, made up in roughly equal numbers of employed men looking for accommodation, unemployed men looking for jobs, and children 'schooling' in Kampala, has a high turnover rate. In any one year most households have at least one temporary visitor of this kind. In another sample conducted at the Kiswa housing estate in Kampala East 78 per cent of respondents claimed to have lived with a friend or relative on first arriving in the city. Such processes give rise to ethnic clusters in multi-occupied dwellings, and in some places small ethnic neighbourhoods. These clusters and enclaves are perceived by outsiders and interpreted by insiders in ethnic terms – thus the heavily Luo area near Kibuli is known as 'Little Kisumu' (cf. Parkin 1969b: 290).[2]

So then, although obligations to help with employment and accommodation derive specifically from ties of kinship and friendship their fulfilment may be interpreted by reference to a wider notion of ethnic solidarity and may result in lines along which ethnic boundaries may be drawn. At the very least the processes entail some degree of interaction among those who share a common ethnic identity. More important perhaps is the idea, particularly strong among Luo and Luhya, that an individual's attitude towards his home people, as expressed in his willingness to help them with jobs and housing, is reflected in his standing or reputation within the ethnic group as a whole. The same applies to the operation of other rural–urban links. For most people 'home' means the sub-county in some part of rural East Africa where they and usually their fathers were born. At Nsambya 85 per cent of the sample houshold heads had spent their annual leave at home, and from most households at least one member, a wife or a child, is absent in the rural home for some part of the year. The ebb and flow of personnel between town and country maintains a constant circulation of goods, cash, and information – on average 9 per cent urban income is sent back in the form of cash and remittances. Most too retain at least an interest in land, though few are active farmers. Thus, each person has some degree of orientation towards a community outside the industry and the housing estate which involves him in obligations and interests costing time and money, and which is perceived as being part of his ethnic identity and a component in his relative status. The same remarks apply to a sphere of activity that is often critical in poly-ethnic systems – marriage.

The marriage patterns of Kampala residents have been documented by Parkin (1966b: chap. 5) and my own data can only support and supplement his findings. In the Nsambya sample seventy-three marriages were recorded and of these only six, or 8·2 per cent, were between members of different ethnic groups. Of these three were between Ganda and Soga, one was Nyoro-Toro, one Nubi-Nyoro, and the last was between a Nyamwezi, from Tanzania, born at Masindi in Western Uganda, and a local woman. All these mixed marriages, therefore, were between individuals closely connected with the Interlacustrine Bantu cultural complex and may in one sense be said to be intra-ethnic. In another study conducted by a medical research worker examining child-rearing practices, fifty-one Luo household heads were contacted of whom only one had a non-Luo spouse, a girl from Lango. That there are so few inter-ethnic unions is not surprising, though I agree with Parkin that one must distinguish between 'permanent' and 'temporary' arrangements. Casual sexual relations are typically inter-ethnic and relatively free, though among Luo and Luhya at least a man is expected to indulge with moderation and discretion. Longer-term interest in the opposite sex is closely supervised by relatives and friends, especially with regard to courtship and marriage. One Luo informant whose interest in Ganda women was felt to be excessive was the subject of an intensive campaign spread over a whole year designed to induce him to marry a girl from his own ethnic group. A continuous supply of eligible girls was brought up from home for his consideration, and on three occasions he was taken or sent on tours of South Nyanza to survey the prospects. Threats were made by his father that unless the man married soon he, the father, would not hesitate to take a fourth wife, a step which would embarrass the man since it would imply that he was too young to marry. Unfortunately the affair was unresolved when I had to leave the field.

Although this young man's obduracy is perhaps unusual and the resistance of most crumbles under the pressure, permanent inter-ethnic unions do sometimes occur. In that event Luo, at least, may bring into play a second line of defence. Another Luo informant married a Gisu girl who was promptly whisked off to Kenya to undergo a stiff course in Luo language and culture. Witnessing part of this one was not clear whether the man's mother and sisters were training the girl to be a good Luo wife or simply making her life so miserable that she would be forced to leave. In fact the marriage survived. A third line of defence exists with respect to children. Another informant established a temporary union with a Ganda girl who bore him a child. When the baby was one year old, by which time the union had broken up, he was removed from the charge of his mother on the insistence of his father's parents and taken home, in this case to North Tanzania. Although both anthropologists and their informants see marriage as a critical symbol of the strength of inter-ethnic boundaries, among Luo and Luhya intermarriage probably occurs more frequently than is generally recognized or admitted.[3] However, since the children of such unions take the identity of one or other of the parents, intermarriage itself cannot be taken, in any simple way, as a measure of the breakdown of ethnic boundaries.

In the related spheres of recruitment to employment, urban accommodation, the maintenance of rural–urban links, and marriage we find a nexus of activities that orientate the individual towards those with whom he shares an ethnic identity and, by drawing him away from the members of other ethnic groups, create and sustain ethnic boundaries. Frequently, too, as we know from the work of Little, Parkin, and others in urban Africa, and in many studies from outside the African continent, this orientation may be reinforced by and expressed in the formal organization of ethnic associations. Once again my material can only supplement the work of Parkin (1966a, 1969a). In the Nsambya sample two-thirds of Luo and Luhya respondents were members of their tribal and/or locational associations, though among other ethnic groups the proportion was found to be as low as 21 per cent. In fact at Nsambya, compared with the areas of Kampala studied by Parkin (Nakawa and Naguru), there was apparently much less active interest in ethnic associations even among Luo and Luhya, an issue which cannot be tackled here. However, the overall impression is one of a strong intra-ethnic orientation. In fact as will perhaps emerge in the subsequent discussion such a picture is too simple.

This section began with an account of status and prestige variables and indicated that by reference to occupation, grade, and so on, the community could be seen as divided into social strata. We then saw something of the extent to which relations among railwaymen are bounded by ethnic criteria. We must now attempt to see how these two principles of organization fit together. Our starting-point for this discussion will be the analysis of the kinds of people that individual railwaymen choose to associate with in leisure-time activities. Any railwayman has a large number of contacts, from among his relatives and friends from home, from neighbours on the estate, from workmates, and from other sources such as churches, sports clubs, and so on. From among these he may select a few who become his close friends. On Nsambya most men have such close associates who frequently meet together to form a small group or clique. These cliques, which are seen by the people themselves as a socially significant phenomenon, consist of those who claim each other as members of 'our group'. Together they go out drinking, to dances, nightclubs, football matches, and so on. Between the members of such a group there is often a complex network of debt and credit, and there may be 'common' property, e.g. a car owned by one, but for the use of all. The group frequently operates as a decision-making unit and a force for social control. Their unity is often expressed through the device of using certain words, phrases, and gestures in a way only understandable by one of their number. They may talk in an elliptical and allusive fashion, especially when discussing sexual matters. On what basis are these groups formed? According to what criteria do railwaymen select their friends? In

TABLE 1 *The composition of small groups at Nsambya*

No.	Occupation	Grade	Educational level	Ethnic composition
i	Labourers in goods shed	Group c	illiterate	Acholi
ii	Loco firemen	Group c	primary	Luhya (Wanga location)
iii	Loco firemen	Group c	primary	Luhya (Samia location)
iv	Loco firemen	Group c	primary	Luo (Alego location)
v	Compound cleaners	Group c	illiterate	Ankole
vi	DTS clerks	B VI–VIII	secondary	Luo, Luhya, Samia
vii	Travelling ticket-examiners	B VII–VIII	intermediate	Soga, Toro, Acholi, Tanzanian
viii	Train-guards	B VII–VIII	intermediate	Soga, Toro
ix	Clerks, all union officers	B VII–IX	intermediate/ secondary	Luhya, Samia, Toro
x	Loco drivers	B VI–VII	illiterate	Luo, Luhya, Ganda
xi	Officers	B IV	secondary	Taita, Gisu
xii	Officers	B II–IV	higher	Lango, Tanzanian
xiii	Officers	B II–IV	secondary	Luhya
xiv	Officers	B I–II	secondary	Luo

Table 1 some information is given on the composition of fourteen such groups.

As *Table 1* shows the key variables underlying the composition of these groups appears to be occupation, the industrial unit in which the members work, grade and hence income, and level of education. Another factor not mentioned in the table is age, all groups consisting of people of roughly the same generation. Most groups had about four or five members. The information on ethnic composition indicates two things. First, low status groups tend to be ethnically homogeneous, while higher status groups tend to be more mixed, though not always. Second, ethnic ties seem to unite people within but not between strata. A simple statement of composition is, however, insufficient. We need to see how groups operate principles of inclusivity and exclusivity. For this purpose I will consider in some detail group number vi.

The members of this group happened also to be neighbours on the estate. *Figure 1* shows the cluster of houses from which they were drawn. The clique consisted of individuals A, B, C, and E. Of the others in the house cluster J was with group viii, G with

FIGURE 1 *A house cluster at Nsambya*

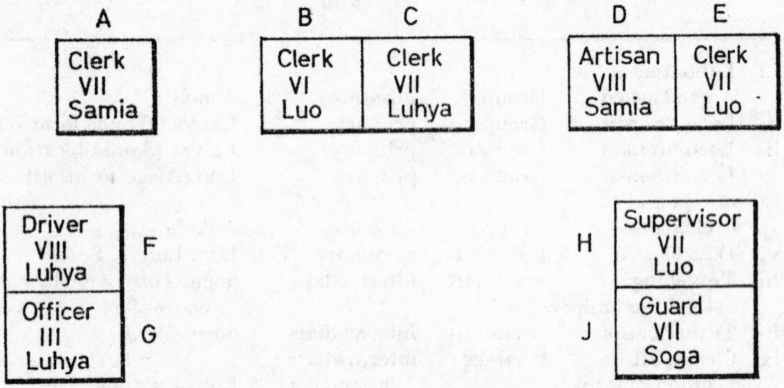

Note: For each householder information is given on occupation, grade (all in Group *B*), and tribe

xiii, and D, F, and H had their own associations not listed in the table. On several occasions F made overtures to C stressing the fact that they were 'neighbours and from the same tribe' and hence should be friends, but was always rebuffed. To the members of group vi, D and H were figures of fun, the former because he was 'always getting drunk' and involved in fights, the latter because of the connotations of his job. He supervised the cleaning of railway carriages and was known as the 'shitman'. Moreover he was said to have pretensions above his status; he could be seen leaving for work each morning in an immaculate white suit and solar topee. It should be recorded that themes of drunkenness, violence, and dirt appear frequently in statements about lower grades and occupations and about other ethnic

172

groups at Nsambya and elsewhere.[4] Also, J was shunned because he had once been charged with theft, though subsequently acquitted. His occupational group had a reputation, justified or not, for adding to their salaries illicitly.

The relationships between B and G and between C and G were interesting. B claimed that formerly he and G had been good friends, sharing his, B's, car on outings to bars and nightclubs. At that time G had been a Grade VI clerk. Subsequently he was transferred to Nairobi on promotion. He had been transferred back to Kampala as an officer and had dropped his former associates. G and C were closely related classificatory brothers who had grown up together in Ebunyore location in Western Kenya. They had gone to the same secondary school, and when G went to the Railway Training School in Nairobi, C had followed him a year later. Thereafter their careers diverged, for G had relatively greater success in achieving promotion. This led to considerable tension in his relationship with C, indeed to its virtual severance. The problems of C and G will concern us again later.

Although the evidence shows that the key factor underlying small group composition is relative status, the significance of the ethnic factor should not be underestimated. Seven of the fourteen groups in *Table 1* consisted entirely of people from the same tribe, and four more consisted wholly or largely of either Kenyans or Ugandans. The emergence of these latter as ethnic categories is noted in the work of Parkin and the phenomenon deserves fuller consideration than can be accorded here. However, inter-ethnic relationships seem more likely to occur in the upper echelons of the status system. To put it another way, with respect to the formation of friendships ethic boundaries appear to be stronger at the lower status levels. Parkin also reaches this conclusion with regard to Nakawa and Naguru when he writes: 'A larger number of lower-status people have more ethnocentrically based recreational activities, friends and neighbours' (Parkin 1969b: 294). At Nsambya this emerges, for example, if we consider the locus of the primary recreational activity, viz. drinking. The higher status groups are much more likely to frequent nightclubs and bars in the city, or at least those bars near Nsambya where European beer and spirits are sold, while the lower status groups tend to drink in unofficial bars (usually in the back room of someone's house) selling home-brewed African beer made from maize, millet, or banana according to the ethnic group.

Combining the two variables of ethnicity and social status we get the impression of a community in which there are strong interactional boundaries between strata and at least in the lower echelons between ethnic groups. In some respects Gordon's ethclass model is not inappropriate. Even the notion of transferability is applicable since there is considerable inter-depot mobility, literally on transfer, and at each depot there is an ethclass structure available into which the new arrival may fit. Such a model, however, is at the best descriptive. It also presents a too static picture of both ethnic and status relations. We have to consider systematic variation in ethnic boundaries, as for example in comparing marriage and friendship for high status persons. There is variation too at all levels in regard to ties which arise out of neighbourhood and work. Although they have not been considered here, such relationships may involve obligations and allegiances which cut across ethnic boundaries even for unskilled workers. In a previous paper (Grillo 1969a) I showed that ethnic ties and the language of ethnic interest appear under certain conditions to be significant resources for those competing for control of the trade union. Note that such competitors are largely middle-status clerks who under other conditions appear to be relatively unethnocentric. Other sources of variation include the possibility that some ethnic groups as a whole might be more or less ethnically inclined or that a group maintains a firmer boundary with one ethnic group than another. Clearly also differences through time should be considered and the extent to which boundaries in a local community are sharpened or blurred in response to distant events and issues. There are also variations between depots and between various areas of Kampala which in the long run also have to be explained. In order to find a model that helps us to understand such variations and also provides a more dynamic framework for the analysis of relationships between those in different ethclass categories I find it necessary to adopt an approach which is more 'individualistic' since it attempts to explain such variations in part at least by reference to the ways in which individuals handle their relationships. The fruitfulness or otherwise of this approach should be judged largely by the extent to which it furthers our understanding of the material.

MAPS AND MODES

Both ethnic and status categories form classificatory systems, cognitive maps, which may be said, following Mitchell, to provide 'mechanisms whereby relationships with strangers may be organized in what of necessity must be a fluid social situation' (Mitchell 1956: 30). They are, however, more than intellectual systems since they carry implications about the codes of behaviour appropriate for particular relationships. These codes of behaviour I will refer to as 'modes'. In the simplest and most general terms these modes include solidarity, respect, avoidance, distance, deference, hostility, and so on, though each may have a specific behavioural component. In the African urban literature interest in these systems derives largely from Mitchell's application of the Bogardus 'social-distance test'. This test has been criticized on a number of grounds including the suggestion that it is a poor predictor of actual behaviour (Banton 1967: chap. 13; Williams 1964: chap. 9). Mitchell himself argues against this in the present volume. The criticism carries less weight if we consider attitudes as measured in the test as the guidelines for ideal behaviour, which may be modified according to context. More significant, perhaps, is the problem that such tests are usually uni-dimensional, measuring an ethnic variable only. This, it may be argued, oversimplifies 'cognitive reality' in that it omits other systems of classification that may also be relevant for the understanding of behaviour. Thus, at Nsambya we would have to include at least the following in any realistic cognitive map: ethnic identity, age, sex, occupation, income, grade, education, work unit, house cluster. In theory such a map may be represented by an n-dimensional matrix, the cells of which are formed by the intersection of the different variables. Any two individuals may locate each other by reference to one or more of the variables and thus attempt to put into operation an appropriate behavioural mode. Physically it is impossible to represent this model. In *Figure 2* will be found a grossly simplified version.

There the dimensions are reduced to two, ethnic identity and a general status identity. It is assumed that each dimension has two values only – same/different, although in fact 'different status' can mean varying degrees of higher or lower. Likewise 'different ethnic group' could refer to one of thirty or more, involving degrees of distance. It is also assumed that for any individual to categorize another as a member of the same ethnic or status group signifies a claim to solidarity, a plus, the opposite signifies distance, a minus. Since there is always more than one dimension available by which to locate an appropriate relationship between two people, there is some degree of choice open to each as to which aspects will be emphasized, which muted. It was clearly in the interest of F in the house cluster discussed earlier to stake his claim to a relationship with C by reference to

FIGURE 2 *Solidarity/distance matrix*

Status	Ethnic group	
	Same	Other
Same	+ + ^{w}	+ − ^{x}
Other	− + ^{y}	− − ^{z}

the dimensions of ethnic identity and neighbourhood. C in turn rejected him by reference to occupation. Similarly competitors for office in the trade union attempted to recruit support by stressing now solidarity deriving from the work unit, now an ethnic tie, and so on. However, freedom of manœuvre is limited by, among other things, the extent to which action and attitude are judged by a public beyond the particular relationship, as we will see shortly.

It will be recalled that Mitchell's discussion of ethnic maps relates specifically to the understanding of casual relationships in unstructured situations. This paper is primarily concerned with interaction not between strangers but with relationships between members of a relatively close-knit community. I would, however, argue that basically the same model may be used for understanding both. Two possible sources of difference between the two kinds of situation are the amount of information available for the purposes of classification and the likelihood of feed-back from one relationship to another or within the relationship at one point in time and another. What information is available to two men meeting casually? This depends in large part on the degree of visibility with regard to the two variables of ethnic identity and status. Visibility means the amount of information that can be gleaned by sensory perception. Visible differences, of course, often form the apparent basis for ethnic classification, or tend to be associated with it. In Ulster Catholics sometimes claim to be able to tell a Protestant at a glance. In a Chicago slum it was found that: 'Clothing, grooming and personal display add another area in which [the] residents can look for and find ethnic differences' (Suttles 1968: 67). This besides differences in language and non-verbal forms of communication. Among Luo and Luhya ethnic differences are openly displayed through the practice, now dying out, of removing different combinations of teeth. Once, out walking with a Luhya man, a stranger approached us on the same path. My friend greeted him in Luo and the man replied. My friend told me that he had identified the man as a Luo because of his teeth. In Kampala where dozens of languages are spoken many people had the knack of being able to place someone ethnically on the basis of a few words overheard at a distance, and many claimed to know a few words of up to a dozen languages, 'To know whether they intend to kill me'.

Relative status is perhaps even more visible than ethnic identity. The stereotypes of the clerk with his suit, white shirt, and tie, and of the porter with his ragged shorts and vest are well enough known to be extensively parodied in Swahili and Luganda popular songs. Thus, each individual has numerous cues that he may offer and receive or choose to accept to help him decide what relational mode he will try to employ. In casual interaction what he actually does may in part be determined by context. In the episode on the path described above both parties were of roughly equal status to judge by appearance. Why then did my friend emphasize his knowledge of Luo? The reason may have been that after the initial greeting he attempted successfully to obtain a favour from the stranger who turned out to be the clerk in charge of a building we wanted to inspect. That is he used knowledge of Luo to stress solidarity in a way familiar to any anthropologist. Although much more needs to be said about casual interaction we should return to the main theme of this paper.

Figure 2, though grossly oversimplified, does indicate four significant combinations of ethnic and social status that recur frequently at Nsambya. In order to simplify still further we may consider what the cells of the matrix imply for a Luo or Luhya clerk in the middle echelons of the industry. In two of the four types of relationship, ego–x and ego–y, there appear to be possibilities for dissonance since two conflicting modes are available, solidarity *and* distance. With the other two there is apparent congruity. Each of the four possible relationships deserves the fullest consideration, but here we will deal with two only. In the case of ego–z, i.e. relationships with those of different, say lower, status and of a different ethnic group there would literally be avoidance, since their paths may rarely cross either at work or on the estate. If they do interact then ego–z is likely to act distantly but politely, invariably uses Swahili, may 'joke' if he wants something done, may employ a certain, rather patronizing, tone of voice. He expects and usually receives deference. It is accepted that they need not greet each other when passing even if they recognize each other as railwaymen. They have no claims on each other. Sometimes, however, these relationships may be used indirectly in political games, as when a Gisu clerk obtained a job for a Luo boy so that the Luo in his section would 'be happy' and support his bid for leadership in the trade union.

The ego–z relationship may be contrasted with ego–y, i.e. lower status members of the same ethnic group. This relationship implies two opposing modes and various responses are possible. Thus depending on the context one rather than the other may be emphasized, or there may be an attempt made to maintain an overall balance between the two by trading off distance in one situation against solidarity in another. Compare, for example, friendship and marriage where this seems to happen. In fact there emerges a publicly acceptable ideal mode appropriate to such relationships which is in some ways a synthesis of the opposing elements and which in some respects resembles a patron–client relationship. In the cases to be discussed later it will be seen that it is with some notion of an ideal mode of this kind that actual performances are compared, and that deviation from the mode, for example by undue emphasis on distance without a corresponding gesture to solidarity, may lead to a bad reputation. Thus, an educated clerk should never stress his knowledge of English or Swahili, though he may switch into the latter as a joke. He must greet people warmly, inquiring after their family and their health. He should shake hands when meeting, though he may expect to be accorded a special deferential gesture in the course of the act. These relationships are also expected to have a specific content which relates to the discussion in the earlier part of this paper. For this includes fulfilment of obligations in regard to jobs, housing, loans, gifts, and so on. He should also play his part as a leader of his locational association in return for which he is accorded power and prestige. He may also expect support should he run for office in the trade union. In short, his standing in the community as a whole may depend on his performance in this relationship.

This general discussion may be illustrated by reference to cases. Take the examples of c and g from the house cluster described earlier. When g first obtained promotion to welfare officer his relatives and friends from Ebunyore were pleased. 'Our man is doing well. Now we shall eat.' However, g forsook his former associates, even those from back home. b's lament that now he saw nothing of g was repeated to me time and again by others. He became, as someone put it, 'a lonely man, a man who walks alone', a phrase used constantly to refer to someone maintaining distance. There is also an implication of *hubris* and indeed in g's case the fates were stirred. A rumour circulated that the police had been asked to check the welfare accounts. g fled from Kampala, a wanted man. Several weeks later he returned, was arrested, tried, and sentenced to eighteen months' imprisonment. Before the arrest his fellow ethnics had been annoyed that g had not approached them with his troubles: 'If he had come to us when he was in debt we would have found the money for him.' They were also worried what members of other ethnic groups would say. When he was arrested several Luhya went down to the place where he was held to ask if they could help. He replied, 'Only if you have money to get me a lawyer'. Being present at the time this remark was made I was made conscious of the shock with which it was received. As a result many claimed that he had forfeited the right to their help. At about this point his father arrived from the rural area and tried to rally support. At his insistence a small committee was formed to collect money. The appeal directed to all Luhya failed abysmally, only a few shillings being subscribed. For example, although c was supposed to be one of the collectors he gave up after a short while and adjourned to the bar.

The case of c was in fact not dissimilar. He too was said to be a lonely and proud man who rarely associated with fellow ethnics in lower grades. If he gave a party at his house they were never invited. He sometimes failed even to observe the elementary courtesies of greeting, doing so consciously since he once gave me a long justification for this behaviour. He had also married a girl from outside his ethnic group, an educated Ganda. The children of this marriage were being brought up more as Ganda than Luhya. Unhappily the youngest of the children died as a baby. At first it was proposed to bury the child at Budo, the mother's home, subsequently, however, c took the advice of an elderly and respected Luhya who argued that the child should be buried at Nsambya cemetery. This man arranged the funeral, collecting several Luhya as grave diggers and inviting another Luhya who was an amateur preacher to say prayers. At the graveside hymns were sung and a short speech made in which c was urged in future not to ignore his relatives and friends from home. In contrast we may consider the case of b, who was c's neighbour. b, a Luo, had also married a girl from another ethnic group, a Toro. As against c's wife who spoke Luhya only reluctantly b's wife spoke fluent Luo to the extent that other Luo on the estate were surprised to learn her ethnic origin. The children were brought up as Luo speakers and played with other Luo children, in contrast with c's who were bilingual and kept under the supervision of a Ganda *ayah*. Moreover b was known as a man who respected other Luo and Luo affairs, being a prominent member of his locational association which met from time to time at his house. He had also, at one time, been a trade union officer, as against c who had once stood in a union election with conspicuous lack of success.

To avoid the suggestion that successful Luo are being contrasted with unsuccessful Luhya we may as a final example take the case of k, not mentioned previously. He is a Luhya who at the time of the study was a Grade ix clerk in the mechanical engineer's office and general secretary to the trade union. κ's brother was also employed by the railway as a Group c fireman. Their relative positions in the railway framework led them into different cliques, κ was a member of group ix in *Table 1*, his brother in group ii. There was, however, no apparent hostility between them. κ, the elder, had done much for his brother, paying school fees, housing him, finding him a job. He had fulfilled all his formal obligations. This also applied to his relations back home, in contrast with c who was reputed never to have sent even his mother a gift. κ never stressed his distance from his brother and other Luhya. On one occasion when we were drinking together in the bar at the Railway Club a Luhya engine-driver, grimy in his work clothes and drunk, came up to κ and reminded him that he was his 'mother's brother' and requested a dance. They waltzed around the bar, κ proclaiming loudly that this was all part of the 'African way of life'. Later in his career κ went to England for three months to study industrial relations. The trip seemed to go to his head and for a while on his return he too became 'proud'. This phase, however, lasted only a short time and he soon returned to normal.

In these cases we have contrasted two responses to the problem of reconciling conflicting modes of behaviour presented by the structural framework. It seems clear that from the point of view of lower status members of an ethnic group there is an interest in ensuring that higher status members retain a sense of solidarity and maintain their obligations. But why should the latter need to operate the system in this way? The answers have been suggested already. First, respect is not automatically accorded to a person in a high position. The content and quality of his relationships with others, especially his inferiors, also counts not only among them, but also among his peers. This, however, merely puts the problem back one stage further. Why should a man be concerned to earn the respect of those below him in the system? Not all, of course, are but those who do clearly obtain certain benefits. Thus, this respect is necessary if he is to compete successfully in those institutions such as ethnic and sports associations and the trade union within which he can obtain power and prestige. Moreover, as I argued in another paper (Grillo 1969b) it should be noted that men at all levels are still dependent for long-term security on retaining a rural base, almost certainly in the ethnic homeland, and for this purpose, if for no other, ethnic ties must be kept in play. Although this model is primarily aimed at explaining the dynamics of intra-ethnic relations it also helps us understand one of the factors involved in inter-ethnic relations between high status people. The mode adopted in the ego–x relationships is clearly affected by the state of ego–y relationships. To put it another way, ego–x and ego–y are interdependent. The state of the boundaries within and between ethnic groups are thus linked. It has not, however, been possible to develop this point fully in this paper.

To summarize the argument let me repeat that the paper began with a holistic approach which attempted to convey an overall impression of the structure of the community when the two organizational principles of ethnicity and social status are considered simultaneously. It was found that the ethclass model, as used in the American sociological literature, has a limited usefulness as a representation of the structure of Nsambya society. It is, however, too static and does not enable us to account satisfactorily for apparent variations and discrepancies. For this reason recourse was made to a more individualistic approach. In this ethnic and status ties are treated as a language of claims that may be employed instrumentally. Claims to solidarity or distance may be made or suppressed, accepted, rejected, or modified according to context and interest. There are, however, significant limitations to the freedom that individuals may have to manipulate their relationships in this way. Adopting one definition of a relationship rather than another, one mode rather than another, may have long-term implications in that attitudes and actions are in the end, in the close-knit world of the railway community, subject to public judgement. It is always open to deny one's ethnic identity or at least to ignore the claims of others on the basis of that identity, but for most people the costs of doing so outweigh the benefits. Given that this remains the case, it seems likely that ethnic identity, albeit in a modified form, will continue to be a significant factor, at least for the kind of people we have considered in this paper.

NOTES

[1] See, for example, Barth 1969: 14; Berry 1965: 46; Gordon 1964: 24; Gulliver 1969: Introduction; Shibutani & Kwan 1965: 47; Warner & Srole 1945: 28.

[2] The techniques devised by Professor J. C. Mitchell for the analysis of clustering, and discussed by him in this volume, are relevant for the data mentioned here.

[3] There appears to be considerable intermarriage in the rural areas where Luo and Luhya are neighbours, e.g. on the borders of Gem and Kisa locations in Western Kenya. Luo seem to make net gains from these marriages.

[4] The theme of animality appears frequently in ethnic and class ideologies. At Nsambya one can hear similar remarks made by clerks about unskilled workers, by Luo about Ganda and vice versa.

REFERENCES

BANTON, M. 1965. Social Alignment and Identity in a West African City. In H. Kuper (ed.), 131–47.

—— 1967. *Race Relations*. London: Tavistock Publications; New York: Barnes & Noble.

BARTH, F. (ed.). 1969. *Ethnic Groups and Boundaries*. London: Allen & Unwin.

BERRY, BREWTON. 1965. *Race and Ethnic Relations*. Boston: Houghton Mifflin.

BLAU, PETER. 1964. *Exchange and Power in Social Life*. New York: John Wiley.

BROWN, JOHN. 1970. *The Unmelting Pot: An English Town and its Immigrants*. London: Macmillan.

COHEN, A. 1969a. *Custom and Politics in Urban Africa*. London: Routledge & Kegan Paul.

—— 1969b. Political Anthropology: The Analysis of the Symbolism of Power Relations. *Man* n.s. 4: 215–35.

COHEN, R. & MIDDLETON, E. (eds). 1970. *From Tribe to Nation in Africa: Studies in the Incorporation Process*. Scranton, Penn.: Chandler Publishing.

EPSTEIN, A. L. 1958. *Politics in an Urban African Community*. Manchester: Manchester University Press.

—— 1961. The Network and Urban Social Organisation. *Human Problems in British Central Africa* 24: 29–62.

FRAENKEL, M. 1964. *Tribe and Class in Monrovia*. London: Oxford University Press.

GANS, H. J. 1962. *The Urban Villagers: Group and Class in the Life of Italian-Americans*. Glencoe, Ill.: Free Press of Glencoe.

GORDON, MILTON. 1964. *Assimilation in American life*. New York: Oxford University Press.

GREENBERG, J. H. 1965. Urbanism, Migration and Language. In H. Kuper (ed.), 1965.

GRILLO, R. D. 1969a. The Tribal Factor in an East African Trade Union. In P. H. Gulliver (ed.), 297–321.

—— 1969b. Anthropology, Industrial Development and Labor Migration in Uganda. In D. Brokensha and M. Pearsall (eds), *The Anthropology of Development in Sub-Saharan Africa*. 77–84. Society for Applied Anthropology Monograph 10, University of Kentucky Press.

GULLIVER, P. H. (ed.). 1969. *Tradition and Transition in East Africa*. London: Routledge & Kegan Paul.

KUPER, H. (ed.). 1965. *Urbanization and Migration in West Africa*. California: University Press.

LUKES, STEVEN. 1968. Methodological Individualism Reconsidered. *British Journal of Sociology* **19**: 119–29.

MACDONALD, J. S., & L. D. 1964. Chain Migration, Ethnic Neighbourhood Formation and Social Networks. *Milbank Memorial Fund Quarterly* **42** (1): 82–97.

MERCIER, P. 1965. On the Meaning of 'Tribalism' in Black Africa. In P. Van den Berghe (ed.), *Africa: Problems of Change and Conflict*, 483–501. San Francisco: Chandler Publishing. 483–501.

MITCHELL, J. C. 1956. *The Kalela Dance*. Rhodes-Livingstone Paper No. 27. Manchester: Manchester University Press for Rhodes-Livingstone Institute.

PARKIN, D. J. 1966a. Urban Voluntary Associations as Institutions of Adaptation. *Man* n.s. **1**: 90–5.

—— 1966b. Types of Urban African Marriage in Kampala. *Africa* **36** (3).

—— 1969a. *Neighbours and Nationals in an African City Ward*. London: Routledge & Kegan Paul.

—— 1969b. Tribe as Fact and Fiction in an East African city. In P. H. Gulliver (ed.), 273–96.

PRICE, C. 1969. The Study of Assimilation. In J. A. Jackson (ed.), *Migration*. Sociological Studies No. 2. Cambridge: Cambridge University Press.

RYAN, ALAN. 1970. *The Philosophy of the Social Sciences*. London: Macmillan.

SHIBUTANI, T., & KWAN, K. M. 1965. *Ethnic Stratification*. New York: Macmillan.

SUTTLES, G. 1968. *The Social Order of the Slum*. Chicago: Chicago University Press.

WALLERSTEIN, I. 1965. Ethnicity and National Integration in West Africa. In P. Van den Berghe (ed.), 472–83.

184

WARNER, W. L., & SROLE, L. 1945. *The Social System of American Ethnic Groups*. Yankee City Series Volume III. Yale University Press.

WILLIAMS, R. M. JNR. 1964. *Strangers next door: Ethnic Relations in American Communities*. Englewood Cliffs, N.J.: Prentice-Hall.

Enid Schildkrout

Ethnicity and Generational Differences among Urban Immigrants in Ghana

THE PROBLEM: THEORETICAL ORIENTATION

This paper deals with the changing significance of ethnic identity among Mossi migrants and urban-born Mossi in the city of Kumasi, in the Ashanti region of Ghana.[1] By comparing the meaning of ethnicity for these two categories of urban immigrants, here referred to as first and second generation immigrants respectively, I hope to show how the significance of ethnicity changes in relation to changes in urban political and kinship organization. For the purposes of this paper, I deal with change by comparing the social and cultural contexts in which Mossi immigrants of different generations find themselves, rather than through a diachronic analysis of the history of the Mossi in Kumasi. The comparison of first and second generation immigrants leads to conclusions about the importance of structural factors and the irrelevance of culture for explaining the persistence of ethnicity as a basis of personal and group identity.

First, it may be helpful to set my own study in the context of past research on ethnicity, with particular reference to studies done in the African context. Since this paper is concerned with the functions of informal and formal urban associations, these remarks are directed to studies on this subject. The problem with many studies which attempt to explain the function, or functions, of complex social institutions is that they tend to generalize from specific cases, thereby running the risk of confusing the general and the particular. While we cannot entirely escape functional explanations,[2] we can attempt to use comparison to arrive at generalizations which fit different conditions under which the phenomenon in question appears. Once we accept this definition of our task, we may of course easily arrive at conclusions which, while valid, are of such generality that they can rarely be wrong, like Cohen's observation that

187

ethnic groups are interest groups (Cohen 1969: 3) or my own contention that we must view them primarily as structural categories, whose specific functions and cultural content may vary from time to time and place to place. This is inevitable; the alternative is to accept explanations that are as situationally specific as they are useless for cross-cultural comparison or generalization.

Many writers have been concerned with the functions of ethnicity in the traditional sociological sense: they have sought to describe the part that ethnic associations play in the social systems in which they are found.[3] For example, it has been noted that in the urban context, instead of traditional kinship groupings, we find voluntary (including ethnic) associations. The functions of these associations have then been described as equivalent to the functions of kinship groupings in rural contexts. In other writings, dealing with the modern nation state, associations in which recruitment is based on ethnicity have been regarded as stopgaps, performing social and political functions that incipient national organizations, such as welfare departments and political parties, are expected eventually to assume.[4] It is worth noting that both these examples, which are representative of much writing on ethnic associations, bring in hypotheses from outside the urban context, in one case from the rural context and in the other from that of the nation. Still other types of functional explanations of ethnicity have sought to show how it helps the individual migrant adapt from rural or urban life, or become integrated into the national polity.[5]

This concern with the functions of specific ethnic associations has taken us away from a consideration of why ethnicity persists when conditions change; functional explanations discuss the meaning of any existing social event or fact in terms of an existent situation, but do not necessarily lead to general explanations. For example, by hypothesizing that urban ethnic groups are substitutes for rural kinship groups, we cannot make any statement about their significance in urban social structure, except to add the inaccurate correlative assumption that certain kinds of kinship groups don't, but somehow ought to, exist in urban areas. If we move away from descriptions of the functions of ethnic groups in specific cases and from the tendency to bring in hypothetical rural/urban comparisons, if we emphasize the

188

need to do some 'comparative sociology' of different urban situations, or of the same urban setting over time, we may be able to arrive at generalizations about the meaning and the range of possible functions of ethnicity in the urban context. This also involves peeling off some of the cultural coating of ethnicity and discussing it in structural terms, in terms of the minimum conditions necessary for ethnicity to persist, regardless of culture and regardless of specific functions in particular cases.

Discussions of urban ethnicity have tended to be heavily descriptive because most writers, at least in the African context, have been concerned almost exclusively with migrants, rather than with settled or town born immigrants. Studies of migrants necessarily involve consideration of two very different social contexts, the rural and the urban. Many discussions of the institutions of urban migrants have, although not always explicitly, taken into account observations and assumptions about both social situations and explained urban institutions in terms of rural ones. This is so, despite Gluckman's (1940), Epstein's (1958), Mitchell's (1956), and others' emphasis on the social situation, because most studies have dealt with recent migrants who are in some ways still involved in their rural social networks. When generalizations are based on a comparison of the rural and urban settings, rather than of several urban ones, the resulting conclusions about urban institutions are likely to be of limited use, for while they may say something about migrants, they say little about urbanism *per se*. Let me take an example from the field of kinship since this is one aspect of ethnicity that concerns me here.

In rural contexts many anthropologists have noted the political importance of kinship groupings. Yet in urban areas we have ignored those advances in theory which help to understand the political and structural importance of kinship, and kinship has been relegated, so to speak, to the nuclear family. Politics and kinship have been described as if they were separate fields of behaviour in the urban setting, rather than as only analytically separable aspects of social action. It has been noted that the idiom of kinship is often used in urban areas and that this is a means of expressing a recognition of common ethnicity. In a metaphorical sense, tribesmen become kinsmen in towns.

189

This observation is accurate as far as it goes, but the conclusion which has often followed, that ethnic associations in urban situations are substitutes for the kinds of kinship groups that are found in rural areas, is too vague to have meaning and in many cases is clearly inaccurate, since both kinship groups (which may have nothing to do with ethnicity) and other expressions of ethnicity, including 'metaphorical kinship', often co-exist in town.

A concentration on studies of migrants, most of whom do not have extensive networks of 'real' kinsmen in town, has led anthropologists to regard urban kinship as something that exists in its 'real' form only in the nuclear family, while all other manifestations of kinship, such as the use of the kinship idiom in ethnic associations, are regarded as metaphorical. A theoretical assumption has entered the argument here and has affected much of our thinking on this matter, even where empirically it does not fit. This is that the awareness of ethnicity is somehow nurtured in the nuclear family and the domestic context, and is then extended by means of a kinship metaphor outside this context to tribesmen who are not 'real' kinsmen. In certain situations, where the nuclear family is the significant domestic unit, and where we are dealing only with migrants who are born in rural areas and who keep up their rural ties, this may be the case (see for example Parkin 1969) but it is by no means a general process that accounts for the persistence of ethnicity or for the use of a kinship idiom to describe relations between members of the same ethnic group. As I hope to show here, certain kinds of domestic situations may diminish an individual's sense of distinct ethnic identity; but then, when ethnicity persists, we must look for alternative explanations. In the Kumasi context the structure of the immigrants' domestic groups definitely mediates against the persistence of ethnic identities based on place or tribe of origin, and encourages the development of a wider sense of identity based upon the culture of the ethnically heterogeneous Muslim immigrant community described below. In this type of situation, we must recognize that ethnicity, in the sense of an identity based upon one's place of origin, persists in the wider social system for reasons that have nothing to do with socialization or with kinship *per se*.

There is, however, much that we can adopt from 'traditional'

190

kinship theory. Specifically, studies of kinship in rural contexts have shown the importance of kinship and in particular of descent as structural principles. It is unfortunate that in the urban context, only the affective, ego oriented aspects of kinship have been emphasized and its importance as a structural principle has been underestimated. As crucially important as networks of real and fictive kin ties are in urban areas, they are not the *only* aspect of kinship that deserves analysis. Descent is an important part of the concept of ethnicity, as it is of kinship, and it is this rather than the affective aspect of kinship that needs to be stressed. Once we place our emphasis on this aspect of kinship theory, the relationship between ethnicity in urban areas and traditional kinship theory may be illuminated.

Ethnicity as I am using the term may be defined at this stage in a somewhat tautological way as the recognition of categories of ethnic identity, defined according to some culturally accepted principle of differentiation. Barth's definition of ethnicity as 'categories of ascription and identification by the actors themselves' (1969: 10) is adequate as a start, although it is worth noting the ambiguity in the word 'actors', a term that may refer to members or to outsiders or to both. Ethnicity also seems always to involve some notion of common origin and descent, even though recruitment and identity may be brought about in other ways. Crissman's (1967) suggestion that we speak of ethnic communities rather than ethnic groups when we refer to the collection of individuals who identify with an ethnic category is also useful. This identification is usually objectively symbolized but it need not be and for this reason it may be difficult for an outside observer to evaluate its significance in a given situation. Obviously, like all social categories ethnic categories presuppose some amount of consensus. I am not concerned with the quantitative dimension of this, but only with the fact that once the categories exist, behaviour may be based upon recognition of them. Ethnicity is relevant in a social situation even if only one actor acknowledges its existence and acts according to norms or stereotypes that he associates with this categorization.

Ethnic communities *may be* culturally differentiated within a particular society, and they may use culturally defined symbols to express their distinctiveness, but I suggest that ethnicity *basically* has nothing to do with cultural differentiation, or, in other words, with cultural pluralism, although it is very often associated with it. This statement can be qualified by adding that this may be shown to be the case only after groups within a society have reached a particular level of cultural integration, such that they lose their distinct cultures but maintain their identity as social categories. Taking this qualification into account we may say that within a given society ethnic communities and groups – corporate or non-corporate – may or may not 'have' different cultures. Like the closely related concept of descent, ethnicity minimally implies a set of social categories giving rise to communities whose members may or may not have distinct sub-cultures. However, in terms of the larger society of which the ethnic communities are a part, the boundaries of ethnic communities are culturally defined. Ethnic group boundaries consist of symbols, and it is perhaps even more important that they be understood by outsiders than that they be accepted by the members themselves. Usually, however, boundaries are defined by *both* insiders and outsiders, in terms of their common culture, not in terms of the distinct sub-culture of any particular community. Any number of criteria such as place of origin, paternal or maternal descent, skin colour, or place of residence, like totems or clan ancestors, may provide symbols for differentiating ethnic communities, and the choice of which principle of categorization and which symbols of this a society adopts are cultural choices. But if in a particular society the recognition of boundaries is *all* that distinguishes one community from another, I would not maintain that they are culturally distinct. It is true that once ethnic communities are differentiated they tend to develop 'content', minimally providing stereotypes about how their members differ culturally from the members of other communities. In some cases there clearly are cultural differences including different value systems and typical behaviour patterns between ethnic communities. And very often, when there are no cultural differences, people try to create them if they want to preserve that identity. But I am still suggesting that we should not regard cultural differences as necessary conditions of ethnicity. It is sufficient that ethnic categories exist; the specific cultural coefficients that may but need not help to distinguish ethnic communities are of secondary importance. Were this not the case it would be impossible to explain the persistence of ethnicity in situations where different ethnic communities lose their cultural distinctiveness or change their symbols of identity.[6] The conseqences of this for the analysis of ethnicity among second generation urban immigrants will be discussed below, and some theoretical problems about the use of the term ethnicity will be reconsidered in light of this data.

THE BACKGROUND: THE MOSSI OF THE UPPER VOLTA

As the Mossi kingdom developed between the fourteenth and nineteenth centuries many different ethnic groups were incorporated into the society. Political incorporation led gradually to social and cultural integration, to a process of 'Mossisation',[7] so that a sense of Mossi identity was created although incorporated groups continued to maintain their separate identities for the purpose of determining political status. Mossi society was stratified and consisted of a royal estate, known as the Nakombse, within which there were ranked subdivisions corresponding to differential rights to hold particular offices; various commoner groups known collectively as Talse in the kingdom of Ouagadougou and as Foulse in the kingdom of Yatenga; and several other incorporated specialist groups such as blacksmiths (*saaba*), Muslim traders of Dioula origin (Yarse), pastoralists of Fulani origin, weavers of Songhai origin (Maranse) and others. The defining and integrating characteristic of Mossi society was its political system: all those who called themselves Mossi, *vis-à-vis* non-Mossi, recognized the right of members of a lineage of the Nakombse group to hold chiefship (*nam*). As the authority of the Nakombse rulers was extended territorially, through conquest and through a gradual process of migratory expansion in search of better farmlands, other groups were drawn into the Mossi kingdom and gradually identified themselves as Mossi. This did not necessarily imply the disappearance of former bases of corporate identity, for these, like Mossi identity, were still relevant in certain situations. Within the Mossi political system, one's ethnic identity ascribed on the basis of patrilineal descent and defined according to the group's common origin, determined one's political status.

The term Mossi does not refer to any specific estate or ethnic group in the society but rather refers to the composite totality which includes many sub-groups, differentiated by distinct traditions of origin, and in some cases by distinct roles and statuses in Mossi society.[8] Cultural integration accompanied the political expansion of the Mossi, making the emergence of a sense of Mossi identity possible. The various groups adopted a common language (Mole), and many other features of common culture: Mossi culture is an amalgam of many separate traditions, but as it developed the constituent groups lost their distinctive characteristics in varying degress. For example, royals whose lineages do not hold chiefships for many years become culturally and socially indistinguishable from commoners. Blacksmiths, Fulani, and Yarse are like commoners in most respects but typically have certain distinctive occupational and ritual roles. Even when these special roles are not performed, and when cultural integration becomes almost complete, as when Yarse become pagan agriculturalists and give up Islam and trading, when royals lose their claim to office, or when blacksmiths marry commoners and give up smithing, an ideology of ethnicity linked to the notion of descent maintains their distinctive social identities. Without this ideology of ethnicity, the Mossi political system could not have functioned as it did.[9]

In the traditional Mossi context, then, we find that as Mossi society developed, ethnic communities lost their distinctive cultural identities in varying degrees; at the same time ethnic categories became status categories which determined differential access to various forms of political and ritual power. Chiefs are conceptualized by the Mossi as an ethnic community; the Nakombse are all related to a single ancestor and all come from the same locality outside of Mossiland (from the south). Various commoner groups who hold access to specific ritual offices relating to the control of the earth, the rain, and so forth, are related in a similar manner. Conceptually these categories remain distinct, even though the cultural boundaries between groups often disappear and individuals may lose their claims to the distinctive entitlements of their status, as when Nakombse become ineligible for office, or when commoners hold political rather than ritual offices in chiefs' courts.

An indication of the extent to which cultural integration and political incorporation occurred in Mossi society may be gathered from the way the Mossi identify themselves and organize their communities when they migrate to other areas. In Ghana, all Mossi groups (Nakombse, Yarse, Talse, etc.) identify themselves as Mossi, and even in the context of *intra*-group interaction the divisions between the various ethnic groups in Mossi society become irrelevant. In the context of the heterogeneous immigrant communities of Ghana, the category Mossi becomes equivalent to the categories of Talse, Yarse, and so on, in Mossi society. That is, the category Mossi becomes a status category within a more inclusive political system. We may take this even further and add that when the status groups are clearly ranked, as they are in Mossiland, we are dealing with a stratified political system, wherein the relations between groups are expressed ritually and do not involve political competition; when they are not clearly ranked or are theoretically equal, we are dealing with a non-hierarchical or segmentary arrangement of ethnic groups, as is the case in Kumasi. There, we will see, since the status hierarchy is unstable, the articulation of ethnic groups is expressed politically, rather than ritually, and competition for status is possible. Although the distinctions between the ethnic sub-groups of Mossi society are irrelevant to a discussion of the socio-political organization of Mossi immigrant communities in Ghana, certain aspects of the traditional political system are relevant. Mossi society was divided into a number of territorial divisions (kingdoms), each of which was controlled by a descendant of the founding ancestor of the Mossi, Ouidiraogo, a putative grandson of the king of the Mamprusi-Dagomba kingdom to the south of Mossiland.[10] Several territorial divisions were recognized in Mossiland (e.g. Ouagadougou, Yatenga, Tenkoudougou, and Boussouma) all of whose kings were descendants of Ouidiraogo and, consequently, agnatic kinsmen of one another. Within each of the main kingdoms, territorial and administrative sub-divisions were recognized, each division having a hierarchy of officials replicating the central administrative hierarchy. Many of the same titles are found on all levels of government, from the village to the central administration, although the functions of specific offices of course varied at different levels. Many officials had functions both in local administrations and as subordinates to chiefs at the next higher level of political organization. The details of this system need not concern us here, but the basic concepts of territorial divisions and administrative offices are relevant to an analysis of the social organization of Mossi immigrants in Ghana.

The migrants I discuss in this paper come from all areas of Mossiland and from all the main groups in Mossi society. In Ghanaian towns many of the first migrants were from the Yarse group, a factor which may have facilitated the conversion of urban Mossi to Islam. The majority of rural migrants are Talse, and high ranking royals are not often found among the migrant population. These factors may have had some effect on immigrant social organization, although since one's identity within Mossi society is regarded as irrelevant by immigrant Mossi this is difficult to determine. In the immigrant communities a man who has gained a chiefship will claim that he is a member of the Nakombse group, since by holding an office he has *nam*, traditionally reserved for Nakombse; yet being a Nakombse is not a qualification for office in Ghana as it usually is in Upper Volta.[11]

Mossi have been migrating southwards from their arid savannah homeland to work in the lush forests of the Ashanti region of Ghana since before Ghana and Upper Volta became respectively British and French colonies. There were, by 1960, approximately 160,140 Mossi in Ghana (1960 Ghana census), and at least 5,000 Mossi in the city of Kumasi, out of a total population of 218,170. The majority of Mossi are in rural areas, working as labourers for Ashanti cocoa farmers. Those working in towns are mainly permanently settled immigrants who have had previous rural experience, and who have decided not to return permanently to Upper Volta. They engage in a variety of occupations, mainly in unskilled labour and trade and express their commitment to the town by buying, or saving to buy, houses there. Like many other northern migrants in Ashanti, Mossi are regarded as immigrants even after they have been in Ghana several generations. Legally, birth does not confer Ghanaian citizenship and even those Mossi who are born in Ghana are aliens, legally, and 'strangers' colloquially.

KUMASI

In the city of Kumasi, the traditional Ashanti capital, the Mossi form part of an ethnically heterogeneous immigrant community known by the Hausa term Zongo, literally 'stranger's quarter'. Just before the turn of the century, when the British overthrew the authority of the Ashanti king and made Kumasi the administrative centre of the Ashanti Crown Colony (in 1901), an area of the town was designated as the Zongo, also referred to as the Mohammedan quarter, or the Hausa settlement. This area accommodated northern soldiers who had fought with the British against the Ashanti. They were known as Hausas but actually consisted of many different peoples. Traders and labourers from northern Ghana, Upper Volta, Nigeria, Togo, Dahomey, and Niger began to settle in the Zongo in large numbers and Kumasi became once again the major market town in the forest region. Today the term Zongo refers both to an area of the town, mainly occupied by 'strangers', and to the heterogeneous Muslim immigrant population, which has out-grown its original neighbourhood but which still recognizes its unity in social and cultural opposition to the local Ashanti population.

I have described the political status of the Zongo community in Kumasi elsewhere, and need not go into it in detail here.[12] Suffice it to say that each ethnic community within the Zongo has a headman, who is not officially a chief,[13] but who holds an informal court to arbitrate disputes within his group, and who acts as an intermediary between his community, other leaders in the Zongo, government officials and the Asantehene, the King of Ashanti. Today, as in the nineteenth century before his power was broken by the British,[14] the Muslims recognize the Asantehene as the ritual 'owner of the town'. Each immigrant headman is ritually installed in office by the Asantehene, and regards him as a patron, one of whose roles is to mediate between the strangers and officials of the Ghana government.

The main ethnic communities within the Zongo are, in order of size, the Yoruba, Hausa, Mossi, Busansi, FraFra (Tallensi), Grusi and Dagomba (1960 census). Regardless of their tribe or place of origin all Muslims in the Zongo recognize that they are united in many ways and a strong sense of community overrides

197

ethnic differences. Among the most important factors leading to social and cultural integration in the Zongo are the following: Islam, which has high prestige, is recruiting converts, preaches a universalistic ideology of brotherhood, emphasizes the importance of the unity of the Muslim community and prescribes many common ways of everyday behaviour for immigrants of varied cultural backgrounds; the use of Hausa as a *lingua franca*; co-residence in several areas of the town in neighbourhoods and houses that are ethnically heterogeneous; common political interests and a common status as strangers, particularly among the immigrants who are not Ghanaian citizens; common economic interests, mainly in trade and transport; extensive networks of kinship and friendship cross-cutting neighbourhood and ethnic cleavages; associations, including the Islamic brotherhoods (mainly the Tijaniyya), athletic and recreational clubs, revolving credit societies and others. While the immigrants abandon many traditional forms of behaviour when they move to the Zongo, they do not become socially or culturally assimilated into the local Ashanti society. Rather a new identity emerges in the Zongo, associated by the immigrants with Islamic values and to some extent with Hausa culture due to the early numerical, economic and political preeminence of the Hausa in Kumasi. Many specific attributes of the Zongo cultural pattern could be described; these involve all aspects of everyday behaviour including language, dress, food, customs, religious, kinship, and economic values, and so on. The immigrants believe that Kumasi Zongo has a distinct culture of its own, and often refer to this as the 'Kumasi constitution', since there is in fact a group of Muslim scholars, *'ulama'*, who meet from time to time to legislate correct ways in which Kumasi Muslims should behave. Whether or not the Zongo actually has a distinct culture, differing in content from that of other Muslim immigrant communities in Ghana, is irrelevant here. What is significant is that Zongo residents feel they and their children are abandoning behaviour patterns and values they associate with traditional tribal culture and adopting patterns they associate specifically with the Zongo community.

Besides Islam, one of the main catalysts of cultural integration in the Zongo is the particular form of domestic arrangements that have developed there. In Kumasi the domestic arrangements provide structural conditions under which culture changes, rather than, as has been observed in other towns, providing a context in which cultural traditions are preserved. In all the neighbourhoods where immigrants live, people from many different ethnic communities reside together. At certain periods in the growth of Kumasi shortages of accommodation have contributed to this pattern, but even in newly developing suburbs, where there is an abundance of accommodation, people from many different groups rent rooms in the same houses. This can probably be explained as an effect of their common status as strangers *vis-à-vis* the Ashanti. The ideology of Islam justifies these arrangements by emphasizing the brotherhood of all Muslims, but the pattern obtains even among non-Muslim immigrants, although somewhat less frequently.

Houses, privately owned by immigrant or Ashanti landlords, or government owned (in two neighbourhoods), are constructed in a rectangular pattern with a series of rooms opening into a central courtyard which functions as a cooking area and as a centre for activity and communication. Rooms are rented from the houseowner, his agent (often a client or relative), or from the government on a monthly basis. A small room (ca. $9' \times 9'$) usually accommodates a nuclear family and this group is often, but not always, a separate economic unit within the house. Men who are in a better economic position hire extra rooms for other members of their families including additional wives, in the same or in different houses, sometimes in different neighbourhoods, depending upon the availability of space. Such arrangements lead to domestic units which are physically located in several houses, since wives may cook in their own houses on the nights their husbands visit, or they may cooperate and cook together in the house of the senior wife.

It is very rare to find houses consisting entirely of kinsmen since almost all houses are built as economic investments and rooms are rarely rented to kin. In a sample of eighty-nine houses (2,500 individuals) owned by first and second generation Mossi immigrants, only one house consisted entirely of a group of kinsmen. It is also unusual to find houses consisting entirely of members of a single ethnic community. There was only one example of this in the sample and it was not the same house in which all residents were kin. In some cases inter-ethnic marriages account for the heterogeneity. In others the fact that rooms are rented to members of different ethnic communities accounts for it. The only discrimination one occasionally finds is on the basis of religious affiliation. Some Muslims hesitate to rent rooms to non-Muslims, claiming that all Muslims are brothers (and implicitly that the all Muslim-house is a kind of pseudokinship unit), and conversely, that living with non-Muslims is undesirable, for the social distance required would be incompatible with co-residence. But this is by no means a general rule and many houses are mixed.

Activities within the house very quickly lead to the social and cultural interaction of immigrants from many groups. Individual rooms are used for little more than sleeping; most other activities are carried on in the central courtyard. Women share a kitchen where each has her own fireplace. They cooperate in cleaning the courtyard and sometimes even in preparing food. Communication between female residents of a house is usually in Hausa and most children who are raised in Kumasi Zongo learn Hausa as their first language. Children form playgroups in these houses and later move out to play with neighbours who also come from a variety of ethnic groups. They are, therefore, socialized with very little awareness of ethnic differentiation. It is only at about the age of seven that most children become conscious of their own and others' ethnic identity, and even then this awareness does not entail knowledge or perception of cultural variability. Children born in Kumasi Zongo grow up in a common cultural milieu, regardless of their parents' ethnic affiliation.

The structure of the domestic unit is important in creating the basis for cultural unity and a common identity among second generation immigrants. Immigrants who are born in Kumasi (*'yankasa*) are not the 'bearers' of different cultures, as are first generation immigrants, yet once they are adolescents they do begin to recognize ethnic categories. The reasons for this, and some of the forms this recognition of ethnicity takes, will be discussed later. Here I want to point out that an ideological basis for ethnic categorizations still exists within Islam even though Islam is a main catalyst of socio-cultural integration. Although the ideology of Islam maintains that all Muslims are 'brothers' and that ethnic affiliation among Muslims, where it exists, should not be a barrier to interaction (including inter-marriage), it also accommodates a lower level of ethnic dif-ferentiation since it admits that agnatic descent is socially significant. One is said to be a Muslim if one's father is a Muslim (although one can also convert). Likewise one is a Hausa or a Mossi or a Yoruba according to patrifiliation. The importance of descent in determining group affiliation, identity, and citizen-ship in much of Africa is well known; here it is apparent that it has been merged with Islamic ideology in such a way that two levels of identity are established: identity as a Muslim and identity as a member of a particular ethnic community defined in terms of one's paternal place of origin. Usually it is the last major migration that is relevant: if a man's father or grand-father was born in Mossiland he is a Mossi; if his great-grandfather was originally a Hausa who migrated to Mossiland, he will probably identify himself as a Mossi but would also recognize and use, when advantageous, the option of identifying himself as a Hausa. So although on one level of social organiza-tion and ideology Islam denies the existence of ethnic categories, on another level, through recognition of the importance of descent, it acknowledges these same divisions.

It is worth adding that the possibility of *opting* to identify oneself as a member of one group or another as suggested above is only possible because of the extent to which cultural inte-gration occurs. Ethnic identity remains important in some situations in the second generation but when the cultural corre-lates of ethnicity are minimal, the possibility of mobility in-creases.

Having described some aspects of the process of cultural integration in Kumasi Zongo and the ideological basis for ethnic differentiation, I now consider some manifestations of ethnicity among first and second generation immigrants.

FIRST GENERATION IMMIGRANTS

Although the urban situation is clearly different in many respects from the rural one, it would be naïve to expect immi-grants suddenly to abandon all the social categories they grew up with when they move to town. I have already mentioned the way in which various ethnic groups are incorporated into traditional Mossi society. Here I would like to pursue the subject of kinship, for among first generation urban immigrants ethnicity is expressed mainly in a kinship idiom and ethnic associations function in somewhat the same way that kinship groups function in the traditional context.

Among Voltaic peoples, including the Mossi, there are two main concepts which are used to describe kinship and descent respectively. The Mole word *doaghda*, which can be translated as room or womb, or as kinship or family, refers to consanguineal kinship through males or females.[15] The word *budu* refers to descent, reckoned agnatically among the Mossi. Members of the same *budu* are described as being all of one kind, and this characteristic (likeness) is based upon ascription by patrifiliation. Thus age and sex categories are not regarded as *budu*. The main ethnic communities in Mossi society – the Nakombse, Talse, Yarse and others – are all described as *budu* since these are agnatically inherited statuses.

The concept of *doaghda* is more inclusive than that of *budu* in that it refers to any kind of consanguineal kinship. Members of different *budu* may or may not be *doaghda*, but members of the same *budu* necessarily are *doaghda*; conversely kinsmen (*doaghda*) are not necessarily members of the same *budu*. Agnatic descent links the members of the same *budu*, while affinal and uterine ties link people in different *budu* to one another. In Mossi society it is not surprising to find that the different ethnic communities are said to be related on the basis of marriages among their founders. Myths of origin as well as actual marriages link the different communities into a kinship network, so that members of the royal (Nakombse) community are symbolically described as the mothers' brothers of the commoners (Talse) by virtue of marriages between their founding ancestors. Joking between classificatory (and real) mother's brother and sister's son is common in this area, and in Mossi society it frequently occurs even when they are only distant classificatory kinsmen, or when they are unable to trace any actual kinship link at all. If we regard the mother's brother/ sister's son relationship as an affinal relationship in the Mossi context, we may say that joking in the idiom of affinity characterizes the relationships between different ethnic communities within Mossi society, that is, between Nakombse and Talse, and between Yarse, Maranse, Silmi-Mossi (descendants of Mossi-Fulani marriages) and others.

In the urban context the Mossi describe 'tribes' or ethnic groups as *budu* (*iri* in Hausa). They regard all Mossi as one *budu*, although they know that in the Upper Voltan context they would distinguish various *budu* within the Mossi category. The Mossi idea of *budu*, then, is similar to what I am referring to as ethnicity in Kumasi Zongo: both concepts divide a population into a set of categories on the basis of a few principles, in this case place of origin and agnatic descent. This is certainly not to say that these are the only possible means of establishing ethnic categories. It just happens to be the case that in both the traditional Mossi context and in the urban situation agnatic descent and place of paternal origin are the primary criteria for ascribing ethnic identity.

I have noted that traditionally in Mossi society joking relationships and myths of origin express the idea that the relationships between different ethnic communities within the society are conceptualized as relations of affinity, while members of the same community are regarded as classificatory con-sanguineal kin, both as *doaghda* and as members of one *budu*. Among first generation immigrants in Kumasi, classificatory kinship terms are applied in such a way that this same distinction is important. Given the irrelevance of ethnic sub-divisions within the category Mossi in the urban context, it is not surprising to find that Mossi apply consanguineal kinship terms to each other. Mossi immigrants, especially those born in Upper Volta, tend to call other Mossi of the same age by sibling terms, while they use parent terms to address those who are older and, as in Upper Volta, to address the headman. The terms which are used in a classificatory sense within the ethnic group are, then, almost exclusively consanguineal kinship terms.

Significantly, in the urban context categorical joking relationships occur almost exclusively with members of other ethnic groups with whom the Mossi have a mythical link of origin. The Mossi do not use affinal terms in a classificatory way and they do not carry on joking relationships among themselves. However, they do joke with the Mamprusi and Dagomba and make frequent references to the kinship links between their ancestors according to their common set of origin myths. This behaviour is identical to that found between ethnic communities within Mossi society, but in the context of the Zongo it takes place between Mossi and non-Mossi. Thus the classificatory kinship terms which immigrants use within the ethnic group are those based on common descent, not affinity which seems to imply a lower order of conjunction. Obviously when I speak of the use of classificatory kinship terms in the urban context I am almost always referring to their use between individuals who cannot trace any genealogical relationship.

In both the traditional and the urban contexts kinship terms are used in what has been called a 'metaphorical' sense. Fortes, in discussing the Tallensi, who are very close to the Mossi in culture, makes the point that 'all social relations implying mutual or common interests tend to be assimilated to those of kinship' (Fortes, 1949: 19). 'A kinsman of any degree is a person in whose welfare one is interested and whom one is under a moral obligation to help in difficulties if possible' (Fortes 1949: 203). Of course this applies in both urban and rural areas, but this similarity should not obscure the fact that there are significant differences in the two situations. In Taleland, as in Mossiland, most individuals have a fairly complete set of kinsmen who are related in varying degrees of genealogical distance. This makes it possible for the rights and obligations implied in the use of classificatory kinship terms to vary according to the genealogical distance between those who use the terms. Rights and obligations will be defined in this way, regardless of the actual facts of performance. In Taleland, Fortes wrote, 'the more distant a genealogical tie is, the more does it become a matter of moral and ritual, rather than jural or economic relations' (Fortes 1949: 18). Thus, in the traditional context close kin and 'metaphorical' kin may be distinguished by different role expectations which are correlated with genealogical distance.

Among first generation urban immigrants, who have very few 'real' kinsmen in town, genealogical distance cannot be used to define rights and obligations between individuals. Consequently first generation immigrants are continually attempting to create institutions and relationships which they can rely upon as they could rely upon kinship relationships 'at home'. They come to town with kinship concepts but without kin. For example, when a Mossi first generation immigrant wants to contract a marriage he looks for someone to fulfil some of the roles which a close agnate would have fulfilled in the north. He will go to a member of his ethnic community, who may be regarded as a *potential kinsman*, and ask him to assume this role for the purposes of the marriage. When the man agrees, he has accepted some of the obligations of a kinsman. These obligations are still defined in traditional terms, for it would be absurd for us to expect all values and all role expectations to change at once simply because a man changes his place of residence. 'Detribalization' in this sense never completely occurs. Once the obligations of, for example, a lineage brother have been assumed, this creates the context of a relationship in which other rights and obligations associated with kinship may be activated. Thus while all tribesmen are potential kinsmen, and may occasionally be addressed by kinship terms, this does not have the very specific meaning it acquires when kinship obligations are voluntarily assumed. Kinship obligations, once established in this way, must be actively maintained through visits, gift giving and mutual assistance. If they are not maintained, kin terms may still be used in a metaphorical sense, but kinship expectations will lapse. In other words, there is no simple division in the urban context, for first generation immigrants, between 'real' and 'metaphorical' kin. The difference between the urban and rural areas is not so much in the definition of kinship roles as it is in the way in which individuals are placed in specific categories: not by birth, but by voluntarily assuming the specific behaviours associated with particular roles.

This gives us some indication of what some of the functions of ethnic or 'voluntary' associations are for first generation immigrants. For people born in the north the recognition of common ethnicity is important mainly, though not exclusively, in the domain of kinship. Thus the headman, who so far has always been a first generation immigrant, is regarded by other first generation immigrants in much the same way that a lineage head (*budkasama*) would be regarded in Upper Volta. He has authority in settling disputes about marriage, divorce, the custody of children, inheritance, debts and many other matters that traditionally would be performed by a lineage head or a village headman, not by a high ranking Nakombse chief. His political authority in Kumasi is severely limited by the urban context, in particular by his position as a leader of a 'stranger' group. Government courts and administrators perform many of the political roles of the traditional chiefs. Nevertheless the urban headman still plays an important role in what the Mossi describe as 'family matters' (i.e. matters concerning only the Mossi *budu*). Disputes involving only first generation Mossi immigrants are settled by the headman and his elders; as long as these stay within his jurisdiction, which is possible so long as both parties are Mossi, they are regarded not as criminal cases but as family quarrels requiring arbitration.

The Mossi headman is cognizant that his role should be regarded in terms of kinship. On one occasion he told a woman whose case he was hearing:

'every woman should remember that when she is with her husband, the chief is her family, because if her husband does something that is not good for her, she must go and report to the chief so that he may call the husband and advise him. . . . It was written in God's book that you will become my daughter. What makes me say this is that whenever you have any trouble with your husband you may come to me and if your husband keeps doing bad [*sic*] I may take you from him. . . . There is no family other than the person who will help you when you are in trouble.'

Although the functions of the headman can be regarded in kinship terms, there are certain aspects of the organization of the Mossi community that resemble the political structure of Mossi society as outlined briefly on p. 195. The Mossi from Yatenga, Fada N'Gourma, and Ouagadougou kingdoms each have separate headmen (Tenkoudougou comes under Ouagadougou), although when the Mossi community was small in the beginning of the century all came under a single headman. Each of these headmen has a series of ministers, who perform court as well as provincial functions. In other words, the Mossi (Ouagadougou) headman has ten titled ministers. Some of them bear Mossi titles, although they admit that their functions differ from the traditional ones, and others have Hausa titles. The functions of these various officials in Kumasi are not highly differentiated; with some slight variations, they all act as advisers to the headman, helping him to reach decisions and arbitrate disputes. Significantly, each official comes from a different area of Mossiland and each, like the traditional Minister in Ouagadougou, is responsible for migrants who come from his territorial area. Thus a Mossi from the town of Kupela would first bring a case or complaint to the Mossi official who holds the Hausa title of Sarkin Fada, because the present Sarkin Fada comes from the Kupela area of Upper Volta. If he cannot settle the case himself, the Sarkin Fada brings the case to the headman.

It is worth reiterating that while the traditional divisions between ethnic communities or estates within Mossi society are not given structural recognition in Kumasi, because of the larger opposition within the context of the Zongo to other immigrant groups, traditional territorial divisions are structurally recognized among first generation Mossi immigrants. The Mossi community in Kumasi is itself defined in terms of its *place* of origin, and territorial divisions within Mossi society have some significance for first generation immigrants. These subdivisions in no way detract from the unity of the Mossi group in ethnic terms, since they are not regarded as ethnic divisions. Outsiders, that is non-Mossi, are not even aware of them and for second generation Mossi immigrants these territorial divisions are not very important: *'yankasa* are Mossi from Upper Volta; occasionally they may not even know their father's town of origin, but even when they do know this, it does not affect social interaction in any significant way. At most, it can be the basis for friendships among them. It is, however, still slightly more important than estate membership or *sondere*, the Mossi patronyms (sometimes called clans), which many *'yankasa* do not know at all.[16]

It is most unusual to find second generation immigrants bringing cases to the Mossi headman and elders. As I will show below, this has to do with differences in the kinship networks of first and second generation immigrants. Also, some of the headman's roles, such as helping new migrants settle into the town, are only relevant to first generation immigrants. These immigrants are very much concerned with the office of headman, whom they regard as a chief and call Mossi Naba, and with the appointments he makes to the various ministerial offices. Second generation immigrants regard the political function of the headman as insignificant since he has no power in Kumasi politics as a whole and is usually unable to command any of the specifically urban resources, such as the allotment of trading licences, house plots, market stalls, and the like. Of course, when the headman takes on additional roles, for instance when he participates in party politics, he may be important to *'yankasa* as well, but this is outside of his role as Mossi headman.

For first generation immigrants Mossi associations are unbounded: the headman and his elders may be called officials of an association but only if it is recognized that membership is conferred automatically by birth. Anyone who comes into the town and who identifies himself as Mossi may regard himself as part of the informal tribal association symbolized by the headman and his elders. There are no occasions at which the whole membership is expected to be present, and the members of the association cannot be enumerated. But everyone does recognize that an association – perhaps a more appropriate term is community – exists, and that they have the right to actively participate or to receive assistance by virtue of their Mossi identity.

The organization of first generation immigrant communities differ to some extent from one ethnic group to another, and these differences correspond to differences in traditional social structure and culture. For example, a traditionally non-centralized group such as the Dagati is organized in Kumasi mainly on the basis of village and clan associations; in Kumasi as in the north there is no headman who has authority over all these autonomous groups. Other ethnic communities, with traditions of chiefship, such as the Mamprusi and the Dagomba have elaborated this institution in the urban setting. This is not the occasion to go into a detailed analysis of these differences, and it is sufficient to note that cultural differences are significant among first generation immigrants, especially in the early years of urban settlement, but that as time goes on the organization of different ethnic communities in Kumasi becomes similar in many respects. Communities that do not have headmen in the early stages of urban residence, such as the Tallensi (known as Frafra in southern Ghana), eventually appoint them, when it becomes clear that a headman can have an important function in the urban context. The traditionally non-centralized groups have much more difficulty in choosing headmen than do those groups with traditions of chiefship; and they also limit the headman's role. But eventually, after they begin to become Muslim and to some extent 'Hausaized', and when they realize that headmen are useful in representing them to outsiders, they appoint them. Cultural differences also gradually disappear among these communities, for after some years they all begin to call their elders by Hausa titles and to ignore their traditional role definitions.

Thus, although there are some cultural differences in the internal organization of first generation immigrant communities, these become increasingly unimportant when we compare the functions that the associations of these immigrants perform. Members of various ethnic communities recognize that their headmen are structurally in similar positions *vis-à-vis* the important political authorities in the town, and that their roles are similar and are determined by the urban context. In all groups the headmen and elders perform limited political functions in the context of Kumasi as a whole, but they can be very important in the daily lives of first generation immigrants.

SECOND GENERATION IMMIGRANTS (YANKASA)

There are two major factors which lead to significant differences in the types of associations formed by first and second generation immigrants. One is the fact that second generation immigrants have a network of 'real' kinsmen in town; the other is that cultural differences between ethnic groups have become minimal by the second generation.

Because second generation immigrants are born in town, they have a set of close kinsmen from birth. These may or may not be members of the same ethnic group. There is considerable inter-ethnic marriage in Kumasi, necessitated by imbalances in the sex ratio among first generation immigrants,[17] and among *'yankasa* sanctioned by Islam and facilitated by the insignificance of cultural differences between communities. A sample of 560 marriages, which included all current marriages of the residents in the 89 Mossi owned houses mentioned above, showed that the Mossi definitely do show a preference for marrying within their own group.[18] Nevertheless, among first generation Mossi immigrants 28 per cent of the men's marriages were to non-Mossi. In the second generation, the percentage of out-marriages increases, so that 37 per cent of male second generation Mossi immigrants are married to non-Mossi women. This increase would seem at first to be due to the more equal balance in the sex ratio of Mossi men and women in the second generation, but since first generation Mossi men frequently marry second generation Mossi women, the number of remaining second generation Mossi women is not as great as the equalizing effect of the birth rate would suggest. Among second generation Mossi men the preference for marrying within the Mossi community is definitely weakened since ethnicity does not entail cultural barriers to inter-ethnic marriage,[19] and since Islam sanctions it. In any case these inter-ethnic marriages show that well over a third of Mossi immigrants who are born in Kumasi have close kinsmen in other ethnic communities. These non-Mossi relatives, with 'real' Mossi kinsmen, perform many of the functions that the headmen, elders and classificatory kinsmen perform for first generation immigrants. Disputes that first generation immigrants would bring to the headman's court are settled within the 'real' kinship groups, which are not necessarily coterminous with ethnic groups, of second generation immigrants. And, of course, they do not need the headman to assist them in adjusting to urban life. This leads to a lack of concern with the office of the headman which is the main focus of first generation immigrants' associations, and to the development of new forms of associations with new functions.

Since the second generation immigrants have 'real' kinsmen in town, they use classificatory kinship terms to address other Mossi much less frequently than do first generation immigrants. They also do not establish the kinds of voluntary kinship bonds that I have described for first generation immigrants. For those born in town behaviour associated with kinship can be correlated with genealogical distance. Moreover, since second generation immigrants often have 'real' affines in non-Mossi groups, they use affinal terms with members of these groups in a different way than first generation immigrants use them; they do not emphasize joking relationships across ethnic boundaries to the extent that I have described for first generation immigrants.

Second generation immigrants do not, therefore, make the close association between ethnicity and kinship that we find among first generation immigrants. When they do form relationships and associations based on common ethnicity, these are not perceived as substitutes for kinship relationships even though they may involve a vague recognition of metaphorical brotherhood. But for second generation immigrants all Muslims are 'brothers' in much the same way as all Mossi are 'brothers'. This vague use of the kinship idiom does not imply that more specific kinship roles can be activated.

As I have indicated, cultural differences are minimal among second generation immigrants although there remains the knowledge that traditionally and among first generation immigrants cultural differences between ethnic communities exist. Kinship relationships and informal associations, such as neighbourhood playgroups among children, sports clubs and religious associations among adults, are not always based upon ethnicity and are often ethnically heterogeneous. The leaders of *'yankasa* associations are people who are respected throughout the Zongo community because they have gained prestige according to the value system of the Zongo as a whole, usually by gaining wealth and Islamic education. Both informal and formal associations are formed among second generation immigrants on the basis of common neighbourhood ties and interests. The number of formal associations is great and many people belong to several. Their functions are varied: some are sports and recreational associations; others are religious, or occupational; and some are formed for specific political purposes (such as a ratepayers' association formed in 1969 to protest tax increases). The number and prominence of these groups in Zongo life attest to the significance of non-ethnic bases of relationships among second generation immigrants.

Nevertheless, just as we find the ideology of ethnicity persisting among second generation immigrants, we also find ethnically based associations among them. Their form and functions differ significantly from the informal ethnic associations of first generation immigrants. As I have shown, the organization of the first generation immigrant community is informal, centred around the headman and his elders. All Mossi, including the *'yankasa*, are automatically members although second genera- tion immigrants rarely participate in the same activities and take little interest in the 'chiefly' offices. In contrast to the kind of organization found among the first generation immigrants, the associations of the *'yankasa* are formal. Given the absence of cultural diacritica to identify members of the *'yankasa* ethnic associations, there are formal procedures for conferring mem- bership, usually the purchase of membership cards and the payment of dues.

First generation Mossi immigrants are seldom explicitly excluded from the *'yankasa* associations, but few of them join. They regard these associations as 'young men's groups' and, in relation to *'yankasa*, identify themselves as elders. To some extent this does reflect a real age and generation difference, in that since migration to Kumasi has decreased, due to unfavour- able economic conditions in Ghana and the development of opportunities for migrants in the Ivory Coast, most first genera- tion immigrants tend to be over forty-five, while only a minority of the *'yankasa* are in this age range. Even so, the tendency of first generation immigrants to refer to the *'yankasa* associations as 'young men's, groups also is an expression of cultural divergence between the generations. First generation immi- grants attempt to apply a Mossi value, that is the association of generational seniority with high status, in the urban con- text.[20] Second generation immigrants see the situation quite differently: for them, Islam and wealth, rather than age, generation or chiefship, confer high status. For them a second generation immigrant, since he is more at home in Islamic Zongo culture, speaks better Hausa and knows more Arabic, has more prestige than an elder born in Mossiland.

There have been formal associations of Mossi *'yankasa* since the 1930s. They are similar in that in the absence of distinctive cultural symbols, they are based upon formal rules which define their organization. They have membership lists, regular dues, elected officials with English and Arabic titles, and written con- stitutions. Regular meetings are scheduled and are conducted in Hausa according to British rules of parliamentary procedure. The agenda of a typical meeting is not, as in first generation immigrants' meetings, concerned with the personal problems of individuals, but rather with planning common activities to strengthen the organization itself.

Most of the associations formed by *'yankasa* have died out after a few years, but when political conditions change, old associations are reconstituted. This is due to the essentially political nature of these associations: they are formed to obtain power, to act as interest groups within particular political situations, and when these situations change, the role of the association changes also. During the 1940s and early 1950s there were several Mossi *'yankasa* groups, but during the height of CPP power, when ethnic, regional and religious parties were banned, the Mossi associations dissolved. After the 1965 coup d'état these groups became active again, for this was a period in which old power groups were broken and new ones were able to make their bids.

Shortly after the coup a group of Mossi *'yankasa* formed an organization known as the Mossi Youth Association (MYA). First generation immigrants were half-heartedly invited to join but only a few of the younger ones did so. Non-Mossi women who were married to Mossi men were admitted into a women's section of the association on the grounds that they would give birth to Mossi children.[21] Although the weekly meetings were conducted in Hausa, one of the purposes of the association as stated on its printed membership card, was to encourage its members to learn the Mossi language. The 'executives' of the association spoke Moré when they could and this was highly regarded, even though in other contexts to speak Hausa well is prestigious among Mossi *'yankasa*. Members were also encouraged to marry among themselves since that would strengthen the Mossi group within the Zongo numerically and would counteract the depletion of the Mossi community through intermarriage. For even though the rule of patrifiliation ascribes Mossi identity to the children of all Mossi men, the economic and political correlates of unilineal descent are lost in the urban setting and the children of mixed marriages can often choose the group with which they identify.[22]

Like the similar *'yankasa* associations of other ethnic groups, the Mossi *'yankasa* adopt certain symbols of their common identity which have no reference to traditional Mossi culture. As I have shown, first generation immigrants' associations differ

from one another organizationally; and these variations reflect
real cultural differences. '*Yankasa* associations of all groups are
similar, with slight diacritical changes in symbolism assuming
great importance. A typical example of this is the importance
placed on the purchase of a distinctive pattern of cloth (*yayi*)
on the main Muslim festival days. Many associations choose a
pattern of 'Manchester cloth' for their members for the major
festivals. The patterns chosen have nothing to do with traditional culture, for the cloth is the common bright cotton print
manufactured in Europe, Japan, Indonesia, and now in Ghana,
and sold by the yard in the market. The pattern chosen distinguishes the Mossi group from others simply by its adoption
by that group as a uniform. Every year, the '*yankasa* associations of each ethnic group choose new patterns, and these designs
become known thereafter as 'Mossi cloth' or 'Hausa cloth' and
so on. In other words, among '*yankasa* the process of cultural
assimilation into the Zongo community has gone so far that they
are unable to appeal to Mossi traditional culture in their search
for symbols of identity. New symbols, neutral symbols in a
sense, such as membership cards and particular patterns of
factory-made cloth, are adopted by the Mossi to signify their
social identity in the face of an evident loss of cultural identity.

Despite protestations that the group was apolitical –
inevitable at the time since the military government (the
National Liberation Council) had banned all political activity –
the potential political function of the MYA was obvious.
Politics, in the sense of the articulation of public or group
demands, replaced kinship as the main focus of Mossi associations in the second generation. This is perhaps understandable
only in light of all the other institutionalized ways of solving
non-political problems that exist among second generation
immigrants. Kinship relationships, neighbourhood friendships,
and a myriad of multi-ethnic associations perform many functions for '*yankasa* that relationships within the Mossi community perform for first generation immigrants. Yet within the
Zongo, and in relation to authorities outside the Zongo, the
Mossi still have to deal with the problem of defining their status
in a competitive environment. They must still find ways of
asserting their identity in a society where everyone, Ghanaian
or non-Ghanaian, has an ethnic as well as a national identity.

In this situation, the Mossi, like all others, must find ways of gaining economic and political power, and for many individuals (though by no means all) identification with the ethnic group is one possible way of increasing the likelihood of success.

The MYA did not violate the National Liberation Council's ban on political activities in any way; and they did not concern themselves with national politics until the ban was lifted and they were approached by candidates running for election. Nevertheless the MYA leaders did make contacts with officials at various levels of government in order to obtain recognition as a formal association (all associations were required by law to register with the government), and to acquire the necessary legitimacy in the eyes of the government and in the eyes of potentially rival organizations.

On the local level the definition of politics presents some problems. According to the 'folk' definition, politics refers to any public situation of intergroup of interpersonal conflict.[23] The MYA's explicit purpose was apolitical in that the group had no intention of competing for or mobilizing support for any sort of public office. Their lack of concern with the office of headman was regarded, by first generation Mossi immigrants, as proof of their apolitical interests. Nor did they become involved in conflicts with other immigrant groups in the Zongo.

However, one of the explicit aims of the association was to make the Mossi community 'strong' (*karfe*, in Hausa). The members met regularly and discussed the relative status of the Mossi *vis-à-vis* other groups in the Zongo. They explicitly encouraged their members to help raise the status of the whole group by achieving prestige within the accepted value system of the Zongo. In other words, their members were encouraged to do well in business, to improve their level of Islamic education, to dress well, and generally to behave in such a way that Mossi identity would be highly valued even by other groups. They were, therefore, competing in terms of the values of Zongo culture, not according to any specific Mossi cultural code. This emphasis is more noticeable among *'yankasa* than among first generation immigrants who, having some measure of cultural identity, do not evaluate prestige and status solely along the scale of 'Zongo values' to which all *'yankasa* subscribe.

CONCLUSION

The differences between the types of associations formed by first and second generation Mossi immigrants, and some general implications of this comparison can now be discussed. There are two themes that I want to touch upon very briefly in this conclusion. First, the question of the importance of culture in ethnicity and second, the relationship between ethnicity and forms of stratification.

Throughout this paper I have been pleading for a structural view of ethnicity. I have maintained that ethnicity is not intrinsically the articulation of cultural differences, even though custom, as Cohen (1969) puts it, is commonly used to symbolize the boundaries between groups. In the past few years many writers on this subject (Barth, 1969: 35; Cohen, 1969; Glazer and Moynihan, 1963) have noted that when ethnic groups become primarily political interest groups, cultural differences change their meaning. Barth for example notes that political confrontations cause groups to become structurally similar and therefore 'comparable' and that this causes a reduction in the cultural differences between them. Obviously this is true for those who are united most frequently on any one side of a structural opposition: in relation to the Yoruba various Hausa groups in Ibadan become united into the Hausa 'supertribe' (Cohen, 1969 : 204 and Rouch, 1956 : 31). In Kumasi, groups of different origins become united not only into supertribes within the Zongo, but also into the Zongo community in opposition to the Ashanti. However, at those points where fusion rarely occurs, as between the immigrants and the Ashanti in Kumasi or between the Hausa and the Yoruba in Ibadan, comparability may not imply more than minimal cultural fusion; nevertheless comparability does imply that some basis of communication exists, and this implies at least some common culture, even if only enough for symbols of difference to be comprehensible.

Whenever fusion, or 'homogenization' (Cohen 1969: 204), occurs we are dealing with the loss of cultural differences and the creation of new bases of identity with new symbols to express this. These may be drawn from traditional culture, or from the actor's idea of this culture, as in the case of the

216

Ibadan Hausa, but they need not be. There may be a seemingly arbitrary 'selection of signals for identity' (Barth 1969: 35) which have no reference to traditional cultural or symbolic systems.

Although the symbols which differentiate an ethnic community need not reflect the cultural individuality of this community, they must have meaning in the larger *context* in which the ethnic community operates. In the case I have described here symbols rooted in Mossi culture are of limited use in the Zongo, for they would mean nothing to the non-Mossi with whom they are meant to communicate. It is, I think, a misunderstanding of the meaning of such diacritical symbols to assume that they imply that real cultural differences exist. If merely the idea of belonging to one descent group or another, having a distinct place of origin, or wearing a different coloured dress, rather than having different values, constitutes a difference of culture, I would agree that ethnic communities do maintain some minimal degree of cultural distinctiveness. However, it does not seem to me that the simple recognition of boundaries implies that the content within the boundaries differs in any objective cultural sense, that is in terms of cultural *values*.

This leads to a minor terminological problem for urban studies, and for studies of complex heterogeneous societies in general. If we accept a structural definition of ethnicity, and if we maintain that real cultural differences between ethnic communities are not crucial and may in fact disappear, what then are the distinguishing characteristics of ethnic groups as opposed to other kinds of ascriptive identity groups? If, on the other hand, we are to insist that ethnic communities are by definition cultural units, then we must admit that when cultural integration reaches a certain level, when cultural differences between ethnic communities disappear, the categories, communities and groups that remain are not 'ethnic', but something else. What? We seem at first to be dealing with an emerging urban segmentary structure (as in the case of the overseas Chinese or the Indonesian Batak clans (Crissman, 1967; Bruner 1971)), for we are no longer dealing with cultural pluralism,[24] but rather with homogeneous segmented societies.

The segments, it is true, look to a past in which cultural

differences were significant to define themselves, but we must still recognize that at a certain stage of cultural integration what we previously spoke of as ethnic differentiation is merely the acceptance of a structural principle of categorization within a society, a society which is coterminous with a culture. If we continue to refer to the differentiated units as ethnic communities, as I have done in this paper with second generation Mossi immigrants, we are left with a minimal definition of ethnicity as being only the acceptance of some culturally defined principle of categorization. The specific functions of these differentiated units and the question of whether they are culturally distinct from one another is then secondary to the more basic acceptance and persistence of a principle of social categorization.

In traditional Mossi society and among northern immigrants in Kumasi, similar processes of socio-cultural change have been described. In both situations culturally distinct ethnic communities are incorporated as social units, and maintain their social and political identity although their cultural identity and functions change. In both cases, however, one persisting function of these communities is to define the status of individuals *vis-à-vis* members of other comparable groups in the society. This very general function remains while other more specific functions change and are reallocated within the larger society. The process of incorporation has in some ways gone further in the case of the *'yankasa* in Kumasi than in Mossi society, where some ethnic communities maintain distinctive political, economic and ritual roles. Nevertheless, a generalization that emerges from this is that as ethnic communities become politically and culturally incorporated into a society, if they continue to exist as corporate units, one of their main purposes is to define social status. Social status, in this sense, may imply hierarchical ranking and complementarity of roles, as in the extreme case of caste systems or in a modified form, in societies like the Mossi; or it may imply a segmented structure in which status groups are theoretically equivalent in rank and similar in role. In the traditional Mossi case, social status based upon ethnic identity defines differential access to political, economic and ritual power; the roles of ethnic communities are in some respects distinct and complementary, and competition between them is not usual. In the Kumasi case, where political and cultural incorporation of second generation immigrants in the Zongo has been more complete and where there is no question of complementarity in the functions of different (but functionally similar) ethnic groups, the status hierarchy that emerges, particularly among second generation immigrants, is unstable. Ideologically all immigrant ethnic communities in the Zongo are equal, yet this theoretical equality is precisely what allows competition for status and power to take place; and it is this competition that justifies the continued existence of the principle of ethnicity in the Zongo.

NOTES

[1] The research on which this paper is based was conducted in Ghana and Upper Volta between 1965 and 1967, with subsequent follow-up visits in 1968, 1969 and 1970. It was supported by the United States National Institute of Mental Health and the Wenner-Gren Foundation. I am grateful to Edward Bruner and Norman Whitten for commenting on earlier versions of this paper.

[2] A valuable discussion of this is found in Davis (1959).

[3] Banton (1957); Epstein (1958); Little (1957, 1959); Pons (1956, 1969); and others.

[4] For example Wallerstein (1960).

[5] For example Mayer (1961).

[6] Similar situations are described by Eidheim (1969: 39), Knutsson (1969: 99), and Blom (1969: 74) as well as Glazer and Moynihan (1963) and Hannerz in this volume.

[7] Marc (1909: 129).

[8] In discussions of the origin myths of the Mossi there has been some question of which group, royals or authoctones or the offspring of the two, are the 'real' Mossi. My position is that no single group is, but that the composite society alone can be identified as Mossi. This argument appears in my dissertation, Cambridge (1969: Chap. 2).

[9] Among works on the Mossi political system are Skinner (1964), Kabore (1966), Tiendrebeogo (1965), Zahan (1967).

[10] At this early date, probably late fourteenth century, the Mamprusi and Dagomba kingdoms were not yet differentiated as they are today. In a common version of the origin myth Ouidiraogo is actually the son of a Mamprusi-Dagomba princess (the daughter of the king of Gambaga) and a hunter of Malinke or Busansi origin.

[11] In the Mossi kingdoms there were some offices reserved for members of non-royal (including slave) lineages.

[12] Schildkrout (1970a and 1970b).

[13] In the colonial period, official chiefs were recognized by the Governor of the Gold Coast, and today (according to the 1969 Constitution) are recognized by the Government (that is, by Regional Houses of Chiefs).

[14] The Asantehene was removed from Kumasi in 1896, and deported to the Seychelles Islands in 1901. He returned to Kumasi in 1924, first as a private citizen, then (1926) as Kumasihene, and finally (1935) was recognized as head of the newly created Ashanti Confederacy.

[15] Fortes discusses the Tallensi meaning of this concept and remarks that the

generic concept of kinship, dɔɣam, 'subsumes all kinds and degrees of genealogical relationship, however remote, through one or more progenitors or progenitrices' (1949: 16).

16 There is one significant exception: Yarse know their patronymic groups and these still are exogamous units even among *'yankasa*. Among other Mossi the *sondere* is not important in town and some people claim that migrants deliberately 'forget' it since they believe witches can attack only with knowledge of the victim's *sondere*.

17 According to the 1960 Ghana census the overall sex ratio (number of males per 100 females) for the Mossi is 283·5. In the older age ranges, which reflect more accurately the situation among first generation immigrants the figures are much higher:

Age Range	M/F Ratio
25–34	376·2
35–44	555·8
45–54	781·4
55–64	762·0
65 and over	577·2

18 I have reached this conclusion by following the formula suggested by Mitchell (1957: 12 ff.). This shows that if there was no preference operating the number of Mossi in-marriages would have been 133·5 in this sample. In fact there were 221 intra-Mossi marriages among 321 men and 233 women.

19 These conclusions were suggested by a survey comparing the marriage preferences of first and second generation Mossi men. *'Yankasa* often preferred Hausa women, regarding these as high status choices.

20 There was also a 'young men's group' among first generation immigrants. This too did not reflect a chronological age group since some members were well over 65, but rather demonstrated the dichotomy between the office holders ('royals') on the one hand and ordinary immigrants ('commoners') on the other. Their leader, one of the headman's elders known by the Hausa title Sarkin Samare, was opposed by the *'yankasa* who thought that a chronologically young man should be appointed.

21 The women's section contained many more first generation immigrants. This may be explained partly demographically: there are proportionately fewer first generation women than men. Also, and most significantly, generation is not nearly such an important determinant of status among women as it is among men. Among men, the type of political role one plays is determined in part by generation. Among women, who play less of a political role, this is not so. Moreover, women derive much of their status from their husbands and second generation women are often married to first generation men. Mossi women's associations therefore were not formed on this basis and women of both generations felt they had common interests. Smith (1959) describes a similar distinction in male and female status systems among the Hausa.

22 Cohen (1969) shows this in his discussion of the urban Hausa. However, while the Hausa were traditionally bilateral in many respects, the Mossi emphasized the paternal line much more. This ideology remains but Islam, with its non-unilineal inheritance pattern, and the shallow depth of urban kinship groups, are factors undermining this.

23 By 'public' I mean those conflicts that directly or indirectly involve the public, not simply conflicts that take place in public.

24 See Kuper and Smith (1969) for a discussion of different types of pluralism.

REFERENCES

BANTON, M. 1957. *West African City.* London: Oxford University Press.

BARTH, F. (ed.) 1969. *Ethnic Groups and Boundaries.* London: George Allen & Unwin.

BLOM, J. P. 1969. Ethnic and Cultural Differentiation. *In* Fredrik Barth (ed.), *Ethnic Groups and Boundaries.* London: George Allen & Unwin.

BRUNER, E. M. 1971. Batak Ethnic Associations in Three Indonesian Cities. Unpublished paper presented to Association of Social Anthropologists, April 1971, London.

COHEN, A. 1969. *Custom and Politics in Urban Africa.* London: Routledge & Kegan Paul.

CRISSMAN, L. W. 1967. The Segmentary Structure of Urban Overseas Chinese. *Man.* 2: 2: 185–204.

DAVIS, K. 1959. The Myth of Functional Analysis. *American Sociological Review.* 24: 757–72.

EIDHEIM, H. 1969. When Ethnic Identity is a Social Stigma. *In* Frederick Barth (ed.), *Ethnic Groups and Boundaries.* London: George Allen & Unwin.

EPSTEIN, A. L. 1958. *Politics in an Urban African Community.* Manchester: Manchester University Press for Rhodes-Livingstone Institute.

FORTES, M. 1949. *The Web of Kinship Among the Tallensi.* London: Oxford University Press.

Ghana: 1960 Population Census. 1964. *Special Report 'E': Tribes in Ghana* and *Special Report 'A': Statistics of Towns.* Accra: Census Office.

GLAZER & MOYNIHAN. 1963. *Beyond the Melting Pot.* Cambridge, Massachusetts: Institute of Technology Press.

GLUCKMAN, M. 1940. *Analysis of a Social Situation in Modern Zululand.* Reprinted as Rhodes-Livingstone paper No. 28. Manchester, 1958.

KABORE, G. V. 1966. *Organisation Politique Traditionnelle et Evolution Politique des Mossi de Ouagadougou.* Recherches Voltaiques 5. Paris: Centre National de Recherche Scientifique.

KNUTSSON, R. R. 1969. Dichotomization and Integration. *In* Fredrick Barth (ed.). *Ethnic Groups and Boundaries.* London: George Allen & Unwin.

KUPER, L. and SMITH, M. G. (eds). 1969. *Pluralism in Africa.* Los Angeles: University of California Press.

LITTLE, K. 1957. The Role of Voluntary Associations in West African Urbanization. *American Anthropologist* 59: 579–96.

Enid Schildkrout

LITTLE, K. 1959. The Organization of Voluntary Associations in West Africa. *Civilizations* 9: 283–97.

MARC, L. 1909. *Le Pays Mossi.* Paris.

MAYER, P. 1961. *Townsmen or Tribesmen.* Cape Town: Oxford University Press.

MITCHELL, J. C. 1956. *The Kelela Dance. Aspects of Social Relationships Among Urban Africans in Northern Rhodesia.* Rhodes-Livingstone Paper No. 27. Manchester: Manchester University Press for Rhodes-Livingstone Institute.

—— 1957. Aspects of African Marriage on the Copperbelt of Northern Rhodesia. *Human Problems in British Central Africa* 22: 1–30.

PARKIN, D. 1969. *Neighbours and Nationals in an African City Ward.* London: Routledge & Kegan Paul.

PONS, V. 1956. The Changing Significance of Ethnic Affiliation and of Westernization in the African Settlement Patterns in Stanleyville. *In* D. Forde (ed.), *Social Implications of Industrialization and Urbanization in Africa South of the Sahara.* Tensions and Technology Series, Paris: UNESCO, 638–69.

—— 1969. *Stanleyville, An African Urban Community under Belgian Administration.* London: Oxford University Press for International African Institute.

ROUCH, J. 1956. *Migrations au Ghana.* Paris.

SCHILDKROUT, E. 1969. *Ethnicity, Kinship and Politics among Mossi Immigrants in Kumasi.* Cambridge University: Doctoral Dissertation. Unpublished.

—— 1970a. Strangers and Local Government in Kumasi. *Journal of Modern African Studies* 8: 2: 251–69.

—— 1970b. Government and Chiefs in Kumasi. *In* Michael Crowder and Obaro Ikime (eds), *West African Chiefs: Their Changing Status Under Colonial Rule and Independence.* Ibadan: Ibadan University Press.

SKINNER, E. 1964. *The Mossi of the Upper Volta.* Stanford: Stanford University Press.

SMITH, M. G. 1959. The Hausa System of Social Status. *Africa* XXIX: 3: 239–53.

TIENDREBEOGO, Y. 1964. *Histoire et Coutumes Royales des Mossi de Ouagadougou.* Ouagadougou.

WALLERSTEIN, I. 1960. Ethnicity and National Integration in West Africa. *Cahiers d'Etudes Africaines* III: 129–39.

ZAHAN, D. 1967. The Mossi Kingdoms. In D. Forde and P. M. Kaberry (eds), *West African Kingdoms in the Nineteenth Century.* London: Oxford University Press.

P. C. Lloyd

Ethnicity and the Structure of Inequality in a Nigerian Town in the Mid-1950s

People do not fight simply because they are culturally different. The reason for those intense struggles which may lead to outbreaks of violence lies elsewhere. It is to be found in most cases I believe, in the competition for two forms of scarce resources – power and wealth: wealth being one of the principal modes of reward in a society, the allocation of such rewards being one of the main elements of power. Tensions within society are likely to be exacerbated under two conditions: firstly, when new resources, hitherto unallocated, are to be distributed, and secondly, when the new patterns of distribution create alterations in the existing ranking of individuals – the basis of the hierarchy being in terms of power and rewards. But in the poorer nations of the world violent struggles which we repeatedly observe are, as often as not, between groups defined not in terms of some precise political or economic interest but of some primordial quality – cultural, linguistic or religious. The cry is not so much 'workers unite' as 'tribesmen unite'. But, though this rallying call is so often effective in uniting people in purposive action, the fears engendered among the masses may be more imagined than real, related more to matters of prestige than to material conditions; these fears may, furthermore, be exploited by certain individuals whose interests are threatened to a much greater degree.

In any society two models may be employed in the perception of the unequal distribution of power and rewards, the system of social stratification. Men may use both, though in any single situation one may be more readily applicable than the other. Thus on the one hand one may see society as open: the rules by which power and rewards are allocated (relating both to ends and means) are seen as legitimate; there is presumed to be consensus. The efforts of the individual are directed towards improving his own position in the social ranking either through

223

individual achievement or through the patronage of those higher in rank – these two modes often being complementary. Alternatively, one may see society as closed – there being an unseen or insurmountable barrier between the 'haves' and the 'have nots'. The rules of allocation are not accepted; rather one seeks to alter them. This is the conflict model. Between individuals cooperation in attaining a common goal is emphasized. Let me repeat, the perceptions of any one person will be derived from both these models, though from each one to a greater or lesser degree, depending on the past experience and the present situation of the individual.

As is well known the cities of the poorer nations have grown rapidly in the last few decades; they are populated overwhelmingly by recent migrants from the rural areas. In Africa, those who now hold the top positions in the modern sector have come, in large measure, from humble homes, their parents being illiterate, near subsistence farmers. Even those who came from the families of the traditional local and rural elite have experienced cultural change in gaining western education and entering a completely new range of occupations. In this process the achieved quality of education is usually stressed, a prescribed level of schooling being demanded for most posts in the public service (which itself accounts, often, for one-half of the nations' employees). Less stressed in the literature, but I feel equally, if not more, significant, is the importance of patronage, both in providing the opportunities for education (in paying fees, etc.) and in subsequently getting jobs. A strong reliance upon patronage as a means of social advancement strengthens the solidarity of those groups defined in terms of primordial qualities at the expense of other groups.

This is so because, in the African context, the patron is most likely to be a member of one's own ethnic group. Just as in the rural area a man turns for help first to the members of his own descent group or small village, so when he comes to the town does he seek the support of those related closely to him by ties of kinship or locality. In fact these are likely to be the only people he knows in the town. (Another type of bond to be exploited is that created by the secondary school – but this affects only the better educated migrant.) The debts and obligations contracted during the first few months in the town, as the members of the ethnic group first of all accommodate the new migrant and find him a job, create a relationship which the migrant subsequently finds it difficult to break. Indeed, the poorer migrant often finds his entire social life encapsulated within that of members of his ethnic group. It is only subsequent to his arrival in the town that he may join other associations which bring him into a close relationship with members of other ethnic groups. Again, in the context of the African town, an appeal to a patron made in terms of ethnic loyalty is likely to have the most favourable result; such an appeal is unambiguous and least constrained by other sectional interests. Conversely, the would-be patron seeking followers, perhaps a politician hoping for votes, is strongly drawn towards an appeal to ethnic loyalties.

The various ethnic groups in a town can be ranked hierarchically and they may be vying with each other for advancement. But equally, the situation may exist in which two ethnic groups are locked in conflict, with others looking on as bystanders. The issue here is the rules by which power and rewards should be allocated.

This situation is exemplified by Warri, a town in southern Nigeria where I lived and carried out fieldwork in 1955–56 (*Map 1*). At that time it did not occur to me to make a systematic study of personal networks, though looking back through my notes I find much relevant information. I was able to collect data illustrating the power and wealth of members of different ethnic groups and can correlate this with the perceived ranking of these groups. For most of the period of Warri's existence the members of the different ethnic groups had lived together in harmony. The major incidents of disharmony centred upon the claims of two ethnic groups for superiority in the town. This superiority was seen at one level in terms of prestige – each group wished to see the town as its capital. At another level each wished to control the town – control being seen to involve the allocation of scarce resources. (Thus, to give one example: Most of Warri's trade is conducted in the town's municipally-run market, with – in the mid-1950s – its 1,800 stalls, as against but 60 shops. When ten new stalls were built there were a thousand applications. It was generally believed that the members of the town council would allocate the stalls

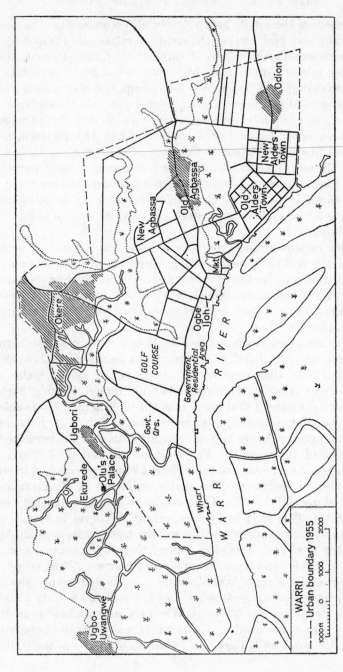

Map 1 Warri, Southern Nigeria

to their friends, i.e. to members of their own ethnic group.) The struggles for supremacy resulted, as I shall outline in a later section of this paper, in a long series of land cases in the courts, in rioting and looting, and in the near-disruption of the parliamentary electoral system.

WARRI TOWN

Warri lies about thirty miles from the sea on the landward margins of the mangrove swamps of the Niger delta (Lloyd 1957). Incorporated within the present limits of the town are Okere, an Itsekiri settlement, and Agbassa, an Urhobo settlement. Ijoh fishermen probably had had camps along the shore of the creek. The modern town dates from the end of the nineteenth century when European firms acquired land on the shore for factories – Bey and Zimmer in 1885, Elder Dempster in 1890 and the African Association in 1898. The British colonial administration established a vice-consulate there in 1891, as a base from which to open up the hinterland. (A similar station was established at Sapele, thirty miles to the north.) The colonial government later acquired a large area of land – at Ogbe Ijoh, in 1906 (this becoming the reservation for government officials and for clerks' quarters) and at Alders Town in 1908, Alder being a government interpreter who had settled in the area. Land here was leased to individuals for private development; Old Alders Town developed mainly in the 1920s, New Alders Town in the 1930s. In 1911 the government acquired Agbassa and its environs, and thus held most of the unused land within the town's boundaries.

Politically, Warri became the headquarters first of the Central Province in 1906 – one of the three provinces into which the Protectorate was divided – and then of Warri Province. Commercially, it developed too. For John Holt Ltd it was the terminal port for their Niger river fleet where cargoes were transferred to ocean-going vessels and vice versa. The United Africa Company's port of trans-shipment was at Burutu but they maintained a large office complex at Warri. The town served as a market centre for a large hinterland, though still rivalled by Sapele, now dominated by its huge plywood factory. (In the late 1950s Warri's importance as a commercial centre seemed to be in decline; but the expansion of the oil fields in its hinterland consequent upon the civil war has made it, once again, a boom town.)

Warri was still a small town in 1921 with a population of only 2,300; by 1931 it had grown to 11,000 and by 1952 to 22,500 – within the 1955 township boundary. (The 1963 population was

TABLE 1 *Residence of self-employed persons (percentages)*

Area	Itsekiri	Urhobo	Ibo	Other	Total	n =
Ogbe Ijoh	12	40	30	22	100	169
Old Alders Town	11	26	53	11	100	428
New Alders Town	14	56	22	8	100	429
Old Agbassa	7	53	25	15	100	530
New Agbassa	6	45	37	14	100	271
Okere	27	27	36	9	100	332
Odion	12	71	14	4	100	534
Total	12	48	29	11	100	2,693

Note: The quantitative data presented here is derived from the tax rolls of the Warri Urban District Council. These rolls separated employees from self-employed persons. The names of employees were submitted by their employers and listed as such. The income cited is that paid by the employer during the previous tax year; it may refer to an incomplete year of work and takes no account of other earnings. Incomes ascribed to self-employed persons are too unreliable to use; such persons are listed under the place of residence and there is of course a probability of substantial tax evasion among certain categories of persons. The ethnic origin of each tax payer was not given in the rolls; it was established by me with the help of several clerks employed by the Council, on the basis of the name of the individual (a fairly sure guide) together with personal knowledge. I estimate that this method gave at least a 95 per cent accuracy.

55,000.) The 1952 population was distributed ethnically as follows: Urhobo 38 per cent, Ibo 28 per cent, Itsekiri 15 per cent, with the remaining 19 per cent predominantly Yoruba and Benin. Historically the Itsekiri were predominant among the earliest settlers together with clerks employed by government and the firms who came from Lagos, the Gold Coast, etc. The immigration of Ibo is the more recent. As figures given below in *Table 1* show, members of the three major ethnic groups are distributed throughout the town. Old Agbassa is still predominantly Urhobo, but in Okere the Itsekiri are now in the minority. The lower rents obtaining in the poorer quality houses here have attracted many of the least-skilled Ibo and Urhobo migrants. Furthermore, in many of the large tenement houses members of several ethnic groups not only co-reside but share common cooking and washing facilities.

Before continuing this description of Warri town, I must outline the background of historical relationships between the major ethnic groups. (Ikime 1969; Lloyd 1957, 1963; Moore 1970.)

The Itsekiri, numbering 33,000 in the 1952 census, traditionally lived on the islands of dry land within the mangrove swamps, on the landward edge of the swamps and along the ocean shore; they practised some agriculture but were also engaged in fishing and salt making. They speak a dialect of the Yoruba language. To the south of them live the Ijoh in a similar environment. To the east of the Itsekiri live the Urhobo (1952 census: 340,000 in Warri province, and nearly 100,000 elsewhere in Nigeria), settled agriculturalists and speakers of an Edo dialect. Even further to the east – their nearest village being 30 miles from Warri – are the Ibo-speaking people. These four languages are as different from each other as, say, English is from Russian; these linguistic differences are paralleled by equivalent cultural differences. Between the Itsekiri and their nearest Urhobo neighbours there existed a symbiotic relationship as the former traded fish and salt for foodstuffs in the border villages.

Originally, the Itsekiri seem to have lived in autonomous villages headed by a chief, often selected for his supernatural powers – apparent possession by a spirit indicating a candidate for the vacant office. But in the fifteenth century a Benin prince founded a kingdom and eventually established his capital at Iwere, also known as Ode Itsekiri, or Big Warri – a village sited on an island in the swamp about four miles from the present town of Warri. Whilst the rulers of Benin soon rejected the proselytizing efforts of the Portuguese, the Itsekiri rulers – perhaps to assert their independence of Benin – welcomed them. Christianity became, as it were, a royal cult. Until the beginning

of the nineteenth century Catholic missionaries resided intermittently in the capital (the death rate was high) and one
Itsekiri king was educated in Europe, took a white wife of noble
birth, and was succeeded, apparently, by his mulatto son.
During this period slaves were exported from Iwere – these
slaves were probably mostly Urhobo who had been expelled
from their own village communities; the Itsekiri did not make
war on their neighbours. The relationship with the Portuguese
at this early period is still very important to the Itsekiri;
'Portuguese' origins are ascribed to heirlooms, loan words are
carefully preserved (Ryder 1960).

The Urhobo remained culturally unaffected by this contact
with Europe. They lived in village communities based largely
on descent and amalgamated into larger units now known as
clans (Bradbury 1957). The largest of these is of equivalent
population with the Itsekiri (1952 census); others number only
a little over a thousand persons. Village government rested
with councils of chiefs in title associations; but although some
titleholders had their appointments ratified in Benin, kingship
in the usual sense of the word did not exist.

The social and political structure of the Ibo resembled, in its
level of development, that of the Urhobo. That of the Ijoh who
lived close to the Itsekiri was equivalent to Itsekiri organization
before the advent of the kingdom.

The trade in slaves began to decline at the end of the
eighteenth century and European ships no longer sailed to
Iwere or to Ughoton, the port lying 14 miles from Benin; instead they anchored outside the bar of the Benin River. Enterprising Itsekiri moved to the lower reaches of the river and
created a much more elaborate middleman role, for they had to
bring their cargoes of slaves, and later of palm oil, from the
markets of the Urhobo hinterland to the sea coast. English
firms later established their 'factories' in the same area. The
leading Itsekiri traders established powerful 'houses' consisting
of their kin, followers, and slaves.

In 1848 the Itsekiri king died and there followed an interregnum lasting for nearly 90 years during which the traditional
political system largely disappeared. Power was wielded by the
leaders of the trading houses, one of whom was recognized by
the British consular officials as 'Governor of the River'. During

the second half of the century one of these traders, Nana Olomu, established a near monopoly of the trade in the river and its hinterland. By the 1890s he was opposed variously by those sections of the Itsekiri who suffered from exclusion from the trade – these were led by Dore (or Dogho) Numa, a prominent member of both the royal and the senior commoner 'Houses'; by those of the English traders who sought independent access to the interior markets; and by consular officials anxious to extend British dominion. A series of events of a type common in colonial history culminated in a little military action in 1894 in which Nana was defeated; he was later exiled.

Dore Numa was made 'Political Agent' and greatly assisted the British in their efforts to 'open up' the interior. Subsequently he was made Paramount Chief of the Itsekiri; an office which he held until his death in 1932. Throughout the first half of this century British administrative officials appeared to show a strong preference for the 'civilized' Itsekiri over the 'bush' Urhobo; this was enhanced by their reliance on the advice of Dore Numa in matters affecting both the Itsekiri and the Urhobo. Itsekiri dominance over the Urhobo was rarely oppressive but a large number of incidents and situations appeared to demonstrate Urhobo inferiority. Thus Warri, seen as an Itsekiri town, was the administrative capital of the whole area. The country of the Itsekiri together with that of neighbouring Urhobo clans was constituted into a Jekri-Sobo Division in which Itsekiri interests seemed to be paramount; although the Urhobo gradually gained independent native authority councils and treasuries, it took a long period of agitation to effect the administrative changes which put the Itsekiri in one Division and almost all the Urhobo in another.

During the nineteenth century no Christian missions established posts among the Itsekiri; a few chiefs sent sons to school in Bonny but education was very limited and most men learned their 'pidgin' in dealing with the English traders. Schools were opened in Warri and Sapele in 1902–3 and most of the early pupils were Itsekiri. Missions and schools did not penetrate Urhobo country until the 1920s and it was not until the mid-1930s that Itsekiri and Urhobo students were equal in number in the Government primary school in Warri. As a result the

Itsekiri held most of the clerical posts in this early period. Thus, of seventeen native court clerks serving in 1922 in this area, seven were Itsekiri and only one was an Urhobo.

This dominant role of the Itsekiri was increasingly contested by the Urhobo from the 1930s onwards as political consciousness and education developed among them and, as the following paragraphs will demonstrate, their role in Warri itself belied the inferiority still ascribed to them by the Itsekiri.

Itsekiri were wont to say, 'The whiteman is god to the Itsekiri, the Itsekiri is god to the Sobo' (a derogatory name for the Urhobo). The Itsekiri remain inordinately proud of their long connections with the European. This is seen by their detractors as sheer arrogance and the Itsekiri is portrayed as a man who holds the train of his wrapper in one hand and his cane in the other – he is thus incapable of manual work and is lazy too. The Itsekiri see the Urhobo as hardworking but as 'bush', commenting upon the scanty nature of their traditional dress, and 'dirty' habits. Itsekiri women are acknowledged by all to be tall, beautiful, and clean; nevertheless Itsekiri men admit that Urhobo women make steadier wives. Both the Itsekiri and the Urhobo see the Ibo as ranking beneath them; 'they are fond of money' (as target workers?) and will do the meanest tasks; most truck pushers in Warri are Ibo and they live in the cheapest and most cramped lodgings; they default in their civil obligations – several migrants will, it is said, share one tax receipt.

I now contrast these popular images with the actual situation in Warri.

OCCUPATIONS

In 1955 a little over 5,000 men were as taxpayers, recorded in employment. Nearly one-half of these were employees in the public services or with the largely expatriate commercial firms; the remainder were self-employed as traders, craftsmen or casual labourers, with of course a few pensioners, professionals, etc.

Over one-half of the employees worked for six large companies – in descending order of size – Holt's Transport, The Public Works Department, United Africa Company, The Nigeria Police, the Warri Township Authority and Elder Dempster

Lines. Each of these employed over 100 men. Eight other
organizations employing between 50 and 100 men accounted for
a further quarter; the distribution of these employees by type
of work – clerical or manual – and by major ethnic group is
shown below. Perhaps the most striking fact to emerge is the
evenness of the distribution. A few divergencies are lost in
summarizing the data. Thus Ibo predominate in the Police Force
and prison services (45 per cent), and also in the Posts and
Telegraphs Department and as crew on the river fleets; con-

TABLE 2 *Occupation of Employees (Percentages)*

(a)	Itsekiri	Urhobo	Ibo	Others	Total	n =
Public service: clerical	10	31	33	27	100	579
manual	10	36	31	23	100	834
Firms: clerical	11	37	28	22	100	356
manual	9	29	42	19	100	778
Total:	10	33	35	23	100	2,547
(b)						
Public service: clerical	22	21	21	27	23	
manual	33	36	29	33	32	
Firms: clerical	16	16	12	14	14	
manual	28	27	38	26	31	
Total:	100	100	100	100	100	
n =	251	841	879	576	2,547	

versely few Ibo were employed by the Warri Township
Authority. The Itsekiri are rather better represented in government offices (18 per cent) than elsewhere, but, despite their
advantages of education in the early years of this century they
do not have a high proportion of teachers. As one would expect
the Ibo are more heavily represented in manual work, the
'other' ethnic groups in clerical occupations (see *Table 2*).

Again, if one looks at the incomes earned by these men one
sees that the Itsekiri have a high proportion of men in the
highest bracket – but only relative to their proportion of the
total population; they still have but one-seventh of such income

earners and but half that of the Urhobo. The Ibo are under-represented at the top. The Itsekiri are well represented in the lowest levels of income (*Table 3*).

When we turn to the distribution of the self-employed persons, a similar picture emerges. More of the Urhobo are traders; Ibo tend to be craftsmen. The table below shows that certain ethnic groups tend to specialize in particular crafts. The Ibo predominate as truckpushers – a lowly occupation, but each

TABLE 3 *Income of Employees* (*Percentages*)

(a) Income Group	Itsekiri	Urhobo	Ibo	Others	Total	n =
over £300 p.a.	14	27	22	37	100	81
£150–£300 p.a.	10	27	30	33	100	362
£70–£150 p.a.	9	29	39	23	100	917
below £70 p.a.	10	39	34	18	100	1,187
Total:	10	33	34	23	100	2,547
(b)						
over £300 p.a.	4	3	2	5	3	
£150–£300 p.a.	14	12	12	21	14	
£70–£150 p.a.	34	31	40	37	36	
below £70	48	54	45	37	47	
Total:	100	100	100	100	100	
n =	251	841	879	576	2,547	

ethnic group is well represented among the jobbers – the casual labourers and intermittently employed; the proportion of Itsekiri jobbers is especially high. Traders and businessmen are among the town's wealthiest and most prestigious citizens. But there were in Warri five times as many Urhobo as Itsekiri in the category of wealthy traders and twice as many Urhobo engaged in other, but equally rewarding, businesses. Many of the prosperous Itsekiri were landlords, though it was often said that they were selling their property in order to maintain their accustomed style of life. Very few Ibo were as wealthy as this. Of the ten lawyers residing in the town in 1955, three were Itsekiri, one was Ibo, one a Sierra Leonean and the remainder Urhobo. The town's sole private medical doctor was an Urhobo (*Tables 4* and *5*).

These figures, taken together, completely dispel the image of

TABLE 4 *Occupation of Self-employed Persons*
(Percentages)

(a)	Itsekiri	Urhobo	Ibo	Others	Total	n =
Craftsmen	6	36	40	18	100	660
Traders	10	62	22	6	100	827
Others (Professionals, retired, etc.)	14	45	24	17	100	257
Truckpushers	7	12	77	5	100	60
Jobbers (casual labourers)	18	46	27	9	100	889
Total:	12	48	29	11	100	2,693
(b)						
Craftsmen	13	18	32	40	25	
Traders	26	40	23	16	31	
Others	11	9	8	15	10	
Truckpushers	1	1	6	1	2	
Jobbers	49	32	30	27	33	
Total:	100	100	100	100	100	
n =	323	1,290	798	282	2,693	

TABLE 5 *Craftsmen (Numbers)*

Craft	Itsekiri	Urhobo	Ibo	Others	Total
Sawyers	4	43	5	3	55
Carpenters	9	26	105	23	163
Builders	11	33	34	19	97
Blacksmiths and Tinkers	1	6	20	1	28
Bicycle repairers	11	11	28	7	47
Tailors	11	85	28	31	155
Goldsmiths	6	31	24	27	88
Washermen	0	4	21	2	27
Total:	43	239	265	113	660

235

Itsekiri superiority. Urhobo and Ibo have obviously taken, by
the mid-1950s, the opportunities provided by the economic
development of the town. The Itsekiri, it is true, do have a
slightly higher proportion of highly paid employees (18 per cent
earning over £150, compared with 15 per cent Urhobo and Ibo);
yet this is completely cancelled out by their numerical inferiority in the town, only 14 per cent of all the highest paid
employees being Itsekiri – considerably less than either Urhobo
or Ibo. The Urhobo have surpassed the Itsekiri as traders,
perhaps because in both the town and its hinterland, Urhobo
exceed Itsekiri in number. The Itsekiri have not become craftsmen, disdaining manual trades; they become instead casual
labourers.

PROPERTY OWNING

The Itsekiri and Urhobo have leased plots of crown land and
built houses in Warri for their own permanent residence and for
letting. The same has happened in Sapele. Neither of the two
ethnic groups has, within its territory, another town which it
might look upon as its commercial and administrative capital,
though Ughelli, the Urhobo Divisional headquarters, is now
rapidly growing. The Itsekiri have always looked upon Warri
as their capital. They have on occasion suggested that property
owning should be a qualification for a local government vote.
But as the table (p. 238) shows, whilst the Itsekiri still do own a
majority of the houses, their value is exceeded by that of the
Urhobo. Furthermore, while Itsekiri men do own 5 of the 8
biggest houses in the town the Urhobo own 23 in the next lower
category against 12 owned by Itsekiri. Again, the Itsekiri are
clearly losing ground to the Urhobo. Itsekiri ownership pre-
dominates in Old Alders Town – the first part of Warri to be
developed for private residence but the Urhobo predominate in
the newest areas – and especially in New Agbassa. The dominance of the Urhobo in Ogbe Ijoh, an area of early settlement,
is probably because new commercial premises have been built
by the Urhobo, perhaps replacing earlier buildings. The Ibo,
though so numerous in the town, have not built many houses
there; the more affluent build in their home villages to which
they ultimately intend to return.

Thus, to an ever increasing degree, it is becoming apparent that Warri, on the criterion of property owning, is fast becoming an Urhobo town (*Table 6*).

GOVERNMENT

I have already mentioned the bias shown by British officials towards the Itsekiri and the administrative arrangements, such as the Jekri-Sobo Division, which facilitated Itsekiri superiority. In the agitation which led to the creation of separate Itsekiri and Urhobo Divisions in 1949, the traditional chiefs and elders of the Urhobo had been allied with the educated elements, organized since the 1930s, in the Urhobo Progress Union (Ikime 1969).

In 1946 Makoro Mowoe, then President of the Urhobo Progress Union, was chosen to represent the entire Warri Province in the Western House of Assembly, thus ending the Itsekiri monopoly of such representative offices in Lagos and Ibadan. He was a wealthy man, with a large house in Warri, and he was much respected by the Itsekiri. The same could not be said of Jesse Ogboru who succeeded Mowoe on his death two years later. Then in 1949, another prominent Urhobo was selected to fill the newly created second seat for Warri Province in the Assembly. It began to appear to the Itsekiri that the numerical superiority of the Urhobo would determine their future success. However, the tide temporarily turned.

Before 1949 the nationalist elements in Warri and Sapele supported the National Council of Nigeria and the Cameroons as heir to the party of Herbert Macaulay. In 1951 the Itsekiri elected two local patriots to represent Warri Division in the new Western House of Assembly – on the platform of the Warri Peoples Party – Chief Arthur Prest and Chief Festus Edah. Prest, a mulatto, had served as an officer in the Nigeria Police Force and had recently returned from studying law in England. Edah had been born and had grown up in the Benin river but his name suggested an Urhobo origin (he later changed it to Okotie-Eboh); he was a very wealthy businessman in Sapele. As was expected, Prest declared his support for the Action Group, Edah for the NCNC, the six representatives from Urhobo Division were also NCNC. The Action Group formed the govern-

TABLE 6 *Property Owning (Percentages of Value)*

(a)

Area	Development	Itsekiri	Urhobo	Other	Total	n	total value £
Ogbe Ijoh	1910 on	28	50	22	100	67	80,000
Old Alders Town	1925 on	64	30	6	100	128	141,000
New Alders Town	1935 on	47	49	4	100	127	115,000
Old Agbassa	indig.	7	92	1	100	116	94,000
New Agbassa	1945 on	7	63	29	100	127	164,000
Okere	indig.	99	0	1	100	181	102,000
Total:		41	47	12	100	746	696,000

(b)

Area	Itsekiri	Urhobo	Other	Total
Ogbe Ijoh	8	12	22	11
Old Alders Town	32	13	10	20
New Alders Town	19	17	5	16
Old Agbassa	2	26	2	13
New Agbassa	4	31	59	24
Okere	35	0	2	15
Total:	100	100	100	100
Number of houses	360	315	71	746
Value £	284,000	331,000	81,000	696,000

ment and Prest became a minister, first in Ibadan and later in the Federal parliament in Lagos. NCNC members held no office. The newly installed Olu of the Itsekiri was also a strong AG supporter and the Itsekiri began to identify themselves – and be identified by others – as following the AG, whilst the Urhobo were represented by the NCNC. The lines were never clearly drawn, however, as Festus Okotie-Eboh had strong Itsekiri support, especially in Sapele and the Benin river area. In 1954 he defeated Prest for the, now sole, Divisional seat in the Federal House of Representatives.

The relationship between the rival ethnic groups and the nationalist political parties coloured Warri local government. In 1939 the Warri Township Advisory Board consisted of three British officials, three representatives of the expatriate firms and three African members – two being Itsekiri and one Urhobo. By 1946, the Board's African membership was increased to include two Itsekiri, two Urhobo and two other members (one of these a lawyer from Sierra Leone resident in Warri). Further reforms gave the Africans a majority. Four officials sat ex-officio, and one expatriate was elected for his ward – the government residential area. In the remaining wards men were chosen by acclamation, with the result – six Itsekiri, four Urhobo, one Ibo and one Sierra Leonean. Some Urhobo alleged, in 1955, that the Resident manipulated the election to ensure Itsekiri superiority.

In 1955 direct elections were held for a new town council set up under the Region's Local Government Law (1952). In the 21 wards, 24 Urhobo stood as candidates (15 NCNC, 6 AG, 3 Indep.); 14 Itsekiri (8 AG, 3 Indep. NCNC, 3 Indep.), 6 Ibo (5 NCNC, 1 Indep. NCNC) and 5 members of other ethnic groups. Whilst the Itsekiri vote was split between the AG and the Independent NCNC, Urhobo and Ibo were competing for the official NCNC nomination; it seems likely that a directive from the highest levels of the party persuaded the Ibo to stand down. Elected were 14 Urhobo (all but one NCNC), 4 Ibo (all NCNC) and 3 Itsekiri (1 Independent NCNC and 2 Independents). These men were by occupation traders and businessmen, professionals, clerks and teachers; one man was a craftsman – a printer. In the instrument setting up the new Council, the Western Region government provided that the Olu should

be the President and that six traditional members should be
selected from among the Itsekiri chiefs. In the event, the six
chosen were all prominent AG members. The division between
the predominantly Urhobo/NCNC popularly elected Council,
and the AG/Itsekiri leadership orientated towards the Olu and
the government in Ibadan, was starkly expressed in this
opposition.

CO-EXISTENCE

The Itsekiri look upon Warri as their own capital city. Yet they
now form a numerical minority; they no longer hold a majority
of the more prestigious occupational positions; nor do they own
most of the residential property. From a position of dominance
in local government they have been displaced by the Urhobo.
Increasingly Warri seems, to the outsider, to be an Urhobo
town. The situations and incidents which I describe in the later
sections relate to the attempts made by the Itsekiri to retain
either the symbols or the reality of their former superiority. But
although tension between the Itsekiri and the Urhobo is never
far below the surface, it must nevertheless be recognized that
daily life in Warri is essentially harmonious.

Firstly, there is quite a substantial degree of intermarriage
between the ethnic groups. The Ibo remain almost completely
endogamous, probably because most of them do not intend to
remain permanently in Warri. But in a sample of school children
in Warri 76 per cent of those with Itsekiri fathers had Itsekiri
mothers, whilst 22 per cent had Urhobo mothers. Whilst
Itsekiri men who marry outside their ethnic group almost all
take Urhobo wives, the Itsekiri women who marry exogamously
choose Urhobo men and those from other ethnic groups in
almost equal proportions. Again, Urhobo men who marry outside their group more often take Itsekiri wives than others. But
only 11 per cent of the sampled children with Urhobo fathers
had non-Urhobo mothers (Lloyd 1957).

In factories and offices there seemed in 1955 to be little
tension between members of different ethnic groups and labour
officers and workers' leaders alike told me that disputes were
rarely interpreted in terms of ethnicity.

Again, I heard no complaints that the newly elected town

council was being partisan in its dealings with the public. I do not doubt that favouritism was shown on many occasions, but here, as in other organizations, men from various ethnic groups are found in high positions, so that the supplicant has no difficulty in finding a patron from his own group to plead his cause. It is perhaps significant that one issue which did divide council members on ethnic lines was the choice of armorial bearings – the Itsekiri wanted the Olu's crossed swords and crown, the Urhobo an emblem symbolizing all the three major ethnic groups.

In the Warri primary schools English was the medium of instruction – pidgin in the lowest forms. The children played without apparent reference to ethnic identity. In the Youth Clubs, too, the adolescents mixed freely. The merits of the members of Warri's national league football team were discussed solely in the context of their skill; nobody ever suggested that there were too many Urhobos or Ibos in the side. My elderly informants insisted that these characteristics of the youth of today do not differ from those of a generation or so ago.

Yet, for the year that I lived in New Alders Town, my neighbours were an Itsekiri trader and chief, an Urhobo who was a senior executive in the Education Department, and a wealthy Ijoh trader. Whilst these men would pass the time of day with each other on meeting in the street, it was very evident that the visitors to their homes were overwhelmingly men of their own ethnic group. Their children were very close companions. How do we account for the difference between generations? The answer must lie in the fact that men of this age and prominence are drawn into the affairs of their own ethnic group – not merely that section of it resident in Warri but more usually the entire group. They were thus respectively involved in the politics of Warri, Urhobo, and Western Ijoh Divisions rather than those of the Township. Furthermore, although inter-ethnic rivalry might overshadow certain issues, most were concerned with matters internal to the ethnic group or Division and related to internal sectional interests and factions. Some, however, *were* issues of the type which I now describe.

241

LEADING ISSUES

(a) *The Ownership of Warri Land*

The town of Warri lies on or close to the margins of Itsekiri and
Urhobo settlement – their villages and farmland so inter-
penetrate that a clear boundary would be difficult to draw.
Much of the agitation over the Divisional administrative
boundaries has been over the 'enclaves'. The leases of land to the
Colonial government were signed by 'Chief Dore Numa of Benin
River and Chief Ogbe Yonwuren (a senior Warrant chief living
in Ugbo-uwange, just outside the present Township boundary)
acting for and on behalf of the Chiefs and people of Warri'.
This wording was crucial in the long sequence of lawsuits from
the beginning of the 1920s to the present. On one hand Dore
Numa's status was questioned; but more important was the
meaning attached to 'people of Warri'. Interpretations ranged
from 'the residents of Warri Township' on the one hand, to 'the
entire Itsekiri people' (excluding other ethnic groups) on the
other. Arising from both issues was the disposition of the rents
received from the leases. Dore Numa received £190 p.a. from the
crown leases; and later the government received huge sums from
the lease of plots to private and commercial builders.

In 1920 the (Itsekiri) chiefs and people of Ogidigben claimed
full and exclusive fishing rights in their area, asserting that they
had never been subject to the Olu of Warri. At almost the same
time the Agbassas claimed the rents paid to Dore Numa for
their area of Crown land, similarly denying the sovereignty of
the Olu. The villagers did not present their cases very well, and
though, in view of the long interregnum it was difficult for the
Itsekiri to prove acts of sovereignty, the weight of evidence
suggested that these two communities had been part of the
Itsekiri kingdom. Judgements confirmed the sovereignty of the
Olu but specified the right of the village communities and their
members to use the land. However, Dore Numa had, in 1915,
written to the Okere people, who were leasing land to the
government for a prison, stating that whilst the Olu was
sovereign over this land, 'such rights have nothing to do with
the ownership and title to the land'; the sum paid for the land
was given to the Okere people.

Soon after the two court cases cited above, members of the

Itsekiri royal family claimed that the right of sovereignty resided in them, not in Dore Numa. The courts had little difficulty in deciding that the sovereign rights cited were not held by the Olu for his family, but on behalf of the kingdom, and that they were rightly held now by Dore Numa. Until his death in 1932, the detractors of Dore Numa were continually claiming that he aspired to the kingship.

Whilst these early court actions confirmed Itsekiri sovereignty over the Township area, later ones, deriving from subsequent leases of land, went further in specifying the nature of those rights and the compensation due on loss of rights. In a court action ending in 1941 between the government and the newly installed Olu and the chiefs and people of Agbassa, concerning land acquired for a cemetery, the Olu had stated that he was willing to receive £15, keeping £10 for himself and giving £5 to the Agbassa. However, the judge awarded £5 to the man farming the land, £15 to the Agbassa community and £1 (being 1s. p.a. rent for 20 years) to the Olu. Later court actions on other land substantially replicated this award. But in 1956, largely, I believe, due to an error in interpreting these judgements, the Governor of the Western Region awarded the Olu a third of the compensation received.

As a result of this favourable award, and with the very pro-Itsekiri attitude of the Regional Government, the Olu began actions not only to claim a third of all rents received – including those from the innumerable private grants of building land outside the Crown area – but also to assert that the Agbassa, in failing or refusing to pay these sums and thus acknowledge the sovereignty of the Olu, should forefeit their rights in the land and become mere strangers.

The second major issue here concerns the disposition of the rents received by the government in leasing Crown lands for private development; such rents ranged from £160 p.a. per acre for the better sited land to £40 for the poorer. In 1943 an agreement was made between the Governor (of the Western Province) and the Olu that a quarter of the rents should be retained by the government for its costs of administration, half paid to the Township treasury (to benefit the town) and quarter paid to the Itsekiri NA in recognition of the sovereign rights of the Olu over the land. Chief Dore Numa had set up an Itsekiri National Trust fund for sums received from land transactions but the colonial government officials felt, at this period, that the Trust did not benefit the entire community. The matter was reopened in the mid-1950s when it was realized that, whilst NAs could legally receive such moneys, the newly created government councils could not properly do so; the Communal Land Rights (Vesting in Trustees) Law was passed providing for the establishment of community trusts with the traditional rulers and chiefs as trustees. The Crown land was transferred to this body. In an award made more on political grounds than based upon past legal judgements, the Regional Government awarded half the Warri rents to the Itsekiri National Trust, half to the government. At the time it was argued that the Olu and his fellow trustees would use the money for further litigation over land, rather than for more productive use. One of the early actions of the Trustees was to commit £100,000 to new building for Hussey College, a school managed by Action-Group-supporting Itsekiri chiefs. The management of the trust was one of the factors in the train of events leading to the exile of the Olu in the 1960s.

(b) *The Title of the Olu*

Chief Dore Numa died in 1932 and the colonial government was prepared to see the installation of a new Olu; Ginuwa II, a lineal descendant of the last reigning king, ascended the throne in 1936. The government did not accede to the request that he should be entitled Olu of Warri.

In 1949 Ginuwa II died and was succeeded by Erejuwa II. The latter was a much younger man, well educated and hitherto a trader. His appointment was not without controversy but he seems to have had the backing of those Itsekiri chiefs later associated with the Action Group. The issue of the title was reopened – with some justification, for not only was Olu of Warri the traditional title, but the Division over which he ruled was now termed Warri Division, and not Jekri-Sobo. But Warri was also the name of the Township and the whole Province and the Urhobo objected that a change of title would infer that the Olu was paramount ruler over the entire Province – there being no Urhobo or Ibo ruler of comparable status. In May 1952 the Regional Government gazetted the new title. Urhobo members of parliament petitioned that the Province should be named Delta, but the government dithered while tension mounted in Warri.

On September 8th, 1952, Chief Arthur Prest planned a political tour of Warri. He was seen by the Itsekiri as the principal agent of their recent benefits from the government and they arranged a grand motorcade welcome. Though anticipating trouble, the police allowed the plans to proceed. Urhobo mobs then attacked the procession and broke it up; in the succeeding days Itsekiri homes – mainly in the small Urhobo market villages – were looted. Two hundred and forty men reported losses amounting to £140,000. The Urhobo refused to sell in the Warri markets, but established new sites within Urhobo territory where the Itsekiri would not venture. It is said that the Oba of Benin secretly sent lorry loads of food to the hungry Itsekiri. In a few weeks life returned to normal, although the memory of these incidents coloured the interpretations of probable outcomes in later situations.

Erejuwa II built a new, modern palace near the creek-side village of Ekurede, a little beyond the Warri Township limits; this was obviously a more convenient site than Old Itsekiri, accessible only by canoe. But this move had rival interpretations. On one hand it suggested that the Olu was trying to strengthen his position within the Township; on the other hand the Itsekiri, seeing control of the Township slipping from their grasp, planned to build a new, modern and purely Itsekiri town around the palace, to which they would soon decamp.

The predicament of the Olu is understandable. Is he to be the traditional ruler of but half of the Itsekiri population – those living in the villages of the swamps, eking out a poor subsistence and heavily reliant on remittances of Warri Division – and even here the Itsekiri were in a minority; of all the Itsekiri wherever they may live; of the Township of Warri which falls within the administrative Division but remains an Itsekiri town only in a symbolic fashion and to the extent that some Itsekiri do look upon it as their permanent place of residence.

(c) *The Electoral Registers*

The early electoral registers in the modern Nigerian State were compiled from the tax rolls. Thus, in theory, all adult men were

registered – almost invariably in the ward where they resided.
Women were, in most areas, disenfranchised. In an attempt to
approach universal suffrage, voluntary registration was in-
stituted. This raised the question – should a man vote where he
ives and pays tax, or in his home village (in the affairs of which
he was still deeply involved)? (Lloyd & Post 1960). In 1955 the
electoral regulations decreed, in complex but relatively unambiguous provisions, that a man should register where he lived
(provided that this was in the Division of which he was 'native')
and had paid his tax for two years; those disenfranchised by this
clause could register in the ward of which they were 'native'.
Many people believed that they had a much greater freedom of
choice. Itsekiri women living in Sapele had no right to register
in that town; so they came to Warri, rather than to the creek
villages where they had probably grown up. So, too, did many
other Itsekiri husbands, who saw their votes being 'wasted' in
a predominantly Urhobo constituency. The Urhobo interpreted
this as a move to pack Warri Township and they brought in
lorry loads of electors from the surrounding villages. The final
register contained over 20,000 names – double the number of
adults resident in the Township. Political party agents, who had
undoubtedly been active in creating this situation, next turned
to objecting to names in order to restore the register to a proper
size. With the adjudicators deciding that the person objected
to should attend to defend his right, most of those who had
come to Warri from outside were removed from the register.

In 1959 the situation was repeated. The choice between
residence and native area as a qualification for registration and
voting was debated at the highest political levels and successive
amendments to the regulations seemed to give the elector an
increasingly greater freedom of choice. The final regulations
gave a choice between voting in one's present place of residence,
or 'the place to which he intends to return'. Other legislation
had referred to 'native' qualifications, clearly intending that the
place referred to should be the one associated with the descent
group of which one was a member – and most Nigerians did so
interpret it. One could not be a 'native' of a modern township,
but one could justly claim one's intention to retire there. Again
an inflated list of registered electors resulted and 13,000 objections were made. Following the rulings made in 1955, Action

Group leaders objected to almost every Ibo name on the register. But this time the Revising Officer placed the onus of proof on the objector, not the person objected to; most of the objections were then withdrawn (Post 1963).

In this election the principal issue for the Itsekiri was not so much the control of the town but their position within the projected Mid-West State to be created by the Federal government. This state, overwhelmingly Edo and Ibo speaking, would certainly have an NCNC majority. During the decade the Olu and the Itsekiri chiefs closely associated with him, were the staunchest possible supporters of the AG. In evidence before the Minorities Commission the Itsekiri leaders had emphasized their cultural ties with the Yoruba, thus claiming continued membership of the Western Region. The election, however, resulted in a victory for Chief Okotie-Eboh over his AG opponent, O. N. Rewane, an Itsekiri lawyer living in Warri and closely identified with the Olu and his faction. Okotie-Eboh could only have won with quite considerable Itsekiri support and his success reflected not only his own personality but also the continuing divisions within the Itsekiri community (Post 1963).

COMMENTARY

In the nineteenth and earlier centuries the 'middleman' role of the Itsekiri, in the slave and palmoil trade, gave them economic superordination over the Urhobo. In the early twentieth century the structure of trade was radically altered. But as the British Administrative officials 'opened' up Urhobo country so new roles were created for the Itsekiri as political agents, court clerks, etc. Though few Itsekiri could hold these middleman roles, the prestige accrued to the entire ethnic group. In time, however, these political roles became obsolete, too.

The Itsekiri looked upon Warri as their new capital, the focal point for their community. But, as we have seen, they have now lost whatever economic and political dominance they once held. The one exception to this general trend concerns the income from the land. In a series of legal actions Dore Numa preserved the Itsekiri rights of sovereignty, though the monetary value of these was whittled down to a token sum. But in the late 1950s it was decided that a substantial proportion of the rents received from crown land should pass not to the community originally holding them – the Agbassa, Okere or Ogbe Ijoh – nor to the people of Warri Township, but to the Itsekiri. The success of the Itsekiri here, and in getting the Olu and his chiefs as traditional members of the new Urban District Council, derived from the support given to the Action Group, the governing party in the Western Region, by the Olu and these same chiefs.

The struggle for these symbols and realities of power heightened ethnic tension in Warri. The rivalry between the two major political parties, the AG and NCNC, polarized this tension; but not completely so, for one faction of the Itsekiri continued to support the NCNC in the person of Chief Festus Okotie-Eboh, whilst some Urhobo were AG supporters.

What had the Itsekiri common man to gain from these struggles? Nearly one-third of the ethnic group lived no longer in the creek villages but in modern towns – Warri, Sapele, Lagos, etc. In Warri they had their due share of the good jobs, though they had conspicuously failed to take advantage of new opportunities in trade and crafts. They were represented on the Urban District Council in proportion to their numbers in the town. And, in any case, the taxes or rents which they paid were unaffected by the political complexion of the local government council.

Why should they then fear Urhobo superiority? Typical responses included 'They might insult the Olu', 'Hooligans might insult my father (a chief) in the street'. A reign of terror against the Itsekiri was predicted. Yet, although the events of September 1952 did provide the Itsekiri with a vivid precedent and although the Itsekiri feared that the Urhobo might abuse them, as they had once abused the Urhobo, everyday life in Warri went on for months without any major incidents of this nature.

Those who gained most in these struggles were the Olu and his circle of chiefs. The Olu sought to increase the status of his title by claiming jurisdiction over all land once falling within the traditional kingdom and including the modern town of Warri; he sought to control the public wealth of this area in the form of ground rents. Some of the chiefs most active in his support seemed to have little income other than that deriving from this 'political' activity. These claims were transformed through the medium of inflammatory speeches, the maintenance of the Itsekiri self stereotype in matters of dress, and through promises of patronage, into issues which could entice the support of the Itsekiri man-in-the-street. Conversely, they were interpreted by their Urhobo counterparts as threats to the economic and political positions which they had won through the 'legitimate' process of free economic competition and democratic elections.

There seemed, in the mid-1950s, to be little immediate likelihood that the Itsekiri would lose their ethnic identity, even though the Urhobo had a reputation for cultural assimilation (two Ibo clans, for instance, having become Urhobo in recent decades). But they were encouraged to believe that a diminution in status of the Olu and his chiefs would be a substantial threat to their own separate identity. It is such fears which seem to produce mob violence – violence which expresses no specific or well articulated interests, at least of the mob.

As I had already indicated not all the Itsekiri supported the Action Group nor were all solid in their support for the Olu. Many consistently voted for Chief Festus Okotie-Eboh, the wealthy Sapele businessman who became Federal Minister of Finance and was killed in the 1964 coup. This split reflected a long-standing division in Itsekiri society between the people living in the Benin River (where Okotie-Eboh was born) and those of the Warri area. Furthermore, the Benin River people looked more to Sapele as their commercial centre and were less interested in the stratagems of the Olu which concerned and benefited (if at all) the people of Warri. The Olu and Chief Okotie-Eboh were leaders of two great factions. But the basis of the wealth of the latter came from his private business and his Federal political office; his electoral support came from Itsekiri, Urhobo and Ibo. So, although he procured what benefits he could for his constituency and although he dressed as an Itsekiri (in as much as one can be dogmatic here, for the Urhobo tended to copy Itsekiri fashions) he did not appeal to exclusively ethnic sentiments. Conversely the Action Group propaganda tended to vilify him as a traitor to the Itsekiri.

I do not wish to minimize the frustration felt by the mass of the Itsekiri as their self-image of themselves accorded to an ever decreasing degree with economic and political realities. But one ought always to look closely to see which individuals gain from exploiting this tension and study the means by which they seek to gain their own ends.

NOTE

The fieldwork on which much of this paper is based was carried out in 1955–56 when I lived in Warri and spent most of my time engaged on an ethnographic survey of the Itsekiri. I was able to revisit Warri for a brief period in 1958 but have not, since that time, had another opportunity to go there. A part of the substance of this paper was given at the WAISER Fifth Annual Conference, Ibadan 1956.

REFERENCES

BRADBURY, R. E. 1957. *The Benin Kingdom and the Edo-Speaking Peoples of South Western Nigeria. Ethnographic Survey of Africa, Western Africa, Part XIII.* London: International African Institute.

IKIME, O. 1969. *Niger Delta Rivalry: Itsekiri-Urhobo Relations and the European Presence 1884–1936.* London: Longmans.

LLOYD, P. C. 1957. *The Itsekiri.* In *Ethnographic Survey of Africa, Western Africa Part XIII.* London: International African Institute.

—— 1963. The Itsekiri in the Nineteenth Century: An Outline Social History. *Journal of African History* 4: 207–31.

LLOYD, P. C. (with K. W. J. POST). 1960. Where Should One Vote? *Journal of African Administration* 21: 95–106.

MOORE, W. 1970. (2nd ed.) *History of the Itsekiri.* London: Cass.

POST, K. W. J. 1963. *The Nigerian Federal Election of 1959.* London: Oxford University Press.

RYDER, A. F. C. 1960. Missionary Activity in the Kingdom of Warri to the Early Nineteenth Century. *Journal of Historical Society of Nigeria* 2: 1–26.

Edward M. Bruner

The Expression of Ethnicity
in Indonesia

In the study of ethnicity the unit of analysis has shifted from
the isolated ethnic group defined by its cultural content to the
ethnic unit as a social category, a form of structure, embedded
within a larger system. Behaviour that had formerly been regarded as traditional may now be seen as emerging as a response
to patterns of interaction and communication among groups;
items of culture as well as but ways of thinking and of evaluating oneself are intrinsically related to the structural position
of one's group in the larger society. Gluckman (1960), for
example, explains urban tribalism in terms of the social context of the town rather than in terms of the persistence of
rural culture patterns in the city. M. G. Smith's (1960) studies
of pluralism treat group relations as a function of cleavages
and segmentation in the nation as a whole, Cohen (1969) turns
our attention to how particular tribal polities share in the
overall allocation of economic and political power, and Barth
(1969) sees the maintenance of ethnicity as based upon interaction rather than isolation and focuses on the boundaries
between groups.

It is somewhat paradoxical, however, that despite the theoretical convergence on the larger system and despite the increasing number of field studies on the emergence of ethnicity
in cities, we have not yet come to grips with conceptualizing
those features of the urban system that are relevant for the
understanding of urban ethnicity. The problem arose in striking
fashion in my own investigations of the expression of ethnicity
in two cities in Indonesia, a nation well known in social science
as the classic case of the plural society (Furnivall 1948). I
found that ethnicity is manifested and experienced very differently in the two cities, and a review of the literature did not
prove to be particularly helpful in elucidating why this should
be so. The expression of ethnicity varied as the urban context

251

varied, and the city itself became a relevant unit of analysis. The problem became one of relating ethnic group interaction and other aspects of social life to urban structure and ecology.

INDONESIAN BACKGROUND

Indonesia, the world's largest island complex, extends 3,400 miles from east to west and consists of thousands of islands populated by 300 different ethnolinguistic groups (Geertz 1963; Pelzer 1963). There are approximately 120 million Indonesians but the population is very unevenly distributed. The island of Java and neighbouring Madura with only 7 per cent of the total territory of Indonesia contains 65 per cent of the population, with an average density of 477 persons per sq. km. The population density of the rest of Indonesia, the so-called outer islands, is 19 persons per sq. km. The important aspects of the social demography of Indonesia are that half the population are members of a single ethnic group, the Javanese, that the vast majority of Javanese live on the island of Java, and that most other Indonesians see themselves as engaged in a more or less continual struggle to keep from being Javanized.

Indonesia has a national culture in that there are national symbols and such national institutions as a civil service, a military organization, and other agencies of the central government but every Indonesian is also a member of an ethnic group in that he is either Javanese, Malay, Balinese, Minangkabau or something else. The national language, Indonesian, exists side by side with various local languages. Home territories on one or another island are ethnically homogeneous; the mixing of peoples occurs primarily in border areas and in such modern contexts as army camps, government offices, and cities. In such modern contexts including the most intellectual circles in the national capital, Djakarta, I have asked literally hundreds of persons if they knew anyone who was just an Indonesian with no ethnic affiliation. My respondents replied that there are a few who do approximate that model, and many felt that the children of some families would eventually lose all ethnic identification, but it was clear that at present there is no readily identifiable community of Indonesians as such. Nor is there any opposition between being a member of an ethnic group and an Indonesian citizen at the same time, for not only is this the normal state of affairs but there is no viable alternative.

An elaborate set of stereotypes or labels define the characteristics of the various Indonesian ethnic groups *vis-à-vis* each other. The Javanese and Sundanese for example are known to be very polite and refined and to control their emotions while the Batak are considered as more expressive and volatile and also as less refined. Some groups are regarded as good businessmen, others are morally puritanical, and there are four groups about whom it is said that one has to be very careful in a dispute because they are likely to fight with knives. Members of two other ethnic groups have the reputation of being food poisoners. Ethnic labels deal with vital areas – emotions, aggression, sex, food.

THE TWO CITIES

My first field study of ethnicity in Indonesian cities was conducted in 1957–58 among one ethnic group, the Toba Batak, in both their rural homeland and in Medan, a town on the east coast of Sumatra. Subsequently, as political conditions stabilized in Indonesia, I returned between 1969–71 for a total of nine months in the field and initiated two different projects. In one, I returned to Sumatra to examine the changes that had occurred among the Toba Batak in village and city, thirteen years after my initial research. The second project consisted of a study of ethnicity among four different ethnic groups, the Javanese, Sundanese, Batak, and Minangkabau, located in the city of Bandung on the island of Java.[1] These two approaches provided new perspectives and it became apparent that my 1958 conclusions (Bruner 1959, 1961, 1963) although valid for Medan in Sumatra were not valid for cities in Java, and the question arose of how to explain the discrepancy.

The expression of ethnicity in the two cities of Medan and Bandung is different not only in terms of the quality of social relationships between members of different groups but also in terms of such other features as the organization of voluntary associations, the performance of rituals, rates of intermarriage, and the depth of the differences between the older and younger generations. These seemingly isolated variables which are often investigated and treated separately are interrelated and form a consistent pattern when viewed in the context of the larger urban structure.

Let us examine the structure of the two cities in the light of some previous urban theories. Louis Wirth (1938) related a large number of social variables to the three criteria of population size, population density, and cultural heterogeneity. Based upon 1961 census data, Medan, the fifth largest city in Indonesia, has a population of one-half million and Bandung, the third largest city, one million, so that both are within the same range; both cities have comparable population densities (9,339 persons per sq. km. for Medan and 12,010 for Bandung); and both are characterized by ethnic heterogeneity although the ethnic mix varies (Milone 1966). Wirth's criteria apply to all urban centres and are not differentiating. The familiar distinction which has appeared in many forms between old indigenous cities and new cities (Redfield & Singer 1954; Southall 1961) is not applicable as both Medan and Bandung developed during the colonial era and are products of colonialism. Other typologies could be cited which distinguish between industrial and preindustrial cities (Sjoberg 1960); between plantation, commercial, and capital cities; or between large primate cities and smaller provincial cities. One could devise an infinite number of arbitrary typologies but the problem in each case for the social anthropologist is to link specific aspects of urban structure to specific aspects of social life.

It would seem appropriate to turn to Furnivall (1939, 1948) as he developed the concept of plural society based upon Indonesian data, and he is referred to so frequently in the literature on pluralism and ethnicity. What is usually emphasized in his writings is the notion of different social orders within the same political unit existing side by side, integrated in the market place, but otherwise separate. But for Furnivall the viability of the political unit depended upon the interconnections between these separate social orders, and in any case he tells us very little about the ethnic groups of Indonesia. Furnivall writes ' . . . in Netherlands India, the European, Chinaman and Native are linked vitally as Siamese twins and, if rent asunder, every element of the union must dissolve in anarchy' (1939: 447). Although Indonesia has had serious problems in achieving economic and political stability in the two decades since independence the country has not dissolved in anarchy and the Natives now appear to be doing reasonably well in conducting the affairs of the fifth largest nation in the world. The plural society for Furnivall refers to 'the European, Chinaman and Native', and not to Javanese, Sundanese, Malay, Minangkabau, and other Indonesian groups. He does not differentiate within the category Native and he has a completely outside or European view of Indonesian pluralism. The presence of the Dutch changed the relationships among the Indonesians, and had this been described it would have provided an invaluable comparative base for later studies of ethnic relations in post-independence Indonesia, but Furnivall did not do so and for our study, has little value.

THE DOMINANT CULTURE HYPOTHESIS

My hypothesis is that the feature of urban structure that differentiates Medan from Bandung and that accounts for the varying pattern of ethnic group relations in the two cities is the absence or presence of a dominant majority culture (c.f. Mercier 1965 and Southall 1956). Medan is a city of minorities and lacks a dominant culture while in Bandung the dominant culture group is the Sundanese, the second largest ethnic group in Indonesia with a total population of approximately 20 million.

To place the hypothesis in broader perspective, the concept of a dominant culture may be divided into three separate components of the larger system that are sociologically relevant to ethnic expression in any multi-ethnic group situation. The first component is the population ratio or the social demography, and not just the fact of ethnic heterogeneity but rather the nature of the particular mix in a given context. The second component concerns the established local culture, if any, and the manner in which members of other groups relate to and articulate with it. The third component focuses on the locus of power and its distribution among the various ethnic groups. The three components then are the social demography, the established local culture, and the locus of power.

Tables 1, 2, and *3* present population distributions for Bandung and Medan in 1930, the last time an accurate census was taken which included data on ethnic affiliation. These data are old but they are reliable and they can serve our purpose. Since

TABLE 1 *Population in Bandung and Medan, 1930*

	Bandung		Medan	
	number	per cent	number	per cent
Indonesian	130,028	77·9	41,270	53·9
European	19,650	11·8	4,293	5·6
Chinese	16,657	10·0	27,287	35·6
Other Asians	480	·3	3,734	4·9
	166,815	100·0	76,584	100·0

TABLE 2 *Ethnic Groups in Bandung, 1930*

	number	per cent
Sundanese	95,769	73·7
Javanese	27,448	21·1
Batavia (Djakarta)	2,223	1·7
Moluccan	1,172	·9
North Celebes	1,114	·8
Malays	688	·5
Minangkabau	632	·5
South Sumatra	374	·3
Batak	120	·1
Other	488	·4
	130,028	100·0

1930 the European population has declined drastically, the Chinese have increased slightly and the Indonesian population has increased considerably. During the 1930–61 period there has been a 600 per cent increase in population in each city, almost entirely due to migration of native Indonesians.

In Bandung we see that the Sundanese total 73·7 per cent of

the Indonesian population, a clear numerical majority, followed
by 21·1 per cent Javanese and then small percentages of many
other ethnic groups. The table is misleading in that some
categories such as South Sumatra are regions, not ethnic groups.
A variety of groups originating in South Sumatra have been
lumped together in the census data, so that there are even more
small ethnic groups represented than indicated in *Table 2*.

The city of Bandung is the provincial capital of West Java,
the homeland of the Sundanese people. Surrounding the city are

TABLE 3 *Ethnic Groups in Medan, 1930*

	number	*per cent*
Javanese	19,069	46·2
Minangkabau	5,590	13·5
Malays	5,408	13·1
Mandailing Batak	4,688	11·4
Toba Batak	820	1·9
Other Batak	1,570	3·8
Sundanese	1,209	2·9
Batavia (Djakarta)	1,118	2·7
Other	1,798	4·5
	41,270	100·0

rural farming communities that are almost 100 per cent Sundanese, and migrants to the city acknowledge that Bandung
'belongs' to the Sundanese. As Sundanese are the most numerous peoples the migrants have more daily contact with them
than with members of their own ethnic group. During the
colonial period there were European, Javanese, and Chinese
sections of the city but now the various ethnic groups are not
residentially segregated.

The Sundanese are the dominant culture group in that they
set the standards of appropriate behaviour in public places,
and most urban institutions are controlled by them and are
operated in terms of their culture patterns. They occupy key
positions of power in the city and it is understood that the
governor of the province, the mayor of the city, the presidents

of local universities, and the heads of major agencies and most branches of the national government will be Sundanese. With some exceptions to be discussed later all migrants adapt to the locally dominant culture. They conceive of the adaptation as a process of individual adjustment but they are responding individually to the larger structure of ethnic group relations in the city. Migrants take a position in the urban system with reference to the dominant culture group and they occupy economic niches made available to them or left vacant by that dominant group. In orienting their behaviour in reference to the Sundanese most migrant peoples change themselves and their culture in the direction of becoming Sundanese-like. This process operates on both conscious and unconscious levels and although it is a reflection of the larger political context it has consequences for individual and group identity, as we shall see.

In Bandung the Sundanese are a numerical majority, are the dominant culture, and have control of political power. The three components of the hypothesis here converge but there are, of course, other cases in which a minority population with an alien culture may have the power, e.g. colonialism. To consider all possible variations would be going beyond the limits of our data, but an interesting contrast is provided by Medan, where there is no population majority, no locally dominant culture and considerable competition among ethnic groups for economic and political power.

Referring back to the data on ethnic groups in Medan in *Table 3*, the Javanese with 46·2 per cent of the Indonesian population are the most numerous group, although not a majority. The Javanese, however, are not indigenous to the area, and most came to Sumatra to work on the plantations as contract labourers. Native peoples such as the Batak refused to work as estate labourers because they considered it beneath them. During the colonial era in North Sumatra the Batak regarded the Javanese as a lower segment of humanity, and referred to the men as coolies and to the women as prostitutes. A number of Batak who had visited Java in the colonial period and who had met aristocratic Javanese for the first time noted with surprise that they were so different from the Javanese labourers in Sumatra. The Javanese in North Sumatra, as lower class recent migrants, did not occupy positions of power and did not serve as a dominant culture model for other ethnic groups. The peoples who were indigenous to the Medan region, and in whose home territory the city was located, were the Malays, the Karo Batak, and the Simalungun Batak, but within the city itself they totalled only 13·5 per cent of the Indonesian population in 1930.

Medan arose as a commercial city within a vast estate complex on the east coast of Sumatra to serve the interests of European planters. By 1930, 46·1 per cent of the population were not Indonesians – they were Europeans, Chinese, and other Asians. Among the Indonesian population almost 52 per cent were migrants from the island of Java. Since independence the percentage of Europeans, Chinese, and Javanese has declined and there has been a large increase in the absolute number as well as in the percentage of native people of Sumatra, particularly the Batak. But the various Batak subgroups do not constitute a majority as they are divided among themselves. Each subgroup conceives of itself as a separate unit and there is an additional cleavage along religious lines between Christian and Moslem Batak.

It will be instructive to examine Medan and then Bandung from the perspective of one ethnic group, the Toba Batak. The group was selected as a basis for comparison simply because I have field data on the Toba Batak communities in each city but the results can be generalized. Later, we shall examine Bandung from the point of view of the dominant Sundanese, but we begin with Medan.

MEDAN

The political scientist R. William Liddle (1970) in a monograph on local politics in Pemantangsiantar, a North Sumatran city very similar to Medan, concludes that 'the most critical principle of differentiation among individuals is ethnic or ethno-religious affiliation' (227), and also 'the most striking findings are the overriding importance of ethnicity' (186). 'For at least the last few decades the inhabitant of Simalungun/Siantar has identified most strongly with his ethnic or ethnoreligious group, and local loyalties and hostilities have been heavily coloured by this ethnic self-identification. Practically all aspects of social life – residence, educational and occupational opportunities, religious belief and practice, friendship, political organization – are today affected by the perception of ethnic differences' (207). Liddle notes that his findings 'seem to be at odds with studies of urbanization and tribalism in Africa' (227) and he refers specifically to publications of the Rhodes-Livingstone Institute, e.g. Epstein (1958). An analysis of the differences between North Sumatra and Central Africa would be beyond the scope of this paper, although one factor of importance may be that both Liddle and I have worked in a postcolonial context, in which the Europeans present were few in number and had almost no political power. A dominant alien European administration tends to solidify diverse indigenous ethnic groups under its jurisdiction. In any case, my findings in North Sumatra confirm those of Liddle as to the pervasive influence of ethnicity and tribal allegiances as opposed to class, and of course we mean contemporary ethnicity that has emerged in modern urban situations and not a rural persistence. In North Sumatran cities most political leaders are dependent upon a support group consisting of members of their own ethnic group, and each urban political party does tend to represent an ethnoreligious group, e.g. the Parkindo party the Christian Toba Batak, the Masjumi party the Moslem Mandailing Batak, and the PNI the Javanese.

The interpersonal consequences of a competitive urban system are that relationships between members of different ethnic groups tend to be tense, lacking in trust, and based on ethnic stereotypes. Certainly close individual friendships do develop but there is always the possibility of the individuals finding themselves involved in a larger confrontation between ethnic blocks which puts a strain on their relationship. It is particularly in situations involving competition that ethnic polarization occurs, and there are many such situations ranging from competition in business to office colleagues vying for the same promotion to teenagers striving for the affections of a girl. It is well known and widely accepted in Medan that if the head of one's office is say a Mandailing he will tend to favour the members of his own group in job assignments and in the recruitment of personnel. Occasionally in government offices one will find that almost everyone in a particular department belongs to the same ethnic group, and if the situation is too blatant it may be called to the attention of the newspapers and create a minor scandal. I asked one Batak department head why so many men in his office were Batak and he assured me that he really did not plan it that way. He was a close informant and we had talked about the difference between particularistic and universalistic criteria. He explained that so many Batak relatives came to him asking for employment and that he did not feel that he could refuse them all. Some were well qualified, and when he had to make a choice between an equally competent Batak and a member of a different ethnic group he would choose the Batak, in large part because he could trust him more. Trust enhances office efficiency and the individual decisions made by the department head were rational, although the cumulative effect adds up to nepotism.

The major line of social differentiation and cleavage in Medan society is undoubtedly ethnic, despite the fact that within each ethnic group members occupy a range of social structure slots in the urban system, differ considerably in level of income, and display a variety of individual life styles. If one plots the interaction network of Toba Batak in non-work situations the majority of ties are with members of one's own ethnic group, and some persons choose the option of encapsulating themselves within the confines of an all Toba Batak community. They do so by withdrawal from as many non-Toba Batak contexts as possible, by full participation in their Toba Batak neighbourhood mutual aid society and their city-wide Toba Batak clan association, by active involvement in the affairs of one of the Toba Batak ethnic churches in Medan, and by attendance at as many of the Toba Batak adat rituals to which they are entitled to participate by virtue of kinship rights (cf. Bruner 1959, 1963). Not all Toba Batak choose this alternative; many, particularly of the elite, extend their ties widely across ethnic lines, but those who do encapsulate themselves find the ethnic organizations and voluntary associations readily available, and they are rewarded by other members of their ethnic community for their involvement in Batak affairs.

There are alliances which crosscut ethnic boundaries. The indigenous peoples, the Malays, Karo Batak, and Simalungun Batak, have formed political action groups in opposition to the

migrants, the Mandailing Batak, the Javanese, the Minangkabau, and especially the Toba Batak, the most aggressive
recent intruders, but the action group has not been successful.
There is some opposition between the Christians, mostly the
Toba Batak, but also many Karo and Simalungun Batak
against the Moslems the Mandailing Batak, Malays, Javanese,
and Minangkabau. The various Batak subgroups have banded
together during some of the sporadic open fighting between
ethnic groups that erupted in Medan during the 1950s, but the
alliances arose on an ad hoc basis and only lasted for the
duration of the actual conflict. All Indonesian groups in North
Sumatra are united in their opposition to the large Chinese
community, with its extensive business and commercial interests tied to the neighbouring Chinese across the Straits of
Malacca in Malaya and Singapore. And finally the people of
Sumatra are together in their antagonism toward what they regard as Javanese control of Indonesia and particularly in their
resentment that so much of the foreign exchange produced on
the Sumatran plantations eventually ends up in the national
treasury in Djakarta, one factor involved in the Sumatran
rebellion of 1958–61 against the central government. Cross-
cutting ties develop but they are temporary, based on particular
issues, and do not generalize to other areas of social life.

The basic predicament in Medan and in the province of North
Sumatra generally is that after the departure of the Dutch
colonial administration, no one indigenous group could gain
control, which led to intense competition to fill the power
vacuum. The situation was complicated by population shifts
due to heavy migration from rural to urban areas, the political
instability of the new national government, the sometimes reck-
less economic policies of Sukarno which led to an extremely
high rate of inflation, the lack of a truly national distinctively
Indonesian culture pattern which could have served as an
alternative to ethnic lifeways, and the uneasy relationship of
Sumatran peoples to the perceived domination by the Javanese
of the national administration located on the remote island of
Java.

Our understanding of Medan will be enhanced by contrast
with the Toba Batak community in Bandung, to which we turn.

BANDUNG

The Batak and other migrants in Bandung realize that the Sundanese are the dominant culture and they adapt to the realities of the urban situation in which they find themselves. As an illustration, if there were a vacancy for the position of supervisor of an office in Medan the Toba Batak would manœuvre and plan so that one of their own might be selected, as they would assess that thereafter they would be favoured, and other groups in Medan would do likewise. If there were a similar opening in a Bandung office it would be assumed that the position would be filled by a Sundanese, or possibly a Javanese, and the other ethnic groups would not enter the competition. The difference between the two cities has profound implications for social life and for ethnic group relations.

The 8,000 to 9,000 Toba Batak are a clear minority in Bandung, a city of one million. It is not possible for them to encapsulate themselves either residentially or socially, as they are too few and too dispersed. In Medan, each neighbourhood has a mutual aid society consisting of the Toba Batak located in the area, and other ethnic groups have their territorially based welfare association. In Bandung there are also neighbourhood associations but membership is not restricted to a single ethnic group; everyone who resides in a given section of the city is eligible to join, regardless of ethnic affiliation. There are fewer Toba Batak adat rituals in Bandung than in Medan, and the clan associations are less active. Thus there are fewer opportunities for a Batak in Bandung to limit himself to distinctively Batak contexts, and there are correspondingly many more occasions for relationships with Sundanese in the neighbourhood, at school, at work, and elsewhere.

The key to understanding social change in Bandung is the process that I have referred to as 'becoming Sundanese-like'. To describe this process, let us begin by taking the perspective of a Toba Batak migrant who has just arrived from Sumatra. The majority of migrants enter the city through a Batak social network and indeed their arrival is usually known in advance. All Batak churches in Java publicly announce at each Sunday service the arrivals and departures of the Toba Batak in their area. The experienced Bandung Batak learn about the new migrant and there is always someone, often a distant clan relative, who welcomes him to the city and who provides a short course of instruction in Sundanese culture and behaviour, designed to help him adjust to life in Java. Most of the instruction takes place over a period of time in informal contexts on a person-to-person basis, but sometimes it is more formally organized. During one period of especially heavy migration a Batak ethnic association met in a Bandung warehouse and held weekly instructional sessions, in seminar-like fashion. The Batak upperclassmen at Indonesia's leading technological university in Bandung, ITB, regularly meet with incoming Batak freshmen, as an extracurricular aspect of the orientation programme.

The content of the instruction varies from recipes for appropriate behaviour in particular situations to the presentation of general rules on such an abstract level that they would delight the most rigorous ethnoscience oriented anthropologist. I witnessed one session on how to drink tea in Bandung. It was explained and demonstrated that in Sumatra the Batak drink all the tea in the cup with gusto while the Sundanese not only handle the tea cup with greater delicacy, but they will only drink slightly more than half, then they place the cup down on the table and announce that they have had enough. The instructor noted with some surprise that the Sundanese never finish their tea, what a waste, and when we Batak do so, he continued, the Sundanese consider us impolite! He said that although the people here may behave in strange ways, we are guests in Sundaland and we must adapt to their standards of tea drinking. After all, he continued, we Batak are emigrés in an alien land and we have come here to make a living, so we are the ones who must adjust. It was a concise lesson, well told, and to the point.

In the instructional sessions it is noted that the Sundanese consider themselves more refined and civilized (*halus*) than the Batak, so that one aspect of the adjustment process consists of learning to become less aggressive, to soften the rough edges and to talk in a lower tone of voice. Aside from the specifics, the covert communication is that in order to survive in Bandung a Batak cannot behave naturally and be 'himself'. He becomes very sensitive to the local culture patterns and he becomes oriented to changing his behaviour.

The migrant to Bandung receives instruction from other Batak on how to behave and he acknowledges that he must discard his village ways and become more refined. He finds it difficult, however, to generalize these prescriptions to all the new interactional situations in which he finds himself and sooner or later he will behave crudely or inappropriately, with the result that he will be laughed at, or embarrassed, or 'put down' by a Sundanese. This hurts, as the migrant quite understandably wants to be accepted in the new urban community to which he has come to make a new life, but the experience represents a new phase in his adaptation to life on Java.

If we take a Sundanese perspective we may better understand what has occurred in the interaction. Most Sundanese have not had much experience with Batak although all are familiar with the Batak stereotype of a rough and aggressive person. The Sundanese and the Batak each approach the initial interaction guided by their own customs and emotional set, and at first they judge the other by their own standards. What the Sundanese define as being crude the Batak interpret as being honest, straightforward, and strong. What the Sundanese regard as refined behaviour the Batak regard as being evasive, insincere, and feminine. Each group feels morally superior to the other and at least initially the behaviour of each tends to validate these stereotypic evaluations. Each group in doing what it thinks is right and proper behaves in ways that the other feels are morally deficient (cf. Braroe 1970). The end result, however, is not an interactional standoff because the Sundanese change their strategy and the Batak change their behaviour.

Within their own cultural system the Sundanese find it difficult to deal with an aggressive person and their initial reaction may be to avoid Batak people, but this is at best awkward if one has a Batak neighbour or office colleague. It becomes very clear, however, that if one shows respect and politeness to a Batak he will take advantage of the situation, or as they say, 'if you lower yourself in front of a Batak he will climb on your shoulder and sit on your head'. The Sundanese learn that one way to handle the Batak is to speak louder and to become more aggressive themselves, and to engage in what they call 'bluffing' behaviour. After all, they are secure in the interaction as they are the dominant power group operating in their home territory. Their main strategy, however, is to let the Batak know in a variety of subtle and not so subtle ways that he is acting in an improper and really rather barbaric manner, which the Sundanese believe. Among themselves the Sundanese comment that Batak eat dogs, which to them is repugnant enough, but they also note that Batak eat people. Cannibalism did exist in the Batak highlands in Sumatra a century ago and all Sundanese are not entirely convinced that the practice has been discontinued. The Sundanese can ignore a Batak neighbour, make life uncomfortable for the entire family, and bring considerable economic pressure to bear if necessary.

It rarely goes this far, however, as the Batak eventually becomes aware of what is happening, he is oriented to change as we have noted, and he begins to experiment with new ways of behaving. After a Batak understands the Sundanese better he accepts even more local patterns and he may become quite skilled in perceiving what the Sundanese define as being refined. One Batak businessman who had lived all his adult life in Bandung took great pride in the fact that he had a deep understanding of Sundanese culture and that he really knew how to handle the Sundanese in any situation. In time, a Batak migrant learns to speak softly, drink tea appropriately, and he observes all the Sundanese rituals of respect. The Sundanese in turn then acknowledge that here is a Batak who is becoming civilized, so they begin to behave toward him in a more human, i.e. Sundanese, way by showing more deference. The process is mutually reinforcing.

With increasing self and cultural awareness a Batak will sometimes begin to manipulate the stereotypes. He fully realizes that the Sundanese regard him as crude and emotionally volatile, but he may raise his voice or even make threatening gestures as a way of manipulating the Sundanese so as to gain his own ends. He acts as if he were angry as a ploy even though he does not feel anger, as he knows that Sundanese prefer to avoid open conflict and overt aggression, but he must be careful not to go too far. The Sundanese too learn to manipulate Batak, sometimes against the Javanese, by appealing to the Batak as a strong and aggressive person, and by flattering him in ways that appeal to his inner conception of himself.

Manipulative behaviour is frequently employed but the Bandung Batak realize that in the long run it is much more effective to play the game by Sundanese rules. More as an outward accommodation than an inner transformation, the Batak acquire a working knowledge of Sundanese culture, learn to predict how the Sundanese will act, and modify their own behaviour in accord with Sundanese standards. This is the very first step in the process by which ethnic labels and what we call 'culture' changes in the course of social interaction. But the process accelerates over time and has unanticipated consequences.

A Batak from Sumatra who had spent four years in a city in Java returned to Medan and described his experiences. In Java he said, he ate less, became thinner, and his voice got softer, but after he returned to Medan he became strong again. He ate more, began to talk loud, and he regained his strength and Batakness. This man's revealing observation suggests that to be Batak is to be crude but also strong and masculine, and that in Sumatra he regained his true self. But those who reside permanently on Java and who raise a family there cannot have this experience of a self regained, because on Java they are not fully aware of a self lost.

The most extensive change occurs among Batak children who have been born and raised in Bandung. They play and attend school with Sundanese children, and they grow up learning the rules of Sundanese culture not as a superficial secondary accommodation but as their first learning experience. The first three grades of the public primary school in Bandung use the Sundanese language as the medium of instruction; in Medan the language of instruction is Indonesian because the school population is so ethnically heterogeneous. In high school in Bandung there are classes in Sundanese culture and all students are expected to write stories and poems in Sundanese. As a consequence the Batak families in Bandung speak Sundanese or Indonesian to their pre-school children, so as to better prepare them for school. Almost all Batak adults in Bandung speak Sundanese, as it is necessary for the men in business and for the women in the market and in the neighbourhood. One Batak educator confided in me with considerable apprehension that he and other adults were very concerned, as most Batak families in Bandung speak Sundanese and Indonesian at home and there were now many Batak children who were barely able to speak their own language. It is a dilemma he said, but what can we do?

An essential component of Batak adat rituals is the sharing of a common meal. In Medan the participants sit on mats on the floor and eat with their fingers; in Bandung they sit at tables and use silverware. In anthropological terms we would say that all participants at the ceremonies in both Medan and Bandung are equally 'Batak', that both variations are equally part of 'Batak culture', and that the Bandung pattern is an adaptation to the Sundanese and to the position of the Toba Batak minority in the urban system of ethnic group relations on Java. For ethnographic completeness we must add that in Bandung before a wedding there is a small private part of the ceremony for the close family, primarily representatives of the wife giving and the wife receiving groups, at which food is shared. At this private ritual the participants do sit on the floor and eat with their fingers but it is always held indoors and Sundanese are never present. At the larger public ceremony to which hundreds and even thousands of guests may be invited, including Sundanese, the Bandung Batak use tables and silverware.

The Batak too see the difference as an adaptation to existing circumstances, and they give a basically situational explanation, in terms very similar to the theoretical positions of Max Gluckman and Clyde Mitchell. When in Bandung follow Bandung practice, and when in Medan follow Medan practice. An adult Batak from Bandung who returns to Sumatra for an adat ceremony feels quite at ease with the Medan pattern of sitting on the floor and eating with his fingers in public. As a child in Sumatra he grew up in that tradition and despite his many years on Java, it is still natural to him. But the striking change in attitude and feeling tone occurs among the Java-born Batak who go to Sumatra for the first time. One Batak youth said that the practice of sitting with a group of men eating together with one's fingers from a common bowl was rather primitive and probably unsanitary. He commented that even though he was a Batak he really felt like a 'tourist' in Batakland, and he soon returned to more familiar surroundings in Java.

To summarize thus far, what begins in Bandung as a conscious accommodation takes on a deeper significance in the second generation and goes beyond a Gluckman-Mitchell type of situational flip-flop, as the Java-born Toba Batak begin to evaluate themselves and other Batak by Sundanese standards. The process of becoming Sundanese-like and of learning the rules of the local game is transformed as the urban Sundanese rules become part of the Batak definition of proper conduct. But the situation in Indonesia is such that the process does not go to completion, as Batak rarely becomes Sundanese. In Barth's terms, they maintain ethnic group boundaries but the cultural content changes. They retain their Toba Batak identity, live in Bandung, speak mostly Sundanese and Indonesian, and practise a culture that is at least partly Sundanese. They are Bandung Batak.

MEDAN AND BANDUNG COMPARED: A SUMMARY

In Medan there is no population majority, no locally dominant culture, and there is competition among ethnic groups for economic and political power. In Bandung the Sundanese are a numerical majority, are the dominant culture in their home area, and have control of political power. The three conditions which I label the dominant culture hypothesis structure the larger urban context and give rise to two different processes of ethnic group relations. In Medan the cleavages between ethnic groups are sharply defined, relationships are tense, and each group tends to encapsulate itself. In Bandung the relationships between ethnic groups are more relaxed and there is more interaction between groups than in Medan. In Bandung compared to Medan there is more intermarriage between members of different groups and the cultural and attitudinal differences between the older and the younger generation within each group are greater.

In Medan there is no common cultural code and no widely shared rules to follow so it is somewhat difficult for the different ethnic groups to relate to one another. They have little basis for predicting each other's behaviour so they tend to remain apart. In Bandung, all migrant groups adapt to Sundanese standards, follow Sundanese rules, and thus share a common code which facilitates interaction. Atjehnese, Minangkabau, and Batak in Bandung relate to one another in Sundanese terms.

What we have accomplished thus far is to state which conditions give rise to which societal consequences, and to isolate two different processes of ethnic group relations. We have established firm links between urban ecology and the larger social system on the one hand, and strategies of adaptation on the other. We have provided models of intergroup relationships guided by symbolic interaction theory. At this point it will be appropriate to introduce two qualifications.

The first qualification is that we have reluctantly but purposely ignored individual variation. Although well aware that persons within any one ethnic group occupy different niches in the urban occupational structure, have different social networks, and interactional strategies based on varying degrees of sophistication, our objective has been to isolate the larger context within which individual adaptations are defined. The second qualification is related to the above, in that depending upon one's position in the system, the consequences that we have described for Bandung occur in Medan and vice versa. To take one example, in Medan there is a top elite consisting of the very wealthy businessmen, high government officials and military personnel, and professionals such as medical doctors. Many of this social class have been overseas for training or business, they speak foreign languages, they interact with the local foreign community, and they relate to one another in some contexts by what might be called an international common code, but it must be emphasized that they do not renounce their ethnic ties nor appreciably diminish their participation in ethnic affairs. These data would represent a contradiction of our major thesis if we were attempting to demonstrate that Medan is one 'kind' of city and Bandung another 'kind', or if our objective were to construct mutually exclusive classes as part of a rigid typology. But as our aim is to isolate social processes and to specify the prior conditions which generate them, the example is consistent with our hypothesis and serves to strengthen our position.

IDENTITY CHANGE AND INTERMARRIAGE

Previously we said that Batak rarely becomes Sundanese, but it does happen. There are circumstances in which the members of one Indonesian ethnic group do change their identity and become something else, and we now consider a variety of ways this occurs.

The Mandailing Batak are an example of a group that defines itself very differently depending upon the context. In Sumatra they refer to themselves by the single term Mandailing and choose not to be known as Batak. They are a Moslem people and they want to disassociate themselves from the crude and Christian Toba, even though the Mandailing and the Toba dialects of Batak are very close. In Sumatra the Mandailing preference for separation is widely known and respected but in Bandung the dominant Sundanese lump the Mandailing and the Toba and the other subgroups together in the larger category Batak. Peoples of Java are not sensitive to all of the finer ethnic distinctions relevant on the outer islands. The Mandailing are then placed in the position of having to explain what kind of people they are to the Sundanese and sometimes they do so by saying that they are really like the Minangkabau, a Sumatran Moslem group located south of the Batak highlands. But on other occasions, especially during periods of political tension in Bandung, it is advantageous for the Mandailing to stand together with the Toba. Then they say to the Toba and to themselves that all Batak have a common ancestor and that all share the same adat, thus they are one people. A Mandailing may be a Batak or not, depending on the situation and although this is a particularly clear-cut example it is not an unusual one, for indeed the phenomenon depicted of presenting oneself differently depending on the context is universal.

As there are large military and educational establishments in and near Bandung many Toba Batak men enter the city as soldiers or as students. According to one estimate the ratio of unmarried Batak men to Batak women is seven to one. The consequence is that Batak men frequently marry Sundanese women. In most of these cases the Sundanese wife will 'become' Batak in that she learns to speak Batak, converts to Christianity, is adopted into her husband's mother's clan, attends the adat rituals, and raises her children as Batak. To become Batak in this case does not mean an identity change, for if the wife is asked her ethnic affiliation she will reply that she is a Sundanese married to a Batak. If her children are asked, however, their first response is that they are Batak, and if prodded slightly they may say they are Batak with a Sundanese mother. At the same time as the wife is becoming Batak and is being incorporated into the Bandung Batak community, the husband and children are progressively becoming Sundanese, not in identity but in culture, and at a faster rate than would otherwise be the case because they have a Sundanese within the primary unit of socialization. The two processes occur simultaneously and are not contradictory but neither are they identical. The Sundanese woman becomes Batak quite consciously and all at once, by accepting the differentiating and visible symbols of Batakness. Becoming Sundanese by virtue of residence in a Sundanese city is a longer term and more subtle process, in which unconscious identification with the dominant power group plays a significant role. To put it in another and somewhat oversimplified way, the child inherits his ethnic identity from his Batak father but most of his culture patterns from his Sundanese mother as well as from his Sundanese peer group.

For centuries, Javanese men have been migrating to Bandung and have taken Sundanese wives. As a rough generalization, if the man is an upper-class aristocrat the children become Javanese but if the man is lower class, isolated from his Javanese relatives, and landless in his home area, then he becomes dependent upon his wife's family and the children become Sundanese. If asked, the children say they are Sundanese with a Javanese father, and indeed there are many Sundanese in West Java who have had Javanese ancestors, whom they acknowledge.

Marriages in the other direction in which Batak or Javanese women marry Sundanese men do occur, but less frequently, probably because most migrants to Bandung are men. Each group, however, has its own cultural explanation. The Batak say that if a woman marries out the children are lost to the Batak community, as they have no clan, which is passed patrilineally, and no wife receiving relatives so that it is impossible to perform the Batak adat rituals. When a Batak man marries out his wife is adopted into his mother's clan, as if it were a matrilateral cross cousin marriage; his mother's father and brothers become the core of the wife giving group and his own lineage relatives the wife receiving group. The pressure to prevent Batak women from marrying out is considerable, and even if the woman runs off with a Sundanese man, her clan relatives do not accept the union but will make every effort to bring her back to the Batak community. The Javanese, on the other hand, explain that they are 'older', that is superior to the Sundanese and that it is not appropriate for an older higher status woman to marry a younger man of lower status. As a concomitant, it is said that Javanese women find Sundanese men too feminine and sexually unattractive.

Sundanese society is characterized by others and by themselves as open and tolerant. Although they appear to give their women away quite freely, they gain in the long run, as the Sundanese incorporate and assimilate the lower class Javanese, who are the most numerous migrant group in West Java.

One theoretically significant finding is that the offspring of intermarriages become neither Indonesian nor mestizo, but rather they take the ethnic affiliation of either the father or the mother. They choose one as their primary ethnic identification and acknowledge the other. In Moslem-Christian intermarriages the family usually settles on one religion, especially after there are children, and they do not remain mixed. If pressed to specify the most important factor influencing the choice of ethnic and religious identification, a first approximation would be that children take the affiliation of the higher status parent, but there are innumerable exceptions. The evidence also suggests that children are not given a real choice but rather, the matter is decided for them by their parents.

Intellectuals in Indonesia and foreign academicians use the term Indonesianization, but the meaning is not entirely clear (Bruner 1973b). Those who migrate to the cities do not lose their ethnicity nor does intermarriage in Bandung result in a merging of separate ethnic affiliations into a larger Indonesian identity. Former President Sukarno frequently called for increased intermarriage as a partial solution to Indonesia's problems but if our tentative findings prove more generally applicable his proposal might have been less effective than he had anticipated.

Another implication of our data, relevant to an understanding of larger patterns of urbanism in Indonesia, is that Bandung urban culture is a regional Sundanese variant and not a generalized metropolitan Indonesian superculture. It might be anticipated that in the central Javanese city of Jogjakarta the rules of the local urban game will be Javanese, and that in urban Den Pasar on the island of Bali they will be Balinese. Although we have not conducted research in other regions, the Bandung pattern may be generalized to other Indonesian cities located in ethnically homogeneous home areas in which migrants adapt to the dominant culture group, and the Medan pattern may apply to other new cities characterized by extensive migration of diverse peoples none of whom is in a dominant power position. If this were the case, then generalizations about all Indonesian cities would have to be modified to take account of the regional variations and of the diverse social processes which occur in what on superficial examination may appear to be seemingly similar urban centres.

One pervasive influence on ethnic relations among all groups throughout the Indonesian archipelago is the role of the Javanese, as it is widely felt that efforts of the central government to foster a national Indonesian identity are in reality a plot to further Javanese political control. Being Indonesianized is equated with being Javanized, with the result that people hold firmly to their own ethnic cultures so as not to be submerged in what they perceive as a Javanese mainstream. To some, and this is an extreme view, the Javanese are equated with the Dutch, as an alien colonial power imposing decisions that are made neither in terms of local cultural categories nor in terms of the local situation.

THE JAVANESE IN BANDUNG

Nowhere is the opposition to the Javanese experienced as strongly as among the Sundanese of West Java. Within the city of Bandung there are almost sixty Sundanese ethnic associations; some are genealogical groups consisting of the Sundanese within one family line; others are designed to advance Sundanese art and dance and to revive Sundanese folk culture; and still others are primarily political in orientation and work for civic improvement. We expect to find ethnic associations among migrant peoples but not among the dominant host population, and the explanation is that they were created in reference to the Javanese. The Sundanese are vehement in their opposition to the Javanese. They trace the origin of the conflict in mythological terms to the year 1357, to a fight between the Javanese kingdom of Modjopahit and the Sundanese kingdom of Padjadjaran. The Javanese won, and 600 years later almost all Sundanese children can recount the story of the conflict and the battle with visible affect and bitterness. The Sundanese, as the second largest Indonesian ethnic group, are reminded daily of the overwhelming political power and numerical superiority of the Javanese.

To recapitulate, the Javanese are the dominant culture in Indonesia with approximately one-half the total population, although they are not a majority in Bandung. The Sundanese are the dominant group in Bandung so that on the level of the city the migrant groups orient their behaviour with reference to them. The Sundanese in turn, although the local power group, see themselves in opposition to the nationally dominant Javanese. And the Javanese do not really understand what ethnicity is about; they are the WASPs of Indonesia.

The Javanese and the Batak perceive other Indonesians quite differently, and they have different conceptions of Indonesia as a nation. To recapitulate briefly a position presented in more detail elsewhere (Bruner 1973a), whenever one Batak confronts another human being a decision is made that the other is either a Batak like oneself or a non-Batak different than self. The most fundamental binary opposition is between Batak and non-Batak, and the differentiation is made on the basis of ethnicity. Indonesians are skilled in distinguishing ethnic identity by such criteria as hair style, skin colour, facial contour, body mannerisms, name, and speech pattern. Although the Javanese are aware of ethnicity their basic opposition is between others as more civilized or less civilized, refined or crude, of higher culture and status or lower culture and status. When one Javanese confronts another he first determines who is higher and who is lower, and he selects from a vast repertoire of respect behaviour that which is most appropriate. This initial distinction is the one utilized and applied to members of other ethnic groups when a Javanese moves outside his home area.

To the Batak the ethnic groups of Indonesia are structurally similar to patrilineal clans. In the Batak highlands the members of a descent unit have a common male ancestor and constitute a biological group, are localized in a geographical area, share traits of temperament and character, and have their own variant of Batak culture and language which is somewhat unique and which has symbolic items of distinctiveness. In the Batak view, Indonesia consists of a number of structurally similar ethnic groups each of which is also a biological unit, is localized in a home territory, and has its own temperament, culture, and language. Just as patrilineal descent groups are little nations within the Batak highlands, so the various ethnic groups are separate nations within the Republic of Indonesia.

The Javanese, of course, do not share this view. They see a homogeneous Indonesia consisting of separate persons who are more or less civilized, and at least in the traditional conception the most cultured and refined were the Javanese nobility. Ethnicity is confusing to the Javanese who point out that members of all ethnic groups in Indonesia have high positions in the government, that all have equal opportunity, that considerable economic development occurs in the outer islands, and that they have never imposed Javanese language or culture on the national scene. An outer islander may counter that nevertheless national power is indeed in the hands of the Javanese, and that the inevitable consequence is that key national decisions are made from a Javanese perspective and on the basis of Javanese logic.

Despite the feeling against the Javanese, there is little sentiment to break up the unitary republic by creating separate states. The rebellions in Sumatra, Celebes, and elsewhere were designed to change the national Indonesian government and not to establish separate governments. There have been severe struggles for power on the national level, especially between the Moslems and the Communists, but only an insignificant minority of Indonesians would want to see their nation fragmented into smaller political units.

Ethnic particularism and exclusiveness is almost universally disapproved if too blatantly expressed, even though everyone is well aware of the strength of ethnic ties. In North Sumatra political parties do represent ethnic groups, but the Toba Batak for example join the Parkindo, a Christian party, and there is no Toba Batak ethnic party as such. Explicitly ethnic political movements have generally been unsuccessful in Indonesia. In Medan there are three Toba Batak newspapers, owned by Batak, and the news coverage and editorial policy favour the Batak. The papers are published in the Indonesian language, although most Batak in Medan speak and read their own language, but according to one editor, the Batak in Medan would not buy a newspaper published in the Batak language. Indonesians rarely talk about ethnicity in mixed groups but they do so frequently and freely in private among members of their own ethnic group. The census of 1970 moreover did not gather information on ethnic group affiliation and the Central Bureau of Statistics does not publish data on ethnic population distributions, not because the information is unimportant but because as one official said it is 'too sensitive'. Political leaders who represent a local ethnic group must participate in ethnic affairs internally within the group, and they must represent their constituents in the national arena, but at the same time they cannot alienate other groups by being too openly ethnic. There are two ways for a leader to commit political suicide; one is to deny his ethnicity and the other is to be too obviously ethnic. In Indonesia, ethnicity must be expressed, but it must be disguised.

CONCLUSION

To write about the expression of ethnicity in such a vast nation as Indonesia based on only 21 months of fieldwork may appear both bold and presumptuous, particularly as we have ranged so widely from Sumatra to Java and to the entire archipelago. I fully realize and indeed expect that future research will correct the inevitable overgeneralizations. But my treatment of the subject is based on the firmly held theoretical position that we must raise our sights and deal with the larger system. I agree with my colleague Lehman (1967) that members of ethnic categories take positions in culturally defined systems of inter-group relations, and although we must describe interactions in context, for indeed this is the heart of our subject matter, the interpretation of the interactions is dependent upon an analysis of the larger system qua system.

The expression of Sundanese ethnicity in Bandung requires a simultaneous appreciation of the demography, the dominant culture, and the locus of power both within the urban system and within the national system, for the Sundanese face in both directions. And Indonesian ethnicity simply cannot be understood from the perspective of Java alone, but must be viewed in the larger context of Java and the outer islands taken together. To deal with systems within systems is a complex matter but the Indonesians do so every day, and their national motto 'unity in diversity' expresses their aspiration for the solution of the ethnic predicament in which they find themselves.

NOTE

[1] The research in Indonesia between 1969–71 was supported at different times by the Center for Advanced Study, the University Research Board, the Center for International Comparative Studies, and the Center for Asian Studies of the University of Illinois, and by the Southeast Asia Development Advisory Group. In the Bandung project I was assisted by three Indonesian anthropologists, Harsojo, Parsudi Suparlan, and Djuriah Utja, and by three University of Illinois graduate students, Hiroko Horikoshi, Caroline R. Wood, and Robert Wessing. I wish to thank them for their many contributions and also M. G. Smith, who made particularly helpful comments.

REFERENCES

BARTH, F. (ed.) 1969. *Ethnic Groups and Boundaries*. Boston: Little, Brown.

BRAROE, N. 1970. Change and Identity: Patterns of Interaction in an Indian-White Community, Ph.D. Thesis. University of Illinois.

BRUNER, E. 1959. Kinship Organization Among the Urban Batak of Sumatra. *Transactions, New York Academy of Sciences* 22: 118–25.

—— 1961. Urbanization and Ethnic Identity in North Sumatra. *American Anthropologist* 63: 508–21.

—— 1963. Medan: The Role of Kinship in an Indonesian City. In A. Spoehr (ed.), *Pacific Port Towns and Cities*, 418–26. Honolulu: Bishop Museum Press.

—— 1973a. Kin and Non-Kin. In A. Southall (ed.), *Urban Anthropology*. London: Oxford University Press.

—— 1973b. The Missing Tins of Chicken: A Symbolic Interactionist Approach to Culture Change. *Ethos* 1: 219–38.

Census of 1930 in Netherlands India. Vol. I Native Population in West-Java. Vol. IV Native Population in Sumatra. Batavia.

COHEN, A. 1969. *Custom and Politics in Urban Africa: A Study of Hausa Migrants in Yoruba Towns.* Berkeley: University of California Press.

EPSTEIN, A. 1958. *Politics in an Urban African Community.* Manchester: Manchester University Press.

FURNIVALL, J. 1939. *Netherlands India: A Study of Plural Economy.* Cambridge University Press.

—— 1948. *Colonial Policy and Practice.* Cambridge: Cambridge University Press.

GEERTZ, H. 1963. Indonesian Cultures and Communities. In R. McVey (ed.), *Indonesia*, 24–96. New Haven: Human Relations Area Files.

GLUCKMAN, M. 1960. Tribalism in Modern British Central Africa. *Cahiers d'Etudes Africaines* 1: 55–70.

LEHMAN, F. 1967. Ethnic Categories in Burma and the Theory of Social Systems. In P. Kunstadter (ed.), *Southeast Asian Tribes, Minorities, and Nations*, 93–124. Princeton: Princeton University Press.

LIDDLE, W. 1970. *Ethnicity, Party and National Integration: An Indonesian Case Study.* New Haven and London: Yale University Press.

MERCIER, P. 1965. On the Meaning of Tribalism in Black Africa. In P. van den Berghe (ed.), *Africa: Social Problems of Change and Conflict*, 483–501. San Francisco: Chandle Publishing.

MILONE, P. 1966. *Urban Areas in Indonesia: Administrative and Census Concepts.* Berkeley: Institute of International Studies University of California, Research Series 10.

PELZER, K. 1963. Physical and Human Resource Patterns. In R. McVey (ed.), *Indonesia*, 1–23. New Haven: Human Relations Area Files.

REDFIELD, R., & SINGER, M. 1954. The Cultural Role of Cities. *Economic Development and Cultural Change* 3 (1): 53–75.

SJOBERG, G. 1960. *The Preindustrial City.* New York: The Free Press.

SMITH, M. G. 1960. Social and Cultural Pluralism. *Annals, New York Academy of Science* 83: 763–77.

SOUTHALL, A. 1956. Determinants of the Social Structure of African Urban Populations, with Special Reference to Kampala (Uganda). In D. Forde (ed.), *Social Implications of*

Edward M. Bruner

Industrialization and Urbanization in Africa South of the Sahara, 557–77. Paris: UNESCO.

SOUTHALL, A. 1961. Introductory Summary. In A. Southall (ed.), *Social Change in Modern Africa*, 1–66. London: Oxford University Press.

WIRTH, L. 1938. Urbanism as a Way of Life. *American Journal of Sociology* 44: 1–24.

Shlomo Deshen

Political Ethnicity and Cultural Ethnicity in Israel during the 1960s

I INTRODUCTION

Multiple Manifestations of Ethnicity

Urban ethnicity is a new field of social-anthropological research
that requires definitions of basic terms and the formulation of
problems. One of the significant accomplishments of the conference in London at which this paper was given was in the
close examination of one specific approach to the field, used
in the recent work of Abner Cohen (1969) and that of some of the
other participants (particularly Gulliver 1969; Parkin 1969).
According to this approach, which may be called the 'political
approach', ethnicity is related primarily, and sometimes solely,
to problems of social organization that are conceived in terms
of politics and the allocation of scarce resources. More specifically, ethnicity is seen to be inherently related to competition
and conflict.

The conception of urban ethnicity in terms of politics and
conflict and their ramifications also implies that the field consists of the study of urban ethnic groups, since political conflict
obviously implies groups that have at least a minimal degree
of corporateness and that engage in political interaction. The
conference did not clearly delineate and define the political
approach to the study of urban ethnicity, and some of the participants used the terms 'ethnicity' and 'ethnic groups' inter-
changeably as if these were coterminous. However, taking into
account the basic datum of urban anthropology which shows
that social groups, in a corporate sense, are not as common in
cities as in peasant and tribal societies, then the study of specifically urban ethnicity, in contrast to ethnicity in other locations, ought to avoid an inbuilt approach whereby the field is
a priori conceived as the study of interacting groups. The

281

fundamental unit of study in the urban field should not, as a
rule, be the 'ethnic group', but rather the elemental components
of ethnicity, namely, particular actions that may be described
as ethnic actions. This leads us to the problem of definition.
My predilection is for a fairly conventional use of the term:
ethnic actions are actions in which a claim to common proven-
ance, ancestry, or culture is potent. Definition however is not
crucial to my present argument but rather the approach to
ethnicity in urban locations which should be through its most
concrete manifestations, specific actions, and not through the
often elusive social groups of the city.

The approach I am suggesting would, of course, lead away
from the merging of the study of urban ethnicity with political
anthropology. This does not deny the evident insight and
efficaciousness of the political approach to ethnicity in terms of
strategy in struggles for power over resources. However, I seek
to develop an approach to those areas in the field of ethnicity,
particularly evident in the urban situation, that 'the political
approach' neither encompasses nor adequately conceptualizes.
This approach tries to show the possibility of existence of
ethnic manifestations that are primarily cultural, and perhaps
not relevant at all to problems of conflict and competition. Such
manifestations might better be interpreted primarily in terms of
strategies to solve problems of identity, belief, and culture, and
perhaps only secondarily in terms of political strategies. This
leads us to consider in the context of ethnicity some of the ideas
and approaches that are currently being developed in the anthropology of religion and the anthropology of symbols, and to
apply to ethnicity some of the questions that emanate from
these sub-fields of social anthropology.

Let me illustrate the limitations of 'the political approach'
from David Parkin's very interesting and valuable paper
(pp. 119–57 above). Parkin notes that the young men's 'companies' of various ethnic groups in Sierra Leone have only had
a very limited political and economic significance, and he continues (p. 145 below):

'I do not wish simply to let the matter of these weakly developed, and probably nowadays atrophied, associations rest
here. It is clear that the 'companies' did not become any

more than a minor component, if that, in the formation of an ethnic political interest group. During the nineteen thirties when they were probably at their most viable, there was simply no apparent need for Temne or Mandinka to organize themselves for economic and political purposes. The significance of the 'companies' is not so much in what they did or did not become, but more in what they might have become. Under different structural conditions . . . these societies might have constituted the corner-stone of a more economically and politically significant association.'

Had Parkin in this paper not restricted his interest in the phenomena that he is discussing to their political aspects, he would also have found significance in what the 'companies' actually 'did or did not become' – surely a central question if one wishes to understand the phenomenon of the 'companies'. But this question, given the political insignificance of the 'companies', can be tackled only by assuming that these associations might have some apolitical, presumably cultural, significance for the actors. Parkin leaves us with no approach for an understanding of these evidently ethnic, though apparently apolitical, associations. He concludes: 'The Temne did not, it seems, exploit an economic "niche", to use Barth's metaphor (1963), at a time when their otherwise socially useful "companies" developed.' To the ultimate question 'Why did they not do so?' there might be forthcoming an answer in terms of the religiocultural problems and dispositions of the Temne, but such a possibility is ruled out if one insists *a priori* on the primacy of the political factor in ethnic activity.

I suggest therefore that the various concrete manifestations of ethnicity be kept conceptually separate. Ethnicity is a very inclusive and highly abstract term which on the level of concrete action is always charged with different substantive content: one can talk of political ethnicity, marital ethnicity, cultural ethnicity, and so on, but in concrete cases it may not always be easy to discern analytically the various kinds of ethnicity. Thus 'ethnicity' is not synonymous with the political expression of ethnicity ('political ethnicity'), or with any other particular kind of ethnicity. Different kinds of ethnicity might operate, or be more prominent, in different social situations individually and at times simultaneously. Inasmuch as one can conceive of ethnic cultural symbols being activated or manipulated in the framework of political conflict, it is also conceivable that such activities appear in the framework of the actors' struggling to solve Weberian 'problems of meaning', questions of life and death, generation and stagnation.

In the following data I document various manifestations of political and of cultural ethnicity in Israel, and I shall attempt to trace their separate and yet interrelated courses of development.

Ethnicity in Israel: General Background

Due to the 'fusion of exiles', an ideal which has been a very potent factor in Israeli society for many years, and the fact that Israeli society is composed of a great number of immigrant ethnic groups[1] from various countries, ethnicity in social life and in local politics has been very much the subject of popular attention. The problems that the ideal gave rise to reached their zenith in the 1950s during which period relationships between various ethnic groups were very tense.[2] This situation led to rioting and the emergence of organized political activity manifested in the form of ethnic political parties. Since the 1960s, however, political ethnic activity has been on the decline.

Simultaneous with the decline of political ethnicity, cultural ethnicity has become stronger in Israel. This expresses itself in such activities as the publication by different immigrants' associations of matters related to their particular religio-cultural heritage, and in the increasing popularity of particular traditional festivities of various immigrant groups. Since the 1960s the traditional memorial festivities of Tunisian immigrants, for instance, attracted ever-increasing numbers of participants; while during the 1950s, the years of mass immigration from North Africa, certain ancient celebrations came close to falling into desuetude.

In this paper I seek to document and illuminate this seemingly paradoxical course of development. I first present data on political ethnicity taken from my observation of Israeli local election campaigns during the 1960s. Then I present data on cultural ethnicity taken from observations of the memorial celebrations of Tunisian immigrants.

II POLITICAL ETHNICITY

I observed local election campaigns in a provincial Israeli town, which I call Ayara, that was established in the 1950s and was inhabited mainly by recent immigrants from various North African and Eastern European countries. There was also a small number of veteran Israelis of European origin. The following is a description of some of the structural changes pertinent to the subject of ethnicity that occurred between 1965 and 1969 in the major political parties of the town.[3]

For about ten years, until 1965, the *Lammed Aayin* (a middle-of-the-road liberal party on the national level) branch of Ayara was virtually a Moroccan ethnic party. Although the national party was indifferent to the particular political demands of its members of Moroccan origin, the Ayara branch pursued a completely independent course. *De facto* it constituted a local ethnic party. The most striking change in Ayara politics during the latter half of the 1960s was the decline of *Lammed Aayin*. In 1965 the party had done well at the polls having gained three out of the eleven seats on the local council, but by 1969 there was a change. The leader of *Lammed Aayin*, a Moroccan, had left the town, and the leadership vacuum created at the top had not been adequately filled by another Moroccan, with the consequence that the main position in the party was taken by a veteran European. This marked a radical change in the character and appeal of the local branch of the party. It lost its attraction for the Moroccan electorate that had formerly supported it with enthusiasm: at the 1969 polls it failed dismally and lost all its representation.

Between the 1965 and 1969 elections, changes relevant to ethnicity had also taken place in *Ma'arakh*, the Israel Labour party, which was the main rival of *Lammed Aayin*. In the past *Ma'arakh* had comprised various ethnic groupings and pressure groups, such as associations of immigrants from Rumania, Tunisia, Morocco, and veteran Europeans. Candidates running for election had been selected on the principle of ethnic representation. The first candidate was always a veteran European, the second an oriental[4] (preferably a Moroccan), and the third a Rumanian. The list had also to include another oriental (preferably a Tunisian) and another veteran. The 1969 composition of the party was more complex than it had ever been before. Four labour parties, divided on many issues, had (for reasons that do not concern us here) merged at the national and local levels to form *Ma'arakh*. While ethnic differentiation had been the main groove that had moulded internal *Ma'arakh* politics in Ayara, the situation became more complex after the merger with the addition of constituent partisan differentiation and loyalty. The unity of this newly organized labour party was conceived at the national and the local levels to be of great importance and was a principle which largely overrode considerations that had formerly affected the decisions of the local party leadership. Internal debate in *Ma'arakh* as to the election of candidates was now on a new factional basis, room having to be found for representatives of the members of the former constituent parties. The increasingly complex differentiation led to a change in the major internal issue in *Ma'arakh*: competition between representatives of ethnic groups shifted to competition between representatives of constituent parties which had been formerly independent.

In *Mafdal*, the National Religious party, the third major party in Ayara, changes had also occurred during the 1960s. Ethnically the local party leadership had become more differentiated. Originally it had been run mainly by Moroccan politicians, whereas in 1969 the party was led jointly by an immigrant from Morocco and by a veteran European. The most interesting development in *Mafdal* was the emergence of a youth faction in the internal politics of the party. Early in 1969 the local *Madfal* branch held internal elections which were contested by one of the local prominent Moroccan leaders with an ethnic slate of Moroccan candidates. Significantly, the challenge of the Moroccan list did not stimulate any other ethnic group in *Mafdal* to comparable activity. The Europeans of *Mafdal*, for instance, were hurt and offended, but they did not take up the challenge as an ethnic group. The opposition to the Moroccan list which crystallized was not in the form of an ethnic opposition, but of a youth faction.[5]

The forthright ethnic approach of the Moroccan faction

touched upon sensitive problems of identity, a deep concern of *Mafdal* youth of Ayara (aged 19 to 24), most of whom are of Moroccan origin with some Eastern Europeans and Tunisians. It went against their aspiration toward a new, Israeli, and modern Jewish, albeit orthodox, image of themselves. Some of them form tightly knit social circles, hold frequent social gatherings, and go together to the movies. They also have their own synagogue. The emergence of the Moroccan faction stimulated the *Mafdal* youth to act as a political faction and to campaign against it, with the result that several of their members were elected to the executive of the local *Mafdal* branch.

The situation that developed in *Mafdal* was analytically similar to that in *Ma'arakh*: the dividing lines of major constituent sections of the party were other than those of ethnic differentiation. In *Ma'arakh* the division was primarily along the lines of membership in the former independent labour parties, while in *Mafdal* it was along the lines of age groups. When *Mafdal* had to select its candidates for the general elections, matters were more complicated than in the past. The list had to include a sizeable representation of the dominant Moroccan element in the party; a veteran European, to satisfy the Europeans of the party and to attract the votes of Europeans; and a candidate on the basis of age rather than ethnic differentiation (as a result of the internal elections). The internal structural developments within the three major political parties of the town thus imply a decrease in the potency of ethnicity as a political factor.

This analysis can be substantiated by a parallel analysis of the 1965 and 1969 formal campaign platforms of the major parties. All promised exemplary handling of ethnic problems and from that respect they make for monotonous reading. However, an analysis of their particular slogans and careful selection of language reveals a remarkable pattern. The 1965 *Mafdal* platform promised the following: 'Item: Closure of social gaps; advancement of the new immigrant, and a true fusion of ethnic groups.' It closed with: 'Our list that is now presented to the voter represents all circles of the public, its ethnic groups and shades . . . We call upon every voter in the town, without any difference, . . . vote *Mafdal*!' Such and similar statements were in an unpublished draft of the local 1969

Mafdal platform with the difference that the terms 'ethnic groups' and 'fusion of exiles' occurred far less frequently. Thus, the 1965 slogan in 1969 became:

'Item: Closure of social gaps through advancement of families blessed with children and of limited financial capabilities in education, housing, and the offering of all government and municipal services, while taking into consideration the financial capabilities of those who require the services.'

In the 1969 version which was finally published, the social policy for ethnic groups was stated more precisely than in earlier versions without however direct reference to ethnicity. Thus, slogans and symbols of ethnic denotation were replaced by a new campaign jargon. While the 1965 and 1969 platforms campaigned for the elimination of the same problems, the 1969 platform was couched not in ethnic parlance but in a socio-economic idiom which, however, strangely enough was used guardedly. There was no reference to the poor or even to 'families with many children', a term repeatedly used in the 1965 campaign, but to 'families blessed with children'. This new phraseology which had become current around that time became common usage in Ayara in the 1969 election and was used continuously, both in oral and in printed propaganda, by all parties. Such linguistic changes in slogans are indicative of underlying, sometimes profound, developments, pointing to the fact that the politicians in 1969 sensed that ethnicity had become a subject which was repugnant. Thus, in 1969 slogans associated with ethnicity were eliminated from the actual campaign jargon. 'Families with many children', a term precise and neutral in value but often critically and denigratingly used, was changed so as to have an explicit positive connotation. The change from 'many' to 'blessed' enhanced one of the most visible features of many oriental ethnic groups, making it flatteringly evaluative.[6]

A comparison between the *Mafdal* platforms of 1965 and 1969 shows the tendency that I indicate quite clearly. While in the draft of 1969 the word *eidot* (ethnic groups) appears a number of times, in the final publication not at all. The phrase 'all circles of the public, its ethnic groups and shades' is replaced by 'all circles of the public'. Another passage reads 'all the various layers (*shekhavot*)', whereas the earlier versions had 'all circles, strata, and ethnic groups'.

A comparison between the 1965 and 1969 platforms of *Ma'arakh* indicates a similar trend. In the 1965 platform, the item 'Fusion of Ethnic Groups' runs as follows:

'We shall continue to deal actively in true fusion: by raising the standard of education, care for families with many children, and causing all those who originated from different countries of the diaspora to participate in the running of civic affairs.'

In the 1969 platform the passage disappeared. To interpret this as a decreasing awareness of social problems in 1969 would be misleading since there is evidence to the contrary. What I am rather arguing is that the politicians in 1969 conceived and projected to the electorate social problems of the town in different terms, thereby showing a new conception of the nature of the problems. Thus, the problem of education specifically referring to ethnicity in the 1965 platform, in 1969 formed part of an elaborate item on education which included a series of projects of a technical and an administrative nature (the putting up of buildings, attracting resident teachers, founding infant creches, etc.). *Inter alia* the article reads: 'Intensification of help, and care for children of families of limited capabilities'.

The article on 'Fiscal Policy' was expanded in a similar manner and in 1969 included a reference to exemptions and reductions that would be granted to 'families blessed with children'. While substantially there is hardly any difference between the 1965 and 1969 platforms, there is a definite change in social outlook. Whereas in 1965 ethnicity was still conceived as a social factor to be grappled with, in 1969, on the level of abstract political platforms, it was almost ignored, and actual social problems, formerly seen as specifically ethnic, were viewed primarily in terms of problems in various areas of life, such as education and housing.

In actual election campaign meetings that I observed in 1969 in Ayara, the decrease in the potency of ethnicity as a political factor is also noticeable. In the 1969 electioneering, politicians claimed that they did not appeal to particular ethnic groups, and they tried to eliminate words pertinent to ethnicity from their campaign vocabulary. A popular slogan that I encountered in 1969, 'The business of ethnicity is finished!', reflects this desire and conception of reality both on the part of the politicians and the laymen who voiced it. In 1965, political rivals sometimes accused each other of catering to the ethnic sentiments of various sections of the electorate (see Deshen 1970, chap. 8). In 1969, however, though some quite imaginative allegations were exchanged between rivals, I only came across one instance in which someone accused a rival of catering to ethnic sentiments.

There were some cases in 1969 where parties mobilized ethnic groups to their support. Thus, in *Mafdal*, the immigrants from Djerba (Southern Tunisia) are a loyal constituent group, both locally and on the national political level. The Association of Immigrants from Djerba and Southern Tunisia issued a newssheet calling upon its 'dear brothers' to vote for *Mafdal*. The leaflet carried the signatures of twelve dignitaries, the major Djerban rabbinical and political figures in the country. It was distributed by the *Mafdal* party centre to local branches such as Ayara where many Djerbans live. It is interesting however to note that the local *Mafdal* politicians were reluctant to distribute the material. Objectively considered, this propaganda was quite suitable since the local Djerbans respected the men who had lent their names to the appeal. From the politicians' reaction to my expression of interest in the material I gathered however that they viewed it as unsophisticated, childish, and old-fashioned. Eventually, the material was distributed among the Ayara Djerbans, but I got the impression that had I not shown interest in the leaflets, they would have been left lying in the local party office. Outspoken ethnicity, as in the case of the Djerban appeal in Ayara, is now generally considered to be in bad taste, and even slightly offensive to those to whom it is addressed, because one assumes thereby that the addressee is still a new immigrant, not fully acculturated in Israel.

The most remarkable development in the 1969 Ayara election campaign was the direction of election propaganda toward various occupational strata. This was particularly *Ma'arakh*'s policy which appealed to such groups as industrial workers, artisans, and teachers. Separate meetings were arranged and the politicians coloured their approaches accordingly. *Ma'arakh* also arranged special campaign meetings for young voters and attempted to develop a particular image that would appeal to that age category as a whole, ignoring ethnic differentiation. Such attempts had been made in the past, but now they were more concerted and most significant is the fact that this time the electorate responded. Many had come to view the occupational categories as meaningful. They attended the election gatherings, not primarily as members of ethnic groups, nor as anonymous individuals, but as members of social formations typical of a society organized along principles of complex differentiation.

The following is a discussion of a *Ma'arakh* meeting of the Division of Industrial Workers, a trade union that *Ma'arakh* was promoting. Approximately 200 men attended the meeting which took place on a Sabbath morning and was addressed by a local labour leader and by the Mayor of Ayara, who was the head of the local branch of the party. The latter remarked *inter alia*: 'Everyone has three families: one's wife and children, the town in which one lives, and the place of work in which one spends a great deal of one's time'. During the meeting various problems of particular interest to the workers present were raised, such as problems of transport to the industrial area and salaries, none of a specifically ethnic shade.

This body had already a formal social organization by virtue of which it gained its name 'Division of Industrial Workers', the term 'division' showing that it was both an entity in itself and a part of a larger whole. It had an official of the general trade union, who specialized in matters that concerned industrial workers in the Ayara branch of the union, and workers' committees, to which the workers attached importance and which, they felt, could obtain material benefits for them in all local factories. In actuality the Division of Industrial Workers was an umbrella organization of the local committees of the various factories. *Ma'arakh* in its campaign among the industrial workers in particular sought to stimulate awareness of the fact that the Division of Industrial Workers was a special organization for industrial workers already in existence within the orbit of the *Ma'arakh*-dominated general trade union; it sought to weld firmly together this organization with the local factory committees, and in general to encourage the existing trend to organize on an occupational basis.

The leaflet that was circulated by the Division of Industrial Workers inviting people to the meeting was both in Hebrew and in French. This fact is of note since the campaigners' approach was evidently more complex than a direct appeal to industrial workers. While they addressed themselves to the electorate of a particular occupational sector, it was on the basis of an internal differentiation, rooted in countries of origin – French being the tongue of recent immigrants from urban Morocco and Tunisia. In the past, campaigning had been primarily, often exclusively, within the channel of existing ethnic and language groups. In 1969 the approach was fused with new tactics of campaigning within the channel of emerging occupational and socio-economic groups.

I have argued so far that campaigning in 1969 took place along lines of complex social and economic differentiation rather than ethnic grooves. I now turn to cultural differentiation between the generations as an electoral issue which stressed another social factor other than ethnicity. My discussion shall focus on a *Ma'arakh* campaign meeting for youth.

The emergence of youth (late teens and early twenties) as a special sector of the Ayara electorate was a direct outgrowth of social and cultural changes that divided the younger generation from their elders. The youth meeting that I observed took place at the party clubhouse with an attendance of about 50 young people. In the course of his speech the Mayor, who also headed the *Ma'arakh* list, declared:

'Though the *Ma'arakh* team for the Local Council is very youthful, we have now added two candidates to our list, Mr Danino and Mr Haddad, who are even younger than the others. This election campaign is quieter than those we have had in the past which shows that the public has matured. The public cannot be bought (*liknot*) any more. The public knows whom to trust. This change of atmosphere is thanks to the younger generation that has gone through the experience of army service. This generation considers matters directly and comes straight to the point; it is not prone to incidental considerations.

In conclusion the Mayor stressed the fact that all should volunteer to help with the campaign during the remaining few days, and that all should go to the polls. The Mayor neither explained the nature of 'incidental considerations' nor what he meant by 'considering matters directly and coming straight to the point'.

The remarks of Haddad, the other local politician present, twenty-five years of age and of Moroccan origin, were brief and trenchant. Haddad was active in the local *Ma'arakh* 'Younger Generation Circle' and appeared prominently on the *Ma'arakh* list of candidates so as to attract young voters. He stated sharply and precisely that he hoped that the election results would be such as to obviate the need for a coalition with *Mafdal* because, as he expressed it, 'the price' of such a partnership would have to 'be paid' primarily by the youth of Ayara. He declared: 'We desire relations of mutual respect with the religious, but they seek to impose on us religious observances. Therefore we must make an effort to succeed at the elections.' Haddad's argument, which was also used in the *Ma'arakh* leaflets to young voters, referred to one of the fundamental issues of Israeli local politics and culture: the attempts of the orthodox to regulate various secular activities, in which they feel there should be cognizance of traditional religious law. An example of this, pertinent to the situation in Ayara at the time, was the problem of the recently opened swimming pool. *Mafdal* politicians, and orthodox persons in Ayara generally, were scandalized by the fact that the pool allowed mixed bathing, and that it was open on Saturdays, thus encouraging transgression of Sabbath laws. Haddad assumed that if election results were to necessitate coalition discussions with *Mafdal*, the religious party would demand certain limitations of the operation of the swimming pool, such as segregated bathing at certain times during the week, and/or obligating bathers to purchase entrance tickets for Saturdays in advance on weekdays. These inconveniences would be felt primarily by those unorthodox persons who made use of the swimming pool facilities, namely the young ones.

This and similar problems of leisure and culture concern the non-orthodox youth of Ayara immediately. They are the matters which the politicians believe will 'be considered to the

point' without 'incidental considerations'. We can only surmise
what the term 'incidental considerations' in this context means.
I suggest that the politicians had in mind considerations that
are not immediately relevant to the social situation as currently
defined, namely the fact of belonging to the social stratum of
non-orthodox youth. Such 'incidental considerations' might
consist in voting for a politician who does not promote a policy
congenial to young non-orthodox people for reasons of ethnic
compatibility with the voter, or in return for a particular
material promise having been made to the voter.

The *Ma'arakh* campaign effort among the younger generation
should be seen in the same light as the campaign among occupational groups. These are attempts at moulding the political
approach along the grooves of social differentiation of a diversi-
fied, industrialized, and modern society in which 'youth' is one
of the meaningful social categories. I have mentioned some
of the problems that are of concern to orthodox youth associated
with *Mafdal*. The substance of the problems differs from those
we are discussing now, but the very attempt of both *Ma'arakh*
and *Mafdal* politicians to seek popularity among youth is of
analytical significance. In both parties youthful candidates
were placed prominently on the lists and the politicians made
much of this fact in their propaganda. In doing so, they have
deepened a social channel of campaigning other than ethnicity
that is rooted in the emerging problems of a particular newly
evolving sector of the electorate.

The conclusion I draw from the election data is that within
the limits of the social situations in which the actions I have
described took place, the potency of political ethnicity has declined. We followed the structural changes within the political
parties, which *de facto* implied a decrease in the weight of
ethnic factors. In election platforms there was a shift from the
formulation of issues in term of ethnic differentiation to the
formulation of the same issues in terms of the spheres of activity
of a welfare state. And, in actual electioneering, we followed the
evolution of channels of electioneering within occupational
strata and age groups of varying culture. This is not to say
that ethnicity or political ethnicity is generally disappearing.
The phenomenon must be viewed situationally. It is for instance likely that expressions of ethnicity in Israel will be more

or less circumspect given the kind of audience present. In an ethnically heterogeneous situation expressions of political ethnicity might be muted because such expressions would be considered improper, even repugnant in that context, while the opposite could be the case in a homogeneous situation. In fact it would not be difficult to produce data to document the continuing potency of political ethnicity in Israel (see my more detailed report on the 1969 elections (Deshen 1972b). But in the kind of social contexts I have been describing, the declining trend of political ethnicity is undeniably there.

Furthermore, when people express a genuine belief that 'the business of ethnicity is finished' they effect the reality of ethnic relations thereby, and indeed to some extent cause that 'business' to decline. This statement of belief is analogous to that of people who express belief or disbelief in the power, malevolent or benevolent, of witches or fairies or any other supernatural being or event. The conceptions of reality are an essential part of reality and through them witches and fairies gain or lose power in the actions of people. Beliefs such as 'the business of ethnicity is finished' should therefore be studied in depth; it would be superficial to dismiss them as mere verbal slogans. It is conceivable that one might sometimes even have to take them at face value. The next step in this analysis would be to specify the precise nature of the social situations in which political ethnicity in Israel does or does not decline, but for the present I leave the problem at that.

III CULTURAL ETHNICITY

The current development of cultural ethnicity expresses itself in a variety of activities. Here I wish to dwell on the growing popularity among immigrants from Tunisia of the *hillula* (plural, *hillulot*), a traditional memorial celebration which had almost fallen into desuetude in the 1950s, the years of mass immigration from Tunisia. During the recent decade *hillula* festivities are being held in an increasing number of localities, and the number of participants they attract is increasing all the time.

About 60,000 to 70,000 Tunisian Jews, either born in Tunisia or of Tunisian extraction, live in Israel. Most of them immi-

grated in the 1950s and are scattered all over the Jewish populated part of the country. In some localities they form sizable
populations. Their style of life which, generally speaking, had
been traditional in their country of origin has greatly changed
as a consequence of the social, economic, and cultural circumstances of life in urban, industrialized, dynamic Israel.

A pervasive feeling of cultural loss besets these immigrants.
They believe that they have declined in religious status, and
this conception of themselves is sometimes expressed quite
explicitly (see Deshen 1972a). Tunisian immigrants also express
longing and nostalgia for the respected traditional rabbinical
leadership of old. When describing Jewish society of the recent
past they tend to idealize it in terms of harmony and piety. The
past, nostalgically recalled as an old cherished culture that is
becoming more and more elusive to them, is an important factor
in the image the immigrants have of themselves. I do not wish
to imply that this factor is constant and uppermost in the minds
of the Tunisians in Israel. Individuals and various groups of
Tunisians differ in this experience, and it is expressed differently
in various situations. There are also other factors that operate
in the image of Tunisian immigrants, such as their individual
socio-economic positions and their identity as Israeli nationals.
I only argue that the Tunisians' conception of themselves is
pertinent in relation to the attenuation of traditional culture.
Later I shall further argue that the underlying reason for the
participants' attendance of memorial celebrations stems, at
least partly, from the kind of image they have of themselves.

Judaeo-Tunisian memorial rites are rooted in the particular
theology of Kabbalism. They initially centred around the death
of pious men which was conceived as a mystical marriage of
their souls with G-d: hence the term *hillula* (literally 'feast' or
'wedding feast') for memorial rites. Kabbalists deemed the
anniversary of the death of a mystic to be an auspicious time
during which mystic secrets of the holy texts were apt to be
revealed. The memorial day of mystics came to be marked by
study, meditation, and prayer. In the course of time memorial
rites also came to be held in honour of persons who had not
necessarily been saintly mystics but who were accorded repsect
because of kinship or other ties. In popular sentiment and
custom these commemorations became joyful and happy

celebrations and some of them attracted multitudes of pilgrims. In folk practice the idea developed that the saint who was being commemorated would intercede with G–d on behalf of the worshipper. As a consequence many people, afflicted spiritually or physically, piously and devotedly make the pilgrimage to the site of commemoration in the hope of being cured or relieved. One might go on such a pilgrimage throughout the year, but most commonly on the anniversary of the mediator's death.

Despite the great popularity of these practices, both among rabbis and the common people, the attitude of many represent-ative figures of the literary tradition toward them is to this day ambivalent. The reason is twofold: first, theologically, some of the popular beliefs run counter to the strict and austere mono-theism of classical Jewish thought; second, from the practical point of view the rabbis frowned upon the boisterous atmo-sphere that developed at memorial celebrations. The mixing of sexes in the crowd was objectionable, particularly since it occurred on hallowed ground, such as a synagogue named after a mystic or by his graveside, and at so auspicious a time as his memorial day.

The current popularity of Tunisian celebrations throughout Israel is not limited to *hillulot* only and is manifest in several ways. One practice is to name newly built synagogues after personalities of the Tunisian Jewish past whose anniversary of death the congregations undertake to commemorate as well as that of other personages whom they wish to honour. Com-pletely new *hillulot* which focus on Tunisian rabbis who died in Israel in recent years have also emerged. The most popular of the new *hillulot* are those in honour of Rabbi Hayim Huri who died in the town of Beersheba in 1957[7] and of Rabbi Hvita Cohen who died in the village of Berekhya near Ashkelon in 1958.[8]

The new *hillulot* started on a very small domestic scale. At first only local people, relatives, and persons who had known the deceased personally attended. Over the years however more and more persons thronged to these *hillulot* which, in some cases, came to attract thousands from distant localities all over the country who previously had not attended. *Hillulot* now take place in many towns and villages that have Tunisian popula-tions.

Commemorating Rabbi Hai Taieb

The following is a description of some of the *hullula* activities
that I have observed at a pilgrimage of Tunisian immigrants to
a synagogue dedicated to the memory of Rabbi Hai Taieb, who
had lived in Tunisia in the eighteenth century. It took place in
the town of Ramla some 30 miles north of Ayara. Among the
distinguished guests were Mr Uzan, Deputy Minister of Agriculture, and Mrs Ghez, a member of parliament, both of them
from Tunisia but members of rival parties.

In Judaeo-Tunisian folklore Rabbi Hai Taieb is considered
a miracle-working saint and was greatly held in awe (Arditti
1904). In common parlance he is always called 'Rebee Hai
Taieb Lo Met' (literally: 'Rabbi Hai Taieb is not dead').[9] This
is a play on the saint's name (the Judaeo-Tunisian name 'Hai'
corresponding to the Hebrew word 'live') that reflects popular
sentiment as to his powers to perform miracles. The phrase
'lo met' is especially emphasized since it reflects the substantive
meaning of the saint's name.

The synagogue of the Northern Tunisian community in
Ramla in which the celebration took place is located in the
oldest and most run-down quarter of the town where buildings
are decrepit, streets are narrow and unpaved and street lighting
is poor. The synagogue itself is quite small. It consists of three
or four ordinary residential rooms converted into one hall,
through the removal of partitions, which has been somewhat
refurbished and renovated by the congregation. On this occasion the street leading to the synagogue was decorated with
brightly coloured lamps and banners welcoming the pilgrims.
Vendors of traditional sweetmeats plied their trades. The
celebration attracted about 1,500 people from all over Israel,
and traffic was so heavy that two policemen were on hand to
direct it. The atmosphere was one of gaiety, exuberance, and
good feeling, with excitement running high. The encounters
among persons were highly emotional. People embraced,
laughed, shouted, and greeted each other ebulliently. Some
said that they had not seen each other for 20 years.

The interior of the synagogue was adorned with many photo-
graphs of scenes from the Jewish quarters of Tunis, such as the
Great Synagogue, and the rabbinical court. Near the Holy

Ark,[10] one of the synagogue beadles was seated with a box of wicks for oil lamps and people were pressing around him trying to buy wicks so that they could light one of the numerous oil containers that hung along the wall near the Ark. It is customary to kindle memorial lights on the anniversary of the dead which is a central ritual at *hillulot*. Despite the noise of the milling mass of people and the selling of wicks, many of the men in the crowd near the Ark, especially those in their thirties and early forties, were devoutly reciting the customary memorial texts. The elders, on the other hand, seemed to be concentrated at the other end of the synagogue, seated around a table laden with food and drink, partaking of the ceremonial meal which is also a central feature of memorial rites.

There was a marked contrast between the expressions of devotion of the men around the Ark as against those around the feasting table and elsewhere in the synagogue. Thus one young man in his early twenties was strenuously pushing his way through the crowd toward the Ark where the memorial lights were burning. He was bare-headed. According to orthodox Jewish custom, men have to cover their heads at all times, all the more in the synagogue, and certainly when one approaches the apex of the house of worship where the Holy Ark is. This custom is very deeply rooted and strictly adhered to in current orthodox practice. Its transgression in the manner of this young pilgrim would normally be considered tantamount to sacrilege. As the young man was threading his way through the crowd, people were commenting to him on his breach of traditional devotional behaviour to which he replied almost pleadingly, 'Yes, yes, true. But what can I do? I *don't* have a cap here!' And he continued to press forward. His demeanour was sincere and pious and there was no doubt of the young man's devotional and religious intent. He was ready to arouse the ire of the people in the synagogue and transgress a commonly accepted norm which he himself adhered to but at the moment could not live up to because of the simple fact that he had forgotten to bring a cap with him. To this young pilgrim it was apparently far more important that he participate in the most significant act of the *hillula*, lighting the memorial light, than that he observe this ancient norm. He was therefore ready to incur unpleasant reactions and behave completely contrary to religious propriety

and normal standards. As a matter of fact, the young man
was not hindered or stopped by other people in the synagogue. The spirit of good humour, joy, and brotherly love
which reigns at *hillulot* fosters an atmosphere of tolerance that
takes in its stride the negligence of the young man. In this
context people forgave behaviour that would have roused their
anger on other occasions. Later at night, in the courtyard of
the synagogue, two men engaged in a noisy and unpleasant
quarrel. Pilgrims who witnessed the incident reacted with un-
belief and shock: 'At the *hillula* of Rebee Hai? It is not good!'
They did not know how to deal with the incident and thus tried
to move away as quickly as possible, to flee the scene of what
in that context amounted to sacrilege. Theoretically people
could have reacted in one of several other ways: ignore what is
in itself a fairly routine incident even in a synagogue; joke
about it; try to intervene and separate the disputers; or take
sides. Their actual reaction of shock and abhorrence was
peculiar to the *hillula* situation. It contrasted sharply yet was
consistent with the reactions to the young man without the
cap. One abhors and flees from strife, whilst a transgression of
traditional propriety is tolerated in good humour: one does not
react by causing more strife and division.

Generally it seems that the men in their thirties and forties were
devotionally the most active and expressive. On the other hand
among the older men, in their fifties and over, at the far western
end of the men's section of the synagogue, opposite the Ark,
seated around the table and enjoying lustily the food and drink,
there were those who were the mainstays of the local congregation. They were now partaking of the *se'udat mitzva* (the ceremonial meal) which is a central feature in many Jewish celebrations, not only at memorial rites.[11] During the course of the
meal religious texts were also read. There was a striking contrast
in the demeanour of these old men seated at the table and the
younger men who stood near the Ark. While many of the latter
were devoutly reciting the texts, among the old men there was
chatter, laughter, joking, and drinking. Some of them behaved
frivolously, pushing dirty forks and salt into the pockets of their
companions.

The implication is not that the old men did not take the
celebration seriously but that there is a difference between the

two kinds of participation; they exhibit different kinds of religious activities, reflecting different kinds of social and cultural needs. The point will be explicated below.

The most formal aspect of the commemoration focused on the Torah-reading table, which is on a raised podium (*bima*) in the centre of the hall of prayer. On the podium stood the distinguished guests who addressed the crowd through a microphone. They drew the attention of all those present, including the reciters of devotional texts and the feasters seated at the table. The master of ceremonies opened with the remarks as to how pleased he was that 'we are all together here once a year, all the Tunisians, all shades (*kol ha' gevanim*), from all places, without any difference'. Then he said that those who would be called up to light the *kandil*, the special seven-branch candelabrum that Tunisian Jews light on *hillulot*, should be generous toward the synagogue fund. He expressed the belief that the merit of munificence on this occasion would cause the army to be victorious. The audience participated audibly: whenever the name 'Rebee Hai Taieb' was mentioned, the cry rose from all throats, 'Lo met!' ('He is not dead!') Mrs Ghez was the first speaker. She expressed her joy at the fact that 'we are all together here' and then proceeded emphatically and with emotion: 'And we must bless all our soldiers that they may return in peace, and that all our wounded recover, that all may marry and have many children, that the Jews of Russia and from the Arab countries may soon come; that all come soon and that many children be born here, and that we receive them all well (*sheniklot otam yafe*), and that the State of Israel succeed and be a light for the gentiles.' After each blessing the crowd roared 'Amen!' many cried out of emotion and the speaker was continuously interrupted with enthusiastic handclapping.

The master of ceremonies then invited one after the other of the seven dignitaries on to the *bima* to kindle the lights of the *kandil* that stood next to the reading table. Each man upon being called up approached the *kandil* and declared formally: 'I hereby kindle a light in memory of Rebee Hai Taieb Lo Met and that his soul be elevated (*le'iluy nishmato*). To this he would add particular blessings for the living such as: 'for the health of my wife', 'that I should make a good living', 'for the health of my children'. One dignitary who was from the town of Ashdod added: 'for the blessing of all Tunisians, and particularly the Tunisian community of Ashdod'.

Discussion of the Hillula Data

Ethnic identity and sentiment were aroused at this celebration by the mere fact of people coming together to unite around ethnic symbols and activities. I seek now to isolate various kinds of ethnic activities in which the pilgrims engaged. Following my general thesis I shall argue that side by side with elements of political activity, cultural activities that are not political can be discerned.

(1) Actions of a political ethnic nature The speeches at the *hillula* by the honoured guests – a deputy minister and a member of parliament – and the explicit acquiescence of the audience may be seen as actions whereby the pilgrims seek to adopt central beliefs and values of Israeli nationalism. They seek to bridge the social and cultural gap between themselves and other Israelis by uniting around nationalist values and sentiments. For it is striking that there was no evidence of ethnic separatism and exclusiveness during the ceremony. The Tunisians, on the whole, are on the lower rungs of the Israeli socio-economic ladder. They certainly do not have less reason than anyone else in Israel to gripe and complain. It would therefore have been natural at an ethnic gathering for them to select rival ethnic groups as targets for complaints and bitterness. Nothing of the sort however occurred, neither at the level of formal activity and speechmaking, nor at the level of informal interaction. On the contrary there were many expressions of general goodwill, of good citizenship, and of nationalist sentiment, such as in the talk about the war, wounded soldiers, and the welcoming of immigrants.

Political ethnicity appears in many guises. It can appear in the form of the separatist activity of an ethnic party, and it can appear in the form I have described. In all such cases the actors seek to solve problems that they conceive as arising from their particular position in society *vis-à-vis* other groups. This leads us toward an understanding of one of the most intriguing sets of problems that confront the student of Israeli society: how do sentiments of national and civic identity under conditions of great social heterogeneity actually emerge? And, in particular, how is such a potentially disruptive element as ethnicity tamed in the heterogeneous Israeli society? The data suggest that manifestations of ethnicity in the forms of ethnic sentiments and identity are stimulated in such a way that they are subservient to general Israeli civic and national loyalties. Ethnicity is legitimized in terms of 'unity in diversity' only; it does not figure as a legitimate end in itself.

(2) *Actions of a cultural ethnic nature* Here we must consider the religious background of the celebration. The stressing of personal problems at pilgrimages, a feature of the Ramla *hillula*, seems to be common to many societies of diverse religion and culture. In the Jewish oriental context, people believe that the merit of the act of devotion will prompt the saint to intercede with G–d in favour of the supplicant. In the particular context of North African Jewish belief, the power of saints to intercede is also accompanied by *brakha* (lit. 'blessing'), a beneficial power that emanates from persons and objects that have had contact with a saint or with his grave. The concept is clearly analogic with the *baraka* of Muslim belief. In Tunisia and in other North African communities, where orthodox Jewish practice was potent and binding, this was only one of many religious and religio-magical practices in which people engaged. Thereby they gained self-justification, felt religiously worthy and pious, and also assured themselves, so they believed, of worldly success. In Israel, however, the pilgrimages we have followed, when viewed in the context of the migration of people from traditional communities in Tunisia to the modern and heterogeneous Israeli setting, are, I suggest, more concentrated as acts of piety. During the process of migration the tenacious adherence to the many minutiae of traditional beliefs and practices is decreasing, and people feel that they are losing hold of the means that lead to self-justification, salvation, and religious integrity. Participating in *hillulot* is one way for the pilgrim to relieve this feeling of anxiety that religiously he is not pious enough and worthy enough. Such participation is an act of concentrated religious fervour, highly dramatic and fused with emotion, and in the present-day social situation of the

immigrant it is far easier for him to take this upon himself than the discipline of constant adherence to a myriad of traditional rituals and practices. Participation in *hillulot* replaces much of the minutiae of traditional practice.[12]

Earlier I described the differential patterns of participation of two age categories. The older generation seemed less devoted than the middle and younger generations. There are also elderly, respectable, deeply pious Tunisians who do not go on pilgrimage at all because they feel that at pilgrimages people are prone to transgressions of traditional custom and ritual, such as in the consumption of food of whose ritual nature (*kashrut*) one cannot be absolutely certain, and in the mingling of sexes where there are such multitudes. The ancient religious ambivalent attitude toward memorial celebrations has not abated and considerations such as these arouse thought and discussion among the devout. One man, with whom I discussed the religiously negative aspects of the Meron pilgrimage (in honour of Rabbi Shimon bar-Yohai who lived in the second century CE) rationalized his own participation by stating, 'For the merit of Rebee Shimon, G–d forgives all their nonsense.' There exists a fourth category, mainly of young people who also do not go on pilgrimage, but for diametrically opposed reasons – they repudiate traditional ethnic and religious practices.

The pilgrimages seem to be acts of devotion by middle-aged and younger persons who feel malaise in their religious existence and who sense that in general their lives deviate religiously from what they were in Tunisia and from what they should be today. Participation in the pilgrimages stems from a feeling of unworthiness (that is rooted in the attenuation of traditional practice) and in the problem of existence that this sentiment arouses.[13] Namely, how does one attain self-justification, and thereby the kind of sensation of order and security that religion can provide? Participating in a pilgrimage enhances a person's religious status in his own eyes. It gives him self-respect and provides self-justification. This view of pilgrimages explains the differential participation of various age categories. The very conservative tend not to go at all. Their religio-cultural and social situation is such that they are not sensitive to the problem of existence to which the *hillula* is related. Absent are also people, mainly youngsters, who seek to repudiate their Tunisian

ethnic and religious traditions. The majority of Tunisian immi
grants fall between these two extreme categories. They increasingly participate because some of their particular problems of
existence resolve themselves in the *hillula*.

The participation of the elders whom I described at the
hillula was not disrespectful but rather in complete accordance
with the *hillula* atmosphere and tradition. According to custom
the ceremonial meal, a central part of the celebration, is an
esoteric act of communion with the realm of souls. It is effica-
cious even when celebrated in a relaxed homely manner, but
the majority of pilgrims in this *hillula* did not participate in
the meal. Instead most of the younger and middle-aged men
were crowded near the eastern end of the synagogue, devotedly
reciting the memorial liturgy. The reason for this cannot be
rooted in any mere spatial factor; places at the table were not
reserved, and while space was lacking near the table, there was
no space anywhere in the small, overcrowded synagogue. The
spatial factor cannot by itself explain the different patterns of
participation. Devout praying was surely not the only alternative left to a man who could not find space at the table. We
will be much closer to reality by assuming that the younger
men were in fact not very keen to mill around the feast table
with the old men. They actually wished to participate in their
own fashion by emphasizing the individual devotional part of
the rites and by understating the communal feast.

IV CONCLUSIONS

I have presented two sets of data, one on election campaigns
that I discussed in terms of political ethnicity, the other on
ethnic celebrations that I discussed both in terms of political
ethnicity and cultural ethnicity. I termed the celebration an
ethnic manifestation because it partly comprises actions that
cannot be conceptualized in terms of politics, and also because
the actions that can be discussed in terms of politics are expressions of communion and not of conflict.

The question now remains as to why political ethnicity, in
the form of political parties and groups that compete with other
ethnic groups, should have declined in recent years and why
cultural ethnicity, that expresses political, cultural, and social

problems in a muted and circumspect fashion, should be concurrently flowering. I suggest two reasons for this development:

(1) The constant changes that the local immigrant society is undergoing. Whereas originally the local society was differentiated primarily along ethnic lines, there began to emerge social groupings based on more complex lines of differentiation, such as religio-cultural and socio-economic interests. Shopkeepers, teachers, and industrial workers constitute occupational strata with common interests which they seek to advance, irrespective of the difference of ethnic background within the strata. This, in the long run, works toward dissolution of ethnicity as a factor of social cohesiveness. At the same time people in the immigrant situation increasingly experience particular religio-cultural problems and needs that are resolved through the symbolic activities of cultural ethnicity as I have outlined in the analysis of the *hillula*.

(2) A temporal event, the virtually traumatic experience of the Six-Day War in 1967, which, more than any comparable previous event in the history of the state of Israel, was highly concentrated in time, packed with action, and dramatic in its outcome. The hypertension of this drama, whose result was seen by many as a miracle, streamed down to all levels of the nation. All strata of the highly variegated and motley society experienced themselves united by the bonds of common peril and salvation, an experience that overrode all the other particular exigencies of various social strata and individuals. While this feeling has since lost some of its intensity, it is still very potent among Israelis. This might explain the increased reluctance to emphasize differences that are deemed rigid, destructive, and divisive.

Finally, I have operated with a conception of ethnicity as a strategy whereby people set bonds of inclusion or exclusion. These bonds have a specific content relative to putative origin or kinship. By this strategy people can solve various problems, both political and cultural. The particular problem that confronts the actors will influence them in the choice of various ethnic or other strategies in order to solve it. Operating with this concept of ethnicity, I have sought to trace the separate courses of political and of cultural ethnicity in Israel, and suggested that there exists an inverted correlation between the two kinds of ethnicity.

ACKNOWLEDGEMENTS

I am very thankful to the many participants in the ASA conference for their comments on an earlier version of this paper. Parts of the data were presented at seminars at Tel Aviv University, and I am particularly thankful to Professor M. Gluckman for his criticism and to my colleagues: A. Aronoff, E. Cohen, L. Mars, E. Marx, M. Shokeid, and S. Weitman, who commented on earlier versions. Mrs A. Sommer-Goldberg helped with editing and styling. I also thank my various sources of financial support: the Social Sciences Research Committee of Tel Aviv University for a travel grant which allowed me to attend the London ASA conference, the Bernstein Fund of Manchester University that financed the fieldwork, and the Association of Social Anthropologists.

NOTES

[1] The people discussed in this paper are all Jews. As such they have much in common, and thus do not constitute disparate ethnic groups in a precise sense. I use the term 'ethnic' only as an analytical term so as to distinguish conveniently between Jews who originate from different countries. The scope of my discussion throughout the paper is limited to the Jewish sector of Israeli society; I am not concerned here with the problem of ethnicity in relations between Jews and non-Jews in Israel.

[2] See Weingrod 1965: 37–44; Bar-Yosef 1959; also Cohen 1968.

[3] For detailed descriptions see Deshen 1970 and 1972b; and for a discussion of the Israeli electoral system of proportional representation see Arazi 1963; also Deshen 1970, chap. 3.

[4] I use the term 'Oriental' to refer to Jews originating from any of the Islamic countries.

[5] See Deshen 1965 for an analysis of another heterogeneous community of immigrants from North Africa in which an ethnic faction crystallized. The development led to the emergence of political opposition in the form of rival ethnic factions. The phenomenon was contrary to what happened here, but that was about ten years ago and in a very different social climate.

[6] At the time of writing (in spring 1971) the new term had already become widely accepted and is now used in mass media. The 'social history' of the diffusion of such terms is an intriguing subject.

[7] For a brief description see Noy 1968: 359–61.

[8] For a discussion of the social context of the *hillula* in memory of Rabbi Hvita Cohen see Deshen 1966.

[9] A grammatically more exact translation is 'Rabbi Hai Taieb did not die'.

[10] The large cupboard next to the eastern wall of the synagogue that contains the *Tora* scrolls. This is the most hallowed part of a synagogue.

[11] For a description of a ceremonial meal see Deshen 1970: 140–7.

[12] For a notion of what this implies see any of the standard codifications of traditional Jewish practice, such as Ganzfried 1961.

[13] Elsewhere (Deshen 1972a) I have discussed in detail the problem of existence raised by the feeling of religious unworthiness.

REFERENCES

ARAZI, A. 1963. *Le Système électoral israélien.* Geneva: Droz.

ARDITTI, R. 1904. Un rabbin tunisien du dix-huitième siècle: R. Hai Taib. *Revue tunisienne* **11**: 489–94.

BARTH, F. (ed.) 1963. *The Social Role of the Entrepreneur in Social Change in Northern Norway.* Bergen: Norwegian Universities Press.

BAR-YOSEF, R. 1959. The Moroccans: Background to the Problem, *Molad* **17**: 247–51. Revised English version in S. N. Eisenstadt *et al.* (eds), *Integration and Development in Israel.* Jerusalem: Israel Universities Press, 1970; 419–28.

COHEN, A. 1969. *Custom and Politics in Urban Africa.* London: Routledge & Kegan Paul.

COHEN, P. S. 1968. Ethnic Group Differences in Israel. *Race* **9**: 303–10.

DESHEN, S. A. 1965. A Case of Breakdown of Modernization in an Israeli Immigrant Community. *Jewish Journal of Sociology* **7**: 63–91. (Revised version in S. N. Eisenstadt *et al.* (eds), *Integration and Development in Israel.* Jerusalem: Israel Universities Press, 1970; 556–86.)

―― 1966. Conflict and Social Change: the Case of an Israeli Village. *Sociologia Ruralis* **6**: 31–55.

―― 1970. *Immigrant Voters in Israel: Parties and Congregations in a Local Election Campaign.* Manchester: Manchester University Press.

―― 1972a. The Varieties of Abandonment of Religious Symbols. *Journal for the Scientific Study of Religion* **11**: 33–41. (Revised version in S. Deshen and M. Shokeid, *The Predicament of Homecoming: Studies in the Cultural and Social Life of North African Immigrants in Israel* (forthcoming).)

―― 1972b. 'The Business of Ethnicity is Finished'?: The Ethnic Factor in a Local Election Campaign. In A. Arian (ed.), *The Elections in Israel, 1969.* Jerusalem: Academic Press, pp. 278–302.

GANZFRIED, S. 1961. *Code of Jewish Law* (the Goldin translation). New York: Hebrew Publishing Company.

GULLIVER, P. H. 1969. Introduction. In *Tradition and Transition in East Africa.* London: Routledge & Kegan Paul.

NOY, D. 1968. *Contes populaires racontes par des Juifs de Tunisie.* Jerusalem: World Zionist Organization.

Ethnicity in Israel during the 1960s

PARKIN, D. 1969. *Neighbours and Nationals in an African City Ward.* London: Routledge & Kegan Paul.

WEINGROD, A. 1965. *Israel: Group Relations in a New Society.* London: Pall Mall Press.

© Shlomo Deshen 1974

David M. Boswell

Independence, Ethnicity, and Elite Status

In this paper I use one case study as a constant reference from which I extract certain themes in the social relations of members of the urban African social elite during a period of transition, first from one town to another and, second, over the period from colonial rule to self government and then independence. I do not intend to dwell at length on the characteristics of urban social networks, which I have already done in another paper concentrating on this particular case (Boswell 1966). However, it must be emphasized that it is only through the analysis of the social network of the man in question, both over time and place, and the content of his relations with network members, that it is possible to define the field and analyse the process of transition.[1]

THE TRIBAL FACTOR

It is the object of this symposium to consider the significance of ethnicity in urban social relations. By that I take the reference in fact to be to that set of categorical relations subsumed under the term, tribe. From other aspects of my fieldwork, it is clear how significant relationships with this common bond may be, whether they are broadly inclusive forms of classification or more specific references to particular sorts of relationship. In fact this forms a major part of the analysis of crisis situations in which those bereaved find themselves in different degrees of isolation, with the result that they or their benefactors have to mobilize assistance according to all, or at least the most effective, channels open to them (Boswell 1969).

Recent analyses of the tribal factor in East African towns have contrasted the perjorative use of 'tribalism' with their observation of alliances with tribal bases. The qualitative difference between these is borne out by comparing the refer-

311

ences of Parkin and Grillo (Gulliver (ed.) 1969). The notion of
tribe as a 'blame pinning device' is a useful one. In Lusaka it
took the form of 'tribal imperialism' and what with reference
to the city council was termed 'this Chibululu business', i.e.
tribal particularism and nepotism was what 'they' do, whereas
'we' have the national interest at heart and select the best
candidates, who may happen to be our friends!

Parkin suggests that "The tribal and non-tribal modes of
explanation were thus used, respectively, by people at the lower
and upper halves of the social ladder . . . those who persist in
tribal explanations may typify the disillusioned or unemployed,
or unsuccessful in general' (Parkin 1969: 285). That is, the poor
are disaffected and talk of exploitation but the rich don't need
to unless they feel threatened or assume a social guilt. Mitchell
stresses the significant difference in the social relations of a
closely-knit, heterogeneous social elite, at present still small in
number (Mitchell 1970: 98–100). This accords with Jacobson's
suggestion that 'The elite's mobility, their movement from town
to town, keeps members of this category incapsulated in their
own friendship network. Elite Africans arrive in Mbale and
make contact with friends they know from other towns. They
transfer from one town to another with the names of their
current friends' friends' (Jacobson 1968: 136). 'Their pattern of
life in town is quite different from that of Mayer's non-elite
migrants, especially in so far as their social network is ethnically heterogeneous' (Jacobson 1968: 137).[2]

However, I cannot say that such a situation reduced the
significance of tribal reference. It was a high status Bemba
civil servant, admittedly in a state of some despondency, who
snapped out one afternoon, 'Ah, those Lozi and their silly king
and all that. If it hadn't been for Queen Victoria, we Bemba
would have defeated them'. Allowing for the fact that the
Bemba never got within several hundred miles of the Lozi at
that time and the absence of any institutionalized joking relationship between them, this expostulation has some relevance.
The point is that high-status people have a greater variety of
social discriminators with which they can justify themselves
and denigrate their opponents. Nevertheless one should not
ignore the chessman-like way in which cabinet posts are allocated and rearranged to take account of significant tribal

factors. Surely, Grillo pin-points the crucial issue that 'In this situation the tribal factor may play an important part as one, but only one, of the weapons that leaders use in the struggle for power. What is basic here is not "tribal rivalry" so much as a system in which competition is fundamentally important and which provides a multiplicity of sources from which the competitors can draw support' (Grillo 1969: 320). That is, people use the weapons and the alliances which come to hand. Just how they use them is well demonstrated in Kapferer's analysis of the social networks of zinc cell-room workers and an Asian tailor's shopfloor (Kapferer 1969, and 1972).

The situation with which this paper is concerned is rather different from those referred to above for two reasons. Firstly my concern is with the impact of many social factors upon a man's social position. Secondly it is possible to analyse the process of change in his social position as it relates to these social factors. One of these is ethnic, or tribal, in character because it is concerned with domestic expectations and styles of life associated with particular kinship patterns and customs. The other is ethnic, in the sense of national affiliation, and is associated with legal status and economic as well as social expectations. Both, of course, reflect upon each other, as well as upon those elite attributes which had been achieved through education, white-collar employment, a middling level of income, and residential exclusiveness. What I want to stress is the interconnectedness of the social factors and the precariousness of any individual's social status and domestic security when any of these are at risk. This case study in fact can provide information on the characteristics of secure elite status just because of the repeated failure of the man in question to overcome all of the social discrepancies he presented in an independent Zambia. He was effectively 'disincorporated'.[3]

THE HALCYON YEARS

Trueman was a twenty-three-year-old Zezuru, whose father, a retired policeman, had come up from Southern Rhodesia to Zambia in 1953, to establish a retail business at first in Lusaka, and then in the Sala reserve some thirty miles from the capital. His father had sent him to Munali, one of the only government

313

secondary schools, where he had passed Form 2 and then left.
Trueman said that he had left because his father said he had
been educated enough, but he had not passed out well enough
to be allowed to continue to the higher forms. He had continued
to take further courses by correspondence up to GCE 'O' Level,
and had taken a short course as a trainee social worker, a
government job which had attracted several of his contemporaries.

As a social worker in Livingstone, a small town on the border
of Southern Rhodesia, Trueman had enjoyed high status as a
government employee with staff-status, a motor-bike to go to
and from the compounds, and a residence near others who enjoyed similar-status posts in the Information and other government departments. His work brought him into contact with
many people much older than himself, including some of well-
established seniority as well as status in the African elite.
Whilst this might have happened anywhere, given the small-
town closeness of Livingstone and the extent to which it was
the Lozi's town, this meant that Trueman established contact
with a wide range of young African civil servants, but also had
access to the tightly-knit Lozi elite. He was nominated to be a
local trustee of the Zambian political party, UNIP, with the
duty of canvassing the European vote, which was critical in the
1962 general election (Mulford 1964).

Two other factors ensured Trueman's integration into the
Livingstone elite. At school he had made many friendships, a
few of which had extended even from his primary school days.
The nature of school-ties is such that, although many may be
contemporaries, only a few are friends. However, given the
small number of those who had passed through Munali, and the
even smaller number who had gone on beyond 'O' level – there
were only one hundred graduates at Zambia's Independence in
1964 – there was always an opportunity for more intense relationships to develop or be reactivated, given their common
status and association in work and place of residence. The
school situation, therefore, provides both the opportunity to
make deep friendships which are likely to last a long time in
some form, and a wider circle of acquaintances from whom
friends may be recruited at some later date in some other place.
The shared experience and the exclusive nature of a highly

selective education system may be the basis for bonds of friendship in situations where other bonds may appear lacking. For others, of course, institutions such as kinship may provide the bonds, as it clearly did for the Lozi in Livingstone. Trueman then had achieved educational status and a potential social network.[4]

The other influential factor in Livingstone was the availability of educated young women of similar social status and styles of life. Trueman and his friends made up a close-knit clique, who founded their own social club with the intention of socializing the older or less educated married women by getting their husbands to bring them into suitable contact with the sophisticated and usually unmarried women, who were studying at the Roman Catholic secondary school, the Elementary Nursing School and the Protestant teacher training college in the town. That the club had to close down because the married men made a set at the unmarried women, and their wives objected, was, to Trueman, an unforeseen development. He laid the blame on the other set in the elite, whom he characterized as heavy drinkers and social reprobates. The situation was one in which not only were the high-status males an elite of closely-knit networks, but their wives and girlfriends were drawn from a parallel set of socio-educational sources, and their joint networks were made up of the same people.[5]

It was not long after this that things began to change in Livingstone, with a critical effect on the Lozi elite and on Trueman. He had already suffered this social setback over the social club. Second, he was affected by a showdown in the political party. With the approach of self government factional rivalries reached a head when a leading Lozi politician was petrol-bombed in Lusaka. This had repercussions in Livingstone, the town of the Lozi, where there was a temporary disenchantment with UNIP. Two of Trueman's friends joined a splinter party which was an offshoot of the ANC and another lost his office in the local party constituency. Trueman was also ousted from his position of trustee in what he termed a wave of 'Bemba imperialism'. At any rate, with a general election based on universal suffrage approaching, there was little need to win the European vote. So he had lost this position of some status also.

During this time Trueman, and two other friends of his, were studying for their GCE and endeavouring to gain entry into universities overseas. One succeeded in obtaining a place and a government grant. The other decided to enter a teacher training college. Trueman also obtained a place at an American university but he could not raise the funds to go. He said that he did not apply to the Government because he was afraid that they would send him to the University of Rhodesia and Nyasaland in Salisbury, Southern Rhodesia (he had actually failed the entrance exam), or to the Oppenheimer College for Social Service in Lusaka, which he regarded as inferior.

By this time he had already resigned from his job in Livingstone. Rather than return there as a failure, he went home to the Sala reserve and helped his father restore his store to a solvent and pilfer-proof basis. He bought a large second-hand car. He then sought employment in Lusaka in a semi-clerical job that made use of his social welfare experience.

We have already seen several significant social developments in Trueman's career. First, there was his considerable ambition to achieve success in the sort of job he obtained. Second, there was the network of young Northern Rhodesian contacts which he developed at school and in Livingstone. In the Federation his status was not that of an alien, but merely that of another of the heterogeneous collection who made up the urban elite. Just how self-conscious was his elite status can be seen in the aims of the social club and the reasons for his selection as a political party trustee. However, when the series of crises came, Trueman's reaction was not that of the others. His elite network decamped from Livingstone and entered opposition politics, higher education, or some of the jobs that were being made available to Northern Rhodesians in the first phase of localization in Lusaka.[6] At this time, however, Trueman still identified himself with the Northern Rhodesian-born members of his social network and, although he maintained links with Southern Rhodesian Nationalist politics, this was within the general context of a commitment to independence, which was shared by all his friends wherever they originated. However, we have already seen the significance of the ethnic factor in political competition for what were fast becoming significant positions of party-political power. The situation exemplifies the relevance of Barth's postulate that 'Colonial regimes are quite extreme in the extent to which the administration and its rules are derived from locally based social life. . . . This allows physical proximity and opportunities for contact between persons of different ethnic groups regardless of the absence of shared understandings between them, and thus clearly removes one of the constraints that normally operate on inter-ethnic relations. . . . In most political regimes, however, where there is less security and people live under a greater threat of arbitrarisms

FIGURE 1 *Trueman's social network during first three months in Lusaka, 1964*

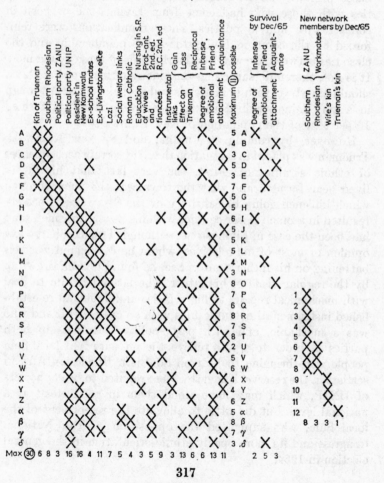

and violence outside their primary community, the insecurity itself acts as a constraint on inter-ethnic contacts' (Barth 1969: 36).

LUSAKA: THE FIRST PHASE OF RESIDENCE

On taking up his job in Lusaka, Trueman moved into one of the houses in the first of the fully-serviced housing estates built for middle-income African residents. During the first three months he maintained or re-established a social network based primarily on his school contacts at Munali, and also his ties with those who had come from Livingstone or been in contact with him in politics. These ramifications were reinforced by the common Livingstone elite membership and the close ties between the wives and girlfriends of these young men. It is not, therefore, surprising that many of his social contacts should have been with Lozi friends and acquaintances. Although in a tiny minority in Lusaka, as a whole the Lozi formed 10 per cent of the population of New Kamwala.

However, by coming to Lusaka, and to New Kamwala, Trueman was placed in a situation that had certain consequences of ethnic significance. First, the very fact that his father lived near Lusaka, and that the town was the place through which kinsmen going to Salisbury or the Sala reserve passed, resulted in a much closer contact with his Zezuru kinsmen than had been the case in Livingstone. Although Trueman had a low opinion of most of his relatives, whom he considered wastrels battening on his father's enterprise, he found himself drawn in by the regular visits of his father. The latter left him to deal with mechanical repairs to his vehicles and Trueman re-established instrumental network links with an ex-school friend who was a mechanic, and with party-political contacts in both parties in order to try to relieve the pressure that local Sala people were bringing to bear on Southern Rhodesian African settlers in the reserve. The latter were reputed to be supporters of UNIP, which may have stood them in good stead at a national level, but did little to alleviate the resentment of the local Sala, who supported the opposition African National Congress and its more openly ethnic orientation in the general election in 1964.

FIGURE 2a *Trueman's kinship links, April 1964*

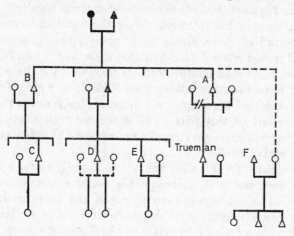

FIGURE 2b *Lozi kinship group in Trueman's network after children's births, at December 1964*

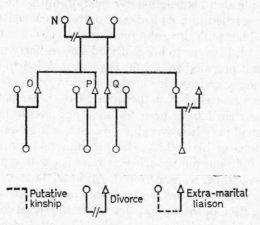

Second, Trueman established links with several Southern Rhodesians, by no means from any one tribal area, who were working or studying in Lusaka and living in the same elite suburb. Given that 10 per cent of New Kamwala households were of Southern Rhodesian origin it is not surprising that they should have been recruited into his network. Once his fiancée arrived in Lusaka, one acquaintance in the street even claimed

putative kinship with him and, although he had avoided them
at first, Trueman himself began to visit them regularly and to
refer to them as his 'relatives'. Given the social and educational
background of these Shona, it is not surprising, during this
critical period when ZANU had split from ZAPU and Southern
Rhodesian African politics were in turmoil, that these friends
should have had sympathies with ZANU, to which Trueman
had also shifted his allegiance.[7] What is significant is the early
development of this pattern of social network relationships,
which were to envelope virtually the whole of his social contacts
by the end of 1965.

The reasons for this shift are various. Firstly it was apparent
to an observer that, although his social network consisted
mainly of social equals earning about the same as himself,
£30 to £40 a month, great demands were made on Trueman,
both by his ex-school friends and the Livingstone set, which
were no longer reciprocated. He was drawn into the marital
dispute of one friend, whose wife's relatives lived opposite him.
This complicated his neighbourly relationships. The mother of
another regarded him as someone onto whom she could un-
burden all her son's domestic problems. A third wanted him to
give him a lift by car to his girlfriend's house forty miles away
but was not prepared to pay for the petrol. A fourth wanted to
borrow money and sent his brother round to ask.

Trueman remarked that 'Because I have a car people think
I must be rich. I have been too kind and people have taken
advantage of me'. However, he could not, in Lusaka, resist the
depredations of his father, who got him to have his lorries
repaired and removed the wheels from his car to replace those
on his own, which were worn out. All in all Trueman, by continuing to present himself in a style that implied elite status, but
in the situation of the capital city where the social context was
different, had potentially over-reached himself. But he had also
ceased to gain anything from these relationships.[8]

In complaining that, in Lusaka, he did not want to become
involved in people's personal affairs, Trueman said that in
Livingstone his own private life and that of his welfare work
had become so confused that he could only disentangle himself
by leaving – the perennial problem of the committed social
worker in a small town community. However, I suggest that in

Livingstone the social situation was different. The demands may have been heavy, but transport was provided by the government and his status was enhanced by the decisive part he was asked to play in the personal lives of clients who were also members of the same elite. He had helped one man in prison for motor-car offences and embezzlement. But in Lusaka he refused to get involved in the troubles following this man's elopement with a Lozi princess's daughter, who was a niece of this same man's divorced wife and politically well connected in the capital.

What had been a part of a social worker's life in Livingstone, and was the experience of an ex-colleague of Trueman's in Lusaka, was no longer necessary nor acceptable after he had left the department of which they were clients. Within three months these network contacts had been pared down but not severed for they could potentially be reactivated if a new situation arose. Trueman had taken on a new role in Lusaka, which had changed the content of his relationship with his ex-clients, although neither his nor their social status had altered relative to one another. Because of his change of residence and the much larger scale of Lusaka's elite, it was also easier for Trueman to take a new role, although the style of life he purported to follow caused amusement to some and irritation to others. What in Livingstone passed for *the* elite, in Lusaka formed part of a much larger middle-income category or class.

However, the second reason for the shift in Trueman's social contacts was the inverse of the first. There were those he excluded, but there were also those who, by the changes in their social circumstances, had no continuing reciprocal relationship with Trueman and who grew away from, or excluded, him. In Livingstone he had held an advisory political office, and even after succumbing to 'Bemba imperialism' his UNIP friends had continued to visit him. In Lusaka they came for meals and to borrow blankets, but they slept in the houses of Zambian ministers. Once they obtained office they ceased to visit any more. For this short, interim period, Trueman was able to take advantage of their new influence, such as in obtaining the release of his fiancée from her teaching appointment to take a course in Lusaka. But this period was a short one. Like the men who asked him for money, he found these friends could

David M. Boswell

only be asked once, and often, as in the case of his scholarship, nothing might materialize. Once they went to live 'in town', these friends did not return to someone now outside their social frame of reference.

If we consider what had happened to the socio-economic status of those in Trueman's social network during those first three months in Lusaka by the end of 1965, we find that almost

FIGURE 3 *Socio-economic status of Trueman's social network members relative to himself*

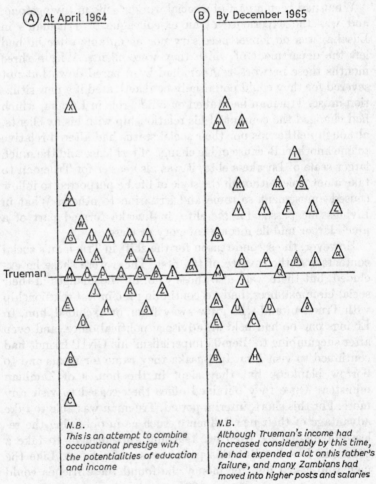

A At April 1964   B By December 1965

Trueman

N.B.
This is an attempt to combine occupational prestige with the potentialities of education and income

N.B.
Although Trueman's income had increased considerably by this time, he had expended a lot on his father's failure, and many Zambians had moved into higher posts and salaries

322

half had achieved posts in the government and other large organizations, which left him behind with his new fellow Southern Rhodesian Africans, who had come up in the wake of the worsening situation in their own country and the hope of commercial expansion in Zambia. Having missed his chance before self government, Trueman had lost it for good, because his birth-place counted against him. He did not wish to become a Zambian citizen even had that made things easier and did not express an awareness of what was happening to him. Zambian-ization had ruled him out, but not his fiancée who was a Bemba. Trueman did not apply and find himself rejected. Rather, he excluded himself by taking action appropriate to an alien. His Zambian friends remarked on the way he never came to see them any more and moved with other Southern Rhodesians.

As early as mid-1964, Trueman's social status largely de-pended on his income, and he took a new job in a commercial company, that promised increments and scholarships. The company had moved up from Southern Rhodesia and was pre-pared to employ other members of the alien Shona elite who lived in the same suburb as Trueman. He had been encouraging his paternal cousin to come up to Lusaka from Salisbury but he stopped doing this. In fact he and his father talked more often about returning to Salisbury, when the political climate had changed there, and reactivated their kinship ties with their home village in a Southern Rhodesian reserve. Trueman's father's elder brother, the village headman, had had some land registered in his father's name at the time of the land husbandry act.[9] They even took on the headman's son again as a driver in the Sala reserve, although only as a wage labourer. He had caused such a catastrophe in his earlier time with them when he had been a kinsman, who expected free access to their equip-ment and resources.

During this first phase of his time in Lusaka after self government, Trueman established new contacts with Southern Rhodesian Africans, and became more closely bound into his father's kinship network. He sloughed off those social contacts which were to him now an unproductive liability, but found himself estranged socially from his Zambian friends who could legitimately enjoy higher expectations and achieve status in the new 'independence elite', because they had the education and the citizenship. Cohen and Middleton suggest that 'the development of citizenship as a specific feature of territorial membership is correlated with the growth of centralized authority and the growth of ethnic pluralism' (Cohen & Middleton 1970: 17).[10] It is not the purpose of this paper to discuss the extent to which this may or may not be so in Zambia amongst Zambians, despite the intention of 'One Zambia, one Nation'. My focus is upon the holder of an ethnic status that became reclassified as an alien status. So far I have only discussed the man himself. Now I want to consider his conjugal relationship and the implications of both different tribal and alien status for this.

LUSAKA: THE SOUTHERN RHODESIAN ALIEN AND THE ZAMBIAN BRIDE

By the end of 1965, when the European Rhodesian Front declared independence unilaterally for their Rhodesia, the transformation in Trueman's social network was almost complete. By then he was established in the oil company, although without any of the increments or scholarships he had hoped for. Zambianization was being extended from the Government service to the City Council and the Mining Companies and no advancement was offered to aliens. By this time he had got one of his cousins taken on as a driver in the same company and was propping up his father's business financially. He was in some financial difficulties himself and could not afford to replace his broken-down car.

Just at this time (which coincided with my leaving the field) Trueman accepted a post in the Lusaka headquarters of the Zimbabwe African National Union, then the minority Southern Rhodesian African political party, whose central office was in Dar es Salaam. Two years before he had been persuaded not to consider such activity by his commercially minded and apolitical father. By this time, with the exception of two school friends whom he had also known in Livingstone, Trueman's social network had not only been reduced in scope but also reduced in size. Almost all his time was spent with other Shona residents of the same suburb, including his putative kinsman, three men he worked with, three political party officials, and two students from the College of Social Service. All were members of ZANU. Almost his whole range of social contacts with members of the Zambian 'independence elite', with his ex-school and Livingstone friends, and with his neighbours had ceased to exist.[11] I have suggested that this change can be understood as one of the outcomes of a changing role, owing to opportunities and even existing status positions being cut off. Trueman now presented himself as a politically conscious young Shona, reacting to the predicament of his compatriots in Southern Rhodesia, which had steadily worsened since the end of the Federation. There seems to have been little expectation of foreign scholarships at that time, because he had even applied for a place at the University College in Salisbury.

At this point it is important to consider the impact of Trueman's social network, role, and status shift on his fiancée. Grace was a Bemba, whose parents had moved to Livingstone at least twenty years before. They were staunch Roman Catholics. She had grown up in Livingstone, where she attended the local Roman Catholic secondary school for girls, and to which she returned as a school teacher after completing her training in a Roman Catholic training college. We have already seen how important this school was in providing the brides for Trueman's friends. Although few of the men were Roman Catholics, their brides came from this school. It had been particularly influential in providing opportunities of secondary education for Lozi girls. Grace was the eldest daughter of a steadily employed but poorly paid and elderly father, who had a large family of children.

Trueman had other girlfriends in Livingstone. One of them, a Shona nurse, sent back his half of a joint-photograph, when she learnt that he had invited Grace to join him in Lusaka. She was disgusted at his choice of a Northerner instead of a sophisticated Southern Rhodesian. However, Trueman was quite explicit in his intentions. He wanted to marry a woman, who would be compliant and domesticated but enabled by him to keep in step with his own social development. When he called Grace up from Livingstone, he was successful, through his ex-school friends, in getting her released from the teaching service and given a place at the Further Education College, for which he intended to pay.

Trueman set great store by Further Education. He intended to gain it overseas but his ambitions for his wife were related

325

to his own. He discussed them with his friends in the presence
of Grace. He was of the opinion that to achieve a successful
marriage 'based on companionship' it was necessary to keep one's
wife in step with one's own educational and social advancement
and to provide her with 'polish'. Such had been the aim of the
Livingstone social club and such was the value of Lusaka's College of Further Education.

At the College, of course, Grace joined several of her ex-school
friends who were the wives or girlfriends of Zambians, at that
time still members of Trueman's social network. Indeed it
looked as though this relatively tightly knit network, joint to
both spouses, would be perpetuated in Lusaka. As we have seen
this was not the line along which Trueman's social network
developed. With the change in his economic and political status,
so his place in the community of the elite shifted. One friend
became a diplomat and moved himself into a new circle. Another
returned with his European bride and a London law degree to
become a magistrate on the Copperbelt. He never contacted
Trueman, despite his close friendship with him in Livingstone.
Others found that Trueman no longer wanted to be involved
with them. This particularly affected his Lozi network members,
with the exception of one man whose wife was very friendly with
Grace, and whose mother got on well with Trueman.[12]

However, although his status and social network were changing, those of Grace were not. In Livingstone she had been a
prominent and well-liked figure in her own right, not just as
Trueman's girlfriend. In Lusaka, at least for some ten months
before they actually married, Grace's social network remained
unchanged. In fact her attendance at the College reinforced her
established, Zambian friendship network. Grace and Trueman
fitted into the new situation differently. The change in his
social network is partly explained by his attempt to socialize
her into a social role and network in line with his own, as a
'Shona' wife and mother.

MANIPULATION OF KINSHIP, NEIGHBOURLINESS,
AND FRIENDSHIP

It is useful to analyse the critical situation that developed in
terms of three categories of relationship or network member-

ship – kinsmen, neighbours and Grace's own friends and educational opportunities. However, it must be realized that all three were closely interconnected at certain or many points, just as were the factors making for the transformation in Trueman's status, activities and network members.

Firstly, there was a significant ethnic difference between the two of a tribal kind. Whilst Trueman claimed to be a modern, educated man he found that, once he contemplated marriage to Grace, the bond between them had ramifications that involved both their kinship groups. Being Bemba, Grace belonged to a matrilineal people and her family refused to countenance any departure from their system and customs. Trueman and his father did attempt to overcome this by saying that they were prepared to pay a much higher, 'Lobola scale', of marriage payment in order to gain the custody of any children born to them. They understood the differences between this and their own, Zezuru, patrilineal practices, but they were unable to understand that what seemed to them the advantages of the one could not be made to outweigh what seemed to be the antiquarian prejudices of the other. In fact the negotiations were drawn out over several months in an attempt to reach a solution.

Just how ingrained the assumptions of kinship normality can be was well brought out by a teaching case-conference at Oppenheimer College that I attended. Based on different assessments of the expected roles of the spouses, students with patrilineal and matrilineal backgrounds took radically different sides in recommending action to resolve the conflict between them. Their European social work tutor assumed that they were demonstrating the typical judgemental attitudes of untrained social workers but quite failed to see the principles upon which the conflict between the students themselves was based.

At several stages, Trueman asserted the significance of his kinship group. I have already referred to the way in which he ignored a Shona neighbour's assertions of kinship, but then accepted them when his Zezuru wife accosted him with a reproach for not having introduced his fiancée to her. She was taken to the house and shown into the kitchen, where this putative kinswoman jestingly explained Grace's future, subordinate position as a wife in their family. Thereafter Trueman referred to them as 'my relatives'. After their baby was born, Trueman had his own mother to stay with them. She lived in Salisbury, being divorced from his father. He had held a second wedding reception at his father's farm after their own church marriage and reception for friends in Livingstone. The church ceremony had been at the insistence of his wife's family, whose concern, he asserted, was based on their fear of the Roman Catholic Fathers whom he held in low repute. Trueman also recruited an Ndebele girl from his father's farm area to work as a domestic servant to help his wife.[13]

Before their marriage, Trueman had emphasized his intention to return to Southern Rhodesia when his education was over and the political struggle won, and he made the point that Grace had now become a Shona and would come to live there with his people. It appeared as though his stated belief in 'companionship in marriage' was partly a response to the norms of domestic life for one enjoying a new, and 'modern' social status, but also a way of evading conflicts introduced by two different kinship systems in an intertribal marriage. Trueman's conception of marriage could not materialize anyway because it only provided for his own generation, which was appropriate to a boy and girlfriend liaison but not to a newly married couple.

Once Grace was expecting a baby and this was born a girl the conflict became more acute. The involvement of Grace's kinsmen became so frequent and important that they forced their way into Trueman's social network. Her mother came to stay with them for the birth, which proved a difficult one, and whenever Grace or the baby was sick afterwards. Grace was her first-born child. The baby's birth brought the marriage payment issue to a head. Grace's father and his brother, who lived in another district of Lusaka some five miles away, regarded the child as part of their family willy-nilly because even the customary payments had not been settled. Trueman had hoped for a son, but the birth of a daughter strengthened the matrilineal ties with his wife's family. Although he used to announce, 'She is a Shona', he knew she would be brought up in a Bemba way. Grace had grown suspicious or jealous of their Ndebele domestic servant and had caused her to be replaced by her own younger sister and then a cousin of hers, who did not have to return to school.

The paradoxical situation was reached in which, at the same time as Trueman was becoming encapsulated within a Shona network and submitting to the demands of his own kinsmen at work and in the Sala reserve, his wife had deepened her association with her own kinsmen. The birth of their baby reinforced this polarization due to the ethnic basis of their kinship differences. Trueman failed to substitute his own for Grace's kinsmen.

The second area in which he was unsuccessful in effecting any lasting change was in his wife's set of neighbourhood ties. A Bemba matron, prominent in New Kamwala and a daughter of the Chitimukulu, lived in the house behind theirs. She was a focal point for gossip, storytelling, and the discussion of custom, which drew in several of her Zambian neighbours, including Grace. As it happened all of them were Bemba, or members of matrilineal tribes married to Bemba men. Grace's mother used to join them when she came to stay and they drank home-brewed beer together. They were all drawn in for the confessions that resulted from Grace's difficult labour.

Trueman discouraged his wife from getting involved in the neighbourhood. When he was present he enforced this estrangement which strained his own relations with the neighbours and led to a series of quarrels. His car finally left the road because they were no longer prepared to help him start it by pushing it down the road. Two refused to help him or give him lifts, because they regarded him as mean and unwilling to reciprocate their favours – a situation similar to that which accompanied Trueman's own earlier rejection of some of those ex-Livingstone members of his social network.

However, although his own ties were broken, those of his wife were not and indeed could not be if she was to remain a social being. Unlike her husband, she had no car, and she was tied to the house by the baby and housework, so the neighbours were an essential source of social contact, help, and advice. Her mother acted to reinforce these ties, but the fact that her husband was at work by day gave Grace scope enough to maintain these links.

In the third area of Grace's friendship links her husband was more successful in reshaping her social network, through his greater ability to determine the frequency and situation of her contacts. Grace had many ex-school friends in the suburb and at the College, most of whom were married or betrothed to members of the Zambian elite, who lived in New Kamwala, or 'in town'. Many lived too far away for her to visit casually without transport, and, because her husband had drawn away from their husbands, Grace's contact with them was limited to the classroom.

However, there were others with whom Trueman encouraged his wife to associate. They were Shona women older than Grace with families of their own such as his putative kinswoman, and the wife of his superior at work, to whose house he used to drive her at weekends much more frequently than to her father's brother. In both cases the husbands were members of his political and work-time network. He even used to invite Shona colleagues and friends to stay in his house with their wives as paying-guests. Her husband's intention was to provide Grace with the company and influence of women of her own educational, and therefore social, status, whose kinship systems and customs were like his own. His aim was now, I suggest, not only to socialize his wife into becoming an appropriate wife of a member of the educated, 'modern' elite, but also an acceptable Shona wife as well. The College could provide the first but was not an appropriate setting for the second. Trueman's own kin could provide the second but not in a way, or at a standard, acceptable to the first.

Trueman certainly achieved some success in restricting his wife's social network. Placed in a situation where the range of options was restricted, Grace became close friends with some of these Shona women. But her social network was never as identical to his as it had once been, because of the significance of her neighbourhood and kinship ties as a housewife and mother. Even Trueman's strategy to ensure the parallel but phased education of his wife up to his own had come unstuck. In fact the difference between them reached its greatest accentuation when Grace was offered the opportunity of a Government grant to study for a Domestic Science Diploma in California, for which as a Zambian she was qualified. Her husband, who did not encourage her any longer, had no alternative but to apply to the University College in Salisbury, and hope to pass his A levels at a second attempt by correspondence. Unlike his wife he had not attended the College in the evenings. By this time, which coincided with my leaving the field, both the neighbours and Trueman's closest friends had noticed the way in which relations were strained not only between their kinsmen, who still regarded nothing as settled and the marriage something as a sham, but between the couple as well.[14]

CONCLUSION: SOCIAL STATUS, ETHNICITY, AND INDEPENDENCE

In this paper I have analysed the different social factors influencing the changing identity of social networks as a gauge of social status, and ethnic alienation during the transition years of independence. It is based on the extended case study of the social network of a young Southern Rhodesian, brought up in Zambia, over a period of two years. This period covered his changes in occupation, educational aspirations, marriage and political identification. From being virtually a Northern Rhodesian African he became a Zimbabwian freedom organizer. He belonged to a patrilineal and his wife to a matrilineal tribe. The significance of this emerged after his wife gave birth to a child.

Ethnicity is, therefore, apparent both as a factor in customary tribal, and national identification. After Zambian Independence, these factors took precedence over those features which apparently tend to unify the social elite – common standards of education, income, occupation, place of residence, and styles of life. In fact, in this case, they determined that the latter must diverge because of the new legal, social, and economic significance of alien status, with all its implications. Behaviour is related to the perception of a situation by others as well as by the actor himself but the process as a whole is that seen by the social analyst.

In the changing membership of a social network it is important to note: (1) the significance of the time factor in the period over which new relationships may be established or old ones reassessed, and the particular categories of association that may be affected; (2) that after a change in residence, old network members will be the first to form nodal points; (3) that changing social status and taking of new roles determine the assessment of reciprocity in relationships; (4) that these are particularly affected even amongst members of the social elite, when the reclassification of citizenship takes place and insiders become outsiders; (5) that changing domestic status due to marriage and parenthood may further complicate the situation due to the introduction of a second party, the wife. If domestic tribal differences are added to those of alien status, then the norms of kinship, neighbourliness and friendship may be expected to conflict, although those apparently based on education and 'modern' elite status did not.

In this situation ethnicity cut across and then reformed Trueman's social network. It is an interesting example of realignment due to a changed ethnic status which accords with Mitchell's suggestion that, 'Ethnic divisions, therefore, tend to follow economic and other social changes leading to a partial coincidence of cultural with economic and social characteristics. . . . As long as people continue to reorganize obligations and rights on the basis of common cultural origins it would appear that clustering of social characteristics is likely to persist' (Mitchell 1970: 99).

In his new situation, Trueman's social network was reformed by the enlargement of two parts of its previously heterogeneous membership, narrowly based upon the coincidence of workmates, political party members, and fellow nationals of one group of tribes. Whereas his network in Livingstone had been narrowly based upon the elite, it now represented only a fragment of the whole of this stratum in Lusaka. The birth of his daughter and the fact of his wife's separate status and greater opportunities as a Zambian citizen accentuated the conflicts inherent in their joint conjugal role *vis-à-vis* their respective kin-groups, their neighbours and their friends, as well as within their own household. Trueman's room for manœuvre was effectively restricted by the limits placed upon his options by the political events and the social situations with which he was confronted.

What has been analysed is the emergent property of ethnicity in a political and in a domestic context, to which other socioeconomic factors are directly linked. Whilst in agreement with the suggestion that 'networks emerge then as a consequence of the local distribution of exchange resources in the population' (Eidheim 1969: 53), it is necessary to look again at Barth's distinction between stratification and ethnicity. 'However, in many systems of stratification we are not dealing with bounded strata at all: the stratification is based simply on the notion of scales and the recognition of an ego-centred level of "people who are just like us" versus those more select and those more vulgar. In such systems, cultural differences, whatever they are, grade into each other, and nothing like a social organization of ethnic groups emerges. Secondly, most systems of stratification allow, or indeed entail, mobility based on evaluation by scales that define the hierarchy . . . Ethnic groups are not open to this kind of penetration: the ascription of ethnic identity is based on other and more restrictive criteria' (Barth 1969: 27). The meaning of ethnicity, i.e. its evaluation, does change. In this case the apparent unity of Africans against Europeans, as colonial rulers of the Federation, gave way to ethnicity based on new national identities and job restriction.

Barth is demonstrably correct to assert that 'a drastic reduction of cultural differences between ethnic groups does not correlate in any simple way with a reduction in the organizational relevance of ethnic identities, or a breakdown in boundary maintenance processes' (Barth 1969: 323). Trueman's common education and activity within the social elite was of secondary importance when the times changed and he became an alien. His domestic difficulties, however, although related to this as far as his wife's social status and prospects were concerned, were such as would probably have arisen in any case if he had belonged to a patrilineal people and his wife's parents to a matrilineal tribe. That he was an alien did, however, force his wife to make friends with emigrés. It is not surprising that Trueman should have chosen this moment to devote himself to Southern Rhodesian African politics as a full-time activity.

ACKNOWLEDGEMENTS

I should like to acknowledge the assistance I received from the Commonwealth Scholarship Fund and the Research Fund of the University of London. During the research I was affiliated to the Institute for Social Research in Lusaka, Zambia, where friendly contacts were numerous and fruitful.

An early version of this paper was read to Professor J. C. Mitchell's seminar in Manchester in 1966, for whose comments I am grateful.

David M. Boswell

NOTES

[1] Diaries and frequent contact with members and ex-members of Trueman's social network over two years made this particular piece of fieldwork possible and their help is gratefully acknowledged.

[2] Argyle's historical observation is pertinent here: 'In that world the Industrial Revolution greatly increased the resources available, but there were still not enough to go round. At the same time democratic and, later, socialist theories spread the belief that everyone was entitled to a share of them. In the general scramble that followed, there emerged numerous, mutually exclusive groups whose members had, or believed they had, certain characteristics in common which enabled them to combine and thus compete more effectively against others who were similarly organised.' (Argyle 1969: 54).

[3] For a discussion of incorporation see Cohen & Middleton 1970: 1–30.

[4] In earlier papers the importance of latency in social network mobilization is more fully discussed (Boswell 1966 and 1969).

[5] See Bott (1957) on social class and joint conjugal role relationships. An impression of this can be seen amongst those who came from Livingstone with wives and fiancées in *Figure 1*.

[6] Zambia achieved Independence in October 1964, but self-government after the ending of the Federation of Rhodesia and Nyasaland in January 1964. In the intervening period the country was ruled by a United National Independence Party government, following a general election in January 1964, under a colonial constitution as Northern Rhodesia. It was during this period that Localization, not officially termed Africanization, of employment became specifically Zambianization (i.e. based on citizenship).

[7] See Van Velsen 1964.

[8] See *Figure 1*.

[9] See Garbett 1963 and *Figure 2a*.

[10] Tyler 1969: 170–71, makes similar claims for a national system of education in East Africa but carries wishful thinking far further: 'The organisation of the colonial education system emphasised tribal, religious and ethnic affiliation and provided no strong basis from which a wider identity might grow through equality of opportunity and full participation in the total system. The development of unified state systems of education and the growth of national education policies will not destroy group identities associated with religion, tribe, or ethnic group, but it can contribute to the formation of an identity based on the wider community through the possibility of full participation and equality of opportunity where previously, during the colonial period, such possibilities were circumscribed.'

[11] See *Figure 1*.

[12] See *Figure 2b*.

[13] There was a large settlement of Southern Rhodesian Africans in the Sala Reserve and Mumbwa District during the Federation of Rhodesia and Nyasaland after the implementation of the Land Husbandry Act in Southern Rhodesia.

[14] Not long after this Trueman went into full-time political work as a Southern Rhodesian emigré freedom organizer. This involved him in considerable foreign travel and absence from his domestic home. Grace did not take up the scholarship but stayed to look after her home and baby daughter. For this latter information I would like to thank Kirsten Alnaes.

REFERENCES

ARGYLE, W. J. 1969. European Nationalism and African Tribalism. In P. Gulliver (ed.), 1969: 41–57.

BARTH, F. (ed.). 1969. *Ethnic Groups and Boundaries.* London: Allen & Unwin.

BIEBUYCK, D. (ed.). 1963. *African Agrarian Systems.* London: Oxford University Press for International African Institute.

BOTT, E. 1957. *Family and Social Networks.* London: Tavistock Publications.

BOSWELL, D. M. 1966. Kinship, Friendship and the Concept of the Social Network. *Conference of the E.A.I.S.R.* Makerere.

—— 1969. Personal Crises and the Mobilisation of the Social Network. In J. C. Mitchell (ed.), 1969: 245–96.

COHEN, R. & MIDDLETON, J. (ed.). 1970. *From Tribe to Nation in Africa.* San Francisco: Chandler Publishing.

EIDHIEM, H. 1969. When Ethnic Identity is a Social System. In F. Barth (ed.), 1969: 38–57.

EPSTEIN, A. L. 1961. Network and Urban Social Organisation. *Rhodes-Livingstone Journal* No. 19: 29–62. Also in J. C. Mitchell (ed.), 1969.

GARBETT, G. K. 1963. The Land Husbandry Act of Southern Rhodesia. In D. Biebuyck (ed.), 1963: 185–202.

GRILLO, R. D. 1969. The Tribal Factor in an East African Trade Union. In P. H. Gulliver (ed.), 1969: 297–321.

GULLIVER, P. H. (ed.). 1969. *Tradition and Transition in East Africa.* London: Routledge & Kegan Paul.

JACOBSON, D. 1968. Friendship and Mobility in the Development of an Urban Elite African Social System. *South Western Journal of Anthropology:* 24 (2), 123–38.

KAPFERER, B. 1969. Norms and the Manipulation of Relationships in a Work Context. In J. C. Mitchell (ed.), 1969: 181–244.

—— 1972. *Strategy and Transaction in an African Factory.* Manchester: Manchester University Press.

MAYER, P. 1961. *Tribesmen or Townsmen: Conservatism and the Process of Urbanisation in a South African City.* Cape Town: Oxford University Press.

MITCHELL, J. C. 1956. *The Kalela Dance.* Rhodes-Livingstone Paper No. 27.

—— (ed.). 1969. *Social Networks in Urban Situations.* Manchester: Manchester University Press.

—— 1970. Tribe and Social Change in South Central Africa: a Situational Approach. *Journal of Asian and African Studies* 5 (1–2): 83–101.

David M. Boswell

MULFORD, D. C. 1964. The Northern Rhodesia General Election, 1962. London: Oxford University Press.

PARKIN, D. J. 1969. Tribe as Fact and Fiction in an East African City. In P. H. Gulliver (ed.), 1969: 273–96.

PAUW, B. A. 1963. *The Second Generation*. Cape Town: Oxford University Press.

TYLER, J. W. 1969. Education and National Identity. In P. H. Gulliver (ed.), 1969: 147–74.

VAN VELSEN, J. 1964. Trends in African Nationalism in Southern Rhodesia. *Kroniek von Africa:* 139–57.

336

S. R. Charsley

The Formation of Ethnic Groups

INTRODUCTION

In Africa the persistence of manifestations of what has usually
been labelled 'tribalism', or even their increase, where it might
naïvely have been thought that they would decline, has attracted
notice for some time. In urban studies the classic work was
Mitchell's *The Kalela Dance* (1956), a direct assault on the
problem of explaining, for the Copperbelt townsmen who were
not tribesmen, the persisting urban significance of tribe. More
recently, and particularly through the work of Cohen (1969), it
has become clear that this significance is not merely a passive
residue among townsmen who have been tribesmen but represents an important social process, a process in which the significance of tribe may grow as well as decline. Cohen has
labelled this 're-tribalization' as the positive counterpart to
'de-tribalization'.

This is within the urban context, but a similar phenomenon
on a still larger scale has also been observed. The political
independence of 'new nations' has often led both to a drive for
national unity and to a perception of tribal division apparently
sharper than in the years of colonial overrule. It was presumably
at least in part as a result of this that anthropologists came in
the 1960s to give much more attention to the concept of the
tribe as a unit, and to challenge what Gulliver has termed 'facile
lay views which conceive of immutable patterns of culture and
tribal alignments that "have not changed for generations"'
(Gulliver 1969a: 13).[1] As an aspect of this development social,
cultural, and linguistic heterogeneity has become itself a focus
of interest rather than merely a marginal complication in a
world of basically homogeneous units (Barth 1969; Cohen &
Middleton 1970). In the analysis of regional and national
relations, as in the analysis of urban populations, tribe has
therefore ceased to be simply a datum, a starting-point, and
has become a matter of process requiring explanation. The

337

establishment, maintenance, and decline of identities, cultural differentia, and boundaries, together with their associated social organization, have become problematical. In part to mark this change, in part to place the African phenomena on a wider stage it is convenient to replace the language of tribe with the language of ethnicity.

By 1969 there seemed to be an increasing measure of agreement among Africanists that persistence and even growth in ethnicity were to be explained 'politically', or even that ethnicity was an essentially political phenomenon (Cohen 1969: 3–5). Explanation was to be found by looking for the interests of the unit concerned and seeing how its members might expect to profit, or at least to avoid threatened loss, from the particular strategy adopted, purposefully or otherwise, in this general area of 'tribalism'. Gulliver, for instance, explains the conservatism of the Tanzanian Arusha and Masai in this kind of way (1969b), and Cohen (1969) similarly explains the 're-tribalization' of the Hausa in Ibadan as relating to the defence of trading interests. As Gulliver in his general introduction to the book referred to puts it: 'the argument runs that it is the concrete politico-economic interests that are the basis of tribe and tribalism – the defence of these against external encroachment and their development according to local preference and advantage', though it should also be noted that he regards this as a 'crude and extreme' statement of the argument since the cultural symbols of common interests 'have an autonomy and a force of their own' (1969a: 32).

In this paper I examine the 'political' type of explanation in relation to a rather different though still African situation of ethnic growth which I have studied.[2] I shall contend that the explanation is inadequate to these particular circumstances and has serious limitations in application elsewhere. I shall suggest that, like many explanations of a basically monocausal type, the factor to which it points may well have special importance in many situations but nevertheless is no more than one among a range of relevant factors. What is needed therefore is a conceptualization or model of the processes involved in ethnicity, processes which I term 'the formation of ethnic groups'. Only this will permit a methodical comparison of the range of situations involving ethnicity and hence a study of all the relevant factors and their relative importance. I make a first and small-scale attempt at such a comparison elsewhere (Charsley 1971); in this paper I cannot go further than to indicate the need for such a conceptualization and my proposals for it.

The situation from which this work springs is in fact an instance of rural ethnicity but the features of the situation are such as to make it more comparable with many of the urban situations studied than with the rural. It is a situation of great ethnic heterogeneity produced by recent and relatively large-scale immigration. It offered the possibility of observing the processes by which ethnic groups form, with an array of different formations at different stages of development within a single social field. There were of course differences between this and any urban situation, as well as resemblances, but these differences have the advantage in the present context of focusing attention upon the matter of group formation. This they do, as will be seen, by eliminating the problem of the relation of ethnic to economically based categories and groupings which has been a major, and I should add a fruitful, preoccupation of much urban work on ethnicity.

KIGUMBA: IMMIGRATION AND ETHNIC HETEROGENEITY

The studies were made in Kigumba, a sub-county of north-east Bunyoro in western Uganda. They were made between June 1965 and November 1966, and again for a period of four months in 1968. The area was one hundred square miles in extent, with its population, then some 12,000 strong, concentrated in its southern half around a main east–west road. A population of this magnitude was however a very recent development. Even since the Census of Uganda in 1959 it had increased threefold: the population then recorded was 3,846, though even this was already the product of considerable immigration. Already by 1959 only 53 per cent (2,026) were categorized as 'Nyoro', the major portion of the remainder (34 per cent of the total) being Kenyan Luyia who had come to Kigumba under a settlement scheme started in 1957. Though boundary changes and the loss of the census sheets for the 1948 Census mean that earlier figures are not available, it is safe to say that before the Kenyans' arrival the 'Nyoro' population of around 2,000 constituted little less than the total population. The good, well-distributed rainfall of the area, the gentle gradients and soils of reasonable fertility mean that a density such as these figures indicate, about 20 per square mile, was perhaps a tenth of the long-term carrying capacity of the land (Charsley 1969: 53–60). Kigumba was therefore in the 1950s, for reasons which I do not need to discuss here, relatively empty, and this was the basis of its appeal to immigrant farmers. It was in response to this basic situation that the immigration of the later 1950s and the 1960s occurred.

The influx was welcomed or even definitely encouraged by both the government of Bunyoro and the local inhabitants. Kigumba had a reputation as a backward and declining area in which human population was retreating before increasing herds of game from a national park immediately to the north, and indeed Bunyoro as a whole was preoccupied in the first half of the century with the smallness of its declining population. It is against this background, together with the lack of any pressure on land resources, that the central and local attitudes to immigration have to be seen. In both quarters a reinforcement of the human population was seen as desirable and newcomers were therefore to be welcomed. Furthermore the welcome, though not completely unconditional, was remarkably free in practice of demands upon the immigrants. The normal form of Nyoro land tenure allowed them to take freely into cultivation any land which nobody else was using and thereafter to have rights to this for as long as they wished to maintain them (Beattie 1954; Charsley 1970). Such land might be obtained either within or quite apart from any established village, but in neither case was obtaining or holding land dependent upon establishing or maintaining local relationships of any kind. The only relationships required were the universal ones of subjection to the law of the land and the payment of tax. This is not of course to say that immigrants never did establish local relationships, only that doing so was not required and in practice, as immigration built up, often not undertaken. This then already constitutes a first resemblance to urban situations, that access to economic resources was basically of an impersonal, universalistic nature.

Cultural and linguistic heterogeneity was a second such

feature. This began within the indigenous population itself, where it was perhaps relevant to the tolerance of immigrant heterogeneity which was almost invariably displayed. There were in fact three indigenous sections since the modern sub-county occupied the borderlands of three of the traditional 'tribes' of the ancient Nyoro empire. To the south were the Ruli, the Bantu-speaking people for whom the Buruli counties to the west and south of the Nile of both Bunyoro and Buganda were named; to the north were the Luo-speaking Palwo or Chope; and in the west began the Nyoro proper, the bearers of the language and culture of the political and geographical centres of the former empire. By 1965 half of the 'Nyoro' population identified themselves as Ruli though not all of these retained the language or any distinctive cultural attributes; about a fifth were Palwo; and the remainder were simply Nyoro, either the few indigenous Runyoro-speakers of the west, or 'assimi-lated' indigenous inhabitants mainly of Ruli origin, or im-migrants from other parts of Bunyoro. A further point of relevance here is that this heterogeneous population was not, as it were, self-ruling. They had for centuries been under the political and to some extent cultural domination of the Nyoro proper. Certainly since the beginning of the colonial period in the 1890s they had been accustomed to receiving their rulers of all but lowest rank as appointees from outside. Often these were Nyoro proper in origin, sometimes displaying the attitudes of superiority towards the north east and its inhabitants which were not uncommon in the central and southern parts of the country. The indigenous basis for immigration was therefore a mixed population accustomed to being ruled by the representa-tives of a central power, with whom there was no complete identification and who were not even necessarily to be relied upon to take the side of native against immigrant should the occasion arise.

The first trickle of the approaching spate of immigration was connected with an unsuccessful agricultural mechanization scheme located at Kigumba in the early 1950s. To provide labour for this a number of Sudanese were recruited from a nearby sisal estate, and some subsequently settled in Kigumba. Their numbers were slightly increased by further recruiting in con-nection with the settlement scheme of the late 1950s already

mentioned, and then vastly increased in the mid and later 1960s
by an influx of refugees coming more or less directly, though
without any official sponsorship or organization, from the
upheavals of the southern Sudan in these years. This later
influx was by no means confined within Kigumba itself. The
numbers involved in this as in the other cases to be considered
are estimated in *Table 1* below.

Luyia from western Kenya were, as already mentioned, the
main people settled in Kigumba under the scheme, but they

TABLE 1 *Estimated Kigumba Populaton, 1959 and 1965–6*

	1959	1965–6
Indigenous	2,026 (C)	2,250
Kenyan Luyia	1,300	2,500
Sudanis	150	500
Lugbara	88 (C)	500
Alur and Okebo	5 (C)	1,100
Kikuyu	0 (C)	500
Rwandans	1 (C)	3,500
Others (residual)	276	1,150
Total:	3,846 (C)	12,000

(C) indicates an exact figure from the 1959 Census, possible only where
classifications agree exactly. Other figures are estimates, those for 1965–6
deriving from household lists compiled and a sample census taken in the
years in question.

did not cease to come when the active phase of settlement
ended in 1959. As the table shows, their numbers continued to
increase subsequently, this being partly the result of a high
birth rate, partly of continuing free and unassisted immigration.
The other major influxes occurred mainly in the mid-1960s.
First there were people from the north west of Uganda, particularly Lugbara, Alur, and Okebo; only a little later Kikuyu
from central Kenya began to come; and finally in late 1964 a
large settlement of Rwandan refugees was officially established.
This is to list the major blocks of immigrants but in fact it does
less than justice to the variety of peoples actually present. Of
the blocks listed only the Rwandan was in any sense monolithic

and the western Kenyans were particularly diverse. Southern Luyia, or 'Maragoli', formed the core of the population but they were accompanied by numbers of northern and central Luyia and such even more culturally and socially different and varied neighbours from Kenya as the Nilo-Hamitic Teso and Nandi and the Nilotic Luo. There were also numbers of the related but Ugandan Gisu. The result was that something like forty languages were in regular use among the inhabitants of Kigumba, and this perhaps gives a more accurate impression of the extreme ethnic heterogeneity of this rural population. To the very limited extent that there was any *lingua franca* in use this was Swahili, but translating and interpreting were conspicuous features of most public and many private occasions.

This heterogeneity and recency of arrival are once again features more readily paralleled in African urban than rural situations, and there were two further features I should also mention in this connection. The first was a high level of instability and residential mobility in many sections of the population, the second a demographic composition showing a relative absence of the old, except in the indigenous section, and in several immigrant sections a marked surplus of men, particularly young men, over women.

If we turn now to consider the economic bases of life the differences between the rural and the urban become more prominent. Though there were important differences between immigrants in their reasons for being in Kigumba and in their interests there, practically all wished to farm, producing maize and cotton as their two main crops, and the great majority obtained most of their subsistence needs and cash income in this way. The prevailing pattern in almost all sections was for people to live on their land and as a consequence there was little nucleation or even concentration of settlement. In the rural situation, therefore, people were not forced into close residential proximity, nor did they have to depend for their livelihood on participation with large numbers of their fellows in organized economic activity. In this may be seen a strong contrast with urban residence patterns and the division of social and economic labour characteristic of towns, both forcing people into a wider range of interaction. Further, although differentiation in both economic activity and wealth was increasing in Kigumba, it was still far from displaying the range of difference found in towns and, with the great majority engaged in small-scale farming, there were not to be found the distinct, ranked categories of occupation such as are produced by a differentiated economy. There was therefore as yet little basis for any crystallization of a pattern of social classes. The absence of any readily established economic classification in Kigumba is important, for it meant that if people were to categorize one another as a basis for social interaction ethnic differences, lacking any economic rival, would almost inevitably have a greater salience in the rural than in the urban situation. It also meant that a problem which has been one of the main preoccupations of work on urban ethnicity since the founding studies on the Copperbelt in the 1950s, in brief the problem of the relation between tribe and class (Mitchell 1956; Epstein 1958), was one which had yet to become significant in the situation studied.

I have noted that settlement in Kigumba was dispersed and that newcomers could settle without the prior establishment of any local relationships. These and the other factors already considered produced a range of ethnic settlement patterns. There were to be found heavily mixed areas, particularly in the vicinity of services and amenities; there were basically indigenous villages with a variety of immigrants around and associated with them in a variety of ways; and there were all degrees of concentration of people of a particular origin, ranging up to the Okebo, the great majority of whom were the almost exclusive occupants of a single tract of country in the west of the sub-county. As a general summary of the situation it is however roughly true to say that, as each new influx began, its members sought out one or more currently largely unoccupied areas in which to establish themselves, and that having done so they tended then to be joined by successors of the same origins. In general therefore a considerable measure of ethnic clustering was to be found.

This does not of course make Kigumba notably different from many towns, but it does perhaps raise the question whether Kigumba was profitably to be regarded as a single social field at all. The answer to this must undoubtedly be in terms of the problem set. Neither Kigumba nor its inhabitants were in any way isolated; significant relationships aplenty reached across its boundaries, not only to adjacent areas but also, as is usually the case with immigrant populations, to distant societies of origin also. Equally, within Kigumba social boundaries were numerous and plain, indeed so much so as to make it an awkward and at times frustrating field of study. Nevertheless from the point of view of examining the growth and development of ethnic grouping by the comparison of different units within the same environment, Kigumba appeared to be a useful if inevitably a somewhat arbitrary field to define. It was a unit in relation to government, the sub-county being at the time by far the most generally significant administrative unit, and the unit to which legal, medical, and agricultural services were attached. Apart from this it was to a considerable extent an economic and educational unit with two main centres, a major and a minor, of shops, markets, producers' cooperatives, and primary schools located on the main road. During the years of the study the major centre was growing strongly and further lesser local centres showed signs of emerging. Kigumba was also a unit of self-identification for large sections of its population at least. It showed every sign, therefore, though not yet by any measure highly integrated, of moving towards integration.

ETHNIC DEVELOPMENT AND ITS EXPLANATION

Although Kigumba in the 1960s remained a rural area in which the great majority of the population got their livelihood from the land, it had therefore attained a degree of ethnic heterogeneity and other characteristics comparable with the towns of Africa. As in these, some but not all of the immigrants formed ethnic groups which generated considerable internal organization. Most impressive in this respect was the group which had come to be labelled 'Maragoli', among whom the idiom of organization was essentially religious. The great majority of the group were members of small congregations of Protestant, particularly pentecostal, denominations. It was these which not only differentiated the Maragoli from other ethnic groups but which also, as I have argued elsewhere (Charsley 1969), formed the basic social units of this community, rather as the hamlet or village might provide the basic unit in another society.

These denominations, of which there were 15 by 1966, provided a segmentary structure for the group as a whole, built up according to principles of organization deriving from the Friends Africa Mission in Kenya, i.e. of congregations assembled into 'Monthly Meetings' and these again assembled into 'Three Monthly Meetings', and so on. This was inevitably modified by the fact that most denominations in Kigumba were isolated from their parent bodies, missionary and independent, usually centred in Kenya, and had therefore to be largely autonomous in spite of their very small size locally. Some had no more than a single small congregation, while others had sufficient to constitute a 'Monthly Meeting' though rarely to go much further. Local expedients to deal with this situation included an interdenominational body which acted in effect as a higher level of organization for about half the denominations, allowing even those with few members locally to participate as segments in larger scale religious activities. Funerals provided the major manifestation of the segmental religious organization of the group as a whole, with Maragoli turning out in force, organized and participating in their denomination groups in a highly distinctive community institution. Further aspects of the way in which the denominations formed a single system were a considerable movement of members and even leaders between denominations, and a marked likeness of religious culture even between denominations with diverse formal religious affiliations. This socio-religious organization was by no means for Sundays only but penetrated into most aspects of life, but even then it did not exhaust the group's total ethnically linked organization. In addition primary schools were run, youth groups were in evidence and male initiation was arranged on an ethnic group basis.

The Maragoli provide the prime example in Kigumba of ethnic development. No other group could compete in the extent or elaboration of its organization, but a few, notably the Kikuyu and the Sudanis, displayed something comparable. Of the major ethnic divisions remaining, Okebo, Lugbara, and Alur might be ranked in that order for their degree of organization but at much lower levels.[3]

Kigumba therefore presents, I suggest, much the same kind of problem as Cohen took up in relation to Ibadan. This is the problem of 're-tribalization', of why there was to be observed in certain instances a process of the creation of reinforcement of ethnic sub-systems and the hardening of ethnic boundaries, rather than of any moving together into a common society. It is also the problem of why such a process should occur more strongly in some groups than in others within a single social field, why it should occur among the Hausa but not among the Ibo in Ibadan, or among the Maragoli but hardly among the Alur in Kigumba. Cohen sees ethnicity, as I have already noted, as essentially a political phenomenon and he sets out to explain developments in the 're-tribalizing' group as a consequence of a need to defend economic interests. No such bald statement can hope to do justice to what is a subtle, many-sided and successful analysis, but it is adequate to my present purpose which is to ask whether the ethnicity of Kigumba can likewise be accounted for in 'political' terms.

A first limitation in this kind of approach which the Kigumba data make apparent is that it has nothing directly to say about the definition of the ethnic units concerned. 'Sudani', 'Maragoli', and 'Okebo' were all widely recognized ethnic group labels but their derivations were diverse. 'Sudani' was a national category, though mediated in practice by tribal identifications since not all Sudanis in fact originated in the Sudan. 'Maragoli' was the place-name form of the name of one southern Luyia tribe, the Logoli; but in Kigumba it often embraced people of other southern Luyia origins and sometimes even all immigrants from western Kenya. The term 'Luyia' was not used. This was to be contrasted with the situation in Kampala where 'Luyia' ('Luhya') was the category in general use (Parkin 1969: *passim*). 'Okebo' finally was what may seem a straightforward tribal label, but as Southall (1970) has made clear, the social boundary between Okebo and Alur was by no means unambiguous. Those who came in Kigumba to be recognized as Okebo were originally, there as elsewhere in Bunyoro, embraced within a single wider category. This was labelled 'Aruru' and shared with the Alur. Kigumba therefore emphasizes the general point with which I began this paper that the definition of an ethnic unit is not simply a datum but is a crucial aspect of the phenomenon of ethnicity, itself requiring explanation. Furthermore, even if, once interests are identified with a particular defined group, their prosecution can explain the growth of ethnicity, there remain the prior questions of why such interests should be seen in group terms at all and why the group to be concerned should be defined in a particular way. In a situation where these do not seem to be live questions, where the structure of the situation is established, an explanation in terms of strategy may seem plausible. To offer it is to take the current structure for granted as setting the terms for the analysis. In relation to some problems it may be justifiable; if, for example, one wants simply to analyse how people use identities and select from within a given range, the approach may be adequate. Usually, however, more is attempted – there is for instance an attempt to deal with social change – and for this such an approach can scarcely provide an adequate base. Too much which is subject to change is taken for granted as unchanging.

But even given the 'structure', will interests explain the kind of ethnic growth observed in Kigumba? A quick glance at the data suggests that it may indeed well prove useful to try to identify interests in terms of which ethnic developments can be revealed as goal-directed, consciously or otherwise, and therefore explicable. The Maragoli are the most obvious candidates for such an explanation. Briefly, they were the main group established in Kigumba under the settlement scheme of 1957–9. As such the scheme was always identified with them and they regarded themselves to some extent, and were often regarded by others, as wards of government. In terms of practical advantages this meant a good deal in the early years, and even after the formal ending of the scheme in 1962, and with it the ending of any special status for the settlers, it left as a residue a specially advantageous form of land tenure in the former settlement area. There 23-acre plots continued to be held unconditionally, whereas under normal Nyoro tenure landholding was formally conditional upon use of the land. Furthermore, as Kenyans they were well aware of the precariousness of immigrants' rights. This they had observed both from their own people's experience of attempting to settle in the countries of their Kenyan neighbours such as the Nandi, and from the experience of the European population in Kenya. To maintain their distinct identity as Maragoli, former settlers and wards of government, as distinct from all the other ordinary immigrants,

348

might well therefore be seen as a strategy for mitigating this precariousness and maintaining at least the material advantage of the special tenure.

A second example looks similarly promising. I have already referred to the way in which Okebo began coming to Kigumba as part of a single category long familiar in Bunyoro under the label 'Aruru'. To this Nyoro attached, exceptionally for them, a distinctly adverse stereotype of violence and dangerous supernatural powers. Almost from the beginning Okebo in Kigumba began to organize themselves apart from Alur and in ways which might be expected to bring their separate identity to wider notice. They settled well apart with their own separate leadership; they developed distinct recreational activities; they established a school of their own; and they took the opportunity of a music contest held in the sub-county in 1968 to send uniformed and beflagged teams to compete. They were almost the only group to act in this way. Here again therefore organization and a strengthening of ethnicity might well be seen as a matter of promoting interests, in this case the interest of escaping from an adverse stereotype.

This, it may be thought, accounts for two of the ethnic groups, the one displaying the most elaborate development and another which, though its organization was still rudimentary by comparison, had far outstripped its otherwise similar ex-partner, the Alur. But what of the other major units, for instance the Sudanis or the Kikuyu? Though these were in some ways even closer to the Maragoli in their development than to the Okebo, I have been able to detect no special interests which may with any plausibility be attributed to them in order to explain their development. It should be remembered that in Kigumba at the period studied economic competition was virtually eliminated by the free availability of adequate land, and competition in the political sphere was similarly depressed by the relative absence of advantages to be sought and by the impartiality and permissiveness of the local administration. There were effectively no local councils and no party politics operating at the period.

It might be argued that every group at least has the interest of maintaining its culture and its boundaries. It is perhaps worth noting first that in the circumstances of Kigumba neither

culture nor boundaries were under any kind of attack, but the
main argument against this point is that it assumes too much.
It assumes that there is always *a* culture to be maintained.
That this is an error can be seen clearly in the Sudani case.
The people to whom this label was attached in Kigumba were
highly assorted in their tribal origins as these are conventionally
classified; there were people of Sudanic, Nilo-Hamitic, and
Nilotic tribes from a wide area of the southern Sudan. Yet these,
together with a small number of people of Congolese and
Ugandan origin, came to constitute in Kigumba a single, readily
identifiable ethnic group, the Sudanis. Having a common culture in any simple sense is therefore not necessary for ethnic
group formation. This one example makes it clear that, from
an analytical point of view, in studying any immigrant population, common culture can never be taken for granted as an
unproblematic starting point for further analysis.[4] Which people
will coalesce to form an ethnic group on the basis of what
common culture is a matter requiring the most careful analysis.
And any common culture which is involved can by no means be
thought of as a simple carry-over from societies of origin; it is
rather something which has to be worked out in the new social
field. I shall be returning to this line of argument later. For
the moment it is sufficient to note that for these reasons any
argument on the basis of general cultural interests does not
appear to offer a useful supplement to the particular interests
outlined above for the Maragoli and the Okebo in providing a
'political' explanation of the total pattern of ethnicity as it
was to be observed in Kigumba.

Indeed even these particular interests need to be considered
more critically. For the Okebo I have in fact no positive evidence that their organization was intentionally directed towards escaping from the adverse 'Aruru' stereotype. In the
circumstances of Kigumba it is doubtful whether in practice
it was even seriously disadvantageous. For the Maragoli I have
again no evidence that the land-tenure matter was more than a
potential interest. Certainly there was no general preoccupation
with it, and although plots within the old settlement were
generally available, it was not uncommon for individuals to
give up the advantage of settlement tenure by moving to settle
elsewhere. As far as maintaining their status as 'wards of

government' distinct from other immigrants was concerned, this likewise is difficult to uphold on closer examination. Maragoli organization showed no explicit concern with ethnic boundaries. Indeed it tended rather to expansionism, to being ready to absorb others of less apparently appropriate origins, even reaching out to the Kikuyu on their first arrival in Kigumba. Further, there was not in Maragoli organization the manifest concern with external relations or with the standing of the group in the eyes of others which has often been reported from towns, for instance by Banton (1965) from Freetown, and which was to be observed in one or two minor sections of the Kigumba population. It was clearly exemplified by the Nyole, southern Luyia neighbours of the Logoli in Kenya and having about 150 members in Kigumba. They maintained a tribal association with associated religious organization, manifestly concerned with asserting and maintaining the separateness of the group, particularly from the Maragoli into whom they would otherwise certainly have been, like other southern Luyia tribes, absorbed. Interests may therefore be important for ethnic development, but they probably do not provide any sufficient explanation in the Okebo case and certainly do not do so for the Maragoli. I conclude therefore that, in Kigumba at least, the 'political' form of explanation is far from adequate.

THE RURAL AND THE URBAN

I have been using my rural data as a test for a hypothesis or explanatory strategy that was developed primarily in an urban context. May it not be that it is adequate to the one, urban, type of social field but not to the other? There is of course in anthropology a strong tradition of making a firm division between the urban and the rural as social worlds. A first answer is that, as I began by discussing, this kind of argument has already been applied across the board to both rural and urban phenomena. A second and stronger answer is to rebut the division itself as far as the present topic is concerned. The making of the division was certainly valuable in establishing the autonomy of urban studies in anthropology, implying, as Mitchell has written (1966: 48), that 'the social relationships, and the norms and values that buttress these relationships in the towns, must be viewed as a social system in their own right'. But the nature and the scope of the divide has perhaps sometimes in the past tended to be exaggerated into a dichotomous system of thought: the town was not only different in certain respects to the country, but it has sometimes been thought of as its very opposite. In many contexts it is clearly both necessary and proper to think of the two as parts of a single field, and there is no *a priori* reason why it should be inappropriate to make comparison between them (Banton 1965; Epstein 1967; Mayer 1961; etc.).

In connection with my present argument there is a particular need to fend off any suggestion that comparison is illegitimate because it is precisely in the field of ethnicity that one of the strongest rural–urban distinctions has been drawn, the classic distinction between rural tribe and urban tribalism established by Mitchell in *The Kalela Dance*. The tribe was viewed as a group of people linked 'in a single social and political system, sharing a common set of beliefs and values', whereas urban tribalism referred merely to 'a sub-division of people in terms of their sense of belonging to certain categories, these categories being defined in terms of ethnic criteria' (1956: 30). As a proposition of general relevance this was certainly an exaggeration, if a useful one, of a real difference. It is an aspect of the dichotomous thinking I have mentioned, based on a view of the town population as totally unstable and heterogeneous, in contrast to the rural population as stable and homogeneous. On the urban side this meant that interaction between 'strangers' was regarded as the characteristic form of relationship, a superficial type of 'categorical' relationship based upon what Mitchell termed 'categories of social interaction'. It was the fact that these categories were often ethnic in nature which was taken to constitute the key characteristic of urban tribalism. In practice of course the degree of heterogeneity, of instability, and the consequent relative importance of categorical relationships are factors which are variable between towns and indeed between different periods in the history of single towns. It may well be that the values of all of these were peculiarly high on the Copperbelt in the early 1950s and before. Rather than starting with a rural–urban dichotomy, I suggest therefore that it may be more useful to start with the notion of a continuum, or more precisely perhaps a set of linked continua, on which not only would towns be variously placed but rural areas could be included as well. In this way more progress might well be made towards disentangling the effects of the various specific factors involved, unbemused by the powerful rural and urban Ideal Types which have been developed.

There is of course a problem in identifying profitable areas of rural-urban comparison (Mitchell 1966: 48), but what I am suggesting is that the classic one chosen in *The Kalela Dance* is in some degree a miscomparison. It is comparing the outward-facing aspect of urban tribalism, focusing on the classifying of people as belonging to other groups, with the internal aspect of rural tribe. As Gulliver and the other contributors to the recent collection on *Tradition and Transition in East Africa* in particular have shown, rural tribe also often has an important outward-facing aspect. Conversely, tribe in town commonly has an internal aspect, with ethnic groups constituting sub-systems of varying importance within the total urban social field. This is not of course to say that there are no important differences between urban and rural situations, but merely that in this field differences are a matter to be investigated and any assumption of absolute difference and hence incomparability is a hindrance to progress in understanding. What is needed, I suggest, is a widening of horizons and the recognition that there is nothing particularly African, or even 'Third World', about 'tribalism'; or rather that the only aspect of it so limited is its label. Under the guise of ethnicity it is a world-wide phenomenon of both rural and urban occurrence.

IMMIGRATION AND SOCIAL CHANGE

On this plane it becomes immediately clear that ethnicity has normally resulted either from immigration, the immigration of rural peoples of varying origins and characteristics into towns, and of free settlers and refugees between regions and nations, or from the incorporation of previously independent social units into one new unit of larger scale (Cohen & Middleton 1970). Ultimately there may well prove to be no fundamental sociological difference between these alternatives, but for the

time being a useful way ahead is perhaps to concentrate on the
former and to regard ethnicity as essentially to do with the
processes of social change resulting from large-scale immigration.
Eisenstadt (1954) conclusively established such a view of
it in sociological theory. I do not suggest that it is the 'right'
or the only perspective on the matter, but merely that it is a
useful one. Though it may have the initial disadvantage of
separating off the incorporation aspect of the problem, as not
resulting from immigration but from the changing environment
of stable populations, it has the more than compensating advantage of imposing a dynamic, 'process' perspective on the
study of ethnicity. In the study of urban ethnicity in Africa,
Banton and Cohen have both already firmly established the
dynamic nature of the phenomenon, and all I am suggesting
now is that it is profitable to take a still wider view, to see
're-tribalization' as a particular instance of the processes of
social change which result from immigration.

S. N. Eisenstadt's work on *The Absorption of Immigrants*
(1954) lays the theoretical foundation for such a development.[5]
His basic contention is that large-scale immigration – and one
must clearly measure scale relative to the size of the unit into
which immigration is taking place – results in social change both
for the immigrant and for the receiving society as well. This
latter is conceived as having a number of universal or compulsory institutions which immigrants are obliged to assume;
they have for instance to attend school, perform military service, pay taxes, submit to the law. To take on these institutions
necessarily means that immigration involves some measure of
change for the immigrants, but this also occurs because of
what happens to the immigrants' own pre-migratory compulsory institutions. These are either directly contradicted or
modified in a clash with their new counterparts, or at least they
are likely to lose their compulsory status. They become in the
receiving society alternatives and options: one may think
particularly of religious and familial institutions, though the
institutions involved in the different ways will vary from one
society to the next. It is this latter aspect of change for immigrants which also constitutes change for the receiving society,
for the alternatives and options provide the basis on which
ethnic sub-systems develop, each sub-system contributing an

element of 'plurality' to the form in which the total society emerges from large-scale immigration.

Eisenstadt stresses that the sub-systems *develop*, and this is the final point of relevance here. They are not simply the prolongation of pre-migration customs and patterns, but are the result of an interaction between these and the values and requirements of the receiving society. In this way ethnic sub-systems come to be patterned in ways that are essentially new but, since all are in part the product of interaction with the same receiving society, in ways that have distinct parallels throughout the range of ethnic groups present if there are several. Though this conception was developed primarily to deal with Israeli data, it is also well exemplified by the American experience as this has been summarized by Jones (1960: 317):

'Each immigrant group, anxious to preserve its traditional ways, at first endeavoured to create a sub-culture of its own. In order to do so it was obliged to develop separate religious, educational and benevolent institutions. But this step alone showed how strong was the pressure towards conformity with the existing American pattern, for these voluntary organizations, none of which had existed in Europe, adopted a common American form.'

Perhaps somewhat surprisingly, considering the great differences of circumstances and scale, the immigration situation in Kigumba was developing in a strikingly similar manner, with one ethnic group after another producing its own religious, educational, and various other forms of organization.

Eisenstadt's is then a 'macro' conceptualization and generalization of processes of immigration. Like much sociology, once stated it may seem to be merely the translation of common sense into sociological terms, but it is of course far more than this since it directly contradicts the 'melting-pot' and individual cultural assimilation views which 'common sense' has at least until recently held regarding immigration and its results. Within its limits it therefore provides an essential basis for the sociological study of immigration, directing attention to the relevant processes to be studied. As I have noted, it receives striking confirmation from the Kigumba data, though this does suggest one slight modification in regard to the significance of the receiving society for the process. In Kigumba the receiving society and its demands were exceptionally weak, yet the same kind of patterning of ethnic developments was still to be observed. It may be suggested therefore that rather than thinking mainly in terms of absorption into a receiving society, in order to generalize the formulation more fully greater attention needs to be given to the forces emerging within the 'pluralistic' society from the interplay of the various immigrant and indigenous elements.[6] For example, 'the existing American pattern' to which new immigrants conformed was surely more the product of previous ethnic development than it was anything proto-American. African urban data would doubtless point to similar conclusions.

The theory of chain migration as it has been developed by Australasian scholars takes the attempt to specify the ethnic processes resulting from immigration to a more detailed, though correspondingly less generalizable, level. It is to be found well expressed in the work of C. A. Price, particularly in his study of *Southern Europeans in Australia* (1963). It is a theory first and foremost of how the changing demographic composition of the body of immigrants affects social development.

According to this theory, what may become a chain of immigration begins with the appearance of a lone immigrant in a foreign land, where he then 'makes good'. As a success, he recruits others of his family and friends, mainly like himself young, often single, men to come out and join him. At this early stage the band of immigrants resulting may well be too restricted in its demographic composition to provide adequately for all its members' requirements. Some are in consequence likely to make contacts outside it, even to the extent of marrying indigenous wives. But this does not happen to all and a second stage in the immigration process is reached when the early arrivals feel sufficiently well established to bring out wives and children, or brides, to join them. With the creation of families in this way the group takes on more permanent characteristics: better accommodation, more secure employment, and more investment in property of various kinds become necessary. At the same time, the earlier moves by some in the direction of establishing ties outside the group are stemmed as the group becomes more self-sufficient and develops its home-based culture. 'Traditional ceremonies and social occasions become more numerous and the customs and values of the old country become more strongly entrenched. . . . Greater attention is given to education and religion' (Price 1963: 113). With community life well established and news of this reaching the society of origin, in the next stage the character of the migration changes as the older and the younger and the less enterprising begin to follow also. This results in a progressive strengthening of the independence and self-sufficiency of the immigrant community. With the passage of generations, further stages may be recognized, but for the present discussion the short-term effects are the most significant and we can therefore leave the account here.

Taken in conjunction with Eisenstadt's stress on the fact that from a sociological point of view immigrants do not simply re-create their society of origin but produce a new synthesis, there were echoes aplenty in Kigumba of the chain-migration pattern. A confrontation between the Kigumba data and the theory helps to throw certain important features of the Kigumba situation into relief as well as to provide a test of the generality of the theory. 'Chaining' had contributed to the building up in several cases of highly inter-connected communities, and there was even some evidence of greater inter-ethnic contacts in the first years than subsequently when ethnic organization had developed and boundaries hardened. But there were also important differences.

In particular Kigumba did not display the same sequence of types of immigrant, from lone pioneers to full families, as the theory puts forward. Migration to Australasia was from all points of view a serious step and in this there was some contrast with Kigumba. There much of the most difficult and longest range migration had been eased by official aid and encouragement in the form of settlement schemes, and much of the rest was relatively short distance, easily accomplished and easily reversed if all did not go well. There was also the impelled migration of the refugees. In these ways relatively broad demographic bases were generally laid from the beginning. Even where there were pioneers on the Australasian model, as among the Kikuyu for example, the level of 'making good' which they required was so low that a matter of months rather than years would determine whether the immigration was to be abandoned altogether or whether wives and children were to be brought to join the pioneer. The characteristic stages were therefore either absent or at least highly compressed. One would expect similar variation in the different circumstances to be found in towns, in some aspects often similar to Kigumba, in others obviously very different. I may also point in this context to an important cultural variable, the extent to which women and children are regarded as needing protection. Even in the Kikuyu case where there was some male pioneering, women, if not children also, generally tended to be regarded more as themselves aids to 'making good' than as luxuries to be afforded when that happy state had been achieved. Again, therefore, the stages were compressed.

One further general difference between a rural area, like Kigumba, of a 'new nation' and even the rural areas of a generally urbanized society, such as Australia, Israel, or America, needs to be noted. This is the greater ease with which the immigrant, even in the short run the single immigrant household, can be self-sufficient in the former case, and the greater extent of the self-sufficiency possible. This arises in part from the economic base in subsistence farming, particularly in an easy agricultural environment such as Kigumba offered, in part from the level of involvement with universalistic institutions which is forced on such immigrants. This is far lower than the level of involvement required of immigrants in a fully modern society. Here clearly is an important variable to be considered also in relation to developments in urban situations.

Nevertheless in general terms the chain-migration theory points to the rate and form of influx as factors significant for social development, and this is well supported by the Kigumba evidence. Where immigrants came in a few at a time over a long period, as was the case with certain groups such as the Lango or to some extent the Lugbara, each newcomer normally accommodated himself to the local society in which he found himself. Where on the other hand a mass influx occurred, the immigrants might almost immediately, particularly in such undemanding circumstances as prevailed at Kigumba, set about creating a social world for themselves.

A CONCEPTUAL MODEL OF ETHNIC GROUP
FORMATION

In preceding sections I have sought to show that the pursuit of interests is by itself inadequate as an explanation for the maintenance or growth of ethnicity, however important it may be as one factor among others. I have argued that in order to be able to compare ethnic situations and examine the significance of the range of variables involved, it is necessary to place the phenomenon within a wider sociological context and to formulate a basic account, or model, of the social processes involved. Since ethnicity has most often resulted from immigration of some kind, I have suggested that theories which have been developed concerning the social changes resulting from immigration provide a valuable guide and starting-point, though not the only possible perspective on the problem. In this final section, therefore, I want to move on from the point of view established by these theories to try to develop a way of conceptualizing the 'creation of a social world' which occurs in immigration situations. What is needed is a scheme or model that will allow the analyst to come to grips with and compare the processes by which heterogeneous collections of immigrants become transformed or transform themselves into determinate arrangements of distinct ethnic groups. Some such general 'theory' or 'model' is, I suggest, essential if the particular and often spectacular examples of 're-tribalization', such as the one Cohen has analysed, are to be seen within a satisfactory sociological context, not confined by the particular features of African towns in the mid-twentieth century.

The overall process needs, I suggest, to be broken down into three components which can be given three well-established sociological labels, 'categories of social interaction', 'community', and 'organization'. I see the process as involving the selection, modification, or even the creation of categories of interaction that will serve to order relationships in the new immigrant situation,[7] the formation of community in relation to such categories, and the creation of organization in relation to categories and community. I use the vague linking expression 'in relation to' here, for the way in which the components in fact relate to one another is both logically and empirically

359

complex. I shall return to the matter below. I cannot here do more than present the scheme together with certain conclusions about its nature and use derived from the empirical analysis of Kigumba immigration. A paper of the present kind does not offer the space to present more than a hint of an empirical analysis of a situation of such variety and complexity, but I carry out such an analysis elsewhere (Charsley 1971).

The concept of the category of interaction in the study of ethnicity derives, as I have already noted, from Mitchell (1956). Such categories correspond to social identities borne by individuals. They are therefore usually labelled according to recognized social entities that pre-date the immigration that gives rise to the ethnic diversity and hence calls for their use, i.e. nationalities, tribes, etc. This gives the impression that the category employed is a simple carry-over from the relevant pre-migration unit. It has been realized at least since Mitchell's paper that the matter is not so simple. As he was able to show for the Copperbelt, certain units which were potentially available as categories, e.g. clans, were not used, and some at least of those that did appear were used with a clearly modified referent, e.g. 'Bemba' for people of a certain region rather than simply for Bemba tribesmen. Exactly comparable processes of selection and modification had occurred in Kigumba: 'Maragoli', for instance, as I have already pointed out, came to signify in many contexts much more than simply immigrants of Logoli tribal origin; 'Aruru' was modified when the category 'Okebo', previously contained within it, gained independent recognition.

Categories of interaction are therefore not to be regarded as something fixed and settled once and for all. The situation at any given moment is best regarded as merely the current state of a continuing process. Empirically there is often a degree of stability over long periods but it is not difficult to account for this in processual terms. The process may be thought of as consisting of a succession of proposals and acceptances or refusals of identities in interaction situations. A private exchange between two individuals is a useful paradigm. A treats B as if he were a member of category a, which may or may not be the category to which A regards himself also as belonging. A is in fact proposing a category of interaction suitable for B in relation to himself in the particular circumstances, and B may accept or reject it. If he accepts it, then the interaction has helped to confirm, establish and define that particular category, but if he rejects it he in turn may propose an alternative; he is not an a but a β. It is then up to A to accept or refuse this, accept it by treating B in such circumstances henceforth as β, or refuse it by denying that B is 'really' a β. In doing this he is again contributing to defining β but this time by excluding B and others like him from it, or by asserting that β 'is really the same as' a, i.e. that from his point of view there is no relevant difference between them. The matter does not of course necessarily end there in any real life situation but this is sufficient for our purposes.[8]

Most interchanges significant from this point of view will undoubtedly be private, but to illustrate the matter more concretely I may cite one interesting public example of the kind of situation envisaged. In 1968, Maragoli in Kigumba organized male initiation and brought a circumcisor from Kenya for the purpose. There was trouble over certain circumcisions and he was ultimately arrested on charges of assault and theft. At a meeting called to discuss what should be done about this, several Luo, non-circumcising, non-Luyia neighbours of the Maragoli both in Kenya and in Kigumba, were present and one attempted to express a view. This constituted in my terms a proposal that he was to be regarded as a member of the category to whom the matter in hand was relevant. He was in fact told to mind his own business; his 'bid' was refused. But others present, including Luyia who had not been involved in the circumcisions concerned since they acted as a separate unit in relation to initiation, participated freely; their 'bids' to be regarded in this context as Maragoli were accepted.

As a public occasion the outcomes here were probably particularly influential for the future, but it is, I suggest, the whole continuing series of proposals and acceptances or rejections in relevant interaction situations which establish and define the pattern of categories.[9] If categories persist it is because 'bids' in terms of them are constantly accepted. Once such a pattern is well established more and more behaviour and organization comes to be predicated on the categorization, or in other language to be structured by it, and the likelihood of its changing lessens. But it is never impossible that a change in circumstances should bring about the refusal of hitherto accepted 'bids', as of course happened in the 'Aruru'/Okebo case in Kigumba. I cannot here examine the empirical determinants of the course the process takes in particular cases any more than to say in conclusion that the Kigumba evidence suggests that the beginning is of great though, as I have emphasized, by no means conclusive importance. How immigration first occurred, the numbers involved then and as the population built up subsequently, and the actions and organization based on the category and through which it comes to represent a known and meaningful unit in the life of the area, these appear to be the crucial factors.

The term 'community' I use primarily in a sense closely connected with the idea of the network as the collection of interpersonal links which can be traced as originating from and surrounding each individual (cf. Barnes 1968; Mitchell 1969). Community exists in my sense to the extent that the networks of any collection of individuals overlap in such a way as to form clusters wherein links are relatively numerous and strong as compared with links between those within and without the cluster. Where ties bunch in such a way as to form detectable discontinuities in the total network, i.e. boundaries, though not usually impervious or wholly rigid ones, I speak of 'community'. This usage is clearly not identical with any of the classical uses of the term, though not I think so far out of line with the thinking implied in them as to be unacceptable. Density of links certainly tends to imply some degree of common interest and some measure of cultural uniformity, at least in so far as the norms and values attaching to the relationships which provide the links are shared (Maciver 1920: 22–3; Barth 1966: 12 ff).

Community and its formation is, I am suggesting, the second crucial element in the process of ethnic group formation that has to be examined. It is one aspect of the 'social deposit' which may build up on the framework provided by categories of interaction, while being at the same time one of the determinants of the categorization. To cite one Kigumba example, the much lower levels of community between Maragoli inhabiting the two ends of the old settlement scheme area had produced a sub-

division of the Maragoli category on the basis of residence into
mutually opposed East and West sections. But at the same
time, once established, this division also affected the level of
community: a relationship of mutual determinance between
categories and community, rather than a one-way causal
relationship, operated.

The processes producing community in Kigumba, and no
doubt more generally, were mainly three. These affected the
various sections of the population more or less strongly and
produced in consequence very different levels of community.
There was, first, chain-migration. This not only brought pre-
existing links to the area of immigration, but through the help
given in initial settlement and in choice of place of residence
ensured that even links which had before migration been only
potential, e.g. those of distant kinship, would often be activated
in Kigumba. Second, there was the local maturation and intermarriage of the rising generation. This provided the possibility
that levels of kinship and affinity would increase within categories of immigrants even where such ties were initially few. It
was particularly relevant to the Maragoli and would doubtless
apply also to the Kikuyu in time if they continued in Kigumba.
And, third, there was organization, the third component of
ethnic group formation, which feeds back into the creation of
community.

'Organization' I use in an orthodox sociological manner as
signifying the combination and arrangement of resources and
roles in order to pursue goals of some kind, creating a pattern
of purposeful human co-activity (Blau 1968: 297–8). Organization may relate to a category or group in one or both of two
ways, through its goals and through its recruitment of personnel.
Defining ethnicity as a 'political' phenomenon is weak in my
view partly because it considers only the former aspect. Where
the category or group is an ethnic one, the organization itself
has to be regarded as ethnic for either reason. Ethnic organization may, for instance, be established in order to promote or
defend some ethnic interest, political, economic, religious, or
cultural, and it is likely then to recruit its personnel from
within the ethnic unit concerned. Tribal or clan associations
or the organization of 'tribal' initiations would be instances of
this. But such organization may also simply recruit from within

an ethnic unit for the pursuit of goals which are not ethnically
defined. Religious organization or forms of agricultural cooperation might be examples of this latter. There may indeed
be circumstances in which it is a condition of the existence of
ethnic organization at all that its manifest objects should not
be of an ethnic nature.

Ethnic interests and goals are important in that their existence is likely to generate organization in relation to them, but
even if they do not exist the mere presence of an ethnic category
and/or a measure of community may give rise to ethnic organization in the second sense. From one crucial point of view at
least it is not possible to separate the types, for both have the
common effect, regardless of whether goals are actually attained,
of reinforcing community. They do this positively by providing
new bases of relationship between members of the unit concerned, and often negatively as well by substituting for ties
outside the ethnic unit which might otherwise exist. For
example, when religious congregations recruiting on an ethnic
basis are established, this commonly leads to withdrawal of
members from non-ethnic congregations. This means the transformation of congregation membership from providing trans-
ethnic to providing intra-ethnic ties. In such ways all ethnic
organization reinforces boundaries, even where there is no
interest involved in so doing.

The precise kinds of organization created will of course depend very much on the circumstances of the immigration and
the character of the immigrants, though there are certain
types of organization, religious, for example, to which immigrants almost universally seem particularly prone. The reasons
are no doubt complex and beyond the scope of this paper to
discuss. In Kigumba, Christian, and to a lesser extent Muslim,
organization was particularly prominent, as also by 1968 was
primary schooling. A number of groups organized initiations,
and there were various institutions of leadership and social
control in evidence. There were a number of forms of recreational organization, and a certain amount of agricultural
cooperation through work-parties. Direct organization for community defence or promotion in any respect was, however,
rare, particularly when compared with at least some urban
situations reported. This was probably related to two factors:

first, the degree of social and geographical segregation possible between ethnic groups in rural circumstances was high, making interaction between groups relatively unimportant; and, second, there was, as I have noted, a shortage of particular ethnic economic or political interests to be pursued in the circumstances of Kigumba. A further contrast between the Kigumba situation and many urban ones was the rarity in the former of individual insurance as a purpose of organization. It may well be that the general need for such insurance is less in the subsistence-based economy of a rural area than in the money-based economy of the town, and at the same time the best and most accessible form of insurance in the former perhaps tends to remain the age-old one of good standing in the community and good relationships with kin and neighbours.

What I have suggested finally therefore is that organization in a general sense is the third component in the formation of ethnic groups, organization on the basis of established categories of interaction and sometimes in pursuit of community interests. On the Kigumba evidence the level of community does not seem to be itself a determinant of the amount of organization, yet the two are related since organization feeds back into community. And community in turn is certainly a factor which may feed back again to influence the pattern of ethnic categorization. This set of concepts provides, I argue, a useful tool with which to tackle the analysis of the process of ethnic group formation generally. I have here in putting it forward suggested the way in which it may be applied to a rural immigration situation. I have also begun using it to compare rural and urban situations. To carry this forward it would of course be desirable to have urban cases analysed in comparable terms. In such a way it should be possible to see 're-tribalization', sharply defined in particular cases, as one type of development of the processes of social change that regularly occur as a result of immigration.

ACKNOWLEDGEMENTS

Earlier versions of this paper were presented to the ASA Conference and to the Anthropology group in the Department of Sociology at the University of Glasgow. I am grateful to participants in both, and also to my wife, for their criticism and advice.

S. R. Charsley

NOTES

[1] Critical examination of the concept of tribe of course reaches back far further: see Nadel 1942: chapter 2.

[2] I made studies in Kigumba focused on immigration and settlement as a research fellow of the then East African Institute of Social Research for a period of about 15 months in 1965–66, and again as a Social Science Research Council fellow in 1968.

[3] The matter of organization of ethnic groups and their comparison in respect of organization is complex. The topic is discussed more fully in Charsley 1971.

[4] Cf. Barth (1969: 14): 'although ethnic categories take cultural differences into account, we can assume no simple one-to-one relationship between ethnic units and cultural similarities and differences. The features that are taken into account are not the sum of "objective differences", but only those which the actors themselves regard as significant'.

[5] Eisenstadt's formulations provided the starting-point for my own research and thinking in this whole area, but I should stress that here I am using only those aspects of his theory that seem particularly relevant to the matters in hand. I am not seeking to evaluate his work on immigration as a whole.

[6] It should be noted, however, that Eisenstadt uses 'absorption' as a technical term defined within and by his theory.

[7] Cf. Barth (1969: 10), who gives 'primary emphasis to the fact that ethnic groups are categories of ascription and identification by the actors themselves, and thus have the characteristic of organizing interaction between people'. Also (*ibid.*: 14) 'ethnic categories provide an organizational vessel that may be given varying amounts and forms of content in different socio-cultural systems'.

[8] Cf. Mitchell (1966: 53) writing about categorical relationships: 'Southall (1961: 39) suggests that "It is rather a matter of external classification than of self-identification". But this is not quite accurate since if Ego orders his behaviour *vis-à-vis* B in terms of a social category it is implied in his behaviour that he identifies himself with a relevant category *vis-à-vis* B'.

Barth (1966: 12–15) offers a comparable though more highly developed account of a transactional process leading to the integration of culture or values.

[9] What I am putting forward is a logical model of an aspect of all social interaction. In most interactions the identities involved will be so well established that such an aspect will be of little interest, but in interactions across or, as it were, near social boundaries, particularly in unstable or new (immigrant) situations, the aspect may be highly significant. As a tool of analysis I cannot yet claim to have tested the model empirically in any more than the casual, incidental manner of the example cited. Nor have I any empirical evidence as to the way in which outcomes may be cumulative in establishing identities and categories.

REFERENCES

BANTON, M. 1965. Social Alignment and Identity in a West African City. In H. Kuper (ed.), *Urbanization and Migration in West Africa*, 131–47. Berkeley: University of California Press.

BARNES, J. A. 1968. Networks and Political Process. In M. J. Swartz (ed.), *Local-level Politics, social and cultural perspectives,*

366

107–30. Chicago: Aldine Publishing; London: University of London Press (1969). Also in J. C. Mitchell (ed.), *Social Networks in Urban Situations*, 51–76. Manchester: Manchester University Press.

BARTH, F. 1966. *Models of Social Organization.* London: Royal Anthropological Institute. Occasional Paper No. 23.

— 1969. Introduction, *Ethnic Groups and Boundaries, the Social Organization of Culture Difference.* Bergen: Universitetsforlaget; London: Allen & Unwin; Boston: Little, Brown.

BEATTIE, J. 1954. The Kibanja System of Land Tenure in Bunyoro, Uganda. *Journal of African Administration* **6**: 18–28.

BLAU, P. M. 1968. Theories of Organizations. In *International Encyclopedia of the Social Sciences*, Vol. 2, 297–305. New York: Macmillan.

CHARSLEY, S. R. 1969. Patterns of Organization in an Area of Mixed Immigration in Uganda. Unpublished Ph.D. thesis, University of Manchester.

— 1970. Mobility and Village Composition in Bunyoro. *Uganda Journal* **34**: 15–27.

— 1971. Immigrants in Uganda, a Study of Social and Economic Development in North-East Bunyoro. Unpublished.

COHEN, A. 1969. *Custom and Politics in Urban Africa, a study of Hausa migrants in Yoruba towns.* London: Routledge & Kegan Paul; Berkeley: University of California Press.

COHEN, R. & MIDDLETON, J. (eds). 1970. *From Tribe to Nation in Africa.* Scranton, Pennsylvania: Chandler Publishing.

EISENSTADT, S. N. 1954. *The Absorption of Immigrants.* London: Routledge & Kegan Paul.

EPSTEIN, A. L. 1958. *Politics in an Urban African Community.* Manchester: Manchester University Press; New York: Humanities Press.

— 1967. Urbanization and Social Change in Africa. *Current Anthropology* **8**: 275–95.

GULLIVER, P. H. (ed.). 1969a. *Tradition and Transition in East Africa.* London: Routledge & Kegan Paul; Berkeley: University of California Press.

— 1969b. The Conservative Commitment in Northern Tanzania. In P. H. Gulliver (ed.), *Tradition and Transition in East Africa.*

JONES, M. A. 1960. *American Immigration.* Chicago: University of Chicago Press.

MACIVER, R. M. 1920. *Community, A Sociological Study* (second edition). London: Macmillan.

MAYER, P. 1961. *Townsmen or Tribesmen*. Cape Town: Oxford University Press.

MITCHELL, J. C. 1956. *The Kalela Dance*. Manchester: Manchester University Press. Rhodes-Livingstone Paper No. 27.

—— 1966. Theoretical Orientations in African Urban Studies. In Michael Banton (ed.), *The Social Anthropology of Complex Societies*, 37–68. ASA Monographs No. 4. London: Tavistock Publications.

—— 1969. The Concept and Use of Social Networks. In J. C. Mitchell, *Social Networks in Urban Situations*, 1–50. Manchester: Manchester University Press.

NADEL, S. F. 1942. *A Black Byzantium*. London: Oxford University Press for the International African Institute.

PARKIN, D. 1969. *Neighbours and Nationals in an African City Ward*. London: Routledge & Kegan Paul; Berkeley: University of California Press.

PRICE, C. A. 1963. *Southern Europeans in Australia*. Melbourne: Oxford University Press.

SOUTHALL, A. 1961. Introductory Summary, *Social Change in Modern Africa*. London: Oxford University Press for the International African Institute.

—— 1970. Incorporation among the Alur. In Cohen & Middleton (eds), 1970: 71–92.

NOTES ON CONTRIBUTORS

BOSWELL, DAVID MARK. Born 1937, Sheffield, England. Studied at Cambridge University, B.A.; University of London, London School of Economics and Political Science, M.Phil.; University of Manchester.

Commonwealth Scholar, University College of Rhodesia and Nyasaland, Salisbury, 1963–65; Research Associate, University of Manchester, 1966–67; Research Sociologist, 1967–70; Lecturer in Sociology, The Open University, 1970– .

Author of 'Personal Crises and the Mobilization of the Social Network' in J. C. Mitchell (ed.), *Social Networks in Urban Situations* (1969), and of other articles on social networks, African urbanization; residential care, mental health, and social organization.

BRUNER, EDWARD M. Born 1924, USA; educated at Ohio State University, M.A.; University of Chicago, Ph.D.

Fieldwork among American Indians, 1951–52, 1968; in Indonesia, 1957–58, 1969, 1971, 1973. Social Science Research Council Fellowship, 1952; Instructor in Anthropology, University of Chicago, 1953; Assistant Professor of Anthropology, Yale University, 1954; Fellow, Center for Advanced Study in the Behavioral Sciences, Stanford, California, 1960; Senior Fellow, East-West Center, University of Hawaii, 1963; Associate Professor, then Professor, of Anthropology, University of Illinois, 1961– ; Head of Department, 1966–70.

Author of various papers on Mandan-Hidatsa and the Toba Batak of North Sumatra.

CHARSLEY, SIMON ROBERT. Born 1939, England. Studied at Cambridge University, M.A.; University of Manchester, M.A. (Economics), Ph.D.

Assistant Research Fellow, East African Institute of Social Research, Makerere University College, Kampala, Uganda, 1965–66; SSRC Research Fellow, University of Manchester, 1967–68; Assistant Lecturer in Sociology, University of Glasgow, 1968; Lecturer, 1969– .

Author of *The Princes of Nyakyusa* (1969), 'Dreams in an Independent African Church' (1973), and of papers on contemporary development in Bunyoro, Uganda.

COHEN, ABNER. Studied at the Universities of London, B.A. (Hons. Philosophy), M.A. (Sociology); and Manchester, Ph.D. (Social Anthropology).

Research Associate, University of Manchester, 1956–61. Appointments at University of London (SOAS): Research Fellow, 1961–64; Lecturer in African Sociology, 1964–70; Reader in African Anthropology, 1970–72; Professor of Anthropology, 1972– .

Visiting Professor of Anthropology, Cornell University 1966–67; Visiting Professor of Anthropology, State University of New York at Binghampton, 1971; Visiting Research Fellow, NISER, University College, Ibadan, Nigeria, 1962–63; Visiting Research Fellow, Institute of African Studies, University of Sierra Leone, 1969–70. Field research in Israel, 1958–59; Nigeria, 1962–63; and Sierra Leone, 1969–70.

Author of *Arab Border Villages in Israel* (1965, 1972); *Custom and Politics in Urban Africa* (1969); *Two Dimensional Man* (1974).

DAHYA, BADR. Born 1927, East Africa. Studied at University of London, M.Sc.

Research Fellow, East African Institute of Social Research, Makerere University College, Kampala, Uganda, 1961–63; Research Associate, University of London (SOAS), 1968–70; Lecturer, University of Edinburgh, 1970–72; Lecturer, University College, London, 1972– ; presently on secondment to Ahmadu Bello University, Zaria, Nigeria.

Author of articles on Arab and Pakistani immigrants in Britain.

DESHEN, SHLOMO A. Born 1935. Studied at Hebrew University, Jerusalem, B.A. (Sociology and Judaic Studies); University of Manchester, Ph.D. (Social Anthropology).

Rural sociologist with Israeli Land Settlement Department, 1961–64; Research Fellow at University of Manchester, 1964–68; Lecturer in Social Anthropology, Tel-Aviv University, 1968–71; Senior Lecturer, 1971– .

Author of *Immigrant Voters in Israel: Parties and Congregations in an Israeli Election Campaign* (1970), and of papers on religion among immigrants from North Africa in Israel.

GRILLO, RALPH DAVID. Born 1940, England. Studied at Cambridge University, B.A., Ph.D.

Research Associate, East African Institute of Social Research, Makerere University College, Kampala, Uganda, 1964–65; Assistant Lecturer in Social Anthropology, Queen's University, Belfast, 1967–69; Lecturer, 1969–70; Lecturer in Social Anthropology, University of Sussex (School of African and Asian Studies), 1970– .

Author of *African Railwaymen* (1973).

HANNERZ, ULF. Born 1942, Malmö. Educated at the University at Stockholm, B.A., Ph.D.; Indiana University, M.A.

Staff Anthropologist, Center for Applied Linguistics, Washington, D.C., 1966–68; Docent, University of Stockholm, 1970– ; Visiting Associate Professor, University of Pittsburgh, 1971–72. Fieldwork in the USA and in the Cayman Islands, British West Indies.

Author of *Soulside: Inquiries into Ghetto Culture and Community* (1969), and various articles on urban anthropology and Afro-American culture.

LLOYD, PETER C. Born 1927, Bournemouth, England. Studied at Oxford University, B.A., M.A., B.Sc., D.Phil.

Research Fellow, West African Institute of Social and Economic Research, Ibadan, Nigeria, 1950–56; Land Research Officer, Ministry of Lands and Labour, Ibadan, 1956–1959; Lecturer in Sociology, University of Ibadan, 1959–62; Senior Lecturer, 1962–64; Senior Lecturer in Sociology, University of Birmingham, 1964–66; Reader, 1966–67; Reader in Social Anthropology, University of Sussex, 1967– .

Author of *Yoruba Land Law* (1962); *Africa in Social Change* (1967), *The Political Development of Yoruba Kingdoms in the Eighteenth and Nineteenth Centuries* (1971), *Classes, Crises and Coups* (1971).

Editor of *The New Elites of Tropical Africa* (1966); co-editor of *The City of Ibadan* (1967).

MITCHELL, JAMES CLYDE. Born 1918, South Africa; Studied at Natal University College, B.A.(Soc. Sc.), and the University of South Africa, B.A.(Hons.) Sociology; Oxford, D.Phil.

Appointments at Rhodes-Livingstone Research Institute: Assistant Anthropologist, 1945; Senior Sociologist, 1950; Director, 1952–55. Simon Research Fellow, Manchester University, 1953; Professor of African Studies, University College of Rhodesia and Nyasaland, Salisbury, 1955–65; Professor of Urban Sociology, Manchester University, 1966–1973; Official Fellow, Nuffield College, Oxford, 1973– .

Author of *The Yao Village* (1956); *The Kalela Dance* (1957); *Network Analysis: Studies in Human Interaction* (1973); co-editor of *Social Networks in Urban Situations* (1969).

PARKIN, DAVID. Born 1940, England. Educated at University of London, B.A., Ph.D.; Commonwealth Scholar and Research Associate, EAISR/MISR, Makerere University College, Kampala, Uganda, 1962–64; Lecturer in Social Anthropology, University of London (SOAS), 1964– ; Senior Research Fellow, Nairobi University, 1968–69; Lecturer in Social Anthropology, University of Sussex, 1971–72. Field research in Uganda and Kenya.

Author of *Neighbours and Nationals in an African City Ward* (1969); *Palms, Wine and Witnesses* (1972).

SCHILDKROUT, ENID. Born 1941, New York. Educated at Sarah Lawrence College, B.A., Cambridge University, M.A., Ph.D. Assistant Professor of Anthropology, University of Illinois, 1970–72; Visiting Assistant Professor, McGill University, 1972–73; Assistant Curator of African Ethnology, American Museum of Natural History, 1973– .

Author of 'Strangers and Local Government in Kumasi', *Journal of Modern African Studies* (1970), and 'Government and Chiefs in Kumasi' in Crowder and Okime (eds), *West African Chiefs: Their changing Role and Status under Colonial Rule and Independence.*

Name Index

Name Index

McVey, R., 279
Mair, L., vii
Maquet, J., xxii, xxiv
Marc, L., 219n, 222
Marcuse, H., xvi, xxiv
Mars, L., 307n
Marx, E., 307n
Mayer, A. C., 82, 100, 114n, 115n, 117
Mayer, P., 110, 117, 120, 156, 219n, 222, 312, 335, 352, 368
Mboya, T., 136, 141
Mercier, P., 16, 34, 159, 184, 255, 279
Middleton, J., 156
Milone, P., 254, 279
Mitchell, H., 32n
Mitchell, J. C., vii, xii, xxiv, 2, 3, 7, 16, 18, 20, 26, 31, 32n, 33n, 34, 135, 156, 175, 176, 183n, 184, 189, 220n, 222, 268, 269, 312, 332, 333n, 335, 337, 344, 351–2, 353, 360, 362, 366n, 367, 368, 371–2
Moerman, M., 25, 34
Moore, W., 229, 250
Morris, H. S., 95, 117
Muhammad, x
Mulford, D. C., 314, 336

Nadel, S. F., 33n, 34, 62, 75, 366n, 368
Naroll, R., 24, 25, 34
Nelli, H. S., 52, 57, 75
Noy, D., 307n, 308

Odinga, 136, 141
Okumu, J. J., 141, 156

Paden, J. N., 21, 35
Parkin, D., vii, xvi, xxiv, 26, 35, 121, 124, 127, 138, 156, 167, 168, 170, 173, 184, 190, 222, 281, 282, 309, 312, 336, 347, 368, 372
Parry, G., xix, xxiv
Patterson, S., 107, 117
Pauw, B. A., 336
Peizer, D., 33n
Pelling, H., 48, 75
Pelzer, K., 252, 279
Plant, M. A., 103, 117
Pons, V., 219n, 220
Porter, A. T., 72n, 75
Post, K. W. J., 247, 250
Price, C., 166, 184
Price, C. A., 356, 357, 368

Redfield, R., 81, 117
Redfield, R. & Singer, M., 254, 279
Reiss, A. J., 76
Rex, J. & Moore, R., 77, 78, 83, 102, 104, 105, 106, 112, 114, 117
Richmond, A. H., 111, 117
Ross, M., 128, 156
Rouch, J., 216, 222
Rudolf, L. & S., 149, 156
Ryan, A., 161, 174
Ryder, A. F. C., 230, 250

Sacco, 47
Sampson, A., xix, xx, xxiv
Schildkrout, E., 219n, 222, 372
Schneider, D. M., 151, 156
Schumpeter, J. A., 101, 117
Schutz, A., 115n, 117
Shibutani, T. & Kwan, K. M., 183n, 184
Shokeid, M., 307n
Singer, M., 149, 156
Singer, M. & Cohen, B., 149, 156, 157
Sjoberg, G., 254, 279
Skinner, E., 219n, 222
Sklar, R. L., 41, 75
Smith, M. G., 122, 157, 220n, 222, 251, 278n, 279
Soloman, B. M., 67, 75
Southall, A., xxiv, 35, 74, 122, 127, 157, 255, 278, 279, 280, 347, 366n, 368
Spiro, M., 63, 75
Spoehr, A., 278
Srinvas, M. N., 149, 157
Steffens, L., 57
Sukarno, President, 262, 273
Suparlan, P., 278n
Suttles, G. D., 44, 58, 68, 75, 177, 184
Swartz, M. J., xxiv, 366
Sytek, W., 127, 157

Thomas, W. I., 115n, 118
Thompson, M. A., 77, 82, 99, 115n, 118
Tiendrebeogo, Y., 219n, 222
Trueman *see subject index under* Zezuru, immigrant from
Tyler, J. W., 334n, 336

Utja, D., 278n

Subject Index

Accra, Kru in, 148
Acholi, 165
  in Kampala, 171
Aden, immigrants from in Britain, 102
Africa
  cities in
    Central, *see* Leopoldville; Lusaka; Bulawayo; Salisbury
    East, *see* Kampala; Mombasa; Nairobi
    North, *see* Tunis
    West, *see* Accra; Freetown; Ibadan; Kano; Kumasi; Lagos; Sapale; Warri
    South, *see* East London
  education in, 224–5, 231–2, 241, 313–15, 316, 325–6, 334n
  missionaries in, 29, 229, 230, 346
  new nations in, 120, 311, *see also* Zambia
  North, immigrants from in Israel, 284, 285, 303, 307n
    see also Tunisians, Moroccans
  tribalism in, xii, 120–1, 260, 311–313, 331, 337–8, 352–3
  Central, 18
  East, 7, 17, 162, 166, 311
  South, 162
  urbanization in, 170, 260
  colonialism and, 45–6
  compared to USA, 37–9, 43, 44, 71–2, 162–3
  voluntary associations in, 143–147
  see also under cities
African Mineworkers Union, 26 *see also* trade unions
Alur, 165
  in Kigumba, 342, 346, 347, 349
Americo-Liberians, xxii
  in Liberia, 144
  in Monrovia, 72n, 148
ancestor worship, 124
Arab immigrants in Britain, 77 *see also* Aden, Yemenis

'Aruru' groups in Kigumba, 347, 349, 360, 362
Arusha, 338
Ashanti, 187
  cocoa farmers, 196
  Confederacy of, 219n
  kingdom of, 197, 219n
  in Kumasi, 197–201, 216, 219n
Asian immigrants in Britain, *see* Pakistanis and Indians
Association of Social Anthropologists, vii, 114n
associations, voluntary, *see* voluntary associations
Atjehenese, in Medan, 270
Aushi, 5, 6, 7, 8, 12
Australia, immigration into, 356, 357–8

Bali, 274
Balinese, 252
Bandung, 263–9
  Batak in, 253, 256, 263, 264–9, 271–2
  Batavians (Djakarta) in, 256
  Celebians in, 256
  Chinese in, 256
  Christianity in, 263
  dominant culture in, 255–9 *see also under* Sundanese
  ethnic identity, change of, 271–3
  Europeans in, 256
  Javanese in, 253, 256, 263, 266, 274–7
  Malays in, 256
  marriage in, 271–3, 274
  migrants in, 263, 264–5, 266, 267
  Minangkabau in, 253, 256
  Moluccans in, 256
  population of, 254
  Sumatrans in, 256
  Sundanese in, 253, 255, 256, 257–8, 259, 263–9, 270, 274–5, 278
Bangladesh, immigrants from in Britain, 86, 87, 94–5, 113
Bank Rate Tribunal, xix

Halifax, 78
Hausa
  in Ibadan, 38, 39, 40, 41, 42, 48, 50,
    125, 126, 127, 143, 146, 147,
    148, 216, 217, 338, 346, 347
  in Kumasi, 197, 198, 200, 201–9,
    212, 215, 220n
  Luo compared with, 125, 126–7
  migration of, xiv
  status system of, 206, 209, 220n
  Tijaniyya Order and, 38, 126, 127,
    146, 148
  traders, xiv, xx–xxi, 38, 39, 40, 50,
    338
  Yoruba and, xiv, xx, xxi, 127, 216
Hindu
  castes in India, 149
  immigrants in Britain, 86
history, xi, xiii, 37, 71–2
housing, xi, 9–13, 29, 179
  of ethnic groups in Britain, 106–8
    Arabs, 77
    Indians, 99
    Irish, 101
    Italians, 114
    Pakistanis, 89–90, 96–9, 101–2,
      102–8, 112
    Polish, 89, 107, 108
    Ukrainians, 89
  estates, *see* Kampala; Nairobi
  in Kumasi, 199–200
  racial discrimination in, 77, 102–3,
    104–8, 112
  slums, in USA, 61
  in Warri, 229, 232

Ibadan, 38, 39, 40, 41, 42, 48, 50, 125,
  126, 127, 143, 146, 147, 148,
  216, 217, 240, 338, 346, 347
Ibo
  in Ibadan, 347
  Union, 143, 144, 145, 146
  in Warri, 227, 228, 229, 230, 232,
    241, 247, 249
    occupations of, 233–6
    politics and, 239
    property of, 236, 238
identity, ethnic, xii–xiii, xv, 2, 22–24,
  26, 29–30, 32n, 38, 39, 95, 136–
  137, 166, 175, 177–8, 192–3,
  194, 214–15, 218, 252–3, 302,
  338
  change in, 271–4, 347
  problems of, 346–50

ideology of ethnicity, 159, 183n
Ijoh, in Warri, 227, 229, 230, 241
Ila, 5, 6, 7, 12
immigration
  in Australia, 356, 357–8
  in Britain
    Commonwealth, 77
    Pakistani, *see* Pakistani immi-
      grants
    in World War II, 84–5, 95, 115n
    see also Britain, ethnic groups in
  in Israel, 307n, 355, 358
    East European, 285, 287
    Rumanian, 285, 286
    Russian, 301
    Moroccan, 285, 286, 287, 292, 293
    North African, 284, 285, 303n, 307n
    Tunisian, 284, 285, 286, 287,
      290, 292, 295–6, 296–302, 303–5
  in Kigumba (Uganda), 339, 340,
    341–5, 350, 355–6, 357–8, 360
  social change and, 353–8
  in USA, 48, 58, 355, 358
    European, 43, 46
    Mexican, 46
    Puerto Rican, 46
    restriction of, 47
    see also USA, ethnic groups in
  see also migration
Immigration Restriction League (of
  Boston), 47
incorporation, 16
Indians, xi, 82, 95
  in Britain, 80
    Bradford, 80
    caste, 96
    Sikh, 86, 95, 96, 99, 115n
  in Vancouver, Canada, 115n
Indonesia, 214, 251, 252–3, 266–7
  Communism in, 276
  Dutch in, 254, 255, 258, 262, 274
  ethnic groups in, *see* Atjehnese;
    Balinese; Batak; Batavians;
    Celebes, north; Chinese; Euro-
    peans; Javanese; Malay; Min-
    angkabau; Moloccuns; Suma-
    trans; Sundanese
  Indonesianization in, 252, 269, 274,
    276–7, 278
  kingdoms in, 275
  marriage in, 273
  politics in, 260, 262, 275
  population of, 251
  rebellions in, 276